Windows
on a
Women's World

Windows on a Women's World

The Dominican Sisters of Aotearoa New Zealand

SUSANNAH GRANT

OTAGO

Published by Otago University Press
Level 1, 398 Cumberland Street
Dunedin, New Zealand
university.press@otago.ac.nz
www.otago.ac.nz/press

First published 2017

ISBN 978-0-947522-42-1

Published with the assistance of Creative New Zealand

A catalogue record for this book is available from the National Library of New Zealand.

Editor: Gillian Tewsley
Design/layout: Fiona Moffat
Index: Diane Lowther

Frontispiece: Stained glass window, Teschemakers.
Front cover photograph: Chanting the Divine Office, St Dominic's Priory, Dunedin
Back cover photograph: see page 263

Printed in China through Asia Pacific Offset

In our time and place we will live as women of truth.

– Dominican Sisters of Aotearoa New Zealand,
Thirteenth General Chapter, 1989–90

Contents

Mary Horn, *Women Waiting*, painting in a Teschemakers windowframe. Private collection.

Acknowledgements

When Sister Elizabeth Mackie first rang me to discuss a history of the Dominican sisters in New Zealand she spoke of the sisters' wish to engage an 'outsider' for the project. I am certainly that: a non-Catholic woman with a young family. Yet in spite of this, perhaps sometimes because of this, the sisters welcomed me into their homes and their churches; they shared their stories and their songs; they opened windows for me on a world that no longer exists, and peered with me through windows on a world yet to come. As I worked through the archives I developed a deep respect for the Dominicans as a group of women, but for me it was my encounters with individual sisters that brought the spirit of Dominic to life.

I am grateful to the members of the Congregation of New Zealand Dominican Sisters for trusting me with this family story, and to the Leadership Teams who have employed me. I have been guided by a Book Advisory Group conisting of Sister Carmel Walsh, Sister Sandra Winton, Sister Mary Horn, Dr Dorothy Page and Dr Peter Norris. They have been unfailingly patient and supportive. Peter has provided me with a home away from home on my research trips to Dunedin, and Sister Paddy McCann and Angela Macmorran helped make the Dominican archives at London Street another home away from home. The Dominican Family in Scotland Street also made me welcome at their kitchen table and in their prayer room. Both Angela and Anne Haines have cheerfully helped with all manner of administrative details. Together with Sister Lorraine Challis, Anne is responsible for compiling the list of sisters at the back of the book. The Dominican Archives Team do a wonderful job, and I am grateful to past and present members of the team for their skill and efficiency. Brian McLennan's work digitalising photographic images for the book has been invaluable.

As well as the Book Group, several other sisters have read and commented on various drafts of the manuscript. My thanks to Sister Elizabeth Mackie, Sister Judith McGinley, Sister Susan Logan and Sister Madeleine McAleese for their careful reading and helpful comments and corrections. During the final stages I have appreciated Sister Sandra Winton's clear-eyed insights and thoughtful wisdom.

Jolene Hannah read the earliest versions of each chapter. She was a kind first proofreader.

Professor Peter Lineham of Massey University also read an earlier version of the manuscript and I am indebted to him for his time, his perceptive observations, and his encouragement.

Sister Mary Horn has been my main contact person throughout the project. She pushed my newborn up and down Dunedin hills while I worked, walked me through the sisters' sacred sites, read multiple drafts and answered innumerable emails at odd hours. I am extremely grateful for her generosity.

Sister Paddy McCann has been a special friend, blessing my family and me with her loving words and uncompromising passion for truth.

I am deeply grateful for the sisters' love and support during the last months of my father's illness. When Sister Roxane Parkinson and Sister Margaret Butler arrived at his funeral on 19 September 2015, having travelled from Johnsonville to Hastings for the occasion, they hugged me and told me they brought all the other sisters with them. Their presence was a special gift.

Mum: I'm so lucky to be able to share with you the big questions about faith and truth that lie at the heart of this book. Daniel, Chloe, Rosie and Christopher: thank you for sharing the little details of everyday family life in which those big questions are rooted. My Gisborne sisters: thank you for walking, talking, dancing, laughing and praying with me over the course of this project. Shaun, Isabella, Beatrice, Francesca, Thomas and Ihaka: thank you for teaching me every day about mercy, justice, love and truth.

My thanks to the fabulous team at Otago University Press, who have prepared the book for publication. Publisher Rachel Scott has made the process smooth from beginning to end. Thank you to editor Gillian Tewsley of Pepperleaf Publishing for her thorough reading and helpful suggestions. Thank you to Imogen Coxhead for proofing, Diane Lowther for the index and Fiona Moffat for her beautiful design work.

Susannah Grant

Abbreviations and terminology

Abbreviations

CCD	Confraternity of Christian Doctrine
CWS	Christian World Service
DSI	Dominican Sisters International
OP	Order of Preachers
OSD	Order of St Dominic
PBVM	Sisters of the Presentation of the Blessed Virgin Mary
PPA	Protestant Political Association
RSM	Religious Sisters of Mercy
S	Sister
SM	Sister Mary
UISG	International Union of Superiors General

Terminology

Nuns/sisters: In the nineteenth century and for much of the twentieth century the New Zealand Dominican Sisters understood themselves both as 'nuns' and 'sisters', and referred to themselves using both terms. In the wake of the Second Vatican Council (Vatican II) the Congregation developed a new identity as ministerial religious women, choosing to describe themselves as 'sisters' – religious who go out into the community, rather than as 'nuns' – a term now commonly used to refer to enclosed religious women. This text follows the usage of the sisters themselves. Both 'nuns' and 'sisters' are used in nineteenth- and twentieth-century contexts. Narrative and analysis of the later twentieth century and twenty-first century uses 'sisters'.

OP/OSD: In the nineteenth century some Dominican sisters signed themselves 'OSD' in reference to the Order of St Dominic. In the twenty-first century most Dominicans sign themselves 'OP' as a means of signalling their membership of the Order of Preachers. The initials function as an important marker of identity, but they are not necessarily used systematically or consistently. To avoid confusion I have not used the initials in this text. Dominican sisters are usually referred to as 'Sister N—', and in late twentieth- and twenty-first-century context they are identified simply by the first and last names by which they are commonly known. Religious sisters and nuns from other orders are identified as such.

St Dominic/St Dominick: The Irish sisters who came to New Zealand in the later nineteenth century used both spellings of St Dominic's name interchangeably. 'St Dominick' was still in use in the early twentieth century but gradually fell into disuse. This text uses 'St Dominic' consistently. Quoted references to 'St Dominick' from nineteenth-century sources remain in their original uncorrected form.

Names: Sisters may be variously referred to by current or previous religious names, baptismal names or nicknames. In the 1970s and 1980s many sisters reverted from the religious names adopted at reception to their birth names, and some continued to use both names. In most cases this text uses the name by which a sister was known at the particular point in time referenced. Appendix 3 provides a list, in order of profession, of all sisters who made first profession – including those who were later dispensed from their vows. It does not include women who spent time in the Congregation as postulants or white novices but who did not proceed to profession.

Prologue

Halt at the cross-roads, look well, and ask yourselves which path it was that stood you in good stead long ago. That path follow and you shall find rest for your souls. – Jeremiah 6:16

So out of the chaos through mist and dark
Dawn emerges,
Journey into the night so as to return
To the place of beginning light
– Mary Horn, 2001

At the crossroads of Smith and Tennyson streets in the city of Dunedin stands a huge concrete building.[1] It is monumental in size and style – the largest unreinforced concrete building in the southern hemisphere.

For more than 100 years, from 1877 until 1981, St Dominic's Priory served as the home of the Congregation of Dominican Sisters of Aotearoa New Zealand. But by the end of the twentieth century St Dominic's was empty. The slate tiles on the roof were cracked and broken, letting in rain that damaged the ceilings and interiors. The exterior concrete walls, which had been plastered over in the 1970s in an ineffectual effort to protect them, had started to crumble. Cracked windowpanes let the weather in – and the birds. Workmen had ripped out basins and pulled off skirting boards, but did not stay long enough to complete the process of refitting the Priory as an inner-city apartment building. Vandals and squatters followed. Now St Dominic's stands derelict, with no apparent purpose. It is owned by the Catholic Diocese of Dunedin, which cannot afford the cost of restoring or developing the building. Heritage New Zealand has listed the former Priory as a Category 1 historic building, which means it cannot be demolished.

Tourists take photographs of the building as a relic from the past – a striking example of Gothic Revival architecture. Members of New Zealand's

Above: Detail of overgrown window, St Dominic's Priory, 2014. Author's collection.
Opposite: St Dominic's Priory, 2014. Author's collection.

Catholic community periodically bemoan the building's state of disrepair and debate options for saving it, and some question whether the 'sorry state' of this iconic building is reflective of the Catholic Church in general.[2]

The Priory has a special significance for the Dominican sisters who lived there – the women who polished the banisters and cleaned the windows, who laid their bodies in prostration on the floor of the chapel, who prayed, studied, laughed and wept within its walls. Many of them feel sadness; others feel frustration and anger at their old home's decline. St Dominic's was a 'place of beginning light' where sisters prepared for religious life and trained as teachers before being sent to staff other congregational convents from Bluff in the south to Northcote in the north.

Its relevance is now historical. None of the sisters have lived there since 1981. Responding to the call of the Second Vatican Council they have reclaimed their identity as members of an apostolic preaching order. They live alone and in pairs, with other sisters and with laypeople, in rural and urban settings, in homes owned by the Congregation, in rented flats and in rest homes. Their identity as Dominican sisters connects them to each other and to centuries of contemplative tradition. Their diverse living arrangements and scattered distribution through the country represent a commitment to engage with the wider community and to share the fruits of their contemplation with others, through their prayerful presence in individual neighbourhoods and their active ministries in education, social justice, pastoral care and spirituality.

Even in its current state the Priory remains an edifice built to glorify God and honour truth. It no longer serves its original practical purpose of sheltering and enclosing a community of religious women, yet its presence is a solid reminder of those women. While its story of construction, growth and decline is intimately bound up with the sisters' story, the two narratives do not always run parallel. As the story of the Priory arcs downwards, the Dominicans' story spirals outwards. The space in between reveals other stories: of transplanted Irish Catholicism evolving into a distinctively New Zealand Church; of colonial Catholic ghettos gradually integrating with an increasingly ecumenical society; and of dramatic shifts in theology since the Second Vatican Council.

The story of St Dominic's Priory illuminates the changing ways in which Dominican sisters in New Zealand have searched for truth and sought to share the fruits of their study and contemplation with their students and with the wider community, how they have read the signs of the times and responded to the needs of the day, how they have sought to praise, to bless and to preach in the past, and how they continue to follow St Dominic in the present.

Mary Horn, *Shadows.*
Artist's collection.

Statue of St Dominic from the boarders' stairs, St Dominic's Priory, Dunedin. Now located at St Dominic's College, Henderson. F2/17, DA.

1. Introduction
The fruits of contemplation

We search for God, Who is Supreme Truth, and then we pass on the fruits of that search to all with whom we come into contact … – Sister Mary Joseph Mercer[1]

One of the most serious Christian reasons for returning to the past is, not just to seek facile comfort, nor to look for some simple formula which will clarify everything and solve all our problems, but to find more space in which to grow in love … – Simon Tugwell[2]

The Dominican Sisters of Aotearoa New Zealand are a Congregation of apostolically active, contemplative religious women. The first 10 Dominican sisters arrived in Dunedin in 1871. After a long period of steady growth, the Congregation numbered more than 170 in the early 1960s. Since then numbers have declined. In 2016 the Congregation comprises an ageing population of 43 professed sisters, with no postulants or novices on the horizon. From the earliest Dominican beginnings in New Zealand until the middle of the twentieth century the sisters were strictly enclosed, serving the Church as teachers. By the start of the twenty-first century they were integrated in their local communities, serving God as preachers in a range of places and professions. But although their lives today are very different, the sisters still identify strongly with their predecessors.

The official Constitutions of the Congregation of the New Zealand Dominican Sisters opens with a statement of Dominican identity: 'Our Congregation is a pontifical institute, canonically affiliated to the Order of Preachers. We have always looked to Saint Dominic as our founder and see ourselves as part of the whole Dominican family.' It makes explicit reference to the Congregation's Irish foundresses, and it gives a statement of common character: 'Our Congregation takes its special character from the inspiration of Saint Dominic, our Irish origins and our life in New Zealand. To this character we must strive to be faithful.'[3]

At the start of the thirteenth century Dominic Guzmán established a community of nuns at Prouille (Prouilhe) in the south of France. The monastery operated as a base for Dominic's friars, and also served as a refuge for female converts from the Cathar heresy. The nuns lived as enclosed contemplatives and followed the Rule of St Augustine: their days were occupied with prayer, penance and manual work.[4] The customary outlining the order's traditions and laws included St Dominic's 'Law of Dispensation':

> *Let the Superior possess, in his own convent, power to dispense the brethren each time that he shall consider it fitting, principally in what might form an obstacle to study, preaching or the profit of souls. For it should be known that our Order, from the beginning has been instituted for preaching and the salvation of souls, and that our very studies should tend in principle, when used with fervour and to the full, to make us able to be of use to our neighbour's soul.*[5]

Hand-painted depiction of the Dominican motto 'Veritas' in a presentation album crafted by the New Zealand Dominican sisters and sent to Sion Hill to celebrate the jubilees of three 'much-revered' and 'well-loved' Irish sisters.
Jubilee Album, SHA.

This was a radically new model of religious life. The order was constituted and defined not by its internal religious life or monastic organisation, but by its ecclesiastical mandate to preach.[6]

When Dominic founded his order there were only two models of religious life: contemplative orders – including the Benedictines, Cistercians and Carthusians – who followed a life of prayer in enclosed monasteries; and active orders – including the Knights Templar, the Knights of St John and the Teutonic Knights – who ran inns and hospitals.[7] Dominic created a new kind of order, both contemplative and active, and demonstrated in his own life the possibility of pursuing an intense life of prayer while preaching God's Word in the world.[8]

From its earliest days the monastery at Prouille was known as the Sacred Preaching (*Sacra Praedicatio*). It was not the 'Place of Preaching', nor the 'House of Preachers'; the very existence of this community of women gathered together to seek God's truth was a form of preaching in itself. The Dominican understanding of preaching is broad: Dominicans preach with their voices, their bodies and their lives. English Dominican Simon Tugwell explains that the preacher must preach 'with all that he is … he must be prepared to take the risk of *being* all that he is, and to let all of that be, in God's hands, an instrument of grace to the world'.[9] In Sister Mary Joseph Mercer's words, 'we enter to love God and we love him not so much by what we do as by what we are'.[10] At a vocation rally in Gore in 1966 she described the charism – the distinctive gift of the Holy Spirit – of the Dominican Order with reference to St Dominic himself:

> *Broadmindedness, intense sympathy, a love of individuals as they are, flexibility, gaiety, together with the other side of his nature – a deep love for God and souls, which expressed itself in prayerfulness, in poverty and penance. This is the personality of our founder and these are the hallmarks – the qualities of what we loosely call the spirit of his order.*[11]

The Dominican charism is encapsulated in three key mottos, the simplest and most profound of which is *Veritas* (truth): above all else, Dominicans are called to contemplate and preach God's truth. The second motto is *Contemplare et contemplata aliis tradere* (to contemplate and hand on to others the fruits of contemplation): preaching proceeds from contemplation. The third motto, *Laudare, benedicere, praedicare* (to praise, to bless, to preach), echoes the wisdom of the first and second.

Three years after Dominic's death in 1221 the Dominican friars made their first Irish foundations in Dublin and Drogheda. In 1644 a convent of Dominican nuns was established in Galway.[12] Despite persecution the Galway nuns survived and set up a school. The nuns at Prouille had begun accepting children to be educated in the Catholic faith at around the same time, in the middle of the seventeenth century, but their school was never more than a temporary measure.[13] In Ireland the Dominican nuns became professional teachers; schools became both their mission and their means of economic survival.

They barely survived. In 1652 the Galway Dominicans were exiled to Spain. Thirty-four years later two elderly sisters returned to Ireland to re-establish the convent. In 1697 bishops and religious orders were officially banished from the country. The Galway sisters took off their habits and lived among friends, while trying to maintain as much of their religious life as possible. In 1717 the Galway convent made a new foundation in Dublin, and although Catholics were legally prohibited from operating schools or teaching, the nuns soon opened a boarding school. Initially the community and the school flourished, but over time Ireland's harsh penal laws took their toll. When the school was forced to close the sisters were left without an income and struggling against starvation. In 1808 the Dublin sisters moved to Clontarf and reopened their school, but once again they were forced to shift. In 1819 they moved to Cabra, where a Dominican convent still exists.

Mary Horn, *Immigrant Sisters*. Private collection.

The Cabra convent became a major hub for the Irish Dominican sisters, who went on to establish several new foundations in the nineteenth century. Their first, in 1836, was close to home, in Lower

SM Anthony O'Reilly on her profession day, 17 March 1898. P1/4/4, DA.

Mount Street, Dublin. In 1840 this community moved to a permanent site on a property known as Sion Hill in the parish of St Mary's, Booterstown, where they established St Catherine's Dominican Convent with a boarding school attached. Sion Hill went on to establish its first mission in 1867 in South Africa. Four years later, in 1871, the convent sent a mission to New Zealand. Of those who volunteered for this mission, 10 were chosen. The eldest, Sister Agnes Rooney, was 59, and the youngest, Sister Bertrand McLaughlin, was 19. They were individuals impelled by curiosity, a need to escape, a sense of obligation, a sense of adventure, a call from God. Each had her own story of leaving Ireland for the Antipodes, and her own experience of life in New Zealand. And on a broader level, all were part of a venture much bigger than themselves; bigger than St Catherine's Convent in Sion Hill or St Dominic's Priory in Dunedin.

The Dominican mission to New Zealand must be seen in the context of the overwhelmingly ambitious project of British imperialism. Stimulated by naval exploration and energised by industrial development and prosperity, the expansion of the British Empire in the nineteenth century was driven by a sense of destiny and propelled by the impetus to improve and control. The sisters were colonists, brought to New Zealand to serve an expanding population of British settlers.

The first New Zealand Dominican sisters were also part of the Irish diaspora. Daphne Pochin Mould, the twentieth-century historian of the Irish Dominicans, describes a well-established Irish tradition of 'adventurous wandering'.[14] In the wake of the Great Famine of 1846–52, Ireland witnessed a period of mass emigration as individuals and families fled their homeland to escape poverty and political conflict. The Dominicans were not pushed from their home convent at Sion Hill by hunger. They were, however, part of a wider demographic pattern that had a major impact on Ireland itself and far-reaching consequences for colonial culture.

At the most basic level, the founding sisters were part of the Christian mission to preach God's Word to the ends of the world. After the suppression of the Jesuits in many countries in the eighteenth century, in the nineteenth century there was a revival of Catholic missions overseas.[15] The Dominican Order had been founded on the model of early Christian discipleship: an early English commentator described the friars as having 'the world for their cell, and the ocean for their cloister'.[16] The Irish Dominican sisters crossed the ocean to live an enclosed contemplative life, but they engaged actively with the colonial culture of nineteenth-century Dunedin.

Like other Dominican convents around the world, the Dunedin community operated on a highly regulated timetable and rigidly observed structures of

Junior classroom, St Joseph's Primary School, Dunedin, 1950s. F2/1/10B, DA.

authority. The prioress was dependent on the approval of Rome and the cooperation of the local bishop, but within the community she reigned supreme. She was assisted by four elected councillors and a number of appointed officials. Religious vows gave every sister a place in community life, but did not make them equal: status depended on position, time served as a sister, and a simple class-based division of labour. Choir sisters were well-educated women who usually served the order as teachers; they prayed the Office of the Church according to authorised constitutions. Lay sisters were usually uneducated women from poorer households, who attended to the community's domestic arrangements and observed less onerous religious rites.

For most of their first 100 years in New Zealand the Dominican sisters continued to live as an enclosed religious community, operating and staffing schools for Catholic primary- and secondary-school children. As in other Dominican congregations around the world, the rules and routines of religious life and the work of teaching took priority over the order's preaching charism.

The Second Vatican Council (known as Vatican II) was a turning point in religious history. Sister Margaret Heath focused in her 1992 thesis on the Council's 1965 document *Perfectae Caritatis*:

> *Before Vatican II a certain lip service was paid to the charisma of the founders in theory but in*

Divine Office in the chapel, St Dominic's Priory, 1960s. P6/12/11, DA.

reality there was an increasing tendency to treat all institutes as more or less identical, and to differentiate apostolic institutes by their works. Perfectae Caritatis *changed all this by enjoining upon all institutes a duty of searching in their history for their true charism and of legislating for themselves accordingly.*[17]

Charged with returning to their roots and rediscovering their original charism, the Dominican sisters joined other religious congregations around the world in studying their origins and laying claim to forgotten inspiration. They remembered their founders. They reclaimed their identity as members of the Order of Preachers. And they liberated themselves from the role of teacher, recalling that Dominic himself had never placed limits on the ways or means of preaching the truth.[18] Gradually they experimented with creative expressions of their charism. The process was often exciting and sometimes painful – and it continues now, in the twenty-first century. Like other Dominican congregations around the world, the New Zealand Congregation looked beyond the classroom into their neighbourhoods, their local parishes and their families.[19]

The Dominican Sisters of Aotearoa New Zealand have made a radical, ongoing commitment to respond to the Second Vatican Council by searching for truth wherever it lies and proclaiming it according to the needs of the times. Some have continued to preach through teaching, some have moved into counselling, nursing and chaplaincy, and others have honoured truth through their involvement in ecological projects and issues of social justice.

The New Zealand Dominican sisters are still closely connected to their missionary mothers, and acknowledge their shared spiritual patrimony as members of the Order of Preachers. They have not in any way rejected or repudiated their history as teachers; rather, they have widened the expression of the Dominican charism to include many different means of preaching God's Word. As Sister Mary Joseph told potential postulants in the 1960s, 'there is room for all talents within the Dominican Order and this again reflects St Dominic's love for individuals and his respect for their individuality.' In her words, 'no two Dominicans are alike'; each was encouraged on her own path 'as yet another way of serving God in love.'[20]

In 2003 three New Zealand Dominican sisters returned to Ireland to participate in the 'Cabra Homecoming', a symposium of Dominican women from Ireland, Louisiana, Western Australia, South Australia, Eastern Australia and New Zealand, whose congregations originated from Cabra. The women shared prayer and contemplation, memories and new stories. They celebrated the past by returning to the ancestral home and looked with hope to the challenges of the future. The New Zealanders led a reflective prayer time on Matthew 16:13–16, and asked the symposium to consider God's vision for Dominican women: 'What is the fresh hope to which we are called in God's Word in our land, in our place?'[21]

From the mid-1990s onwards, other New Zealand Dominican sisters have made pilgrimages to Ireland and to Dominican sites in Europe. At an individual level these trips provided sisters with spiritual refreshment and space for contemplation. At a congregational level they brought the New Zealand foundation full circle, connecting the New Zealanders with international Dominicans, re-energising the Dominican charism, and integrating the Congregation's past with its present and future.

S Joan Bennett preaching in the Little Sisters of the Poor Sacred Heart Home chapel, Dunedin, on the occasion of S Winefride Morris's 100th birthday celebrations, 25 April 2014. Bishop Len Boyle listens from behind. Private collection.

> *By our past we are challenged to maintain a deeply contemplative life, liturgical prayer, zeal in proclaiming the Word and an ability to adapt to changing needs. As we constantly renew our life we treasure our traditional freedom of spirit, balanced attitude to law and joyful acceptance of all that is human.*[22]

While the New Zealand Dominican sisters acknowledge their Irish founding sisters and cherish their contemporary connections with Irish and international Dominicans, they developed a distinct identity as a congregation. They are proud of their New Zealand heritage and intensely interested in social and political issues that affect New Zealanders; they are committed to celebrating and caring for the environment in which they live; and they are

Tapestry created for the New Zealand delegation to display at the Cabra Homecoming Symposium in 2003. The banner was designed and made by Sisters Noreen Murphy, Cecilia Kennedy, Molly Griffin and Bernadette Fox. DA.

Celebration of S Elizabeth Mackie's Diamond Jubilee, 1 February 2016. **Back**: Sisters Lorraine Challis, Judith Robinson, Maureen O'Hanlon, Susan Logan, Nola Gleeson, Janice Ogilvy, Paddy McCann, Patrician Hannan, Mary Horn, Marie Twomey, Joan Hardiman, Mary Anna Baird. **Middle**: Sisters Molly Griffin, Madeleine McAleese, Elizabeth Mackie, Cecilia Kennedy, Margaret Quinn, Adrienne White, Jacqui Ryan. **Front**: Sisters Margie Fahey, Joan Bennett, Sandra Winton, Judith Anne O'Sullivan, Cecily Sheehy and Father Kevin Toomey. Private collection.

active in their multicultural local communities. In 2011 the New Zealand Dominican sisters formally accepted a Māori name for their Congregation, Ngā Whaea Arahi Rongo Pai o Aotearoa.

Glory, story and truth

This book sets out to share the stories of the Congregation of New Zealand Dominican Sisters. It draws on existing stories of Dominican life and acknowledges wider perspectives from religious, social, economic, political and women's history.

In the nineteenth century and for much of the twentieth century, religious life received very little attention in the writing of New Zealand history. Religious histories were denominational and institutional; they were written to glorify founders and forebears and to validate the present. But several key figures have recently added breadth of subject and depth of critical analysis to studies of New Zealand's religious history. Allan Davidson, Peter Lineham and John Stenhouse, among others, have engaged with stories of religious experience in robust, often controversial terms. They have motivated a new gen-

LEFT: Born in Dunedin in 1925, Monica McCarthy was educated by the Dominican sisters at St Dominic's and the Sisters of the Mission in Christchurch. She graduated from Otago University with an MA in 1945, and from 1945 until 1949 taught at Marlborough College. In August 1949 she entered the Dominican novitiate, and made her first profession on 9 May 1951. SM Augustine spent more than 10 years researching and writing *Star in the South* – a labour of love, fitted in around regular community life and a full-time position at St Dominic's teaching English, Latin, mathematics and science. S, DA.

eration of religious historians in New Zealand, and have forced an increasing recognition of the significance of religion in our past. Geoffrey Troughton and Hugh Morrison, in their introduction to a 2013 collection of essays on Christianity in New Zealand history, describe the current state of religious history in this country as 'flourishing'. 'Rumours of religion's demise, it seems, have been greatly exaggerated. If anything, "God is dead" is dead.'[23]

The New Zealand Dominicans first appear in historical literature in the late nineteenth century. Cardinal Patrick Moran's *History of the Catholic Church in Australasia* describes their arrival and early success in Dunedin in glowing terms.[24] J.J. Wilson's 1910 history of the Catholic Church in New Zealand similarly praises their patience and forbearance in the face of difficulties, and notes 'the remarkable spread of the community in a comparatively short space of time'.[25] The Dominicans are presented as handmaidens of the Church and their success is perceived as part of its progress in New Zealand. 'And thus,' writes Wilson, 'the Church in New Zealand unfolded gently – emerged like the petals from an opening rose-bud.'[26] Catholic nuns did not feature at all in more general histories of New Zealand.

Sister Mary Augustine McCarthy's book *Star in the South*[27] formed part of the New Zealand response to the Second Vatican Council's call for religious congregations to return to the inspiration of their founders. Published in 1970 to coincide with the centennial celebrations of Dominican life in New Zealand, *Star in the South* was written primarily for the sisters themselves. It is a scholarly depiction of the New Zealand Congregation and its progress. Anecdotal evidence suggests that Sister Mary Augustine was instructed to write a chronicle and was given little leeway for analysis. Her *Mother of the Missions*, published in 1989, focuses on New Zealand's first prioress, Mother Mary Gabriel Gill, and can be seen as an accompanying volume to *Star in the South*.[28]

Star in the South sits alongside five other histories of female New Zealand religious orders. Between 1952 and 1983 the Sisters of Mercy, the Religious of the Sacred Heart, the Sisters of Compassion, the Sisters of St Joseph of Nazareth and the Sisters of St

Joseph of the Sacred Heart published congregational histories, most of which celebrated the centenary of their arrival in New Zealand.[29] These histories were written either by a member of the order or by someone closely associated with the sisters.[30] Sister Mary Augustine's histories also form part of a broader Dominican family history: they contribute an antipodean perspective to the wealth of international literature produced by Dominicans in the 1960s and 1970s in response to the Second Vatican Council.[31]

The Council's impetus to historical research coincided with other developments in historical method and interpretation. Postmodernism, postcolonialism and dramatic social and political change transformed cultural and academic landscapes in the second half of the twentieth century. Spaces opened in the historical record for the voices of those who had been previously marginalised, and women's histories, class histories, indigenous histories and gender histories proliferated. A third development also occurred. History had traditionally focused on significant events and powerful figures, but now, new methodologies such as oral interviews and cross-disciplinary research brought the personal histories of individuals increasingly to the fore.

In New Zealand these developments contributed to an increasing recognition of women in history, and of religious experience. In his 1978 *Brief History of the Catholic Church in New Zealand*, Ernest Simmons acknowledges the contribution of religious women to the Catholic education system.

> *The sisters gained much from their dedication and one can only be filled with admiration for their goodness. It is more difficult to find anything to admire in the blindness that prevented the bishops, the clergy and the laity from seeing that they were building a Church on the bent backs of the nuns.*[32]

Michael King's 1997 history of Catholics in New Zealand, *God's Farthest Outpost*, applies broad brushstrokes and a personal approach to the history of the Church. He acknowledges the service religious women provided to Catholic communities: 'I knew even then what I would prefer to do: being a priest was a lot more fun than being a nun.'[33] In 1995 Mark Williams edited a collection of essays by New Zealand writers reflecting on their Catholic heritage and its impact on their art.[34] In her chapter, Bernadette Hall acknowledges the influence of her schooling at St Dominic's in Dunedin: 'Catholicism gave me brilliant teachers.'[35] That same year Dominic O'Sullivan, in *Faith, Politics and Reconciliation*, examined the Church's response to issues of discrimination, prejudice and racism in Australia and New Zealand.[36] Jane Tolerton's 1994 collection of edited oral histories, *Convent Girls*, added a layer of personal perspective to the literature. Marian Hobbs was one of those interviewed: educated by the Dominican sisters, she resented the restrictions of life at St Dominic's, the paucity of resources and the limits on academic enquiry, but she also acknowledged the confidence and leadership skills she gained from the nuns. There was 'a feeling that women could do anything, and not just a feeling, but the example of the sisters'.[37]

In 2001 Jenny Collins, a past pupil of Dominican schools, conducted in-depth interviews with eight Dominican sisters for her master's thesis; the interviews focused on the sisters' teaching philosophies and methodology and their religious lives.[38] Collins saw her research as part of a shift.

> *Religious women are breaking the silence that has in the past surrounded their lives. Long regarded by themselves and society as outside the purview of sociological and historical inquiry, they are beginning to speak out. In New Zealand they no longer shy away from questions and research about their experience of life in the cloister.*[39]

More recently, religious women around the world have begun sharing their own stories more freely than ever before. Pauline O'Regan's 1987 story of life as a New Zealand Sister of Mercy, *A Changing Order*, is a deeply human account of religious life. She writes of smoking her 'last fags' and attending her last movie before entering the convent in Timaru in 1942. She describes a life 'sometimes beautiful, sometimes bizarre', and writes with heartfelt honesty about the impact of the Second Vatican Council on her Congregation.[40] In 1997 Jessie Munro's biography of Suzanne Aubert, the founder of the Sisters of Compassion, won the Montana Book Awards.[41] Academic historian Ann Trotter wrote the history of Mary Potter's Little Company of Mary published in 2003,[42] and Diane Strevens, another academic with an interest in church history, wrote *MacKillop Women* (2008), a history of the Sisters of St Joseph in New Zealand.[43] Both books use archival sources and oral histories, and both follow similarly narrative trajectories, observing the expansion and contraction of each order and identifying the Second Vatican Council as a crucial turning point. Sister Susan Smith's *Call to Mission: The story of the Mission Sisters of Aotearoa New Zealand and Samoa* (2010) also looks at the impact of the Second Vatican Council on local religious congregations.[44] These local histories – and a growing number of international histories of women religious – reflect the increased openness of many congregations after the Second Vatican Council; and a growing interest on the part of outsiders in a way of life that was previously hidden from view.[45]

Sisters at the 1995 Congregational Chapter: Helen Bergin, Molly Griffin, Brenda Fitzgerald and Mary Anna Baird. P9/2S, DA.

Truth for our time: sources and structure

The Dominican sisters have had a significant impact on Catholic education in New Zealand, and a profound influence on individual lives. Yet many non-Catholics in New Zealand have not heard of the Dominicans, and even Catholics might have difficulty distinguishing between the Dominicans and the Mercy or the Mission sisters. This book looks at the lives of Dominican women in the past and present; it identifies the changes that have affected the Congregation and explores the spirituality that still holds them together and connects them to the larger Dominican family.

The Dominican archives, housed in Dunedin, are extensive and exceptionally well maintained. In recent years the sisters have prioritised their archives as a means of preserving their heritage and making their stories accessible. The archives are dense with material that covers every aspect of Dominican life, from accounts for music lessons to school magazines and legal files. They provide a wealth of detail about the sisters' lives and activities both before and after the Second Vatican Council.

In addition to archival research for this book, I have used oral interviews to allow the sisters to speak for themselves. Between 2010 and 2013 I recorded interviews with 27 sisters. I also gathered

Sisters and pupils in front of St Catherine's Dominican Convent, Invercargill. FEB/L.2, DA.

written personal profiles containing reminiscences and observations from 30 sisters. These helped bring life and meaning to the bare bones of analysis.

As I read through the archives and listened to sisters' stories, the three Dominican mottos of 'Truth', 'Contemplate and hand on to others the fruits of contemplation' and 'Praise, bless, preach' became unifying themes. The shift from a transplanted Irish Dominicanism to a distinctively New Zealand Dominicanism with international connections formed another strong thread. I was also interested to see the way the sisters have responded to change in wider New Zealand society in the wake of events such as the two world wars, economic depressions and population expansions, as well as to wider cultural forces such as feminism, indigenous protest movements and environmentalism.

The impact of the Second Vatican Council is inevitably a defining theme of the book. The Council serves as a hinge between two quite distinct periods in Dominican life in New Zealand: there are many continuities that span both periods, but there are also radical differences that mark the mid-1960s as a watershed in New Zealand's religious history.

The present period of transition is another theme that emerged. As they face the challenges of ageing and declining membership, the Dominican Congregation continue to search for new and creative ways to share their charism with current and future generations.

2. Historical overview
The story of a southern star

Across the turbulent waters of the Tasman Sea lay New Zealand and journey's end. It was a land of promise ... – Mary Augustine McCarthy[1]

The first Dominican sisters arrived in Dunedin in 1871. They began teaching immediately, and over the next few decades established convents and schools throughout Otago and Southland. By the mid-twentieth century they had several foundations in the North Island. Now, in the twenty-first century, the sisters are still spread from Auckland in the north to Invercargill in the south. Their lives are radically different from those of the Irish nuns who preceded them, yet their mission – to preach God's truth in Aotearoa New Zealand – remains unchanged.

From Sion Hill to the Robin Hood Hotel

The sisters were invited to come to Dunedin and were accompanied on their journey by the new diocese's first bishop, Patrick Moran. Bishop Moran had a close relationship with the Sion Hill Dominicans.[2] As Bishop of Dardania and vicar apostolic of the Eastern District of the Cape of Good Hope in South Africa he had applied for nuns from Sion Hill to staff schools at Port Elizabeth. Moran's request provided the impetus for Sion Hill's first overseas mission, established at Port Elizabeth in Eastern Cape Province in 1867.[3] In August 1870, after accepting his new posting to New Zealand, Moran visited Sion Hill to ask for more Dominican sisters for a foundation in Dunedin.[4]

Sion Hill's Annals record the details of an extensive process of questioning, consultation and consensual decision-making by which the community's sisters considered Moran's proposal. After the bishop's initial visit, Dublin's Vicar General Monsignor Forde visited the convent and met privately with every professed member of the community. Having ascertained unanimous support among the sisters, he granted consent for the new venture on behalf of Cardinal Cullen. The community then held a Special Chapter to formally vote on the decision, and to consider how many sisters could be spared for the mission and how much money should be allocated to the new foundation. The sisters also had input into the composition of the new mission. A system of anonymous envelopes gave every sister the opportunity to offer herself for service; and it allowed them to identify members of the community who were necessary for home service and should thus be excluded from selection. Once the cardinal had considered both lists, the prioress and the council of Sion Hill proceeded to select the superior of the new

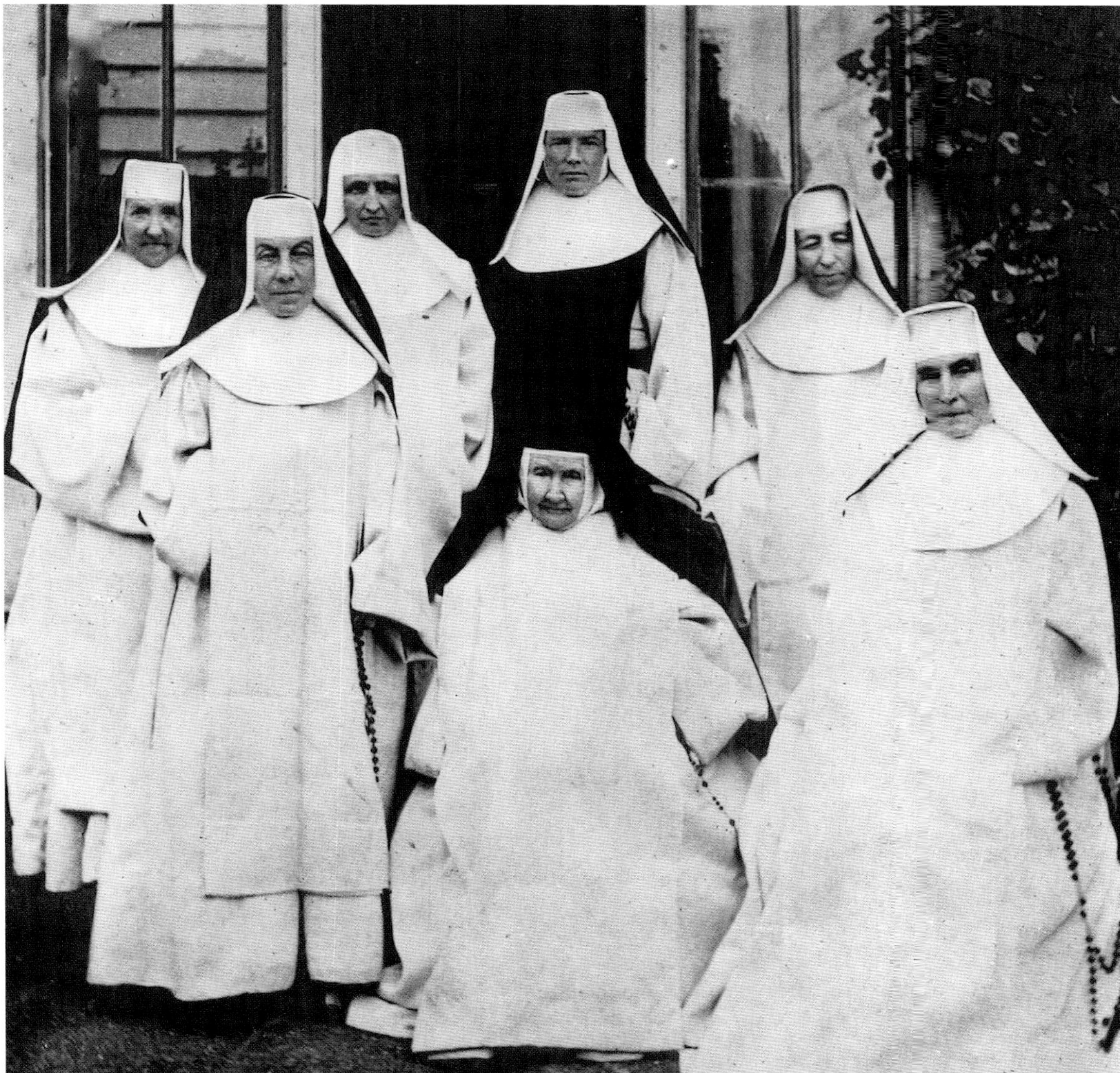

Seven of the 10 founding New Zealand Dominican sisters, 1895. **Standing**: MM Catherine Hughes, MM de Ricci Kirby, MM Bertrand McLaughlin, SM Peter Jordan, MM Vincent Whitty. **Seated**: MM Agnes Rooney, MM Gabriel Gill. P1/3/5, DA.

mission, and those who would accompany her. On 1 October the names of the 10 sisters chosen for New Zealand were announced to the community. Mother Gabriel Gill, appointed as superior of the new mission, was 33 years old. She took with her Sister Mary Agnes Rooney (59), Sister Mary Francis Sullivan (44), Sister Mary Vincent Whitty (38), Mary Catherine Hughes (40), Mary Gertrude Dooley (33), Mary de Ricci Kirby (33), Sister Mary Bertrand McLaughlin (19), Sister Mary Lucy Tracy (43) and Sister Mary Peter Jordan (21).[5]

Before they left Ireland Bishop Moran drew up a simple letter of agreement. As Bishop of Dunedin he undertook 'to provide a suitable house and Schoolrooms, to provide plain, necessary furniture and also to secure the services of a Chaplain till such time as the Community be enabled to pay a Chaplain's salary'. Moran further promised to respect the sisters' internal independence and assured them that 'in reference to the Rules of the Community, there will be no interference whatever on his part'. For their part, the Sion Hill Dominicans agreed to send out 10 qualified nuns to teach two schools – a high school and a 'poor school' – at their own expense.[6]

Preparations 'on a tremendous scale' began immediately. 'Trunks, in dimensions rivalling lesser Arks, appeared, and were filled to the brim with every domestic, ecclesiastical, and conventual requirement, that the idea of a new country, still inhabited by cannibals, suggested.'[7] Four days later, on 5 October, the sisters left Sion Hill for New Zealand; it was Sister Mary Bertrand's twentieth birthday. They drove from Sion Hill to Kingstown and, the next day, sailed from Kingstown to Southampton.[8] On 10 October they boarded the *Glendower* and departed Britain.

The journey was eventful: only two days after departing the *Glendower* was nearly shipwrecked. While the crew struggled to keep the vessel off the rocks the sisters remained with Bishop Moran in the saloon, 'His Lordship expecting at each moment to be obliged to pronounce the last Absolution'. Despite some seasickness, the nuns enjoyed life on board ship. The normal rule observed at Sion Hill was relaxed. In contrast to the silence of the convent refectory, mealtimes on board were full of 'fun and amusement, keeping time with our knives and forks which go so briskly with our tongues'. In the midst of the excitement the nuns did miss the normal rhythms of Dominican life, however. 'The only drawback to our happiness,' wrote Sister Mary Catherine, 'is the impossibility of finding a quiet corner of the house wherein to say our prayers.'[9]

Christmas Day on board the *Glendower* was a memorable one: the religious travellers celebrated multiple Masses; at midday they observed six large whales passing close by the ship; and in the evening a mutiny arose on board: some of the sailors had broken into the stores of spirits and, having 'partaken too freely', had to be put in irons. Later in the evening a storm arose and, with the passengers in danger, all hands were freed to save the ship.[10]

The *Glendower* arrived in Sydney on 2 February 1871. After a few days there, and then a few days in Melbourne (where they were offered the best sites in the city as an inducement to stay), the Dominican sisters embarked on the final leg of their journey. They left Melbourne on a steamship, the SS *Gothenburg*, on 11 February and arrived at Port Chalmers in the Otago Harbour at 7.25am on Saturday 18 February 1871, where they were met by an enthusiastic crowd of Catholics.

At this point, Catholics comprised about 10 per cent of the European population of Otago. The locals had met at the Octagon in Dunedin early in the morning and travelled overland to the port to greet the new arrivals. After a brief welcome there, the bishop, sisters and attendants continued on to the town. It was a hot day and they stopped for refreshments near Mt Cargill at the home of the Coleman family.[11] They arrived at St Joseph's Church at midday. Father Moreau, SM, Otago's first resident priest, greeted the sisters and the bishop at the church gates and led them inside. They recited the Te Deum and celebrated Benediction of the Blessed Sacrament. The party then adjourned to the schoolroom, where Catholic groups from around the diocese presented addresses of welcome to the bishop and the 'religious ladies' who accompanied him. John Griffin, speaking on behalf of the Dunedin City Congregation, described the nuns' arrival as a blessing: 'like their noble Sisterhood throughout the world, they will be the consolers and comforters of the poor and afflicted, the unequalled instructors of the young, and, in the saintly simplicity of their unsullied lives, an impressive example to all'.[12] The formal welcome was followed by 'a sumptuous banquet' at the presbytery.[13] After months at sea, a long hot ride in a dusty, bumpy carriage and an afternoon of speeches and ceremony, the sisters must have been more than ready to settle into their new convent.

Father Moreau and the reception committee had arranged for the bishop to live at the presbytery and the sisters at the vacant Robin Hood Hotel. When they inspected the hotel, however, they found it far from ideal; it was, protested Mother Gabriel, 'just a shed, offering no protection against bad weather'.[14] Famous in Dunedin 'as the abode of rats', it was also heavily mortgaged[15] and altogether unsuitable. Instead the sisters moved into the presbytery on Dowling Street and the clergy moved up the road to a small rented cottage on Bell Hill. Sion Hill's annalist described the cottage as 'a wooden shanty, open to wind and weather', and praised Moran for his 'noble self-sacrifice' and 'the honourable manner in which from the start he sought to carry out his agreement with his Nuns'.[16] This temporary arrangement continued for the next seven years.

Roughing it

The presbytery that served as the Dominican sisters' first home in Dunedin was a seven-room house built of Oregon pine. It was more solid than both the Robin Hood Hotel and the cottage on Bell Hill, but it was still disappointing. 'I little thought,' wrote Mother Gabriel, 'that our anticipated "St Dominick's Priory" was to be represented by a little wooden box.' The house had a beautiful view of the sea and the hills, but it was 'exposed to every inclemency of weather' and 'decidedly in the poorest aspect for heat'.[17]

The house was, however, lavishly furnished. The reception committee had decorated the presbytery with the best furniture available, seeking to adopt a suitable style for a bishop's seat. When the sisters took up residence they felt they were 'living on velvet'.[18] For the first few days local Catholic ladies visited regularly to ask if there was anything else the sisters required and assure them that there was 'plenty of money in hand' to meet their needs. But as Sister Mary Francis revealed in a letter home to Sion Hill, all was not as it seemed. Some assurances to Bishop Moran about the state of the diocese were all 'quite false'. Very soon after their arrival the sisters began to hear rumours and 'strange stories', and realised there was actually no money to pay for all their fine things. It seems that collections had been taken up to defray the cost of preparing accommodation for the bishop and the sisters, but nobody knew where the money had gone. 'Really it is hard to know the truth here,' Sister Mary Francis wrote; but, undaunted, she described the debacle quite cheerfully, adopting a spiritual approach to a very worldly problem.

> *There is absolutely no money in hand … and as to the preparation for the nuns, now that we know the truth, they would make you laugh. Mind that*

The Dominican sisters' first home in New Zealand – Father Moreau's presbytery. F2/1/1, DA.

is what you are to do, don't fret about them. It is no good and besides there is no real reason to fret. The cross is the true happiness of a new foundation. I know I never felt happy here till I knew we had a good heavy one, and now that I am sure we shall have to rough it even far more than I anticipated, I am quite jolly.[19]

When the bills for outfitting the presbytery were presented to Father Moreau, he referred them to the bishop, who must have been overwhelmed. Before leaving Ireland Moran had promised to provide the Dominican sisters with suitable accommodation. He had made his invitation and based his promise on the understanding that Dunedin had the means to support both bishop and nuns. Mother Mary Gabriel was only sorry that 'our poor Bishop was to go through so many hardships and troubles on our account as well as his own'.[20] When the bills arrived, she took charge.

This first glimpse of Mother Gabriel in action in New Zealand is revealing. She was a female immigrant who had spent the whole of her adult life in a cloistered religious order, and who had arrived with nine other women dependents to a life in New Zealand that was not at all what she had expected. She described the promotional pamphlet she had read before embarking as nothing but a 'tissue of falsehoods'.[21] Upon close acquaintance she 'did not think there could be any climate in the world so bad'; she had a dim impression of the colony's state of commerce and society; and the accommodation provided for the sisters was unsuitable. Where others might have quailed, though, Mother Gabriel proved herself a woman of action. She remedied the situation by engaging with the clergy and the community

Left: MM Gabriel Gill, superior of the Dominican mission to New Zealand.

> *Oh! She is Mother of the Missions,*
> *All her children call her so;*
> *First and bravest of the brave few,*
> *Who have taught us God to know.*

– Mary Augustine McCarthy, *Mother of the Missions: Mother Mary Gabriel Gill OP (1837–1905)* (Dunedin: St Dominic's Priory, 1989). P1/2/1, DA.

and holding those responsible to account. First she got hold of the receipts and checked that everything charged for was there. Then she returned as much as she could. Dunedin's tradesmen proved very obliging and agreed to take back all that she asked. Under pressure from Mother Gabriel, Father Moreau also obliged: he made a substantial contribution to the last outstanding bills. After a couple of days of 'great fuss and work' the luxuriously fitted presbytery was stripped of superfluities and transformed into a simple priory.[22]

On Monday 20 February, two days after the sisters had arrived and settled in to the presbytery, they took charge of Dunedin's Catholic girls' school. A boys' school and a girls' school had been running since 1863, taught by lay teachers and supervised by Father Moreau. Both schools were housed in the old wooden provincial government buildings[23] on the hill above the town, immediately below St Joseph's Church. Within a month the sisters had enrolled about 75 children in St Joseph's Primary School. This was a 'free' or 'poor' school, where most students paid one shilling per week to attend.

A week later, on Monday 27 February, the sisters opened a girls' high school for day pupils, which they initially named St Catherine's. At first there were just two students,[24] and an infant class attached to the school consisted of six primary students – four girls and two boys. The children at St Catherine's paid higher fees than those at St Joseph's. The sisters' original intention to open a convent boarding school had to wait – their temporary quarters in the presbytery were far too cramped to do so respectably. 'When this will be,' wrote Sister Mary Francis, 'depends on the Tin [the money] which has not yet come in.'[25]

The sisters also accepted private pupils for piano, singing and harp lessons. In a letter home to Sion Hill Sister Mary Francis Sullivan described the 'delightful concord' of eight pianos playing simultaneously in a small wooden house as too much for her 'nervous sensibilities'. 'Don't you think I perform a heroic act when I urge the children most energetically not to lose a moment of their practice time?'[26] In addition the sisters offered tuition in painting, flower-making, art, needlework and languages (French, Italian, German and Spanish). Their days were more than full. School fees supplemented by private tuition fees and donations allowed them to pay their bills. 'We have earned enough for our support,' wrote Sister Mary Francis, 'and the people are very good in sending us presents of provisions so our bills are not heavy that way.'[27] One parishioner, Miss Hayden, sent the sisters dinner every Sunday, and others sent ducks, geese and produce.[28]

Bishop Moran, meanwhile, was still struggling to come to terms with the straitened circumstances of his diocese. On Thursday 23 February he called a meeting at St Joseph's, where he addressed a large audience on the absolute necessity of providing an appropriate dwelling place and school buildings for the Dominican sisters who had come to teach their children. He explained 'how much he had been deceived and the heavy responsibility he had incurred', and warned 'that unless they assisted him liberally in acquitting himself of it' he would have to send the nuns back home.[29] The meeting passed a resolution to raise the necessary funds and appointed a committee to advance the cause.[30] The sisters told Moran he should focus not on them but on building a suitable church: 'We are quite satisfied to go through any amount of roughing it,' wrote Sister Mary Francis. They told Moran they would be happy to live in the presbytery's outhouses so that he could move in to his rightful home, but the bishop would have none of it.[31] In pastoral letters and sermons from the pulpit he exhorted his parishioners to come to the aid of the 'good ladies who have made such great Sacrifices for the diocese'.[32] The Catholic community eventually responded, but not as generously as Moran had hoped. He himself made several large donations to the convent building fund, but it would be some time before the sisters were in a position to purchase their own property.[33]

In December 1871 the Dominicans held a huge fundraising bazaar.[34] Preparations were intense. Mother Gabriel, who had been ill for two months, spent her convalescence writing letters and answering questions about the bazaar, receiving visitors bearing contributions, and distributing tickets for the art union.[35] The first meeting of the bazaar committee, on 13 November, was a rather unedifying affair. Mother Gabriel assured the Irish sisters back at Sion Hill that they would have laughed to see her surrounded by all 'the chief Catholic Ladies of Dunedin', though 'ladies some indeed did not prove themselves such'. 'I had to give them an exhortation on Charity, honesty and honourable dealings, and such subjects as I never anticipated having to place before a respectable assembly called together for so noble an end as the erection of schools for the benefit of their own children.'[36]

Once they had been called into line, the committee began preparing for the bazaar. Mrs Edwards, the wife of the Anglican vicar, visited Mother Gabriel to say that the ladies of her congregation would be patronising the bazaar 'to the utmost of their power'.[37] Members of the public donated all kinds of goods, from jewellery to livestock. Several Catholic women formed a sewing group to produce articles for sale, and the sisters themselves worked on pieces of embroidery and illumination.[38]

The bazaar, which opened on 26 December, was to take place over four days but was such a huge success that it was extended for another four days. The stalls sold a wide range of goods, and St Patrick's Brass Band, the St Joseph's Choir and other musicians entertained the crowds. Altogether the bazaar and the art union, drawn on the final night, raised £2000 for the convent fund.

While the sisters continued fundraising and saving to purchase their own property, they adapted the presbytery. After a year in Dunedin and several requests from parents, they embarked on alterations to cater for boarding students. Work, financed by the bishop, began on extending the main house in February 1872, and in October a new laundry and other outbuildings were erected. Even then, room was tight: there was only one suitable dining room, and the sisters had to wait for their meals until after the children had eaten.[39]

When an ideal house for the bishop came on the market, the sisters loaned Moran the £2000 raised at the bazaar. 'Rockmount House' on Rattray Street was a new, two-storey Italianate house close to the church grounds. The sale went through on 17 April 1872, and Moran promised to repay the sisters' loan within three years.[40] He was better than his word: he repaid the loan in November 1873 so that the sisters could purchase a property at Wakari for their boarding school. The main property was £2000, and the sisters also purchased a smaller adjoining property, which gave them 80–90 acres (32–36 ha.) of land in total. With alterations to the buildings to make them suitable for a convent and boarding school, the final cost amounted to £4800. Seven sisters stayed at the convent in town, and Mother Gabriel and four others shifted out to form a new community at Wakari. Known variously as St Dominic's Priory and the Priory of Mt Sion, the Wakari convent school received its first boarders on Tuesday 27 January 1874.[41] By a year later it had 83 students.

Wakari served as the site of Dunedin's Dominican boarding school for two years. At the end of 1875 the sisters decided it was too far from the city for use as a school; they retained it as a holiday house.[42] In May 1877 the Jesuit fathers took over the Wakari property and Bishop Moran refunded the sisters' purchase price.[43]

The nuns were now under pressure from increasing school rolls. Bishop Moran invited the Christian Brothers to Dunedin and, at the start of 1876, they took charge of the boys' school.[44]

A purpose-built priory

The sisters now refocused their attention in the city. Bishop Moran paid Father Moreau £300 for the land immediately below the old presbytery on the corner of Smith and Dowling streets and gave the property to the Dominicans. In August 1876 work began on levelling the ground and excavating for foundations. Local architect Francis Petre drew up the plans for the convent, which was to be made of poured or massed concrete – a relatively new technique in the 1870s. Photographs of the plans were distributed around the diocese in an effort to raise interest and prompt donations. The sisters held another art union with 122 prizes, including works by European and New Zealand artists and an altar piece gifted to the Dominicans by Pope Pius IX.[45]

More than a year after work began the sisters moved into the new Priory on Rosary Sunday, 7 October 1877. How excited they must have been to have a permanent, purpose-built building after nearly seven years of waiting, planning and praying. The convent was built on four levels. The basement with an entrance off Dowling Street housed the kitchen, the furnace, the lay sisters' recreation room, two bathrooms, a lumber room, a coal cellar and a scullery. The first floor included the main entrance hall entered from Smith Street, a visitors' parlour, the chapter room where the sisters would hold formal community meetings, the refectory, the community room where the sisters spent their recreation time and the prioress's office. The second and third floors housed the novitiate rooms, the infirmary and the sisters' cells or bedrooms, which were small and spartan but had at least one window in each and, as the *New Zealand Tablet* reported, an 'abundance of room for one individual'. The building had gas lighting and electric bells. The *Tablet* reporter, who visited in August 1877 before the nuns moved in, was highly impressed.

Every visitor to the structure in its present state must be struck with the provision made for air, light and cleanliness. To obtain these requisites without entailing bleakness or bareness, it must have required high architectural skill. The result, however, is admirable, for, while the most ample means are afforded for such in the plan of the building, the effect of the whole interior is extremely pleasing. A house, in fact, has been provided that throughout is suggestive of the end for which it is has been erected, evidently suited to the requirements of the religious life, and, although of respectable and even of fine appearance, presenting nothing that would recall a building fitted up for worldly purposes. An air of earnestness pervades it.[46]

A century later, prominent Dunedin architect E.J. (Ted) McCoy described the building as 'a tribute to Petre's engineering skill'. McCoy believed the Priory was one of Petre's finest works; he referred to its 'controlled, chaste design', 'strong urban feel' and 'powerful architectural rhythm'.[47]

The Priory is a physical symbol of nineteenth-century religious ideology, designed to enclose the sisters and exclude outsiders. The building has a striking number of windows – all placed high on the convent walls: people passing by cannot see in, nor can they easily gain access to the interior. Most of the building is surrounded by a solid concrete wall. The main room for receiving visitors was the parlour, accessed through the grand entrance hall. A door leading off the entrance hall opened onto a special internal staircase for the doctor to ascend to the infirmary without passing through the rest of the convent. The prioress also received visitors and conducted business in her office at the back of the building. The *Tablet* reporter described this room as 'a species of outer chamber, for into the interior of the Convent the rule of St Dominic forbids strangers to penetrate'.[48]

With the nuns in the Priory and the bishop in his own new residence, the old presbytery was transformed into schoolrooms and dormitories for boarding students. As soon as the Priory was finished the bishop began fundraising for a cathedral – also designed by Petre – to be sited adjacent to the Priory between Smith and Rattray streets. Work began in May 1878 and the cathedral was completed in May 1886, though Petre's plan for a tall spire over the transept was never realised.

Moran's fervour eventually encouraged a generous response from Otago's Catholic parishioners. Diocesan financial records for the period from 1871 to 1886 reveal a total expenditure on churches, presbyteries, schools and convents of £80,268 17s 4½d, all raised from parish donations and collections. The largest single project was the cathedral at a cost of £20,000. The cost of the bishop's residence was £3600. The total budget for the Priory was £7700, and around £900 for St Joseph's Girls' School. The Christian Brothers' schools and residence cost £4300.[49] In these early missionary years, Moran's main priority was establishing the Church as a presence in the province: the cathedral and the bishop's residence were institutional symbols of influence and authority. His other main priority was education. He was zealous in his support for Otago's Catholic schools, and as the accounts reveal, he saw the Dominican sisters as his main allies in educating the region's Catholic children.

Although Bishop Moran fundraised on the sisters' behalf and included the details in diocesan records, he made no claim on their convents or schools. The Dominican sisters were never affluent but they were financially independent from the outset. They acknowledged their first bishop as their religious superior, but engaged with him as collaborators in joint mission. Their friendship with Moran established a model of partnership that bolstered the sisters' sense of their own identity and ability to exercise power in commercial affairs and in relation to the Church.

St Dominic's Priory. F2/1/11B, DA.

Expanding and extending

The Dominican sisters arrived in Dunedin 10 years after gold was discovered inland at Gabriels Gully in 1861. The city was rough, as the sisters observed, but it was booming. The economy slowed in the 1870s, but Julius Vogel's immigration and public works schemes encouraged development, and Dunedin became firmly established as New Zealand's largest and most important industrial and commercial centre. As Otago's population grew, school rolls expanded and opportunities opened up for new schools in other areas. The Dominican sisters very clearly saw the 'finger of God' directing their progress elsewhere in New Zealand.[50] Even after recession set in during the 1880s their schools continued to grow. Sister Mary de Ricci Kirby was very aware of the economic downturn and its impact. 'The times are very bad,' she wrote to her uncle in Rome; 'numbers of poor creatures [are] out of employment and almost starving, a thing before unknown in Dunedin.'[51] Yet the Catholic community maintained its support for the sisters and their schools, and the sisters attempted to meet the community's need for more teachers and more schools.

In 1874 Father Coleman travelled to Europe and returned with additional priests for Dunedin and nuns for the convent.[52] In 188[illegible] Moran made another trip to Europe and he too returned with priests and with women to join the Dominicans.[53] By 1882 there were 35 Dominican sisters in New Zealand, including 14 novices.[54] But they needed still more. The early letters from Dunedin to Dublin are peppered with appeals: 'Do Mother send us a couple of professed sisters. We do need them so badly.'[55]

Rosary Convent, Oamaru, 1882. P12/5, DA.

Motivated by Mother Gabriel's missionary zeal the Dominicans expanded beyond Dunedin. After several months of intense planning and fundraising they established their first branch house in Invercargill at the start of 1882. In June that year Mother Mary Gabriel visited the new convent to arrange for school rooms to be built to replace the 'wretched' rooms initially in use. Sister Mary Alphonsus accompanied her; she observed that even under 'very great and very trying' difficulties, 'the thought of the poor little children's souls' seemed to steel the prioress 'against discouragement, a feeling that under the circumstances might beset the bravest heart'. The main difficulty was financial. As Sister Mary Alphonsus observed:

> *It is difficult to await the cheques from the Bank of Divine Providence, which come in when God sees fit to send them. There is a latent feeling that if one knew the exact position of the Bank one would turn burglar, break in and take out not less than £10,000.*[56]

In September 1882 the sisters established a community in Oamaru and, in the same month, they took over the care of St Patrick's Catholic School in South Dunedin. At the start of 1883 four sisters set up a community and opened St Joseph's School in Queenstown.[57] Sister Mary Agnes wrote home to Sion Hill asking how the Irish sisters liked the New Zealanders' 'mania for dispersion'.[58]

In order to keep their communities functioning and schools staffed, and to maximise the missionary momentum of the early 1880s, the New Zealand Dominicans needed more nuns. They believed that Irish nuns were the best means of keeping convent standards high, but several Irish novices who had travelled to Dunedin had left religious life before taking their final vows. Mother Gabriel wanted reliable nuns with sure vocations who were fully trained in Ireland before incurring the cost of their passage to New Zealand. Sion Hill could not continue to staff the colonies. Cardinal Edward McCabe, Archbishop of Dublin, was quite firm on the matter: he believed that Sion Hill had 'done enough' for the missions already by sending out some of its 'best and most useful subjects' to South Africa and New Zealand.[59]

Undeterred by ecclesial politics, Mother Gabriel determined to establish a New Zealand novitiate in Ireland. In 1886 she returned to Dublin where the sisters of Sion Hill welcomed her warmly, and within a couple of months two professed nuns had left to join the Dunedin mission. Despite a series of early difficulties Mother Gabriel eventually established her novitiate at Beaumont, a property situated in the countryside at Drumcondra on the outskirts of Dublin. She soon had six young women eager to receive the habit.

Although the novitiate was technically established under the diocesan authority of Bishop Moran in Dunedin, it depended on clerical assistance from Dublin. Depressed economic conditions in Ireland in the mid-1880s seem to have contributed to strained relations between Mother Gabriel and the Irish archdiocese. Dublin's Archbishop Dr Walsh was initially friendly but became increasingly determined to repudiate any assumed responsibility for the New Zealand novitiate. Mother Gabriel had hopes that Beaumont might continue with support from other colonial foundations, but without adequate funding the novitiate was forced to close.

Queenstown community, 190[illegible]. SM Ignatius Ralph, SM Xavier Hart, SM Michael McCarthy, SM Virgilius Mannion. P2/[illegible]

At the end of 1887 the first Beaumont recruits arrived in Dunedin – four professed sisters and one postulant – and Mother Gabriel returned at the start of 1888 with one professed sister from Sion Hill, one novice and seven postulants.[60] In 1889 Bishop Moran travelled to Dublin again and returned with 10 more young women for Dunedin's Dominicans,[61] incuding two of his own nieces, Sarah (Sister Mary Brendan Murphy) and Kate (Sister Mary Evangelist Murphy).[62]

As the Dominicans established their presence and reputation in New Zealand they attracted colonial applicants. Jane Neylon was the first local woman to join the Congregation; she received the habit and the name Sister Mary Joseph on 8 Janu-

In the nineteenth and well into the twentieth century the New Zealand Dominican sisters relied on regular infusions of Irish personnel. In 1889 Bishop Moran accompanied 10 young women on the journey from Dublin to St Dominic's Priory, Dunedin. **Standing**: SM Cataldus (Bridget) Kavanagh, SM Benedict (Nora) O'Connor, SM Brendan (Sarah) Murphy, SM Dympna (Margaret) Connolly. **Seated**: SM Virgilius (Kate) Mannion, Kate Murphy (SM Evangelist), SM Frigidian (Bridget) Butler, SM Ita (Mary) Connolly. P1/5/2, DA.

ary 1876.[63] In 1879 two young women entered from Dunedin: Sister Mary Rose (Teresa Anne) Cantwell was born in Australia, and Sister Mary Dominic (Mary) Williamson in Ireland. The first New Zealand-born woman to join the Dominicans was Kate Scully, born in Auckland in 1861. She made her profession on 4 September 1883 and took the name Sister Mary Dominic.[64] The following year two more young women entered from New Zealand (one of Scottish birth and one English). In the 1890s equal numbers of Irish and New Zealand women joined the Congregation, and by the late 1900s most novices and newly professed sisters were New Zealanders, although Irish women continued to enter until the mid-1950s.

All these new recruits put increasing pressure on space at the Priory, and in 1889 the sisters held another art union and bazaar to raise funds for an extension. On 13 October Bishop Moran laid the foundation stone for the extension,[65] which provided space for St Dominic's College as part of the Priory. Students and sisters now lived and worked in the same building, but the sisters' section of the Priory was strictly out of bounds to pupils. The new

ABOVE: Congregation, 1892. [illegible]

LEFT: SM Joseph Keylon. Born in 1854 in Ireland, Jane Keylon emigrated to Otago with her family in 185[illegible]. She received the habit and took the name SM Joseph on 8 January 1876, and made her first profession on 1 May 1878. She served the Dominicans as cook, refectorian, infirmarian and laundress until her death in 1946 at the age of 92. [illegible]

Interior of Teschemakers Chapel. F8/10/1, DA.

school building was officially opened on Rosary Sunday, 5 October 1890 – marking the twentieth anniversary of the first sisters' leaving Sion Hill for Dunedin. Priory and school together formed an 'imposing architectural pile, situated on a hill open to the ozone-laden breezes of the Pacific, and commanding from all points an unrivalled view of the city and suburbs, of mountain, valley, bay and ocean'.[66] At around £8500, the Priory extensions put the Dominicans in heavy debt. Bishop Moran, who had visited Ireland earlier in the year, had arranged for a loan of £1000 from Sion Hill to be repaid in regular instalments over 30 years. The balance was paid off gradually from the proceeds of art unions and bazaars.[67]

In 1900 work began at the Priory on the Chapel of the Immaculate Conception. The chapel was graced with an altar of Carrara marble and illuminated by three stained-glass windows depicting the Immaculate Mother of God, Pius V and St Thomas Aquinas.[68] The chapel was connected to the main building by a glass cloister: 'On account of the wet weather sometimes prevalent in our latitude, this sheltered promenade is practically, at such seasons, more serviceable than an estate.'[69]

Otago's population was still growing and the Dominicans continued to expand. At the start of 1891 four sisters established a community in Milton. In 1893 three sisters moved to Lawrence, where the school was across the road from the convent; this required a special dispensation from the bishop to allow the sisters to cross from one side to the other. He also granted permission for the sisters to walk to and from the railway station when travelling.[70] In May 1889 three sisters formed a community in Cromwell. The Congregational Annals record that the 'self-sacrificing sisters, aware of the need of imparting to the children of this town the blessing of a Catholic education, decided to endure the isolation of Central Otago'.[71] At the start of 1900 three sisters established a community at Bluff. Since there was seldom Mass there on a Sunday the sisters travelled down on Monday and returned to Invercargill every Friday.[72] In March 1912 five sisters set up home not far from Oamaru at Teschemakers, a two-storey homestead of 20 rooms with 25 acres (10 ha.) of land gifted by the McCarthy family. The Dominicans later purchased 54 acres (21 ha.) of adjoining land, and in 1914 the McCarthys gave a further 54 acres. In 1913 the sisters began teaching at St Mary's School in Kaikorai, Dunedin. Each day they travelled there and back from the Priory by cable car and on foot, until 1922 when a small community moved into a branch house on Taieri Road to be closer to the school.[73]

The sisters expanded their mission beyond New Zealand, too. In 1898 Dr Kelly, the newly consecrated Bishop of Geraldton in West Australia asked Mother Gabriel for nuns from New Zealand to open a Catholic school. The council approved the proposition as 'a providential and desirable opening', though Dr Kelly 'gave no hope of anything but hard work'. 'Are you willing,' he asked the Dunedin Dominicans, 'to do for God what the miners will do for gold?'[74] The Bishop of Dunedin approved the new foundation, but only on condition that it could be made without depleting the staff of the sisters' existing schools.[75] Unlike the New Zealand branch houses, the Australian foundation was to be an independent convent with its own superior. In April 1899 Mother Gabriel, at the age of 62, left Dunedin to pioneer the new mission at Geraldton with five other sisters. The West Australian foundation became fully independent in 1902, and established its own new foundations at Leonora in 1903 and Day Dawn in 1905.[76] Mother Gabriel died at Day Dawn in April 1905.

The mission to Western Australia: SM de Ricci [illegible] and SM Gonzales Wall travelling by horse-drawn buggy. F6/7/6A, DA.

A colonial congregation

By 1886 the majority of Pākehā (non-Māori) living in New Zealand had been born there, and in 1907 Britain granted New Zealand status as a dominion and officially recognised the country as a 'self-governing colony'. By 1900 roughly half the New Zealand Dominican sisters were Irish and the other half New Zealanders, yet their communal identity was still firmly based on allegiance to 'the saintly traditions of the Dominicans in the Older World'. Letters home to Sion Hill reiterated a strong desire 'to clasp hands across the wide ocean' that separated Ireland from New Zealand and 'to tighten the bonds of sisterly affection' between Dublin and Dunedin.[77] The New Zealand congregation was still an essentially Irish community living according to a medieval European rule.

The outbreak of World War I in 1914 reinforced New Zealand's loyalty to Britain but also contributed to a developing sense of national identity. To some extent the Dominican sisters were sheltered from the war by their enclosure, but they felt its impact through letters from relatives and through the children they taught. In 1914 the children of St Dominic's gave up their usual end-of-year prizes so the money could be given to the Belgian Relief Fund.[78] The sisters also felt the effects of the war on the general cost of living. In November 1915 Prioress Mother Mary Cecily Mulcahy applied for permission from the bishop for the sisters to save money by travelling second class on the railways, but Bishop Verdon declined.[79] Enclosure – which could be more strictly observed in first class – was more important than economy.

In October 1918 the influenza epidemic arrived in New Zealand. It had a catastrophic impact, killing 6700 people – the equivalent of more than a third of the country's war casualties.[80] Dominican schools, like other establishments, closed to prevent the disease from spreading.[81] There are tales of sisters going out from St Dominic's in Dunedin and from Teschemakers in North Otago to nurse the ill in their local neighbourhoods.[82]

In Otago and Southland the Dominican sisters lived in a European world. Their pupils were the children, grandchildren and great-grandchildren of Catholic emigrants. In 1921 Catholics comprised 12.2 per cent of the Pākehā population of Otago and Southland; Presbyterians made up 48.9 per cent and Anglicans 23.2 per cent.[83] Catholic parents were still strongly encouraged to send their children to Catholic schools. In 1926 over 60 per cent of Catholic children aged between five and 13 were attending Catholic schools.[84]

Religious education and school funding had aroused strong sentiment since the colony's earliest days – although there was, in general, a distinct lack of sectarian angst in New Zealand in the nineteenth and early twentieth century.[85] The Dominican sisters always received Protestant pupils, and the leading members of Dunedin's Protestant community actively supported the Priory's bazaars and other fundraising endeavours. When Pope Leo XIII died in 1903, Sister Mary Louis observed in a letter home to Ireland that the flags on all the government buildings in Dunedin were run up at half-mast – 'a great mark of respect in such a non-Catholic city'.[86]

In the build-up to the 1919 general election 'a storm of religious bigotry' hit the country.[87] The Protestant Political Association (PPA), established in 1917 to combat 'rum, Romanism and rebellion', stirred up underlying tensions by focusing on events in Ireland, Catholic educational policy, and the exemption of the Catholic clergy from conscription. The storm was intense but brief, and by the early 1920s the PPA's influence had waned.[88]

Catholics, meanwhile, closed ranks. Catholic sense of identity and solidarity in New Zealand were

Left: In 1904 the congregation sent a beautiful presentation album to Dublin to celebrate the jubilees of three senior Sion Hill sisters. At the turn of the twentieth century the ties between old and new homes were close: New Zealand is represented as a sunny southern home and Sion Hill as the 'old home … ever dear'. Protected by a heavy wooden cover carved with Dominican images and inlaid with intricate silverwork, the album contains photographs of the New Zealand convents and their communities. Each page is decorated with delicate botanical paintings and finished with gilt. Some photographs are adorned with British floral specimens; others are surrounded with New Zealand imagery, including pohutukawa flowers, flax, toetoe and cabbage trees. The flyleaf bears the simple greeting 'Kia Ora' below a small painting of a kiwi and native flora. SHA.

underpinned from the start by shared cultural and class values. Most Catholics in New Zealand in the nineteenth and early twentieth century were of Irish descent.[89] They developed their own institutions parallel to those of the general community, and attended Catholic schools, sports clubs, dances and other social organisations.[90] They were overrepresented in the poorer suburbs and, in Dunedin, were more likely to occupy lower paid, unskilled jobs.[91]

Catholic cohesion was the vital context for the growth of Dominican schools in the early twentieth century, and for the growth of the Dominican Congregation. In the 1910s the Congregation grew to over 100 members: 39 professed between 1910 and 1919, 28 in the 1920s and 42 in the 1930s.[92] As the Congregation grew the proportion of New Zealanders steadily increased. Yet the connection to Sion Hill remained strong. There are frequent requests for postulants and professed nuns in the correspondence from Dunedin to Dublin: 'We are really in want and we always like to keep an Irish sprinkling in our Novitiate.'[93] In June 1924 Sister Mary de Ricci, the second to last of the founding Irish sisters, died. 'If you can only fill her place now with a few good subjects I'm sure she will obtain for you special graces in return,' wrote Sister Mary Peter 'for we are anxious to keep up our union with home and to have always in the novitiate some novices with the Irish faith.'[94] There was still a sense that Irish-trained nuns were somehow superior to their colonial counterparts. 'Get us numbers if you can Mother,' urged Sister Mary Peter in the same letter, 'they will always be welcome if only they were trained and professed at home it would be the best way of all for them, for then they would have the foundation which would be the real help through life.'[95]

Two Irish girls – Annie O'Sullivan and Alice Finnigan – arrived in Dunedin to join the Dominican novitiate in the middle of 1924. They settled in well and made their first professions in 1927 as Sister Mary Colman and Sister Mary Patrick. At the end of 1924 Prioress Mother Mary Cecily Mulcahy wrote asking for 'a few more helpers from the Emerald Isle'. The New Zealanders were eager to expand. James Liston, then coadjutor bishop of Auckland, had written to the Congregation in 1923 asking for their help and offering a choice of three locations. 'But you see,' wrote Mother Cecily to Sion Hill, 'our want of members keeps us back. Is it not too bad? The Sisters of Mercy are stepping into most of the places now and if we can't do something soon all the good places will be gone.'[96] The Dominican community had been reduced by death and ill health, and several lay sisters had contracted tuberculosis.[97] In March 1925, with several Irish choir postulants already about to embark for Dunedin, Mother Cecily wrote to Sion Hill again to ask if 'a couple of strong young girls' could be induced to come to New Zealand as lay sisters.[98] Mother Cecily was herself one of the Beaumont-trained sisters and her correspondence with the sisters at Sion Hill was based on personal relationships. 'Wouldn't it be just lovely if you could come and visit us and bring out a band of postulants,' she wrote to her old friend Mother Mary Pius, 'we want your advice on so many things.'[99] 'A right royal welcome awaits you … a hundred thousand welcomes.'[100] Urgent requests for postulants continued over the next few years. After several cases where Irish girls had travelled to Dunedin to join the Dominicans and had either left the convent or had developed tuberculosis, Mother Cecily asked if Sion Hill would be willing to give future postulants a trial before sending them out.

> *It is too great a risk to take them out here without some test as to their vocation and health … We rely on your help and charity in this matter and your great zeal for souls and the welfare of this great Mission in far away New Zealand. We are growing old and worked out after all our strenuous years and surely Our Dear Lord will come to our aid.*[101]

With a growing congregation and ongoing demand for a separate Catholic education system, the Dominicans expanded once again. They opened their first North Island convent and school in 1932. The Congregation had first considered an Auckland foundation in 1909 when the sisters were offered a house at Huntly but, after three years of internal discussions, negotiations with the bishops of Dunedin and Auckland and two formal community votes, they abandoned the project.[102] In 1920 they looked north again. The council believed that although the warmer climate would be 'most desirable and beneficial to many of [the] sisters', the Congregation did not have enough available sisters. 'The prospects of success of a foundation at such a distance from the Mother House did not seem sufficient to warrant the undertaking.'[103] A year later the Auckland Bishop James Liston made a formal invitation to the Dominican sisters to establish a school in his diocese. Although they were still constrained by numbers, the sisters were persuaded by the 'spiritual and temporal' advantages such a foundation would offer to both 'the community and the Order', and resolved to accept the invitation as soon as possible.[104] More than 10 years later, in January 1932 they opened a new convent and school at Helensville, just outside Auckland; and a year after that they opened another convent and set up a school at Northcote. They opened a third at Blockhouse Bay in 1962 and, in 1967, a high school at Henderson. They also opened two schools in Invercargill: St Albert's Convent in 1939 and St Bertrand's in 1944.

LEFT: St Bertrand's Convent, South Invercargill, established 1944. P13/4C/3, DA.

BELOW: Opening of St Dominic's Convent, Helensville, 1933. P3/8/3, DA.

S Gemma Finlay teaches a group of deaf primary school students at St Dominic's School for the Deaf, Feilding, 1969. Jane Cuff, Miiria Storey, Roydon Seymour-East, S Gemma Finlay, Susan Allen, Christina van der Hooft, Rosemary Brouwers. F14A/5/22, DA.

In 1944 the Dominican Congregation embarked on a new venture, establishing St Dominic's School for the Deaf at Island Bay in Wellington. The school opened in March with seven pupils; Prime Minister Peter Fraser attended the official ceremony. In 1953, with 40 pupils, the school moved to a larger property out of Feilding. St Dominic's School for the Deaf was a special community. The students were all boarders, and many of them started at the school as young as three or four years of age. Sister Paddy McCann taught at St Dominic's from 1974 until 1987. 'You had to be a mother and a teacher and other things, all at the same time … For me the most important thing was that the children recognised Jesus in what I was doing for them and that I, in my turn, recognised Him in them.'[105] St Dominic's closed in 1989, but the Dominican sisters remained heavily involved in deaf education and closely connected with New Zealand's deaf community.[106]

As the Congregation and its school rolls increased, there was once again pressure on space at St Dominic's Priory. During the early 1920s singing lessons had to be given in the novitiate, and at one stage standards one and two were taught in the glass cloister. The novitiate was housed in the sisters' first convent – Father Moreau's old presbytery – which stood behind the new chapel. There were plans to replace it as early as 1916. It was eventually demolished to make way for a new novitiate building in 1928. Called St Teresa's, the building included two large classrooms on the ground floor with space for the novitiate above. On 2 February 1929 the first 15 postulants moved in, including 10 girls recently arrived from Ireland.[107] A newly developed garden area beside the new novitiate was known as the 'Vatican Garden'.

School rolls were still rising. In 1937 the Dominicans built Rosary Hall on Rattray Street, which contained a school assembly hall, four classrooms and a science laboratory, all fitted with modern radio extensions so they could listen to the special radio programmes that were being produced at the time for secondary schools.[108] The laboratory bore the name of St Albert the Great, a thirteenth-century Dominican scientist.[109] The new building was initially connected by a covered walkway to the novitiate building and the primary-school classrooms. In 1944 it was extended and linked to St Teresa's by a new wing that included three more classrooms and a basement. The first floor, called St Hyacinth's, was used as a sewing room, and the second floor was divided into St Agnes' for commercial classes and St Catherine's for homecraft.[110]

During World War II, air-raid shelters were constructed below the bank leading to St Joseph's School and along the bank below the tennis court. The sisters and school pupils received lessons in first aid and home nursing. In response to the strains of wartime economy the sisters made school sewing lessons 'as useful and practical as possible'; they focused on mending, adapting clothes and refitting garments for younger family members.[111] Prioress General Mother Mary Dominica McKay instructed that each sister should have a small suitcase packed in case of emergency. She personally had no fear that the 'Japs' would come: the Dominican sisters would remain at their posts, preserving community morale and providing 'a source of strength and encouragement to others'. She urged the Dominicans 'to increase our fervour in prayer, our fidelity to Holy Rule, our acts of penance, to draw down God's blessings on this distracted world'.[112]

Independence and identity

The Dominican Congregation reached a peak in the 1950s with over 170 professed sisters, most of whom were born in New Zealand, and in 192[illegible] the Congregation elected its first New Zealand-born prioress, Mother Mary Teresa Lynch. All subsequent prioresses were also New Zealanders.

In April 1933 the New Zealand Dominicans received formal papal recognition as a separate congregation and approval of their own constitutions, as well as the right to the full Divine Office – they had previously said the briefer Little Office of the Blessed Virgin Mary in common with Sion Hill. With 141 Dominican sisters (87 choir sisters, 33 lay sisters and 21 novices) living in 13 convents around the South Island, they were a well-established presence. They still honoured their Irish mission heritage, but the Dominican sisters were now a New Zealand religious community.

That is not to deny that there were lingering cultural tensions. In 1935 Prioress General Mother Reginald Quilter warned her Congregation of the need to suppress 'anything approaching Nationalism' in 'our Dominican family':

> *It is not the first time that those in authority have had to give this warning and to forbid the use of expressions such as 'the Home Sisters', 'the New Zealanders', 'the Irish Sisters', as being destructive of the unity which is so strongly impressed in the Rule of St Augustine under which we make profession … We cannot be said to be of one mind when a sharp and offensive division in nationality is drawn. There has been much pain caused and many violations of charity have been the result of heedless comparisons and sometimes even of foolish boasting.*[113]

In order to 'avert the danger of a divided house', Mother Reginald called on her superiors to 'discountenance and fearlessly correct' anything that might tend to foster nationalistic sentiment. In the context of interwar global relations she reminded sisters that 'Patriotism is a virtue, Nationalism a vice'.[114]

In the mid-twentieth century there was a surge of young people entering religious communities; American religious academic Sandra Schneiders writes of a 'vocational tsunami' beginning in the 1940s and peaking in the mid-1960s.[115] After nearly two decades of war, economic depression and international crisis there was a renewed emphasis on the domestic sphere and a strong focus on security and stability. People sought safety and personal meaning in religion. Church attendance rose and revival spread through mainstream and evangelical Protestant denominations, as well as the Catholic Church. New Zealand enjoyed a prolonged period of general prosperity, economic expansion and ongoing labour shortages after the war. Real incomes increased and there was less inequality.[116] There was an upswing in marriage and birth rates with the return of servicemen; and the Catholic fertility rate was even higher than the rate for the rest of the population.[117]

Opportunities for higher education and career advancement were still limited for women of all denominations. Before the 1960s most Catholic women faced a choice between marriage and motherhood or convent and community. It was not a simple choice: those who entered the convent removed themselves from the outside world. Paradoxically, the choice of convent over family gave some women access to education and career paths from which they would otherwise have been excluded. Although they were technically cut off from the world in order to focus on God, semi-enclosed apostolic religious communities also offered women the potential to engage with the world on a practical level. Some orders trained their sisters as nurses and social workers, and the Dominicans, with their charism and their history of educational work, trained many of their sisters as teachers. Most Catholic children in New Zealand at this time were taught by nuns. Catholic girls who felt a vocation to teach often followed their teachers' example and entered the convent.

From the mid-1960s onwards, however, a growing number of women left religious life. They had felt called to serve God and called to teach, but in time realised they were not called to vowed religious life. As winds of change swept through society and through the Vatican, religious and secular women embraced creative new ways of serving God in active ministry within the home, the wider community and the church. But from the 1930s to the early 1960s the convent seemed the best place for many young women to answer God's call to service.

St Dominic's Priory was full to overflowing. Sister Mary Borromeo was prioress in the early 1940s, heading a community of 20 choir sisters and eight lay sisters. The Priory's schools continued to grow. In 1942 there were 35 boarders at St Dominic's College, with 71 day pupils in the secondary school, 102 day pupils in the primary school and 50 pupils at St Joseph's, the free primary school.[118] That year 145 students learnt piano, violin, singing and elocution from the sisters at the Priory.[119] Sisters also supervised devotional Catholic lay societies known as sodalities, including the Children of Mary, the Legion of Mary, the Maria Goretti Guild, the Guard of Honour of the Sacred Heart, Young Catholic Students and the Eucharistic Crusade.[120]

The growing rolls at the primary and secondary schools were putting a strain on space and staff.[121] In 1958 St Joseph's School and St Dominic's Primary School merged and became St Dominic's (the name changed to St Joseph's School in 1975). By the early 1960s the primary school was forced to expand into the old Christian Brothers' High School building.

Santa Sabina Convent, North East Valley, Dunedin, established 1933. [illegible]3/1/8[illegible].

In 1946 the sisters opened Dominican Hall, a hall of residence for young Catholic women attending the University of Otago and the Dunedin Teachers' Training College, with an initial community of three sisters and 20 students. Demand for accommodation grew steadily and, in 1952, the sisters purchased an adjoining property to accommodate a total of 43 students in 1953.[122] In the late 1970s factors that included changes in city council building codes and fire regulations and a trend toward student flatting meant that university and teachers' college halls of residence struggled to balance dramatically increased financial pressures and falling rolls. Some were forced to change their model of accommodation, and others were forced to close. Dominican Hall closed at the end of 1978.[123]

The Dominican sisters facilitated the Dominican fathers' expansion into education in New Zealand.

At the start of 1949 two Dominican priests settled in Auckland, where they initially worked as chaplains and relief priests. In 1950 when the Catholic teacher training college Loreto Hall opened, Dominicans Reverends E.J. O'Leary and D. Fitzmaurice joined the teaching staff. On 7 March 1948 Bishop Whyte of Dunedin had written to the Australian Dominican fathers inviting them to establish a residential hall for university and training college students. Very Rev L.T. McArdle and Rev D. Crowley arrived in Dunedin a year later. The Dominican sisters owned 10 acres (4 ha.) of land on the slopes of Pine Hill adjoining Santa Sabina Convent in North East Valley. After a vote by the entire community they gifted this property to the Dominican fathers.[124] The foundation stone of Aquinas Hall was laid on 7 March 1952 and the hall opened in January 1954. 'The way has been difficult,' wrote Father McArdle, and 'the progress slow, but in no small way the cooperation of the Dominican sisters has been a staff of support and encouragement all the while.'[125] The sisters' generosity and practical assistance at the opening ceremony was 'a revelation of Dominican solidarity and deep living faith'.[126] This pattern of cooperation continues to the present.

The Dominican sisters in Invercargill, Central Otago, Oamaru and Auckland were also faced with growing school rolls. Large classes were often difficult to manage, and fitting in the long hours of work between communal observance of the horarium (the daily schedule) could be stressful. Maureen O'Hanlon recalls that the sisters were trying to live two different lives at the same time:

> *We were still enclosed and praying all the hours of the Divine Office; keeping silence throughout the day – at least supposed to be! At the same time, I was actively involved in teaching [primary school]. I took individual pupils for Speech and Drama lessons before and after school. There wasn't much of a let-up in the weekends as I also taught on Saturday mornings. Any free time in the weekends, I was planning school work for the following week.*[127]

The Dominican schools needed more teachers than the Priory could supply. In some schools it was necessary to employ secular teachers to fill the gaps,[128] and even then, state school inspectors complained about the size of some Dominican school classes.[129] In 1951 Prioress General Philomena McCarthy travelled to Ireland on a recruiting mission. She also visited holy sites in France and received an audience in Rome with Pope Pius XII, who blessed her quest for postulants. In September 1952, after a year abroad, Mother Mary Philomena returned to Dunedin with five Irish postulants. Mother Mary Gonzaga, who had accompanied the prioress general overseas, returned to New Zealand six months later with four more postulants. Over the next few years, nine more Irish postulants travelled out to join the New Zealand Dominicans.[130]

From the 1960s changes in Catholic theology and in wider popular culture intensified the inherent tension the Dominican sisters experienced between contemplation and action, enclosure and mission. Some sisters still came from Ireland, but by the 1960s the Congregation had established a distinctive New Zealand identity. Mother Philomena McCarthy, prioress general from 1944 until 1956, articulated the Congregation's mission as a patriotic pledge:

> *Let us all strive to be true daughters of St Dominic, and to do all in our power for the general good of the Order and its work for souls, that it may go from strength to strength in this fair land of ours, that through our loyalty and devotion to God, to Our Blessed Lady, to Holy Mother Church, and to our beloved St Dominic, New Zealand may truly deserve the title of 'God's Own Country'.*[131]

MM Jordan McCormick with Pope Paul VI, 1970. F14A/7H, DA.

Winds of change

The 1950s was a time of widespread political, social, economic and technological change in the Western world. In Rome there was an intellectual shift as Catholic theologians explored and integrated techniques from modern biblical criticism, literary theory and science. In January 1959, less than three months after his election, Pope John XXIII gave notice of his intention to convene the Second Vatican Council. It was time, he said, to open the windows of the Church and let in some fresh air. Opening on 11 October 1962 and closing under Pope Paul VI on 8 December 1965, the Council heralded a period of openness and spiritual renewal in the Church, characterised by a spirit of dialogue and freedom. The New Zealand Dominican sisters were far from the action but were intensely interested in the Council's activities and progress. Carmel Walsh, who made her first profession in 1962, recalls it as 'a very exciting time, when these new documents were arriving, some in French, some in Latin. We were riding the crest of the wave.'[12]

The New Zealanders enjoyed a direct connection with Rome. In 1961 Sister Mary Jordan McCormick and Sister Mary Genevieve were sent from Dunedin to study at the Regina Mundi Pontifical Institute on the banks of the Tiber. Established in 1954, Regina Mundi offered spiritual and theological formation for religious women, who were not then allowed to study at pontifical universities. After two years of personal development and academic training in an environment buzzing with the latest theological developments, Sister Jordan returned to a position as mistress of novices at St Dominic's Priory. In 1969 she was elected prioress general. Sister Jordan's training in contemporary theology had a real impact on the sisters, novices and school students. Sandra Winton, who attended Sister Jordan's religious education class at St Dominic's, noted: 'It was new and it was interesting … We all felt that for once it was a subject that you could get interested in, and enthusiastic about, and think about and learn some stuff and that was really good.'[133] Two years after leaving school Sandra entered the Dominican novitiate with Sister Jordan as her novice mistress.

> *As novices … she tried to train us in a different way, to a slightly different spirituality. She wanted us to be independent and to think for ourselves, and she also – which was very different for our novitiate – she wanted us to be able to have good human friendships with one another.*[134]

Sister Jordan 'advocated a much more human way of life',[135] according to Sandra. Paddy McCann describes her as a 'trailblazer for change'. Sister Jordan's path as prioress general was difficult and lonely, but she did 'beautiful things' for the Congregation, such as initiating changes in the habit, reforming community chapters and creating more space for reflection and contemplation. Just as importantly, 'Jordie taught us to love … and one of the greatest things she taught us was to have a sense of gratitude.'[136]

With official documents from the Vatican and personal letters from the sisters at Regina Mundi, St Dominic's Priory was not really far from the action at all. The winds of change blowing through the open windows of the Vatican set off strong southern currents. In the mid-1960s there was an initial process of experimentation in the New Zealand Congregation as a whole and in individual communities. Joan Hardiman thought it was 'brilliant'; 'There was sort of an energy everywhere.'[137] Raewyn Benzie, who made her first profession in 1968, recalls a constant state of flux as the Congregation amended its rules and constitutions, modified the dress code and adjusted to new patterns of living. 'We only knew change for years really.'[138] There were times when the younger women, who often initiated and motivated change, clashed with older segments of the Congregation. Dominican sisters had worn the same clothes, sung the same liturgy and followed the same lifestyle for several hundred years. After generations of dependable stability even small changes could be disconcerting and sometimes painful.

The liturgy was one of the first issues covered by the Second Vatican Council. Promulgated in December 1963, the Constitution on the Sacred Liturgy, *Sacrosanctum Concilium*, encouraged greater lay participation in the liturgy. Papal permission to celebrate Mass in the vernacular had a huge impact on religious as well as laypeople. In March 1964 the four lessons before the Easter Vigil Mass at St Joseph's Cathedral in Dunedin were chanted in English.[139] In October of the same year Vespers was also sung in English 'with all the Congregation participating'.[140] For Mary Horn, as for many others, the English liturgy transformed the experience of the daily Office. Mary had not studied Latin at school so she did not understand the Latin prayers. The Office was beautiful, but it was just 'something that you did'. Praying in English and understanding the psalms 'was like a big opening up'.[141]

The council's emphasis on ecumenism, formalised in the 1964 Decree on Ecumenism, *Unitatis Redintegratio,* sanctioned increasing interaction with Christians who were not Catholic. In 1965 several sisters from the Priory attended a university seminar on 'The Church and Unity', with lectures by both Catholic and Protestant clergy including priests from Holy Cross College and Professor Lloyd Geering from Knox College.[142] Other Dominican convents around the country also enjoyed increasing contact with Christians of other denominations. In June 1965 the sisters of Rosary Convent in Oamaru participated in combined hymn singing in the Methodist Hall – 'a very friendly affair'.[143] In August 1965 the sisters of St Catherine's in Invercargill entertained five members of a local Methodist Bible class who wanted to ask questions about the Catholic Church.[144] Sister Joan Hardiman was a founding member of the Council of Christians and Muslims. Sister Jacqui Ryan was a founding member of the Auckland Catholic Diocesan Commission for Ecumenism and Interfaith Relationships.[145] For sisters who had grown up in staunchly Catholic homes and then been cloistered in the convent, the shift toward ecumenism sometimes seemed quite extraordinary.

The Second Vatican Council promulgated the Decree on the Adaptation and Renewal of Religious Life, *Perfectae Caritatis*, on 28 October 1965. The decree called on individual religious congregations to return to the spirit of their founders and update their constitutions in line with contemporary conditions. The New Zealand Dominican sisters responded immediately: they met in their convent communities to discuss the decree's implications and potential. For some this was a period of great excitement. For others it was difficult and unsettling – they were accustomed to living under directive leadership and comfortable with the status quo, and even the process of meeting in community was awkward and uncomfortable. There were moments of tension and ongoing challenges within each community, but most sisters engaged with the Council's call for renewal in their own lives and in their Congregation.

The initial stages of cautious experimentation soon gathered momentum. From 26 December 1968 to 18 January 1969 the New Zealand Congregation of Dominican Sisters held the first session of a Special General Chapter at St Dominic's Priory to consider the Congregation's charism and constitutions in relation to Council teachings and modern needs. The chapter made several provisional changes to the Congregation's constitutions and ordinations, and an additional list of general recommendations. The changes were experimental but still binding.[146] A year later they met again and the earlier changes were confirmed and, in some cases, extended.

The Special General Chapter opened the way for a greater level of involvement with the wider community. Beginning with Sister Mary Peter Higgins, sisters became involved in the Confraternity of Christian Doctrine (CCD) religious education programme, visiting students' families in their homes. Teaching sisters enjoyed full participation in science and social studies fieldtrips. They attended night classes for professional development. Some sisters joined Māori language classes. Increasing ease of egress enabled individual sisters to engage with and contribute to special interest groups. In 1973 Sister Mary Chanel Horn was a committee member of the North East Valley Combined Churches Easter Festival, secretary of the Religious Association and a member of the Otago branch of the New Zealand Council for Educational Research. In 1976 Sister Mary Thomas Dunn and Sister Mary Teresa Roughan became the first of several sisters to train as counsellors with Lifeline.[147] In 1977 the sisters resident at Dominican Hall in Dunedin believed they had 'availed themselves of nearly every lecture and conference that has been offering in or around the city during the last three years'.[148] At the Convent of Our Lady of the Sacred Heart in Queenstown, hospitality became a large part of the community apostolate: priests, religious and other visitors frequently visited and shared meals with the sisters.[149] These were radical changes for an enclosed contemplative order.

The Special General Chapter also opened up community life within the Congregation. Each convent was encouraged to experiment with various aspects of communal living and religious observance. At St Dominic's in Feilding the community embraced a more relaxed communal life and enjoyed the freedom to prepare some of their own meals.[150] At St Dominic's Priory the sisters found that sharing ideas through formal community meetings, spiritual discussions and liturgical chapters helped 'to create a deeper spirit of community'.[151] Other communities struggled with change. At Northcote the superior reported that 'very little has been done regarding "experimentation" – the reason could be that the Sisters, generally, favour our traditional form of Chapter.'[152] The Santa Sabina community in North East Valley held 'beneficial' discussions on the constitutions, but there was some concern 'that we are not yet quite open to each in saying what we truly feel'.[153]

The New Zealanders were not alone in their struggle to adapt. In 1970 Mother Jordan travelled to Rome for an international meeting of superiors general. Superiors at the meeting 'spoke freely of the many difficulties arising out of the rapid, and often far-reaching changes' that occurred in the wake of the Second Vatican Council.[154] Mother Jordan acknowledged that the way ahead was not 'an easy straight road'. Following the promptings of the Spirit meant 'a readiness to move onward with suffering, a readiness to move forward perhaps in darkness, experiencing a continuing transformation'.[155] In 1975 Father Vincent de Couesnongle, Master of the Dominican Order, urged Dominicans around the world to respond to the difficulties they faced with courage:

> *Our life cannot be easy. What we need above all is courage … The courage of St Dominic then is the courage of someone who, far from being shackled to a particular past because it is the past, takes his stand on the essential and permanent values that the past enshrines in order to look straight ahead and go forward: courage for the future.*[156]

In New Zealand, too, the transformation of religious life was dramatic. By the 1980s many sisters had returned to their baptised names. Most had adopted a secular style of dress. Communities had changed the way they ate together, prayed together and worked together. In little more than a decade the Council had effected massive change in the New Zealand Congregation of Dominican Sisters and in other religious congregations around the world.

Moving out

The 1970s was paradoxically a period of renewal and reinvigoration and of contraction for the New Zealand Dominican sisters. The mid-century heyday was well over. The changes in modern life that had motivated and informed the Second Vatican Council had offered Catholic women new opportunities for teaching and serving God as laywomen. Vocations had declined sharply since the mid-1960s and several professed sisters had left the congregation. By the 1990s there were fewer than 100 sisters and by 2010 there were 60. But the group, although it was diminished and its members were older, was more passionate and committed than ever.

Inspired and motivated by the promptings of the Second Vatican Council, the New Zealand Dominican sisters had scrutinised every aspect of their congregational life and routines. The experience was different for each community and for each individual sister. In general terms the Congregation responded to the signs of the times with a steady shift towards increasing freedom and a new emphasis on personal responsibility. At the same time they moved towards a more cooperative style of leadership: the prioress general and her councillors were replaced with a leadership team.

Most significantly, the New Zealand Dominicans reclaimed their patrimony as preachers. The Council's call for religious foundations to return to the charism of their founders led the New Zealand sisters back to St Dominic – a radical preacher who had

S Patrice Bolger (left) and S Judith McGinley (kneeling right) with the Walarano Women's Club, Vanuatu, 1986.

aligned himself with those in need and always stood firm in the interests of peace and justice. The new openness of religious life offered sisters the opportunity to explore this call as a group and as individual women. Some continued to preach through their teaching; others shifted into adult education, chaplaincy, parish work, social work, spirituality, art and ecology, proclaiming God's name in their work and their lives. Many used the skills they had developed as teachers in their chosen new fields. The sisters were no longer limited by their role as teachers. The process was gradual and the journey sometimes painful, but the New Zealand Dominicans were liberated into the world as preachers.

One of the most radical new ventures of this period was a mission to the New Hebrides (now Vanuatu). In 1979, with the country on the brink of independence from France and Britain, the Apostolic Delegate for New Zealand and the South Pacific invited the Dominican sisters to establish a mission in Vanuatu to assist the French-speaking Catholic schools with English language training. The Congregation engaged in an intensive process of discernment. Some expressed concern that the Congregation should first 'sort out our own personnel problems', but many responded positively, identifying the invitation as a call that could 'generate new life and hope in our Congregation'.[157] Twenty-two sisters of all ages volunteered for the mission and,[158] on 27 January 1980, during a special Mass in the chapel at St Dominic's Priory, Sister Joan Hardiman, Sister Mary Patrice (Helen) Bolger and Sister Sandra Winton were formally assigned to the mission of Walarano. They left Dunedin two days later.[159]

For political reasons the sisters did less formal school teaching in the New Hebrides than they had anticipated. Instead they found themselves involved in community work, working with Catholic women's

Left: Sandra Winton spent five years in Vanuatu from 1980 to 1984, where she arrived with no training and totally unprepared. She found her time with the local women of Walarano a life-changing experience of 'immense learning and [a] privilege to work in another culture'. F18/10/1C, DA.

clubs, cultivating neighbourhood gardens, teaching religious education and technical skills to girls, training catechists and developing friendships with the local people. There were many challenges, but they settled and formed close connections.[160] Sister Sandra Winton wrote home to the sisters in New Zealand:

> *Any work has to be done carefully, tactfully, quietly – sometimes it feels as if I'm doing nothing. The essential of evangelisation, changing hearts, is a slow process, and out of my hands. There are not many opportunities to speak, but Melanesians watch everything, so what I am and do matters. I have to show and live faith, hope, fidelity, charity that makes no difference between persons, forgiveness … Not much is said but the eyes are always watching.*[161]

In 1984 when the Congregation considered withdrawing from the mission, locals urged them to stay. 'Your sisters understand and carry out their work for us in a way that we like. They have shared our lives, helped anyone who asks, eaten with us in our villages. We need your sisters.'[162]

In June 1988 the Leadership Team decided to close the mission in Vanuatu. The number of active sisters in the New Zealand Congregation had continued to decline. At the same time, the Melanesian Church was ready to assume a greater level of responsibility and independence.[163] The Walarano mission had an ongoing impact: as Sister Patrice reflected, the challenge of living as strangers in a foreign land provided 'opportunities of living Gospel values, sometimes in the extreme'.

> *Now in New Zealand I see sisters challenged to communicate with the New Zealand other culture, the other churches, and the poor. And I see too the Vanuatu experience fitting into our future evangelization in New Zealand. The people of Vanuatu have evangelized us and are evangelizing us for our future work.*[164]

As the Congregation aged and shrank and moved into new apostolates, the sisters gradually passed their schools into lay care. Raewyn Benzie was the last Dominican principal of St Joseph's Primary School in Dunedin. In her final year at St Joseph's she made a deliberate effort to prepare the lay teachers and parents for her departure and support them as they took on additional responsibility for religious education.[165] The administrator at St Joseph's Cathedral was very disappointed when he learnt there would be no Dominican sisters on staff in 1981. 'I know there are many problems and difficulties in teacher appointments today, but the continuity of Dominican sisters in the Cathedral Parish School since Bishop Moran brought out the sisters for this purpose, has now been broken.'[166]

St Joseph's Primary School continues to thrive as an integrated Catholic school, but St Dominic's College no longer exists in its original form. By the early 1970s the buildings on Rattray Street were in a very poor state and there were no funds available for repair work. The cost of hiring lay teachers soared. Financial problems were compounded by sheer lack of space – nearly 1000 children were packed into four separate schools on two and a half acres (1 ha.) surrounding the cathedral. Carmel Walsh, the principal at St Dominic's, knew the situation could not continue and took a practical approach to the problem. In 1976 St Dominic's amalgamated with the Mercy sisters' St Philomena's high school on the St Philomena's site, under the new name Moreau College (honouring Dunedin's first parish priest).[167] Carmel Walsh was deputy principal of the new school, and other Dominicans continued to teach at Moreau. There were challenges – learning 600 students' names in one weekend, merging timetables for St Dominic's language-oriented classes and St Philomena's more commerce-focused classes, and switching uniforms – but in general it was a smooth transition.[168] In 1986 Moreau College was integrated into the state education system,[169] and in 1989 the college amalgamated with St Paul's High School, established by the Christian Brothers, to become Kavanagh College.

In a way, the Priory's schools were its raison d'être. The Priory was built to house a large group of teachers in close proximity to their classrooms. From 1981 the primary schools of St Joseph's, St Mary's Kaikorai and Sacred Heart in North East Valley were fully staffed by lay teachers. As the Dominicans gradually left their classrooms in the late 1970s and moved out into other positions in the community, the Congregation adapted living arrangements to meet their changing needs. In 1979 four Priory sisters moved out into a small house in suburban Dunedin. The community that remained was small and the Priory buildings were large, but the sisters worked hard to 'build and sustain a strong community spirit'.[170] For several months of 1979 five Cambodians who had come to New Zealand as refugees lived in the novitiate building and, a year later, a Vietnamese extended family spent several months living in the building.[171]

When the Ninth General Chapter met at the end of 1980 the sisters considered the Priory and some of the other older convent buildings according to the current priorities of the community and the apostolate. They asked themselves whether the building allowed the sisters to meet the needs of the people they wished to serve.[172] With great sorrow, they voted to close the building.[173] Margaret C[illegible] recalled the practicalities: 'cleaning out the accumulation of over 100 years of "left luggage" was quite a task!'[174]

It was one thing to leave the Priory but another altogether to dispense with the building. When the chapter delegates voted to close the Priory they had assumed the building would be demolished. In January 1981 the sisters contacted the Dunedin City Council to have the Priory removed from the council's list of historic buildings. The Historic Places Trust (now Heritage New Zealand) immediately indicated that it would oppose the application and attempt to save the Priory. In the meantime, the sisters offered the Bishop of Dunedin first purchasing option. After several months Bishop Kavanagh made it clear that he did not want to buy the Priory, although he did want the sisters to transfer ownership of the small strip of land on which the cathedral steps were built to the diocese.[175] The bishop was interested in the rest of the land for school purposes, but only once the Priory was removed. He would not purchase the Priory himself, but nor did he want the sisters to sell to anyone else for fear that the building would be put to some 'undesirable use'.[176] The Dominicans were stuck.

In October 1981 they received notice that the Historic Places Trust intended to classify the Priory as a Category One building requiring permanent preservation. The sisters opposed this classification, but lost. The Priory was eventually registered as a Category One building on 15 February 1990. The trust's listing identifies the Priory as an important part of the ecclesiastical precinct of St Joseph's, occupying a commanding position in the townscape above Dunedin's commercial centre. Its innovative design and style, and the engineering skill demonstrated in its construction, mark it as one of New Zealand's most notable Victorian buildings.[177]

In 1981 St Dominic's went on the market. Over the next two years the sisters continued negotiations with the Historic Places Trust, the bishop, lawyers, real estate agents and structural engineers. Parts of the Priory were found to lie on diocesan land, and other parts were found to be structurally unsafe. The cost of restoration was entirely prohibitive.[178] The sisters really wanted the Priory to pass to the diocese, but although Bishop Kavanagh showed sporadic interest, he was not prepared to commit diocesan funds to the purchase. In March 1983 the sisters finally signed a deed of sale. Dunedin solicitor John Dowling signed the deed on behalf of a Dunedin Catholic family trust, which purchased the Priory (excluding the chapel) for $70,000. Initially the name of the purchaser was kept secret, but he was soon identified as Dunedin priest Father Kevin Keane.[179]

When Father Keane died the Priory passed to the Diocese of Dunedin. In 2005 the diocese sold the main Priory building to a North Island property developer, who planned to transform the convent into upmarket inner-city apartments. The sale was subject to several conditions and eventually fell through, but not before builders had started pulling apart internal joinery and removing fittings. In 2009 Stuart Young, general manager of the Diocese of Dunedin, told media that the Church could not afford to develop the building; even preservation was beyond their means.[180]

For the Dominican sisters, leaving the Priory was part of a bigger shift. Since the mid-1960s the Congregation had begun a process of increasing engagement with the secular world. The Priory was a concrete symbol of pre-Vatican II monastic life, an inheritance from Mother Mary Gabriel and the other founding sisters. Selling and leaving such a legacy was hard, but it confirmed the New Zealand Congregation's true identity as ministerial religious women who were committed to praise, to bless and to preach in their local communities and the wider world.

In September 1982 the general council purchased a two-storey brick house on Scotland Street to serve as the Congregation's centre of administration. Scotland Street now houses the Dominican Family Community where three Dominican sisters, one Mercy sister and a Dominican father live together in a contemplative community engaged in a range of active ministries.[181] The Congregation's administrative centre is located around the corner and up the hill on London Street, in a house that accommodates visiting sisters and laypeople, houses the Congregation's archives and provides office space for the Congregation's administrative and financial personnel.

Since leaving the Priory, the sisters have lived in various forms of accommodation around the city, as individual and community needs have changed over time. In the 1980s five sisters lived in St Brigid's Community in Tainui: Sisters Mary Teresita, Mary Winefride, Mary Ambrose, Susan and Mary Madeleine were involved in a range of missions: congrega-

Southland Street community, 2014. S Joan Bennett, S Judith Anne O'Sullivan, Father Kevin Toomey, S Mary Hepburn RSM. DA.

S Winefride Morris serving at the St Vincent de Paul op shop in Dunedin. SDA

tional administration, pastoral work, study, teaching, synod, Catholic Presbyterian dialogue, St Vincent de Paul, Catholic Women's League, board of trustees, mothers' group and parish visitation. They described their lifestyle as 'Ordinary, stable, sensible, accepting, hospitable!'[182] They met together daily for prayer and a shared meal, and shared the responsibility for community leadership. The sisters were free to dress as they chose, they had the opportunity to pursue their own interests like gardening, tramping and films, and each was given a small personal monthly budget. The house catered for women living active lives but also provided space and time for contemplation.

Some communities began to include laypeople. In 1987 Jan Ogilvy, Clare Mackenzie, Margie Fahey, Sandra Winton and laywoman Jacqui Clayton lived together in community in London Street. It was 'a riot … good fun', Sandra recalls.[183] The following year Jan and Sandra formed a community in York Place with laywomen Brigid Inder and Marie Walker. The community joined together in daily prayer using the psalms and the scripture of the day. 'Our prayer is real and related to life and so gives life. It is simple in structure, but open to enrich community life and feed mission. It fleshes out personal, individual prayer. It is good prayer for us.'[184] Leadership was shared, involving 'the whole of life not just household but prayer, relationships, apostolate, life of the group, care for one another. We feel that it is an excellent way of living that we value highly.'[185]

In Auckland and Invercargill, which had also housed large convents of Dominican women, the same process was occurring. Individual sisters were encouraged to take increased responsibility for their lives, including their living arrangements. After years of very close communal life some sisters sought and received permission from the Leadership Team to live alone. Sister Mary Gerardine was one of the first, in North East Valley. She found it a liberating experience: 'My present situation, living alone, has given me every opportunity for a fulfilling chance to live my life as I feel it needs to be just now.'[186] Raewyn Benzie shared a house with four other sisters in View Street in Invercargill in the 1990s. The others moved away one by one and she found herself living alone. The experience was 'very freeing', but she kept in constant touch with the other Invercargill sisters: 'We are a community really, just not under the same roof.'[187]

Such a dramatic change in the structure of community life was difficult for some sisters, and presented a challenge to the Congregation as a whole. Sisters could no longer expect that all their needs would be met in their immediate living environment. The wider community of the Congregation and other communities that individual sisters belonged to provided networks of support. Recognising community life as a 'creative ordeal', the Tenth General Chapter of 1986 agreed that sisters should be free to live in a form of community that met their needs, whether it was a traditional structured lifestyle incorporating a set timetable and the saying of the Office, a flexible lifestyle open to different ways of living and praying together, or an individual lifestyle.[188]

The practical arrangements involved in adapting to altered living circumstances created their own challenges. Convents were sold, houses bought and rented and households relocated, often several times over. Like the Priory, other large buildings were hard to let go. In 1987 Bishop Boyle asked that St Albert's and St Bertrand's in Invercargill be made available for the diocese to purchase for the use of St Teresa's and St Patrick's schools. After a period of discernment the Leadership Team agreed to sell; they assured the wider Congregation that their decision had 'evoked much emotion and pain', and asked the sisters to 'pray for and affirm each other as we again let go of a precious past to look with hope and courage into uncertain tomorrows'.[189] In 2011 the largest commu-

S Jacqui Ryan and S Marie Therese Smith, the youngest and oldest sisters present after locking the chapel door for the final time at Teschemakers, 19[illegible]. Teschemakers was a special place for the sisters. The sale of the land and convent was painful, and ongoing uncertainty over the property and the future of some chattels has been difficult. [illegible]

nity of Dominicans living together consisted of three sisters. Of a total Congregation of 56 sisters, 24 lived alone. For nearly all of them, these living arrangements entailed a dramatically different approach to contemplation and community from the life they had lived in the mid-1900s as novices and nuns in the Priory.

They no longer live together in the same way, but the Dominican sisters are still very much a family, and as they lose more and more of their fellow sisters 'that connectedness that we have with one another' becomes increasingly precious.[190] In the twenty-first century sisters have far greater freedom than the nuns of the nineteenth and early twentieth centuries. They take responsibility for major decisions affecting their lives, and for their own daily prayer life and study. 'In a sense it's the same and in a sense it's different,' says Sister Jan Ogilvy. Even though it may be expressed differently, 'the heart of Dominican life' is still there;[191] the pattern of Dominican life – the rhythm of contemplation, study, community and mission – is the same.

Since the mid-1960s the Congregation of New Zealand Dominican Sisters has steadily declined in size, and no new members have joined since the mid-1980s. Some sisters still see a place for the continuation of the Dominican charism in New Zealand in its current form. Most have shifted their focus to supporting laypeople in the development of the Dominican family in New Zealand. As Mother Constance wrote in 1976, 'declining numbers concern some sisters but St Dominic does not appear to have worried about such things.'[192] In the early 1990s the Leadership Team looked directly to the future:

> *The truth is, no one has joined us for years. It seems to us as a team that the key thing is to create life-giving communities where there is a genuine commitment to the poor, a felt spirit of love and enlivening prayer … The future of our form of religious life is in God's hands, and we need not be anxious about that. The true thing of our call NOW asks for our energy and creativity whoever and wherever we are.*[193]

3. 'God stepped in'

Becoming a Dominican sister

What I love most of all about being Dominican is that we are making life's journey together – singing, dancing, hobbling, crying – with our arms around one another. – Judith McGinley, 1998[1]

✣

Vowed Dominican life entails a profound commitment to the body corporate. The Dominican Sisters of Aotearoa New Zealand are *sisters* – despite wide-ranging circumstances of birth, personality differences, various theological perspectives and disparate lifestyles and occupations, they are called to live as family. Their identity as sisters gives meaning and belonging. It also involves challenge: to create meaning, to foster belonging and to keep the body spirit-filled in its search for truth.

Each woman who has joined the New Zealand Congregation of Dominican Sisters has made her own personal journey to the order, but all have completed an extended process to become members. Although there were major changes made in the late twentieth century, the process has always been systematic and demanding, requiring nothing less than the laying down of self. Some women never completed the process; others left the Congregation after years of membership. The process of leaving has been painful for those who left and for those left behind.

Called to the convent

Every woman who has entered religious life has her own personal story. Some New Zealand Dominicans have spoken and written about their experiences. A few tell of mystical encounters and supernatural promptings. Many reflect on a persistent sense of vocation beginning in childhood. Some were stimulated and encouraged by the suggestion or example of Dominican teachers.

Until the 1960s a record was kept of each aspirant's motive for joining religious life. In the nineteenth and early twentieth centuries the emphasis was on saving souls – usually the aspirant's own, but also her family's. The Catholic Church taught that religious life was a 'higher calling'. Those who responded to the call received God's special favour; the convent shielded them from worldly distractions, and training according to the traditional rule led them ever closer to God. Florence Hart, who entered in 1895 and became Sister Mary Xavier, wanted simply 'to save my soul'. Mary Ann O'Reilly (later Sister Mary Anthony) entered in the same year because, like others who recorded the same motivation, she felt 'sure that it was God's will'. Imelda Gaffaney (Sister Mary di Pazzi) wanted 'to love God as much as I can, to

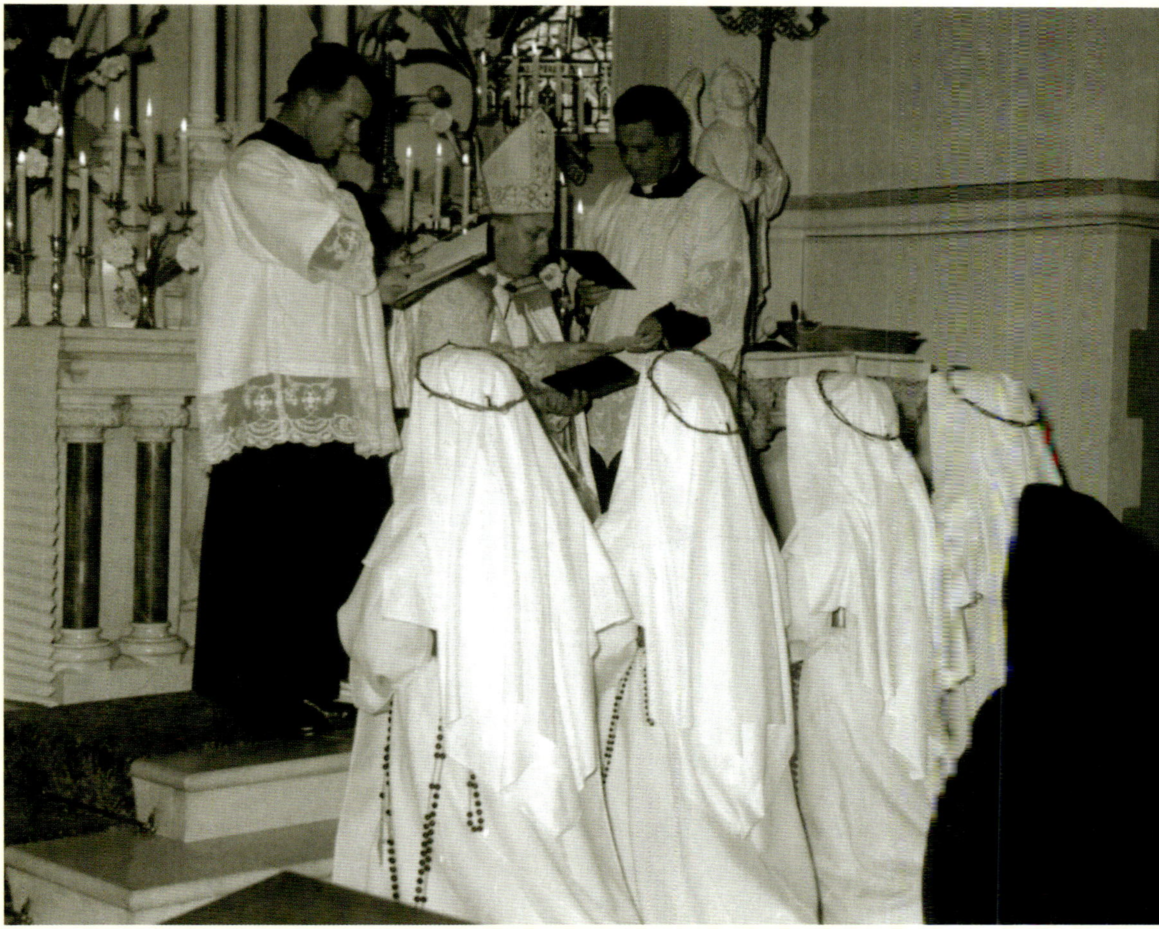

Reception of the habit, 4 October 1958. Lorraine Challis (SM Roberta), Bernadette Che[illegible]e (SM Bern[illegible]dine), Mary Horn (SM Chanel), Brenda Fitzgerald (SM Christopher). P5/[illegible]/7, [illegible].

serve Him as best as I am able, to save my soul and that of my brothers and father and to make reparation for sin'. Alice Meenan (Sister Mary Magdalen), who entered in 1913, expressed her motive in elaborate fashion: 'By mortification and sacrifice to become more devout and nearer contact with my creator thereby being assured of a crown of everlasting glory.'[2]

Those who entered in the 1960s seemed to come to the convent with rather more equivocal motives. They lived in a world that was questioning every element of the established order. These women were far less certain than their predecessors. They came to test and to seek. 'To find out if this is my vocation and to do the will of God.' 'To learn the truth, that being, to love God and be able to pass that love on to others.' 'Couldn't get rid of the idea that perhaps I should follow Christ as religious.'[3]

Sister Mary Basil Geoffrey (known to her family as May) had a sense of being guided in her decisions, and of being specifically chosen to become a 'Bride of Christ'. May was about seven when the Sisters of Mercy visited her family farm in Naseby. It was the first time she had seen a nun.

> *My mother told us that we were blessed having Sisters in our house. A few days later we were sitting round the tea table and Mum told us she had had a strange dream the night before. One sister came back to visit her. Mum asked the sister why she came alone. The sister replied she didn't need a companion because one of her daughters would become a sister. Mum looked straight at me. I knew then that I would be a sister someday …*

A few years later the family visited Dunedin and May encountered her first Dominican sister. 'I thought I was seeing an angel!' She told her mother then that she wanted to be a Dominican.[4]

Judith Anne O'Sullivan felt the call to religious life as a student at St Dominic's College. Because she knew the Dominicans so well she had decided to join the Missionary Sisters of the Society of Mary. When she was just about to enter, God came to her in a vision telling her to stay with the Dominicans.[5]

Sister Mary Genevieve wrote of a 'gradual growth in decision', but she also described receiving a sign from God when she was 14 years old. Her experience was of 'liquid light' and was repeated many years later when Sister Mary Genevieve was on retreat in Dublin.[6]

Phyllis Fox (Sister Gertrude) was a devout young girl. She was very close to her father, and every morning she used to trot along beside him to Mass at the Christchurch Cathedral. This routine gave her 'a great love of the Mass and prayer', and 'love of the Mass set up a personal relationship with the Lord'. Sister Gertrude can remember the exact moment she decided to join the Dominicans. She was on a bus in Invercargill at a corner where there was a shoe shop; other people on the bus were chattering away 'and it seemed to be so inconsequential in a way, you know, I thought I wanted to do a bit more with my life than that, and that's when I decided'.[7]

Mary Baird (Sister Mary Anna) was a young teacher with a great social life when 'God stepped in' on the golf course. She had occasionally thought about religious life, but with several job offers and a 'super wardrobe' she struggled with the idea. Out on the golf course, at a hole in the rough that she can still visualise, she felt an 'absolute urge or call – "You go home and write to Catherine Laboure and do something about becoming a Dominican."' She decided to try Dominican life for six months but told her sister not to touch any of her clothes. She is still a Dominican sister.[8]

Paddy McCann was deeply attracted by the lives of the Dominican sisters who taught her at St Catherine's in Invercargill, and over time the daily Mass became important to her. 'It was kind of like God

Reception, 3 December 1964: Sandra [illegible] (SM Bede), Raewyn Benzie (SM [illegible]), Margaret [illegible] (SM Margaret [illegible]), David Starr. The three young girls are the postulants' flowergirls. [illegible] DA.

was preparing me ... it was about God taking care of me ... putting that yearning in my heart.' When she told her family she was joining the Dominicans, her Uncle Bill asked if she wasn't just entering the convent to escape from home. Paddy herself was sure of her vocation – 'whatever means that God used to get me here I got here'.[9]

Some young women left romantic relationships to enter the convent. Raewyn Benzie was not a particularly devout teenager, but at around 16 she was visiting her aunt and uncle in Queenstown one weekend when 'it just hit me'. The experience stayed with her. Later on, Sister St James encouraged her. Raewyn had already discussed marriage with two different boyfriends, but 'this feeling' that she should try religious life just 'wouldn't leave me alone'. Eventually she made the decision to 'try it out and get it off my plate and then I'd come home again and things would be back to normal'.[10]

Roxane Parkinson was another young teacher with a great social life when she felt the call to religious life. She had had several long-term boyfriends but couldn't commit to engagement. 'Deep down' she wanted to 'give my life to God'. Roxane had been taught in turn by the Mission sisters, the Mercy sisters, the Sisters of St Joseph (the 'Brown Joes'), the Sacré Coeur sisters – and the Dominicans. She hadn't liked any of them, in their black and brown habits, until she came to the white-robed Dominicans. 'I loved the Dominicans immediately. They were full of joy and life and friendliness. They seemed to be real people ... I felt at home with them.' Ultimately, for Roxane, becoming a religious sister was 'about making a total gift of your life to God'. Dominican teachers, Monsignor Hussey and other priests and her family and schoolmates all encouraged and supported her in her vocation.[11]

Several Irish sisters recall Dominican teachers and visiting New Zealand sisters as important influences in their lives. Annie O'Sullivan (Sister Mary Colman) was born in 1902 and attended secondary school at the Dominican College at Eccles Street in

Dublin where she met Sister Mary Felicitas, a sister of Mother Mary Bertrand, one of New Zealand's founding sisters. Sister Mary Felicitas told her about the New Zealand Dominicans and how they needed help. After finishing her education and working for two years in France, Annie sailed for New Zealand to join the Dominicans.[12]

Anne O'Neil grew up in Dublin, where she was educated by Dominican sisters. Listening to the sisters' 'angelic voices' singing in choir was a deciding factor in her decision to enter the convent. When she met visiting New Zealand sisters Mother Gonzaga and Mother Philomena, Anne recognised in them 'the same spirit of joy and love of God' that animated her Irish Dominican teachers. She decided to join the New Zealand Congregation, confident that doing so 'would fulfil my desire to give my life to God and also to be a teacher, and be part of their wonderful liturgical experiences'.[13]

Susie Logan studied for her teachers' certificate at the Froebel College in Sion Hill. She got to know the Dominican sisters there and admired their open-mindedness. 'Something else, the call of God's spirit, urged me to think of religious life.' When New Zealand Dominicans visited Sion Hill she thought 'a new life, a new country could be exciting'.[14]

Barbara Dwyer grew up in Ireland in a staunchly Catholic family. She had wanted to be a nun teaching in a missionary country for as long as she could remember. A Dominican school teacher had a strong influence on her – 'she was a such a true friend and so happy as a nun'. When Barbara was in primary school she gave her name to visiting sisters from Africa and New Zealand, and eventually she came to New Zealand in 1953.[15]

Sister Loreto Meehan grew up in a series of small towns in the central North Island. The family went to church together, but if there was no Mass (because services were irregular in some places) Loreto, who was a devout child, would climb the hill behind the house with her prayer book and say the prayers herself. She was often in church as a teenager. 'Why don't you take your bed there?' asked her mother. Loreto was forced to leave school at 13 to contribute to the family income. After a series of jobs she went to work in a bank and became one of the first women tellers at the Bank of New Zealand. She had a happy social life and loved golf. Every Friday she went to confession. She had thought of religious life but knew it wasn't for her. There was a sense, however, of wanting something more; 'not a dissatisfaction, but I was searching I think …' One day the priest asked her a series of questions and the next week he told Loreto she had a vocation, to which she replied, 'I don't want one, thank you very much.' Eventually she visited the Dominicans and made arrangements to enter, but she told her mother not to give away her golf clubs as she was sure she would be home again after six months.[16]

For some sisters the call to religious life was experienced as a simple sureness that had always been there. Lorraine Challis joined the Dominicans in 1959 at the age of 20. She had felt 'a sense of call to the religious life' from a young age.[17] She has seen many changes since entering the convent and has coped with them 'because of the sense of rootedness which has remained constant – a call from God to live as a Dominican woman, wherever and in whatever way that may be'.[18]

In the mid-twentieth century, making the decision to enter religious life was not considered a particularly radical choice. Patricia Hannan, who attended St Catherine's College in Invercargill in the mid-1950s, was one of 12 girls from her class to join a religious congregation.[19] Patricia was in form three (year nine) when she decided she would join the convent. 'At first, I was appalled with this decision, but somehow knew it was what was to happen.'[20] Carmel Walsh went straight from school to Otago University and stayed

Beautiful brides, 4 October 1958. Lorraine Challis, Bernadette Cheyne, MM Tarcisius Toomey, Brenda Fitzgerald, Mary Horn. P13/7/5, DA.

Reception of the habit, 4 October 1958. SM Roberta (Lorraine) Challis, SM Christopher (Brenda) Fitzgerald, MM Tarcisius Toomey, SM Chanel (Mary) Horn, SM Bernadine (Bernadette) Cheyne. P5/7/7, DA.

at Dominican Hall. She entered the convent before she finished her degree: 'I'll give it a go, get it out of my system,' she thought. At the time, she recalls, 'it was quite a normal thing for people to do'.[21]

Others also expressed an element of prosaic inevitability. For Sister Marie Eugene Nicolson the decision to apply for admission to the Dominican novitiate was 'a natural choice'. She had spent four years at Teschemakers and five years at St Dominic's in Dunedin. She knew and admired the sisters and she wanted to be a teacher.[22] Dominican life was also a natural choice for Catherine Tither, who grew up in a strong Catholic family with the encouragement of Dominican teachers.

> *No doubt I would have been a teacher. The sisters were good role models of teaching as well as religious life. I hated boarding school but grew to love the sisters (mostly) ... Mother Patricia said, 'You come where God calls you'. The path was clear.*[23]

Most Catholic families in this period recognised and valued a religious vocation. As Elizabeth Mackie recalls, it was quite normal for high-school kids to consider religious life: 'we would sit in the milk bar, and if we had any money we'd eat cheese rolls and talk about did we want to be nuns'.[24] In Joan Bennett's words, the theology of the time presented a vocation to religious life as 'a very special way of loving and serving God'.[25]

Theological developments in the latter half of the twentieth century had an influence on vocations to religious life. The Second Vatican Council's emphasis on the priesthood of all believers empowered some people who previously might have taken religious vows to respond to God's call as laypeople, serving Christ and the church in their communities. At the same time, the rapid pace of social and political change, and the women's movement in particular, opened an unlimited range of new roles to women who might otherwise have entered a convent.

Vowed religious life was an increasingly unusual choice by the early 1980s when Jacqui Ryan joined the Dominicans. She knew she wanted to enter by the time she finished school, but she spent several years working and studying, and then a period of time travelling, before she finally entered in 1982. When her school pupils asked her why she had become a Dominican she responded with questions of her own:

> *How did your mother know to marry your father? How did your father know to marry your mother? Because there was something special about them? What made her stand out above all the other women that your father had ever known or met? There was something special about the Dominicans that was so intangible that I couldn't even put my finger on it, but it showed itself in the lives of the women that I saw ... and so that's why I chose the Dominicans.*[26]

Leaving families, losing daughters

Catholic families were enormously proud to claim religious members. Vocations were considered a blessing that reflected honour and glory on the home in which they were nurtured. When Mother Agnes Rooney, one of the founding sisters, died in 1902 the Annals praised her parents: 'In such Irish homes the seed of religious vocation germinates inevitably as a crowning blessing from God on parents who fulfill their sacred obligations with fidelity.'[27] Yet sending a daughter to the convent was a sacrifice. The enclosed Dominican life meant that after her final profession a young woman might not see her family again. She would not attend important family events such as weddings and funerals. She could correspond with her family and perhaps see them in a supervised set-

The Gavin family, Queenstown, 1963. Mrs Gavin, Deidre Gavin, SM Stanislaus (Kathleen) Gavin, Monsignor Jim Gavin, SM Agnes (Moira) Gavin, S Mary of the Nativity (Ethel) Gavin, Des Gavin, Baby Gavin, Dorothy Gavin.
F5/3/20, DA.

ting within the convent, but she was not at liberty to interact with them freely as a daughter and sister. Her commitment to God and to religious life meant total immersion in her new family at the cost of her family of origin. In 1957 a formal report from the Congregation of New Zealand Dominican Sisters to the Holy See described parental opposition as the main obstacle for aspirants to overcome in order to follow their vocation.[28]

Mother Mary Gabriel Gill ran away from home to join the Dominican sisters. Born in 1882, Victoria Gill was educated by governesses and at schools run by the Presentation and Ursuline sisters before she attended the Dominican sisters' school at Sion Hill. When she was 15 her parents took her on a tour of the Continent to introduce her to society. Almost immediately she had a suitor, and it seems that her parents were happy to accept the match. Victoria, though, had other plans. One cold winter's night, 'the ground covered with snow thickly frozen, I fled from my home and all I loved for Him who called me to be His Spouse'.[29] Seven months later she was formally welcomed into the Dominican novitiate, and she received the habit and the religious name

Sister Mary Gabriel of the Most Blessed Sacrament on 17 August 1853. Her father became a generous benefactor to his daughter's new religious family.[30] Mother Gabriel's mother died in 1882, and when she heard the news several months later she wrote of her deep sorrow and of her concern for her surviving parent:

> *my poor desolate Father who is now alone – of 13 children I am the only survivor and separated from him as far as distance, on this globe, permits. I do not regret this, trying as the thought is sometimes to nature – I rather thank God that He gave me the grace and the good sense to abandon for His love my sunny, happy home, while it was full of attractions, instead of waiting until I should have few or no sacrifices to make for Him.*[31]

Mother Gabriel understood that the sacrifice was not hers alone. In the 1880s when she returned to Ireland to set up the New Zealand novitiate at Beaumont her father was a frail old man. Mother Gabriel was a fiercely independent, strong-willed woman, but her reflections on returning to New Zealand in 1887 reveal a deeply human pain as she mourned her father and acknowledged his loss. 'He cannot long survive the shock of this renewed sorrow and sacrifice – parting from his only surviving child. But I thank God for giving him and me an opportunity of giving Him a new proof of our love.'[32]

Helena Carroll (known as Lily) also ran away from home to join the Dominicans. She was the only daughter of prominent businessman John Carroll, who was Dunedin's first Catholic mayor from 1890 to 1891. Lily was in her early twenties when she began visiting the Priory to drop off secret parcels of the necessary requirements for entry. She entered in February 1889. When the family realised where she had gone, Lily's brother John junior was sent to St Dominic's to reclaim his sister, but although he 'fumed and thundered', she remained. She received the habit in September 1889 with the religious name Sister Mary Agatha and made her first profession on 15 July 1891. 'The church was packed and as the novices entered the sanctuary the shining toes of gentlemen's best shoes were visible as the wearers stood on the seats in order to obtain a better view of the mayor's daughter.'[33]

For non-Catholic families it was especially hard to lose a daughter to the convent. Katharine Mary Josephine Dickinson of Invercargill (later Sister Mary Cecilia) entered the novitiate in July 1897 at the age of 26 'to devote myself to the service of God'. She received no help from her parents and brought no dowry, as neither of her parents was Catholic and both opposed her decision.[34]

Honora Jimima (Mima) Falconer was born in Oamaru on 19 April 1897. Her mother was a Catholic but her father was not. On Sundays Mima's mother would sneak the children out through a window to get to Mass, and at one point she threatened to burn the children's new velvet dresses if her husband continued to keep them from Mass. Despite her father's antipathy to the Church, Mima was allowed to be educated at the local Dominican school. She entered the Dominican novitiate in Dunedin at the age of 34, received the habit on 28 July 1913 and made her first profession on 16 June 1915, when she became Sister Mary Alphonsus.[35] Like her mother, Mima had had to fight for her faith. Her brother had a vocation to the priesthood, so Mima had stayed at home to earn enough money to put him through Holy Cross College.[36]

Sister Dominic (Janet) Swindale was brought up in the Church of England but the example of her Dominican secondary school teachers led her to become a Catholic. 'The thing that impressed me was their respect, the respect they had for the unique human dignity of each child in school. It really struck very deep with me.' Sister Dominic's parents and grandparents were very upset at her decision to convert. 'Well, if you want to make a mess of your life,' said her mother, 'then go ahead and make it!' They insisted that she wait until she turned 21, and the local priest advised her to comply. Sister Dominic converted on her birthday. She entered the convent at 26, and by then her father was actually quite proud – 'he was tickled pink'.[37]

Three sisters joined the Dominicans from the same Catholic family: Anne McAleese made her first profession in 1941 as Sister Catherine Laboure; Monica, who was eight years younger, made profession in 1950 as Sister Mary Madeleine; and Kathleen, a year older than Monica, made profession in 1956 as Sister Marie Grignon. One of the girls' brothers became a priest. Their parents were immensely proud. Sister Madeleine used to catch the bus down to the university with Sister Augustine. She remembers an episode when her father was ill in hospital:

> *When we got onto the bus there were no seats but sitting in one of the seats with a big suitcase was my mother. Dad was in hospital. I wasn't allowed to go and see him because of our rule! Apparently he was very very sick and nearly died … Mum was going to get him to take him home, that's why she had the suitcase with his clothes in it. She got up and gave me her seat. I will never forget it … I was so overwhelmed. That was typical of my mother. Even though I was her daughter, the fact that I was a sister took precedence …*[38]

The Dominican rule separated sisters from their family members in the outside world, and it also kept them apart within the order. Until the 1970s blood sisters were not allowed to live in the same convent. Sister Madeleine and Sister Catherine Laboure 'swapped' several times between Teschemakers and Dunedin. In 1982 they both moved to Oamaru

Honora Jimima Falconer (Sister M. Alphonsus) S, DA.

where they taught at St Kevin's and later developed active pastoral ministries in the community.

The Fox family were very proud of their Dominican sisters. Eldest daughter Margaret made her first profession as Sister Mary Ceslaus on 1[illegible] September 1933. Phyllis, fourth of the five Fox children, made her first profession on 11 September 193[illegible]. The sisters were never placed in the same convent.[39]

Sister Maria McDonald remembers a profound awareness of her parents' support on the day of her final profession on 24 May 1[illegible], a day for which I had worked so hard – the fulfilment of my childhood dream'. Recognising the collective effort of those who had prepared me throughout the years – my parents, teachers and my colleagues who trained with me,' Sister Maria was conscious of the joy and pride of my parents that a child of theirs was chosen by God to serve him in religious life'. 'Religious life was indeed a challenge for us but we did not realise, in our youthfulness, that it was our parents who were also challenged and far more heroic at a time when they could have done with our help.'[40] Sister Mary Columba McHugh, who was in the novitiate with Sister Maria in the early 1940s, was keenly aware of her parents' sacrifice:

> *Entering religious life in 1941 was a challenge! My mother had made me wait another year as she thought Dominican life was too enclosed for a country girl. Four of my brothers were away at the war in the army and airforce (Kean, a pilot, was shot down in France six months after I entered). My two sisters were nursing in Northern Ireland and my youngest brother went boarding at St Kevin's, Oamaru, the same week as I left home. Imagine leaving my parents!*[41]

Catholic parents were usually supportive of vocations in the family, but they commonly objected to their daughters entering the convent straight from school. Sister Marie Eugene's father insisted she get a qualification and a 'taste of life' before she entered the convent. He wanted her to have some time as an 'ordinary teenager'.[42]

Roxane Parkinson wanted to enter the convent as soon as she left school. The Dominicans suggested she stay on at St Dominic's as a parlour boarder and do her teachers' 'C' certificate and music studies, but Roxane's parents insisted she go to teachers' college. She went to Wellington Teachers' College and then taught in Lower Hutt; she entered the novitiate at the age of 21. Roxane's brother William left home to become a Dominican priest (Father Joseph) in the same month as his older sister entered the convent. Their parents were supportive: 'I think … they were both quite proud really.' Roxane's younger sister Molly, who was 16, stepped straight into her big sister's wardrobe.[43]

Joan Bennett was sure of her call from the age of 15 but knew she needed time before she joined the Dominicans. After two years working as a shorthand typist in a city insurance office she posted her application to the Dominicans in March 1960. Even though she was happy with her decision, Joan found her parents' grief almost impossible to face. When it came to time to leave home to enter the convent 'I simply could not bring myself to say goodbye … I couldn't trust myself to face the sadness.'[44]

Jan Ogilvy's boyfriend tried hard to convince her that God did not want her to join the Dominicans. Her parents were heartbroken at losing their only child, but they did not try and stop her. At the time Jan did not realise just how much strain they endured. Her father didn't speak her name for a whole year; he was convinced she would be home in time for Christmas dinner.[45]

Sandra Winton's parents were initially both unhappy about her decision to join the Dominicans. Her best friend was supportive and eventually her mother was, too – 'it wasn't easy but she understood; she wanted what I wanted'. Her father and his Presbyterian aunts were strongly opposed to the idea. Sandra entered in the late 1960s when rules around enclosure were gradually being relaxed. She had not been in the convent long when her mother had a car accident and Sandra was allowed to visit. Sister Teresa came to visit, too, and made a strong impression on Sandra's father: 'I don't feel so bad about it now she's with nice people like that.'[46]

It was not just parents who lost their loved one to the convent; siblings also had to adjust. Judith Robinson was the oldest of 12 children, five of whom died in early childhood from a rare genetic disease. Her youngest sister Janet died just after Judith entered the convent. A few years later, when Judith was teaching at St Teresa's back in her home town of Invercargill and her two younger sisters were at high school at St Catherine's, their mum sent them both to Judith for after-school speech lessons so they could get to know each other again.[47]

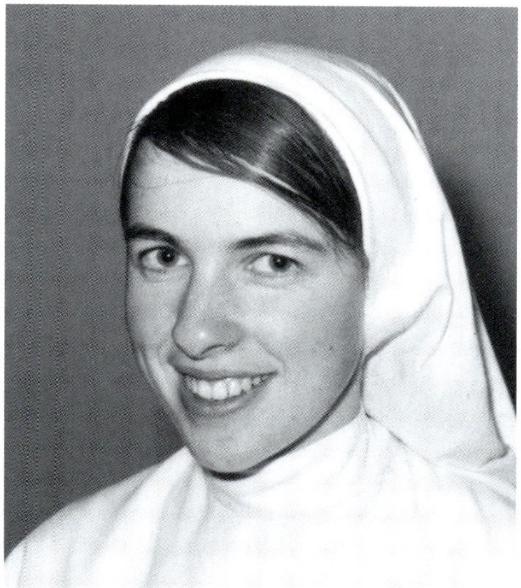

Left: Helen Bergin as a white novice, [illegible], DA.

Below: SM Alphonsus (Patricia Hannan) and her oldest sister, SM Ignatius (Catherine Hannan), who joined the Sisters of the Home of Compassion. Patricia Hannan and her siblings grew up in a strong Catholic family and attended Catholic schools: 'I grew up in a Catholic ghetto, though I wasn't aware of this at the time, and then, wouldn't have wanted it any other way.' Of the 50 girls in Patricia's fifth-form class at St Catherine's College in Invercargill, [illegible] joined religious congregations. Patricia Hannan, Personal file, [illegible]

Helen Bergin's family members were all supportive when she decided to join the Dominicans. She was the oldest of eight. The second oldest was Michael, who wrote to tell her that although he could never commit his life in that way he thought she was wonderful. The next brother, Paul, joined the Marists a week before Helen entered the convent. Their youngest sister was eight and their youngest brother only six when Helen entered: 'I hardly knew them in a way.' All of them cried when she left home. Two weeks after Helen left, Michael died in an accident – so her parents and younger siblings had lost all three older children in less than a month.[48]

After finishing school in Invercargill at the end of 1955 Patricia Hannan entered the novitiate on 24 May 1956. She waited to join with her schoolfriend Mary Concannon, who wanted to be a debutante first.

> *Mum and Dad took me to Dunedin by car. We stopped on the side of the road for lunch, which we all thought would be my last tasty food. We ate muttonbirds (which my father cooked expertly) and drank beer. When we reached the Priory, I was very relieved to find the [illegible] Studebaker parked outside – I wasn't sure Mary would actually turn up. I remember piling on the [illegible] lipstick, saying to myself that if those nuns were going to kiss me, they were going to [illegible]. We went in, Mary and I went away to change into black frocks and veils, and we then said goodbye to our parents – who agreed to meet up in a pub outside Dunedin to console one another.*[49]

Families such as the Hannans and the Concannons must have welcomed the loosening of enclosure in the 1960s with great delight. For the sisters themselves, being able to spend time freely with their families was a huge joy. Sisters who had thought they might never see their childhood homes again found themselves nursing elderly parents, participating in family celebrations and developing close relationships with younger members of their extended families.

The novitiate

The New Zealand Dominicans did not advertise for postulants in magazines or newspapers, but they did send recruiters to Ireland and they also took part in 'vocations drives' within New Zealand. At one of these events in the 1950s Mother David Stark explained the process for joining the Dominicans:

> *What qualifications are needed for a girl to become a Dominican sister? Basically, the same as those required by any religious order: a right intention, a normal Catholic life, normal good health and an attraction towards the type of work done by the order …*[50]

Most entered the convent in their late teens or early twenties. The rule and constitutions of Sion Hill, which the New Zealand Dominicans initially followed, required that all applicants be at least 14 years of age.[51] The constitutions developed for the New Zealand Congregation in the twentieth century did not specify a minimum entry age; they included rather more general statements. The 1989 Constitutions required that a candidate 'show appropriate human and spiritual maturity, an aptitude for living in community, generosity and suitability for our Dominican way of life'.[52] Candidates also had to supply references and a medical certificate. The 1989 Ordinations required the Congregation's leadership to undertake 'prudent consultation' within the community and with those who knew the applicant well in the world before accepting her for formation.[53]

Traditionally, women entered religious life with a dowry: in 1939 the dowry for choir sisters joining the New Zealand Dominicans was set at £1000, and by the 1950s it was £100. The dowry could be remitted in part or in full, especially in cases where the candidate was already qualified as a teacher. On entrance the dowry was legally made over to the congregation, but remained inalienable during the sister's lifetime. After the sister's first profession it was invested and administered by the convent, and the income was used for the benefit of the congregation. On the sister's death the dowry became the property of the congregation, but if she left the order she took the dowry with her (though not any added interest).[54] Lay sisters, who were usually from less wealthy households, were not expected to bring a dowry.

Both choir and lay sisters left their material possessions behind when they entered the convent. They did not, however, go empty-handed. Getting outfitted for the convent was a major undertaking. Postulants were expected to go in with all they would need for the rest of their lives, including blankets, sheets, towels, underclothes, shoes, and large quantities of white calico for making petticoats.[55]

In effect the Priory ran two separate novitiates: one for lay sisters and one for choir sisters. Those admitted for training as lay sisters were required to show such 'humility, penitential spirit, good sense, and bodily strength, to afford just grounds of hope, that they will render service as to the spiritual, as to the temporal interests of the Community'.[56] Before a woman was accepted for training as a lay sister she served one year as a secular, functioning essentially as a servant. Once she had been accepted for reli-

The Novitiate, 1896. **Back**: SM Evangelist (Kate) Murphy, SM Ursula (Mary) Mintern, SM Teresa (Ann) Lynch, Julia Shannon, SM Regis (Annie) Houlihan. **Front**: SM Xavier (Florence) Hart, MM Antoninus (Teresa) Mullany, Mistress of Novices Mary (SM di Pazzi) Miscall, SM Genevieve (Susie) Downing. P1/4[illegible]2, [illegible].

gious life she became a postulant, and after at least one year of postulancy she spent two years as a simple novice before taking vows. During this period of preparation lay sisters were given practical training and also educated in Christian doctrine and the obligations of religious commitment. The mistress of lay sisters instructed her charges in the 'exterior ceremonies of the Order … but also in the spiritual life, mental prayer, progress in religious perfection, recollection, mortification, resignation and other similar virtues'.[57] The New Zealand Congregation's 1908 Constitutions described lay sisters as an important part of the community:

> *Let these sisters, during the time of their probation, be fully instructed, and impressed with the deepest conviction, that the accomplishment of the Divine Will, which is the soul of perfection, consists in the faithful discharge of their duties, however humble and laborious. Let them, in a spirit of peace and loving conformity with the Divine Will, seek, in the midst of their labours to draw consolation from the reflection, that their poor and humble condition brings them to the closest imitation of their Divine Lord and Master.*[58]

Choir sisters entered the convent as postulants. A postulant wore a simple black dress and spent her time becoming familiar with the Dominican lifestyle. If she was already trained as a teacher, she taught in the schools. After six to nine months as a postulant she received the Dominican habit and began a year of intensive spiritual formation as a 'white novice'. She did not teach during this period, but in every other way led the full life of a Dominican sister. After about a year the novice made her

RIGHT: Irish postulants visiting McCarthys' farm, 1929. P3/5/1, DA.

BELOW: Reception of novices, 4 September 1929. P3/5/3, DA.

The Novitiate, 1929. **Back**: SM Declan Butterly, SM Veronica Kearns, SM Stanislaus Gavin, SM Amata Nolan, SM Damian Sligo, SM Raymond Redwood, SM Bartholomew Fitzsimmons, MM Tarcisius Toomey, SM Enda Treacy, S St Anne Brennan, SM Imelda Hynes, SM Ignatius Cournane. **Middle**: MM Elizabeth White, SM Marjory Fitzgerald, SM Teresita Dunne, SM Columbanus Cribbin, SM de Sales Lynch. **Front**: SM Ina Fraser, SM Ita Maloney, SM Canice Lowe, SM Oliver Dooley, S Marie Therese Smith. GP3[illegible]/2.[illegible]A.

first profession, vowing obedience to the mother prioress and exchanging her white veil for a black veil. Black novices usually spent another year in the novitiate, but were often required to fill teacher vacancies in other Dominican communities. After three years the temporary vows of first profession were renewed for life. At this final or perpetual profession the sister accepted a gold ring to wear on her right hand as a mark of her consecration to God.

Both first and final professions were momentous occasions in a sister's life. Family and friends gathered to celebrate with the Dominican community. In the period before Vatican II these ceremonies offered the sister's family a rare opportunity of access to her new life and community.[59]

The clothing ceremony, which was part of reception into the novitiate, was particularly beautiful. Until the end of the 1960s young women arrived at the ceremony dressed as brides. Sometimes their dresses were specially made, but often girls would borrow a gown from a recently married friend. After accepting the blessed habit before the altar, the postulant would retire to change and would return to the chapel dressed in white Dominican robes. The ritual was powerfully symbolic of a complete renunciation of the world and all its trappings.

Honour Smith was 17 years old when she entered the Priory as a postulant, and 18 when she received the habit in September 1929. She remembered that for her, the months of postulancy sped by very quickly. By August the postulants were all busy sewing habits, petticoats, guimpes and headdresses: 'The workroom was a hive of activity. The senior novices helped, and by the start of September they were ready.[60] Honour and 13 other young women received the Dominican habit on 4 September 1929 in a service held at St Dominic's Priory. Bishop Whyte officiated. Local priests and about 150 family members and friends joined the Dominican community to celebrate. Honour received the religious name Sister Marie Therese.

> *A touching sight it was when the religious, clothed as brides, each carrying a lighted candle symbolic of the light of Faith … and attended by a tiny maid as a train bearer, advanced up the chapel, [and] kneeling before the Altar asked in all humility to be admitted to the Holy Habit of St Dominic. The procession then reformed and left the Chapel … Presently into the chapel came 14 white-robed Dominicans, each to receive from the Bishop's hands her rosary and crucifix, and the new name by which she was to be henceforth known.*[61]

When Janice Ogilvy was received in 1969 she was the last New Zealand Dominican sister to dress as a bride.[62] In the early 1970s final profession ceremonies moved from the Priory to the cathedral. What had been a private function attended by invited guests became part of the everyday parish Mass. In 1972 Paddy McCann and Judith McGinley were two of the first to make profession in public. The shift symbolised the loosening of Dominican enclosure and emphasised the bond between religious orders and the people of the diocese they served.[63]

The novitiate itself was conceived as a period of religious formation to prepare the individual for religious life. Until the 1960s novices had no communication with professed community sisters, except in the school environment. For the white novices who were not teaching, the novitiate was an extremely isolating experience: apart from some household chores, their days were devoted entirely to spiritual exercises and religious study. They provided each other with support but were warned against forming 'particular friendships'. For many women the novitiate was a time of trial – cut off from their family and friends, excluded from the wider community of Dominican sisters and overwhelmed by the rituals and rules of a new lifestyle, they often experienced feelings of extreme dislocation and loneliness.

The novitiate served as a real test of vocation. Novices were free to leave the convent at any point in their training but, in reality, the culture of the pre-Vatican II novitiate discouraged questions or expressions of doubt. Until the mid-twentieth century the question for most women was not 'Will I continue?' but 'Will I be allowed to continue?' Regular examinations were designed to ascertain each novice's progress and suitability for religious life. They were tested on their knowledge of doctrine and their understanding of the obligations of religious life, and senior sisters also used this opportunity to gauge the seriousness of a postulant or novice's intention to persevere in religious life.

Sister Marie Therese Smith was one of the first young women to live in the new novitiate building opened in 1928. 'Despite the ups and downs of those years,' she says, she had happy memories of her first years as a Dominican and as a teacher in the company of her novitiate companions. By the time she joined the community in the Priory building she 'felt ready for whatever the future might hold'.[64]

From the 1870s right through until the 1970s cleaning was part of everyday life in the novitiate. Sister Marie Therese recalled wielding heavy wooden blocks covered in wet sacks to prepare the stained wooden floors of the new novitiate building for waxing. Another 'arduous task' was cleaning the high windows overlooking the two large classrooms on the ground floor.

> *This entailed climbing on to the roof of the corridor. On one memorable occasion two of us were left stranded on the roof after one tidy novice had put the ladder away. As we could not raise the*

Novices in the library, 1954. P5/12/3, DA.

> *alarm; we climbed up the sloping slate roof above the front end of the stone cloister and from there got in through the window of the Art studio behind the chapel! And after all that we were late for the afternoon lecture!*[65]

It was an undeniably demanding life, yet many of those who entered in the period before Vatican II accepted the strict regime with equanimity. Sister Maria McDonald made her first profession in May 1943. 'Our generation expected to be challenged – and we were not disappointed. Everything was timetabled and we were expected to be in the right place at the right time.' The full programme of religious studies included study of the Divine Office, the breviary, the vows and the congregational constitutions, and although there was also plenty of domestic work to be done, 'life was not burdensome.'[66] Sister Mary Columba belonged to the same generation as Sister Maria. 'I expected there to be big challenges – the ups and downs made me strive to be better.' She and her contemporaries knew they were always free to leave; their worry was rather that we would be sent away.'[67]

Sister Basil Geoffrey, who made first profession in 1939, had no difficulty in adjusting to convent life. She had lived at St Dominic's as a boarder for seven years, so she knew the convent's rhythms well. 'We had our ups and downs,' she recalls, but she knew that the novice mistress had her best interests at heart. 'Most of the time it was peaceful and we enjoyed our recreation time together and had fun.' Sister Basil's main concern was the lack of heating in the novitiate building; she was continually getting

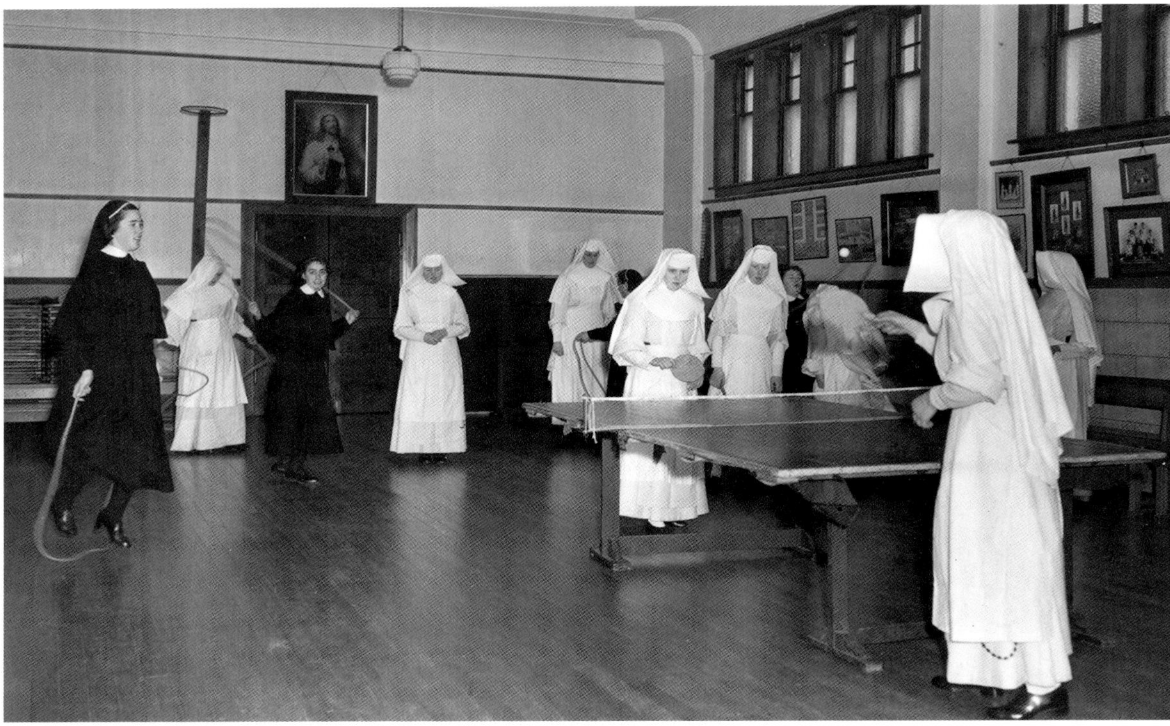

Novices and postulants playing table tennis, 1954. P5/12/6, DA.

bad colds, and one day Mother Gonzaga said, 'If you keep getting colds you had better pack up and go home.' The warning made Sister Basil very anxious: 'I wanted to be a Dominican sister with all my heart and soul.' [68]

Lorraine Challis entered the convent in the 1950s. She spent her novitiate with a group of 15 to 20 other women and found support in being one of a group who were undergoing similar changes in lifestyle.[69] Roxane Parkinson was also part of 'a big crowd'. On her first night in the novitiate she remembers thinking: 'Golly. It's just like a big boarding school.'[70]

Barbara Dwyer was 16 years old when she travelled by boat from her home in Dublin to enter the novitiate in Dunedin. She was very happy in her new life as part of a large novitiate group that included several other Irish girls. Their novice mistress Mother Tarcisius was 'a holy lady' who 'gave us great guidance in our Spiritual Formation'. Although she never wanted to go 'home', Barbara missed her parents and her brothers and sisters very much, especially at Mass and Benediction. 'I was in the right place, but missed being with my family.'[71]

Sister Loreto Meehan found the novitiate a very negative experience. The rules were so 'silly' and so rigid. Newcomers were appointed an 'angel' – an older novice who would guide them through the foreign rituals and routines. On her first night in the convent Loreto's angel gave her a long list of instructions. As soon as she got to her room Loreto wrote down all the things she shouldn't do on the back of an envelope. She found it difficult adjusting to life with a group of young women. At 25 she was several years older than most in her group. Some of the younger girls were just out of school – they used to cry and have rows. Eventually Loreto made great friends with some of those who were closer to her own age, and she came to understand that the younger women had not experienced the same freedoms she had enjoyed before entering the convent.[72]

Maureen Connolly's main recollection of the 1950s novitiate is of the lack of freedom. She too appreciated Mother Tarcisius and the depth of spirituality she incorporated into the formation programme. But having left Ireland as a teenager to travel to New Zealand and join the Dominicans, Maureen struggled to adjust to the lack of independence. 'Every minute of every day was totally organised and controlled … Frequently I asked myself what I was doing there.'[73]

Maureen O'Hanlon, who entered St Dominic's novitiate on 22 August 1954, recalled: 'Everything was so very different … We were strictly enclosed and followed a fairly rigid timetable … What a change of lifestyle this was from the freedom enjoyed as a young girl just out of school!'[74] Mary Concannon also joined the Congregation in the 1950s. Her description of life in the novitiate is brief but pointed. 'The less said the better – we were taught how to pray and I appreciated that. I still wanted to make profession when the time came.'[75] Sister Mary Adrienne's description of her experience is even more succinct: she felt like 'a fish out of water'.[76]

Many of those who entered the novitiate in the 1960s were aware of things beginning to shift in the Church, and of change in wider society. The strict rules and peculiar customs that governed life in the novitiate seemed stranger than ever. As applications for entry declined and the novitiate shrank, the support and sense of camaraderie enjoyed in earlier years was harder to maintain. Mary Anna Baird made her first profession in [illegible]. Her time in the novitiate was 'difficult and lonely'. She came to appreciate the silence, the spiritual reading and Gregorian chant – 'all these began to fill my soul'". But the rigid timetable and the lack of time for school preparation was deeply frustrating. Occasional picnics and bushwalks were 'like "good" for my BEING'.[77] Raewyn Benzie found the rules and regulations governing novitiate life utterly bizarre: it was 'a way of living that made no sense to me'. While she has not dwelt on it since, Raewyn has wondered why she persevered with such a strange and difficult

SM Benedict (Danielle) [illegible] taking vows, 24 October 196[illegible] [illegible]

The Novitiate, 1957. **BACK**: SM Michael (Mary) Concannon, SM Gerardine (Carmelita) Collins, SM Agatha (Catherine) Hurley, S Peter Julian (Judith) Baird, SM Alphonsus Hannan. **MIDDLE**: SM Regis (Joan) Hardiman, SM Stephen (Judith) Hobbs, SM Timothy (Patricia) Rabbit, SM Norbert (Maureen) Connolly, SM Gregory (Hazel) McDonald, SM (Maureen) Ligouri O'Hanlon. **FRONT**: Katherine (SM Helena) Gibson, S John Baptist (Gloria) McGee, MM (Josephine) Tarcisius Toomey, SM Denise (Roxane) Parkinson, Annette (SM Cecily) Sheehy. F14A/7, DA.

life. It was her own internal conviction rather than the novitiate experience that kept her going.[78]

Jan Ogilvy entered the novitiate by herself. She was the first to try a new postulant's uniform – a white blouse instead of black, and a black pleated skirt with black suede shoes. Her novice mistress was Mother Mary Jordan McCormick, 'a very forward looking person' whom she respected immensely. Jan experienced her one-on-one training as a real gift,[79] but adjusting to life in the novitiate was still hard: 'It amazes me still today how I stayed.' The main problem for Jan and for others was the lack of time to prepare for teaching.[80]

The period of postulancy changed considerably in the 1970s and 1980s. In 1976 the New Zealand Dominican General Council agreed to comply with the Church's wish that postulants live outside the novitiate.[81] As the number of aspirants fell away, the form of pre-novitiate training adapted to meet individual needs. In the 1980s several women who were interested in vowed Dominican life were offered the opportunity to live with a Dominican community and experience religious life before they applied formally for entry to the novitiate. The women who trialled this method of pre-formation appreciated their experience and affirmed the communities who welcomed them, though none chose to persevere with religious life.[82]

Jacqui Ryan enjoyed a unique novitiate experience. She entered as a postulant in 1982 and made her first profession in 1984. Jacqui was the only active member of the novitiate in the early 1980s. At times it was lonely. Dominican life was far more open and liberal than in preceding decades, but there were still rules and restrictions to adjust to. Jacqui had been raised in a highly politicised family. She remembers her novice mistress reminding her that the novitiate was designed as a period of spiritual development, and preventing her from reading a political column in the *Listener* – 'it was like somebody had put a tourniquet around my arm; it was cutting off this life-blood!'[83]

Since the mid-1980s a few young women have expressed interest in vowed Dominican life but none has continued on to enter the novitiate.[84]

Celebrating S Jacqui Ryan's first profession, 1984.

Leaving sisters, losing sisters

Since the first 10 Irish Dominican sisters arrived in New Zealand in 1871, 285 other women have joined the community.[85] Of these, 31 left the convent before taking religious vows, and 50 left the convent after taking vows. Each departure was felt as a loss in the community left behind.

Those who left before profession did so with canonical approval. Whether they were asked to leave or chose to return to the world themselves, these women understood that the novitiate was designed as a temporary trial period. This does not mean that parting from their new community, leaving a way of life they had felt called to and starting afresh in the world was not a difficult and painful process.

But leaving after profession was far more grave. Professed sisters had made a lifelong public commitment to serve God as a member of the Dominican order. Applying for dispensation from religious vows was a long and complicated process. Because the Congregation of New Zealand Dominicans is an institute of pontifical right, permission to leave can only be granted by the Holy See. The process can take months or even years. Once formal dispensation has been granted a woman is free from all the obligations of her profession.

In the first 60 years of Dominican life in New Zealand, only two professed sisters left the order. The constitutions labelled anyone who made a 'rash departure' from religion an 'apostate'. If a woman returned to the convent after running away she fell to the very bottom of the established hierarchy, though choir sisters always ranked above lay sisters.[86] Outside the convent, women who had abandoned religious life also fell to the bottom of the established social hierarchy.

Gerty Walsh was one of several young Irish women who travelled out from Dublin to join the

New Zealand Dominicans in 1924. Dunedin's Bishop James Whyte travelled with them. When they were still on board the boat Gerty told the bishop she had no real vocation, she had only joined the group to get out of Ireland. The bishop took great pains to ensure that she made it safely with the others to St Dominic's Priory in Dunedin, but the evening after her arrival Gerty told the mistress of novices that she would not stay. The bishop and the sisters 'reasoned with her' and the prioress recorded that Gerty 'settled down and looked happy for a couple of days', but on the evening of 10 March she disappeared after night prayers. The gates were locked so Gerty tried to climb over the fence, but the Priory had been designed and built to enclose the community – there was no way out. After this incident Gerty was moved from the novitiate to the children's infirmary. Prioress Cecily Mulcahy 'thanked God that she was under our roof instead of roaming the wicked steps of Dunedin'. Gerty was adamant that she would not stay in the convent nor return to Ireland. The sisters arranged for her to stay at the convent in Invercargill where she would help the lay sisters with housework duties while she completed arrangements to travel to friends in America.[87]

The sisters were disappointed in Gerty's behaviour and regretful of the cost involved in bringing her out from Ireland to no apparent purpose, but they were sympathetic to her situation. They saw that she had no true vocation, and as Mother Peter wrote, it was 'a good thing that she knew her own mind from the beginning'.[88] By July 1924 Gerty was working as a maid for a Catholic family in Invercargill, giving 'entire satisfaction'.[89] Later that year Sister Mary Cecily wrote to Sion Hill with a 'surprise': Gerty had decided she 'would never be happy until she was back in the convent'. Though she felt no call to teaching, Gerty wrote a humble letter asking for readmission as a lay sister. She had been deeply affected by the death of Sister Mary Colombiere (Kathleen Ryan), who had travelled out with her from Ireland. Having been in Dunedin only a matter of months, Sister Mary Colombiere died from tuberculosis in October 1924. She was professed on the day of her death.[90]

The general council decided to give Gerty another trial.[91] She received the postulant's cap and the religious name Annunciata on 25 March 1925.[92] The bishop and the prioress both wrote to Sion Hill for prayers that Sister Mary Annunciata would persevere. A few months later she was doing 'very well – ever so happy and most useful and generous', but Gerty never made profession.[93]

Sister Mary Ceslaus (Ann) Corcoran was born in Tipperary in 1889 and made her first profession at the Priory in 1910. Her brother was a priest in the Diocese of Dunedin. In February 1927 Prioress Sister Mary Cecily Mulcahy wrote to Sion Hill for help with an unfolding 'emergency'. Sister Mary Ceslaus had had to be placed in psychiatric care (presumably Seacliff Lunatic Asylum): she had apparently never had a vocation and wished to return home to Ireland. Doctors agreed that this was the best course for her health. Ann was dispensed from her vows and accompanied home.[94]

Three professed sisters left the Congregation in the 1930s, three in the 1940s and four in the 1950s. In 1936 Sister Mary Bernadette (Catherine Bourke) was dispensed from her religious vows after 12 years professed. She followed all the correct procedures and although she had not brought a dowry when she entered, she left furnished with 'a full outfit', the means of returning home safely and an assurance of an allowance of £1 per week for the following six months.[95]

A period of 'declaustration' often preceded dispensation. In the 1940s a perpetually professed sister 'who had partly lost her reason' and was 'threat-

SM Constance (Margaret) Quinn, S Micaela Dillon, SM John (Barbara) Menzies, SM Antoninus (Valerie) Dibley, 1960s. Margaret Quinn is still a Dominican sister. In the 1990s Micaela Dillon left the Congregation to establish her own congregation at Whanganui in connection with the Society of St Pius X. Barbara Menzies was dispensed from her vows in 1992, and Valerie Dibley was dispensed from her vows in 1981. P6/12/3, DA.

ened with insanity' was taken home by her parents. Doctors advised that she should stay in a psychiatric hospital but her parents chose to take responsibility for the woman. The apostolic delegate granted permission for her to remain outside the convent until her health was better or until she applied for and was granted formal dispensation.[96]

In the swinging 1960s 'freedom' and 'rebellion' became passwords for social change. Popular music flooded the airwaves, hemlines rose and political protests established a new brand of 'cool'. As society changed, the Church did too. The Second Vatican Council worked to open the Church to the world it served, responding to the signs of the times and meeting new needs. In 1964 the Council issued the Dogmatic Constitution on the Church, *Lumen Gentium*. Recognising laypeople together with clerics as 'the people of God', *Lumen Gentium* and other council documents affirmed the 'priesthood of all believers'. The Church called laypeople to exercise apostolic responsibility in their daily lives as 'leaven in the world', they would manifest God's love and spread Christ's spirit.

For Catholics drawn to seek and serve God this theology opened up radical new possibilities. All of a sudden it was possible to serve God as well and as fully as a laywoman in the community as it was as a nun in a convent. In this context, the restrictions of semi-enclosed religious life became even more grating to those already grappling with ambivalence toward their call. Seven professed sisters left the New Zealand Dominicans in the 1960s

Judith Graham (née Hobbs), who was professed in 1956 as Sister Stephen and left in 196[illegible], has published her story of leaving the Congregation in *Breaking the Habit.* For Judith the process was painfully protracted. From the beginning she found the separation from family and friends very difficult. She believed that God wanted her at the Priory for the perverse reason that she did not want to be there: 'it was a sacrifice'.[97] Family life was what she really wanted 'and the renunciation of it got harder by the day'.[98] She asked to leave several times, but Prioress General Mother David always sent her away on a holiday, assuring Judith that she would 'never be happy' in the world.[99] In 1961 one of the girls who had entered the novitiate with Judith left the convent for secular life. 'We all felt as if someone had died. There was a brief, impersonal announcement and the novitiate was bathed in sadness. She was never mentioned again – it was as if she had gone to another planet.' Convent gossip appeared to confirm the assumption that leaving could only ever lead to unhappiness. 'The sister who left, left with the stigma of failure and she would feel guilt forever.'[100] Eventually Judith's discontent became unbearable and she ran away. She returned almost immediately, but after several more attempts to leave over the next couple of years she eventually applied for and was granted formal dispensation from her vows.[101] Judith was left fragile and exhausted in the immediate wake of her departure. The community she left behind also suffered. Mother David wrote to the Congregation of the 'crisis of defection of one of our members'. She seemed to feel a sense of responsibility: 'We are in conscience bound to bring to light anything that could have been instrumental in precipitating such an action, wrong and all as it was.'[102]

As more women left (16 in the 1970s and nine in the 1980s), those who remained struggled. Some sisters felt angry and betrayed; others experienced sorrow and grief. Some questioned their own vocations. 'It was a big shift and it was hard.'[103]

Kathleen Thomson joined the Dominicans in 1959 and made her first profession as Sister Mary Andrew in May 1961. Despite the emphasis on external rules in the novitiate, Kath and her contemporaries grew extremely close. 'We were young and resilient and could laugh at the strange and hilarious things which happened constantly.' Kath taught in Dunedin, Invercargill and Bluff before she moved to Feilding to work at St Dominic's School for the Deaf. 'I felt very suited to community life. I loved the company of many of the sisters.' After a difficult period in the 1970s Kath spent 1981–82 studying at St Joseph's Institute for Deaf Children in St Louis in the United States. She returned to Feilding in January 1983 'to cold indifference, a depleted staff and students, no interest in my study and experiences and bewilderment and confusion as to what my role was'. Kath lurched into 'the worst four years of my life'. 'Over these four years I tried everything I could to survive but in the end I had to trust in my own integrity and face the heartbreak. I had reached the end of my life as a Dominican sister.'[104] The process of leaving was agonisingly painful. Eventually Kath engaged a lawyer to act as an intermediary in her dealings with the prioress general. He negotiated a settlement with the Congregation and Kath's aunt helped her establish a new life in the secular world.

Over time the Congregation as a whole became more accepting and supportive of those who left. The 1976 Constitutions made it clear that any sister who left was not entitled to claim compensation for her services to the Congregation, but did acknowledge 'an obligation in charity to see that she is provided with whatever assistance she needs to take up secular life'.[105] By the time the 1989 Constitutions and Ordinations were drawn up the official language had shifted. The constitutions laid out the formalities around withdrawal, exclaustration and readmission.[106] The ordinations provided that any sister leaving the Con-

Judith Graham (née Hobbs) visiting S Marie Therese Smith, MM David Stark and S Margaret Quinn. Judith Hobbs made her profession as SM Stephen in December 1956 and, after a long and difficult process, she was dispensed from her vows in July 1967. P9/19/1, DA.

gregation be given help to make the transition. The sisters committed to providing those who left with the financial resources to begin a new life, and also to providing spiritual, moral and social support.[107]

Barbara Menzies grew up in Dunedin and attended St Joseph's Primary School and St Dominic's College. She was 'a fairly romantic and devout child' with 'predictable daydreams about devoting my life to God and good works'. After leaving school she completed an Honours degree in English at the University of Otago. She entered the novitiate in January 1973.

> *The sisters' primary occupation as educators was one which I admired and wished to take up myself. The prospect of living in community intrigued me, and I was also attracted by the choral office … It seemed to me a life that balanced work, prayer and a strong sense of mission, though I had no idea how good a match we would be.*[108]

Barbara spent the next 20 years living as a Dominican sister. In the 1980s a developing interest in liberation and feminist theologies placed her increasingly at odds with members of the clerical hierarchy. As she moved into anti-racism work the Congregation provided ongoing support. 'I believe that the work they trusted me to do contributed to our ongoing exploration of Dominican mission in Aotearoa.'[109]

Barbara's alienation from the Catholic Church slowly crystallised in the painful realisation that she could not logically or honestly continue as a member of the Congregation of Dominican Sisters. Having witnessed others departing over the years and experienced for herself the strain on those left behind, Barbara was determined to manage her exit from religious life 'in a way that articulated my debt to the Congregation and my love for the sisters'. She wrote an explanatory letter that went to each community, and she wrote individually to every sister she had lived with and been close to. She followed up with personal visits to each of the communities she had lived in. 'During the process of leaving I encountered great kindness and affection, together with genuine distress and sincere efforts to understand my decision. There was mutual sadness about the change in our relationships with one another.'[110]

The Leadership Team supported Barbara throughout the leaving process and made 'considered, practical provision' for her wellbeing. Barbara was officially dispensed from her vows on 15 January 1993, 20 years after joining. Although she is no longer a member of the Congregation, she continues to identify herself as a member of the Dominican family.

In the 1990s the language used to speak about sisters who had received formal dispensation became more supportive and inclusive. In 1996, as part of their 125-year jubilee, the New Zealand Dominicans extended an invitation for 'all women who have been part of our Dominican life to join us in our celebrations'. The jubilee year was seen as an opportunity 'to honour the life and gift of these women and to seek mutual forgiveness and reconciliation for any past hurt'.[111]

In 2006 Kathleen Thomson initiated the idea of a regathering of sisters who had left. Organised together with four sisters and another woman who had left, the regathering took place over a weekend in May 2008 at Holy Cross College in Mosgiel. About 60 women attended – 35 sisters and 25 women who had left. For Kath it was 'a precious and healing time'.[112] For Barbara Menzies it was 'an amazing and inspiring time together – and a wonderful unlooked-for opportunity to reconnect' with women she had lost touch with.[113]

For many women like Kath and Barbara who are no longer members of the New Zealand Congregation of Dominican Sisters, the years they spent living, working and praying together in committed community cannot be disregarded or forgotten. Even if for only a brief moment in time, these women planted their feet on shared Dominican pathways. Their journeys have been shaped by Dominican values. And they in turn have impacted others and helped shape the Congregation's path forward.

Barbara Menzies (SM John) and S Margaret Quinn at the 2008 Regathering. Private collection.

The meaning of membership

The processes involved in both joining and leaving the Congregation of New Zealand Dominican Sisters are legalised and lengthy. Membership of the Congregation is not lightly sought or granted. Missing records make it hard to establish concrete figures, but it is likely that roughly 20 per cent of all the women professed as New Zealand Dominican sisters

2008 Regathering, St Dominic's Chapel. Private collection.

over the last century and a half have been dispensed from their vows. Most have stayed, but those who left helped shape the local Dominican communities in which they lived. Their departure had a deep impact on those communities and on the Congregation as a whole. Though their absence is still felt, these women are now recognised as members of the wider Dominican family.

Each woman who has joined the Dominican Sisters of Aotearoa New Zealand over the last century and a half has made sacrifices to become a member of the order. In the nineteenth and early twentieth centuries sisters sacrificed family. In the late twentieth century, rekindling and maintaining relationships with parents and siblings has brought special joy to many sisters. But whatever the nature of their relationships with their families of origin, Dominican sisters also provide each other with family. Membership of this family entails particular rights and responsibilities as a professed Dominican sister, but it also bestows on each sister a network of relationships based on shared experiences, mutual understanding and an overriding commitment to each other as Dominican sisters.

4. 'A TOTAL GIFT OF YOUR LIFE'

From enclosure to immersion

Her aim is to be devoted to the Lord in both body and spirit. – 1 CORINTHIANS 7:34

NEW ZEALAND'S DOMINICAN SISTERS are heir to a religious tradition of absolute devotion to God based on total separation from the world. St Dominic's first female followers formed a community at Prouille in 1207 and the convent was officially enclosed in 1294. The community functioned as a centre of prayer. In the late medieval period and in early modern times nuns were confined to the cloister; they were only permitted outside its walls for legitimate purposes approved by the bishop. In the seventeenth century the Dominican nuns established a fragile presence in Ireland. Their struggle to survive in penal times necessitated extreme adaptations of the rule. For much of the seventeenth and eighteenth centuries the Irish Dominican sisters lived as 'secular ladies': they dressed in modest contemporary clothing, ran schools and accepted secular parlour boarders. Although political turmoil prevented them from implementing the full rule in practice, they honoured the law of enclosure as a sacred ideal. Religious persecution eased from the nineteenth century onwards and the Dominicans resumed their enclosure but continued to operate schools. They remained true to the first nuns at Prouille by living in community and observing a common religious life. Teaching provided the Irish nuns with security of income and with sacred purpose, enabling them to pass on the fruits of their contemplation to others.

Bishop Patrick Moran understood the sisters' charism and valued their enclosure as a personal religious sacrifice and also as a form of Christian witness to the wider community. In 1870 when he requested Dominican sisters for the mission to New Zealand, Moran was asked if he would not be better to take sisters who went out among the people. 'No,' he replied, 'it would be better for the people to come to the Sisters rather than the Sisters come to the people.'[1] Moran envisaged the Dominican nuns functioning as a spiritual focal point for the local Catholic community.

In the years before the Second Vatican Council, the New Zealand Dominican sisters were semi-enclosed. They were required to engage with their students, were allowed restricted contact with their families and, where necessary, were permitted to interact with school parents and other laypeople. Yet they rarely emerged from their convents. Physical separation from the outside world served to represent and reinforce their repudiation of worldly affairs in favour of spiritual sanctification.

MM Cecily Mulcahy. P2/4/4, DA.

Enclosure had its purpose, but it was always difficult to balance with the mission of teaching. The Second Vatican Council offered the New Zealand Dominicans an extraordinary opportunity to resolve this inherent lifestyle tension. In the spirit of *Perfectae Caritatis* the Congregation returned to its roots. Over the last few decades of the twentieth century the New Zealand Dominicans developed an ever more creative focus on mission and a correspondingly less intense focus on the traditional rules of enclosure. The nuns became sisters: ministerial religious integrated and embedded in their local communities.

Enforcing limits

From their earliest days in Dunedin the New Zealand Dominicans followed strict guidelines to maintain a 'holy distance' between themselves and the world. The outer door of each convent was always kept locked. Visitors were only ever received in the parlour, which was always located on the outer edge of the building. Interaction with outsiders represented a test of religious purity. Unless they had a formal dispensation, sisters who received visitors were required to have a companion present. Before speaking with her visitor, a sister had to present herself for a few moments before the Blessed Sacrament 'to implore the light and grace of Jesus Christ to preserve her heart from the least sin, or breath of the spirit of the world'. Visits were kept as short as possible, 'that is, as far as obedience, charity or the avoidance of giving offence' allowed. Sisters had to 'guard carefully' for the duration of each visit, taking special care to avoid listening to worldly news or disclosing community information to outsiders. They were never to accept visits for the 'purpose of entertainment'. Rather, they were expected to employ 'a holy and cheerful demeanour' to show 'worldlings how sweet and holy is the yoke of the Lord'.[2] If workmen were needed in the convent the prioress was only permitted to speak to them with a companion present. When a doctor was called to the convent the prioress and another sister accompanied him at all times and gave notice of his presence by ringing a little bell to warn the other sisters to stay either in the choir or in their cells until he had departed. Every year the prioress visited each of the Congregation's branch convents to ensure proper observance of the rule, and even for these visits she had to obtain specific permission from the bishop. The bishop and other clergy were allowed in the convent for the purposes of preaching or performing other spiritual services. Schoolchildren also crossed backward and forward between the outside world and the convent grounds, but they never went beyond designated school boundaries. The nuns' living, eating and sleeping quarters were sacrosanct. The earliest New Zealand constitutions urged sisters 'that, in consecrating themselves to God in this holy state, they have entirely renounced the world, and shall be bound to a strict and faithful observance of enclosure'. After making profession they were allowed to pass outside the bounds of enclosure only with the written permission of the Bishop, or 'for such weighty reasons as are assigned in the sacred Canons and apostolic Constitutions – such as fire, robbers, malefactors or any evil that would cause immediate death'.[3]

These limits were too strict for Mother Gabriel. Intently focused on the community's mission and on the health of her sisters, she sought to adapt the rule of enclosure to meet local needs. In 1884 she sent three sisters who were unwell to Queenstown. She had already obtained permission from the Bishop of Dunedin, but Mother Gabriel used this case to press her contacts in Rome for a more general leniency of enclosure.

> *Our numbers are so limited and our works so heavy and important in the cause of religion that I had no scruple in giving orders contrary to the rule of enclosure in my desire to restore the failing health of three valuable and holy teaching nuns. Did I do right?* [4]

Mother Gabriel sought help from Archbishop Kirby, Rector of the Irish College at the Vatican. She asked him to procure for her 'full authority' to exercise her own judgement in moving sisters from one convent to another for health reasons or for school duties. She also asked 'high sanction' for her own freedom of movement. Mother Gabriel was an active manager. She felt deeply responsible for all the sisters in New Zealand. An annual visitation to the local branch convents was not enough: she wanted to be free to visit whenever 'a necessity' occurred – whether that was for class examinations, to solve practical problems or to offer spiritual wisdom. Although she had no immediate trip planned, she also sought a general permission to travel to Europe in the interests of the order in New Zealand:

> *I am too enthusiastic a Dominicaness to wish to transgress any of the precious rules or to dispense myself, even with the Bishop's permission, in any important matter. What I ask is merely to free my conscience from embarrassment in the future …* [5]

Like Mother Gabriel, successive prioresses also negotiated the boundaries of enclosure with ecclesiastical authority. The Priory's Book of Permissions provides a written record of requests and responses. In December 1910 Mother Mary Cecily Mulcahy asked permission for a few of the sisters to accompany the visiting Sisters of Mercy from Wellington on a tour of some places of interest around Dunedin. Bishop Verdon declined his consent. In February 1911 she asked permission for the Invercargill and North East Valley convents to have telephones installed. Verdon agreed, with the stipulation that two sisters must always be present when the telephone was in use, and it was on no account to be used for private conversations.[6] On 31 May 1923 Mother Cecily asked for and received permission to visit the cemetery. Later that year she asked if the sisters could go across from the Priory to St Joseph's Hall to conduct practices for an upcoming school concert; Monsignor Mackey signed his consent. On 3 January 1927 Mother Mary Teresa Lynch asked permission for Sisters Mary Dominic and Cecilia to go for a month's holiday in the North Island. The bishop granted his consent on the understanding that the holiday also included congregational business. In 1930 Mother Teresa asked permission for two sisters to travel to Christchurch and spend a week with the Sisters of the Mission to learn the Montessori method of teaching. Bishop Whyte consented. In the same year he also granted consent for Mother Mary Reginald and Sister Mary Dominica to attend the Catholic schools conference in Wellington.[7]

At a superficial level the relationship between bishop and convent might be seen as systematically enforced subservience. At a deeper level, the bishop's involvement in enforcing enclosure also represented institutional protection and support. During this period Dunedin's bishops and Dominican prioresses worked in close collaboration. They provided each other with mutual support, based on a shared vision for colonial Catholicism. In 1931, 60 years after the Dominicans had arrived in New Zealand, Auckland's Bishop Liston echoed Moran's original vision for convents of enclosed Dominican sisters as loci for Catholic education and spirituality. While they were discussing the proposed Dominican foundations at Northcote and Helensville, Dominican priest Father Finbar Ryan suggested to the bishop that more 'active' nuns might be better suited to these particular locations. The bishop demurred: he believed that the Dominican Rule was entirely suitable, 'because of its providing such a centre of prayer'.[8]

In reality it was the prioress who controlled enclosure. Every sister in the convent had knowingly vowed herself to enclosed life. The basic limits were taken for granted, but it was the prioress who determined exactly where the boundaries lay and under what circumstances they should be expanded or contracted. The bishop was her backstop. She engaged him on her terms to fulfil the obligation of procuring consent in specific instances. In a few rare and extreme cases where sisters broke enclosure, the prioress used the bishop as her envoy in the outside world.

Mother Mary Reginald Quilter, prioress general from 1933 until 1939, used congregational letters to manage the limits of enclosure. In February 1935 she issued a long letter to the superiors of the local branch convents. Mother Reginald was particularly concerned about sisters' relationships with clergy. She reminded sisters that prolonged private conversations were never allowed, not even with priests. 'Far too much about our private affairs is known in clerical circles. Very great imprudence must be imputed to some of our members and even the graver fault of disloyalty. If the Rule were observed such fault would be rare, if not absolutely unknown.' Mother Reginald encouraged her superiors to monitor and correct junior sisters to ensure that all 'sentimentality and frivolity should be utterly discountenanced'. She expected sisters to be modest in all their interactions, preserving the 'dignity which should distinguish a religious' by guarding not only what they said but also where they directed their eyes. 'It is not becoming,' she warned, 'for a sister to smile up into the eyes of either priest or layman, or to endeavour to attract special notice in any way of the ways known to women of the world.' Enclosure bound the sisters to a code of behaviour that was set on the inside but also monitored on the outside. 'Those who come in contact with nuns expect to find them ladies, even if they do not understand the spiritual side of their lives.'[9]

MM Bertrand McLaughlin, MM Reginald Quilter, MM Teresa Lynch, 1927. P3/10/1, DA.

Mother Reginald's words highlight the inextricable connections between social, cultural and religious codes of behaviour. The Dominican prioress was head of her own little world, governing her community as a spiritual disciplinarian. Yet the Priory was also part of Dunedin's class system: the choir sisters who taught in Dominican schools were expected to act as ladies, and the lay sisters who performed the bulk of the Priory's domestic chores were perceived as members of the working class. The prioress enforced not only traditional religious values but also contemporary social and moral standards among her sisters, and in the classroom the sisters imparted these standards to the students they taught.

In December 1937 Mother Reginald issued another warning letter. 'I think it is my duty to call your attention to a few points of rule or of customs which are not as strictly observed as formerly, and the neglect of which can but weaken or even destroy religious discipline.'[10] She reminded local superiors

Bishop Liston speaking at the opening of the new Teschemakers building in 1923. Clergy and dignitaries sit on the stage; the nuns are segregated on a balcony at the side. F8 [illegible]

that the outer gates of all convents should be punctually locked at six o'clock every night. Correspondence was also subject to strict limits: sisters were permitted to write family letters once a month, although more frequent correspondence was allowed in the case of death or illness. Quoting from the constitutions, Mother Reginald urged sisters 'to refrain from needless correspondence, lest indulgence of desire for this kind of intercourse with persons outside their convent tend to destroy their spirit of detachment from the world'.[11]

At the start of 1939 Mother Reginald believed that standards were slipping again. Superiors were empowered to slit open all letters 'and read if they consider it advisable to do so', and to dispose of any parcels from outsiders. Mother Reginald also reminded her sisters to ask permission every time they used the telephone, and long telephone conversations were forbidden. As ever, Mother Reginald was concerned not only with internal observance of the rule, but with the image her sisters projected to the outside world. Too much interaction between the convent and the world might weaken respect for the sisters; and it would certainly do 'no good to souls'.[12] Lest the sisters fall into laxity during school holidays, she issued a directive at the start of December 1939 that no visitors should be admitted to any of the Dominican convents during Advent, and no letters should be sent until Christmas Day. Sisters travelling by train during the holiday period were to refrain from speech, 'except when politeness or necessity requires it, and then they will speak in a low tone and briefly'.[13]

Mother Reginald's successor Mother Dominica McKay, was particularly sensitive to comparisons between the enclosed Dominican sisters and 'active orders' of 'visiting sisters' such as the 'Mercies' (the Sisters of Mercy).

The sisters should take every opportunity of speaking to the children of the greatness of the Dominican Order, its glorious past, the wonderful work achieved by it through the centuries, not least that done by our own sisters since their coming here in 1870. We must combat the pernicious heresy that active orders are more suitable for present-day needs. Our life of prayer and contemplation overflowing into our active work must be shown to be the means of combating the evils of the present day.[14]

The ordinations passed at general chapters served to reinforce specific features of enclosure and respond to changing social conditions. The General Chapter held at the end of December 1939 passed several ordinations relating to enclosure. Automobiles were not accounted for in the Congregation's formal constitutions, so the chapter passed an ordination to restrict their use. The chapter also established that secular visitors should be discouraged when sisters were required to stay in hospital, and the Congregation was reminded that a 'little bell' should be rung whenever a workman was present in the house.[15] The General Chapter of 1950–51 passed an ordination prohibiting sisters from attending teacher training refresher courses in the evenings.[16] Six years later, however, in recognition of the increasing importance of professional education, the General Chapter passed an ordinance permitting attendance at evening refresher courses.[17]

Mother Mary David Stark's report to the Holy See for 1953–57 affirms her determination to protect her sisters from secular life. Sisters were allowed out of the bounds of the convent for 'just and grave reason' only, and for the shortest amount of time possible. They were not allowed 'by reason or colour of a vacation' to spend time with their parents. Sisters were not allowed to spend time with visitors inside the convent without a companion, or for frequent or protracted visits. Mother David was adamant that no visits were allowed that were 'evidently useless' or 'dangerous', or that threatened to disturb the community's religious exercises or spirit of piety.[18] The rules governing contact with the outside world were so tight that it usually did not matter where sisters lived in relation to their relatives. In 1956, however, Mother David and her council decided that sisters with relatives in Invercargill would not be stationed there as the frequency of family visits had become 'an abuse'.[19]

The physical environment of the convent reinforced the boundaries laid out in the rule. The Priory in Dunedin and the other Dominican convents around the country were designed to impose very real physical limitations on their inhabitants. Sister Mary Adrienne White, who made her first profession in 1950, recalls an environment that allowed sisters to focus on 'Jesus and Me': 'The windows in the chapel and the high walls outside were to keep "the world" out.'[20] For some this was a wonderful thing – the opportunity to concentrate solely on God, to be freed from distraction and absorbed entirely in the daily routines of spiritual devotion. For others the transition to life in this set-apart world was difficult.

Judith Graham's memoir of life in the convent gives a strong sense of the physical reality of life at St Dominic's Priory in the mid-twentieth century: 'The view over the city and harbour from the long narrow windows was superb but I felt a world away from the city below in this concrete fortress.'[21] Although she had lived at St Dominic's as a boarding student, Judith did not realise how different her life would be when she entered the nuns' enclosure.

The first thing I noticed was how bare everything was. In the boarders' building there were pictures on the wall of the stairwell. Here there were none. Four flights of bare stairs went up to the top floor. They looked more like outside steps with their metal banisters and wire grilles. Mother

Tarcisius showed us our bedrooms – only they weren't bedrooms, they were called cells. They were partitioned each from the next but the walls did not go right up to the ceiling, so we could hear but not see our neighbours … In the cubicles of the boarding school we had mirrors and hand-basins and we could make our rooms personal with pictures of our family. But here there was nothing but the polished wooden floor, a narrow bed with a horsehair mattress, grey blankets, one pillow and a pure white bedspread. Each cell had a small window which opened only slightly, and was painted over white, so you felt like Macbeth, 'cribbed, cabined and confined'. There was a wooden table and chair, a cupboard and a plain enameled jug in a stand. The only ornament on the wall was a crucifix.[22]

SM Dominic Swindale and SM Louise Tim[illegible] on their way from Feilding to Wairoa to visit SM Dominic's grandmother. When they stopped at Kopua Monastery the abbot, Father Joseph, insisted on checking the car for them. F14A-7, DA

Marie Twomey, who made her first profession in 1960, found the separation from her family very hard; not being able to visit her home was 'almost painful' and she was acutely aware of the effect on her parents. As the only daughter she found her parents' deaths traumatic, and her brothers did not cope with the large family home 'crammed with treasures and books' – 'If only you could come home and sort out,' they wrote to her. Marie had nightmares and dreams of sneaking home, and began to have trouble sleeping.[23]

Joan Bennett, who entered the convent in 1960 and made her first profession in November 1961, accepted enclosure as part of her commitment to Dominican life. 'We did not leave the convent precincts except for holidays to another convent, or medical visits within the city or town,' she says. Joan never felt locked in – she had made her vows with the expectation of lifelong religious enclosure.[24] Nola Gleeson entered at the same time as Joan. She missed her family at first but adapted quickly – 'those people become your family … the ones you're living with.'[25]

Negotiating new boundaries

In the 1960s the General Chapter responded to the invitation of the Second Vatican Council to reassess the ancient boundaries of religious enclosure. The first major change came in the chapter of 1962–63, not long after the first council sessions. The Congregation of New Zealand Dominican Sisters passed an ordination allowing sisters from Ireland and other countries to return to their homelands to visit parents and relatives. For women who had travelled to New Zealand in their teens and early twenties expecting never to see their families again or to set foot again on home soil, this was an astonishing and wonderful gift. The change signalled an increasing awareness of individual needs and openness to the secular world. Other small changes were also granted: the sisters at Lawrence and Cromwell were allowed to ask permission from the prioress general to go for long walks in the holidays, and all sisters were allowed to ask permission to visit seriously ill parents, brothers or sisters in hospitals or institutions. Yet the 1962–63 Chapter reaffirmed many of the other traditional boundaries of enclosure. Communication with parents, priests and seculars was still restricted, newspapers were still prohibited, and visitors were still banned during Lent and Advent.[26] Enclosure was still understood as a spiritual discipline enabling religious women to focus their time and energy on God.[27]

Some sisters found the pace of change frustratingly slow in these early stages. In the mid-1960s Patricia Hannan was stationed at Dominican Hall and studying at Otago University. When she ventured outside the convent she was required to have a companion. Another sister at Dominican Hall was also studying at the university, but the two women were attending different classes and it was not always practical to walk to and from the university together. Carrington Hall was across the road, so they often asked one of the boys to walk with them to and from class. 'When the superior asked if we had a companion, we were always able to say, yes; and it didn't occur to her to ask for details.'[28]

The annual visitation of local communities gave the prioress general an opportunity to address any blurring of the boundaries of enclosure. In 1964 Mother Mary David Stark reminded the Northcote community that television represented an intrusion of the outside world. Television sets were not to be hired except for special occasions, and then only with the permission and supervision of the prioress. At Santa Sabina Convent she noted that some sisters were using the telephone too freely, carrying on long conversations with seculars 'with the result that silence is broken and charity forgotten'.[29] In 1965 the Helensville and Northcote sisters joined throngs of other religious women at a private screening of *The Sound of Music* at the Plaza Theatre; the convent corridors rang with singing for weeks afterwards.[30]

The Special General Chapter of 1968–70 initiated a thorough process of revision. The first session, held between December 1968 and January 1969, made numerous alterations to the congregational constitutions. Egress was still controlled by the prioress general but the conditions under which it could be granted were far more relaxed. Sisters were permitted to accompany school children on excursions and cultural visits, and to attend local educational meetings, religious seminars and conferences. Usually sisters were not permitted to travel alone, however superiors were given leeway to decide when exceptions could be granted. If a sister was posted in a place where her family lived she could apply to spend one day a year at home, and sisters were permitted to visit their family home when a family member was seriously ill or dying. The conditions under which outsiders were permitted to breach enclosure were also loosened: confessors, chaplains, doctors, workmen and others were allowed within the sisters' enclosure 'whenever it is deemed necessary for the fulfilment of their respective duties'. Superiors were still expected to control correspondence but letters were expected to pass through their hands sealed rather than unsealed, as previously. In a radical departure from tradition sisters were permitted to have meals with visitors, to share morning tea with lay staff members and to eat with school children when on picnics, fieldtrips and social functions, and they were permitted to correspond with outsiders during Lent and Advent.[31]

At the second session of the Special General Chapter, held between December 1969 and January 1970, these changes were confirmed and the conditions of egress were relaxed even further. Sisters were permitted to visit business establishments and shops 'where necessary', and to visit their families regardless of location.[32] They were still expected, however, to maintain a high degree of formality in their interactions with the outside world. A handbook of rules printed in January 1970 reminded sisters not to answer the door to callers while wearing an apron. At public lectures and social gatherings they were advised to exercise tact, discernment and courtesy. The council recognised that some sisters had spent most of their lives in religious isolation. It advised that before sisters stepped out of their convents – whether for school outings, study or family visits – they should make themselves familiar with the rules for pedestrians in city traffic.[33]

As the Congregation experimented with the limits of enclosure, the prioress general's role became even more important in clarifying the details of specific situations. In January 1970 Mother Jordan revoked the experimental one day at home; instead, sisters could apply for permission to visit home from their local superior, who would use her discretion to grant visits for varying lengths of time.[34] In June 1970 Mother Jordan found it necessary to remind the sisters at the Priory that home visits were allowed only with the express permission of the local superior – it seems that some sisters had been making 'extraordinary expeditions' without the required permission.[35] At her annual visitation of St Catherine's Priory in Invercargill in 1971 Mother Jordan urged sisters to consider their increased freedom of egress within the balance of spiritual and community interests. She asked them to be 'reasonable' in their requests to go out of the convent, 'weighing well the reasons for seeking these permissions, realising too, that the nature of our work puts a constant strain on us and that we need sufficient rest if we are to be courteous to one another, and to the children in our classes'.[36]

The Eighth General Chapter, held in the summer of 1974–75, approached enclosure in the context of personal rights and responsibilities. Recognising 1975 as the International Year of Women, the chapter called on Dominican women to acknowledge their shared sisterhood with women throughout the world and to accept their additional obligations as religious women. The chapter exhorted Dominican women to display the 'courage of distance'. It permitted greater egress and increased social contact with the outside world, while maintaining the obligations of a consecrated life of poverty, prayer, professional dedication and responsibility to community life.[37]

The Congregation's revised Interim Constitutions of 1976 emphasised freedom and personal responsibility, but still reserved ultimate responsibility for the limits of enclosure to the prioress general. Local superiors were entitled to give permission within general limits fixed by the prioress general. When a sister was on holiday she was permitted to stay with her family. Sisters were still not permitted to go out unaccompanied at night without 'grave need'. They were encouraged to approach their requests for egress with an attitude of obedience and courtesy. Both the sister who requested egress and the superior who allowed it were expected to ensure that absence from the convent did not disturb community life or impede observation of religious devotions. 'In all questions of egress a balance must be maintained between charity to the community and charity to those outside it.'[38]

The gradual relaxation of the rules of enclosure in the 1960s and 1970s had a profound impact on individual sisters. Lorraine Challis entered the convent in 1958 and made her first profession in October 1959. Her father, who was not a Catholic, found her decision to become a nun very hard to accept. He first visited his daughter in the convent

S Virginia (Judith) Robinson and S Ligouri (Maureen) O'Hanlon in the Fiat given to St Dominic's Convent at Feilding by Father Klimeck OP, 1970s. F14B/5/1, DA.

four years after she entered. When he died in 1968 Lorraine was able to visit her home for the first time since joining the Dominicans. Later she enjoyed visits with other family members and spent time at home helping her mother recover from a cardiac arrest.[39] In the late 1990s Lorraine lived on her own in Milton, providing 'a Dominican presence in a rural area'. Her ministry focused on adult education involving personal growth programmes, spiritual direction and retreats. Although she had never anticipated living alone, her lifestyle was an integral aspect of her ministry: she was fully available to whoever needed her, whenever they needed her, and she experienced a strong sense of belonging in the local community – 'a mutual sharing and support'.[40]

Roxane Parkinson made her commitment to Dominican life in the mid-1950s. Her family travelled to Dunedin for her reception and profession ceremonies and wrote to her in the convent once a week. In 1969 Sister Denise, as she was known then, enjoyed her first visit home to her parents since 1955. A month later her father died and she travelled home for the funeral. In the 1970s Roxane was living in Henderson in West Auckland. She was a member of the Congregation's general council and travelled regularly to Dunedin for meetings, and on her way south she always stopped in Wellington and stayed a few nights with her mother.

The relaxation of enclosure also opened up opportunities for overseas travel. In 1965, out of the blue, Roxane was sent to Rome to study at Regina Mundi. She was present for the promulgation of the Document on Religious Life, and for the closing of the Second Vatican Council on 8 December 1965. During her years in Italy she visited Siena, Monte Cassino, Assisi and Aquino, and afterwards she travelled through Germany, England, Ireland and France. Roxane now lives in Johnsonville where she enjoys close contact with her sister Molly in Lower Hutt. Her brother Bill is a Dominican priest in Auckland and her brother Phillip lives nearby in Raumati South. She commented, 'I've never been so close to family on a regular basis since I left home.'[41]

Judith Anne O'Sullivan came from a very close and happy family. She entered the convent as a 19-year-old on 7 March 1960: 'I thought my Mother's heart would break.' Both parents and all six siblings came to drop her off at the Priory amid 'copious tears'. She was often homesick as a postulant, yet she believed in her call. Having family visits only once a month was 'a great deprivation'. It was wonderful when things began to change in the mid-1960s and sisters were able to visit their families at home – 'this was like a miracle and a great joy'. Judith Anne spent five years in Rome from 1979 until 1983, an experience she describes as 'pure gift'. In 2007 she travelled with her three siblings to Italy, where she attended the Dominican Sisters International Conference. The four O'Sullivan sisters continued on to Ireland together, and Judith Anne then travelled to the United States where she spent three months in the Dominican Ashram in Adrian, Michigan. She has also travelled in the Asia–Pacific region in various leadership roles for the New Zealand and International Dominican sisters.[42]

As prioress general from 1975 until 1985 Margaret Quinn was directly involved in the process of relaxing enclosure. She understood the personal cost: when her father died Margaret was prioress at Teschemakers. The funeral was only about 45 minutes' drive away in Timaru, but Margaret was not permitted to go. When her mother died 10 years later Margaret was living in Dunedin. By then the rules had changed and she was allowed to travel to the funeral. Decades later Margaret still grieved for her father; she insisted that 'the changes were right'.[43]

Responsible obedience and community cohesion

As individual sisters explored new freedoms and renewed connections with family and friends in the outside world, the Congregation worked towards a new understanding of community identity. The Dominican women of the 1970s made the same vows at profession as the Dominicans of the 1870s, but they were not nuns. They were apostolic sisters held together not by walls or rules, but by a shared call and a conscious commitment to communal religious life.

In the late 1970s four Dominican sisters – Susan Logan, Imelda Windle, Helen Bergin and Patricia Hannan – moved out of the Priory. They wanted to live a simple lifestyle in a normal neighbourhood. Their move to Silverton Street in Andersons Bay caused controversy within the Congregation. Not only had the sisters left the Priory under [illegible], they had opened up the possibility of others [illegible] centralised convents and moving out into the world.

Sister Judith Anne also had a vision for a new kind of Dominican community embedded in the life of the local neighbourhood. In 1977 she wrote to the general council from St Albert's Convent in Invercargill advocating selling the Congregation's larger convents such as St Albert's so that sisters could live in 'simpler homes and thus be a more effective witness to poverty and availability'. She envisaged smaller Dominican communities 'where we could open up our home more to the people and thus be more in touch with the realities of today's world'.[44] By the early 1980s more sisters were asking for permission to live in smaller communities and follow a different lifestyle.[45]

In 1981, when Raewyn Benzie first approached the prioress general with the idea of living in a small community in a normal house, she wrote of the need 'to look deeply at our life of prayer, our life in community and our reaching out to others'.[46] As the limits of enclosure loosened, Raewyn found herself increasingly engaged in the wider community. At times the experience was empowering; at other times it was challenging. Applying for a job herself rather than being sent to a new community and issued with instructions for her next appointment was 'a huge thing'. Even being invited out for coffee by colleagues was a new experience – sequestered in the convent and protected from outside influence, she had never heard of a flat white or a latte.[47]

Located in the country outside Oamaru, Teschemakers had been the Congregation's most isolated convent. In 1980 it was reinvented as a retreat centre offering 'open-house hospitality' to church and community groups. The first community – Sisters Denise, Imelda, Anthony, Loreto, Gregory and Gerardine – lived, prayed and worked together as a team with separate areas of responsibility,[48] and over time they welcomed others to join their Dominican community life. During their first year of operation, Dominican priest Father Roman Carter spent several months there as resident chaplain: he ministered to the community's spiritual needs and ran weekend scripture courses and retreats that were open to all. Father Ambrose Loughnan, also a Dominican, joined the Teschemakers community in 1981, and Father Bernard Maxwell soon followed. Ambrose had worked with Dominican sisters in the Solomon Islands, where they ran the schools and he ministered to the parish. He notes that Teschemakers was a new experiment: 'our roles were no longer defined and we were endeavouring to become a joint Dominican partnership. We had to discover our roles ourselves by working in them and then by deciding how to define them.' Although it took some time, there were 'not very many squeaking joints that could not be overcome' with 'a little of the oil of charity on both sides'.[49]

SM Winefride Morris, S Mary Concannon and SM Jordan McCormick at Tainui, 1980s. F9/17B, DA.

In June 1980 the community welcomed Pam Heaney, a young laywoman who came to share fully in the sisters' life and work at Teschemakers; she served as the coordinator of school camps and youth activities. Other laypeople also came and went. In 1985 Connie and Tony Hassan became part of the extended community. Cecily Guest worked with the community in March 1987; Judith and Bruce Challies lived in the main house for a year from March 1989 as members of the community; and early in 1989 Sharon and Paul Mitchell and their family joined the extended community. Community prayer life was open to all. At times it was a struggle to meet all members' needs ecumenically and inclusively. Community life at Teschemakers was 'creative and energising, stimulating and exciting'.[50] But openness to outsiders brought challenges, too, with different forces pulling in different directions.

Teschemakers met a need in the Christian community. Groups came from all over the South Island

Teschemakers, [illegible] **Back:** SM Am[illegible] SM Therese, S[illegible] Challis, SM [illegible] Scully, Father [illegible] Loughnan, S E[illegible] McDonald, SM [illegible] Stark. **Front** [illegible] Anne O'Sullivan, S Marie Two[illegible]

and from many different churches. It was a special place for those who lived and worked there during its time as a boarding school, and for those who spent time with the community in the 1980s and 90s. It remains a sacred place for many Dominican sisters, a place 'to walk in freedom and beauty, an intangible beauty and quality of atmosphere that is a gift to be part of and very conducive for contemplation and silence'.[51]

At the Tenth General Chapter in August 1986 the Congregation recognised and embraced the challenge of maintaining unity in the midst of rapid change: 'We reaffirm the importance of community in enabling us to answer the call to mission, and its central value in our lives as the place where we can be at home, accepted and loved for ourselves, and at the same time be challenged in our growth.' Recognising that each sister belonged to a range of communities within and beyond the Congregation, and that the Congregation was itself an important community, the chapter acknowledged that 'people understand and express community in different ways.' Accepting this diversity, the chapter encouraged communities 'to search out ways of providing a life-giving environment' for those they included.[52]

Until the loosening of enclosure the Dominicans cared for elderly sisters within the Congregation. Most of the aged and infirm lived in one of the upper storeys of St Dominic's Priory and, later, in Santa Sabina Convent. Since the 1990s several elderly sisters have lived in local rest homes. In the late 1990s Sister Mary St Anne Brennan moved to Calvary Hospital in Invercargill. She had never anticipated living in a rest home, but she adjusted well, integrating Dominican observances into her new lifestyle. 'The morning routine is always the same: rise about 7am, shower, breakfast ... Mental Prayer, Office, Rosary, Mass ... reading, lunch. In the afternoon Office and so on as in a Convent.' Later in the afternoon she enjoyed the company of visitors.

Teschemakers staff, 1989: Danielle Melton, Mary Anna Baird, Judith Challies, Bruce Challies, Marie Therese Smith, Ian Schneiderman (not staff), Roxane Parkinson, Joan Marie McClusky, Mary Concannon, Marie Twomey, Pauline Lynch (not staff). F9/11/1, DA.

Teschemakers Cooperative, 1992. **Back**: Paul Mitchell, Gerrit Sonnenberg, Danielle Melton, Susan Healy. **Front**: Jane Sonnenberg, Marie Grunke, Vera Gray, Sharon Mitchell, Mary Horn. F11/11/1, DA.

'It is extraordinary whom one meets here,' she wrote. 'People I have not seen for 60 years or more, and others whom I last saw in a school room.'[53] Sister Mary Declan Butterly moved into St Catherine's Home in Auckland in 1993. The home, run by Mercy sisters, offered daily Mass and Sister Mary Declan was able to observe the Office and the rosary in community with other residents. The other Auckland Dominicans visited her often.[54] Despite the Congregation's elderly sisters no longer living in exclusively Dominican communities, they are honoured and cared for by other Dominicans who live close by, and cherished by the group as a whole.

The current constitutions of the New Zealand Dominican Sisters do not include any references to enclosure. Sisters are encouraged to take personal responsibility for their lives and living conditions, but are also bound by a vow of obedience to live a consecrated life in community.

> *Our vow commits us as individuals and as a community to search for the will of God and unites us in the task we do for the Church. In our personal and community struggles to find and realise God's will we enter both into the mystery of our own lives and into the mystery of Christ's passion, death and resurrection. If we are faithful to this commitment, we witness that it is only in submission to God's will that people become truly free and truly themselves.*[55]

Freed to identify their own needs and desires in the context of God's call to religious service, the New Zealand Dominicans of the twenty-first century live in a diverse range of situations. Some live alone or with one or two other Dominican sisters, and some share homes with laypeople or other religious men and women. All move about the towns and cities they live in with full freedom to engage with the secular world; in fact, this is now understood as part of their preaching mission.

In 1995 Sister Mary Clare Timpany embarked on a new mission on Waiheke Island: she formed a community with her natural sister Joan, who was a sister of the Home of Compassion. 'Hospitality is our joy so our home is open to all who come. Many come to pray, others for relaxation and some for a listening ear,' Clare writes. The sisters became involved with local groups that were concerned with 'the needs of the world, our earth and its people'. They helped young parents with children. In the absence of a parish priest they worked in the local parish community, taking joint responsibility with other members of the parish for evangelisation, formation, caring and liturgy. Clare and Joan formed deep connections and made many friends on the island. In Joan's words, there was 'plenty of opportunity to grow in human care and understanding'.[56]

In the 1990s Margaret Butler ran the Catholic parish in Bluff. She expressed her experience in a poem:

SM Clare Timpany and her sister Joan relaxing in their garden on Waiheke Island. RA, DA.

> *Living alone*
> *makes this ministry possible,*
> *allows for the development of gifts*
> *I didn't know I had,*
> *and challenges me to face*
> *the very deepest parts of my being.*
> *At a little distance from community*
> *I relearn the value of community:*
> *day to day sharing and stimulation*
> *and the rubbing off of rough edges.*[57]

Helen Bergin lives in community with Carmel Walsh in Mount Albert, Auckland. She teaches theology at the Catholic Institute of Theology, and describes her work as 'deeply Dominican'. She finds motivation for her mission in community life – 'the motivation that keeps me going as a Dominican especially comes from those I live and pray with, particular from our common exploration of the Word of God, our seeking for truth and celebratory times together'.[58]

Dunedin Airport, 11 May 1966. The first Irish-born New Zealand Dominican sisters to return to Ireland to visit their families: SM David Stark, SM Canice Lowe, MM Catherine Mary (Amata) Nolan, MM Enda Treacy, SM Veronica Kearns, SM Teresita Dunne. P6/5/1, DA.

The New Zealand Dominican sisters no longer own any of the large purpose-built convents of earlier times: those have been sold and repurposed or demolished. The loss of this physical legacy has caused real grief for some sisters. Others have embraced the freedom of living beyond the symbolic bounds of the old convent walls. In 1990 Cecily Sheehy and Clare Timpany lived in a small house in May Road, Auckland: 'Living in a place without a Dominican history has given us an opportunity to create our lives (without conditions or expectations).'[59] Cecily now lives on her own. She sometimes misses companionship and help around the house, but she is happy. 'I feel more part of community living alone than I would if I was with somebody.' She takes part in regional Dominican meetings and social get-togethers, and spends time visiting the older sisters. 'We're all pretty well friends,' she says of the wider congregation, 'We all love one another.'[60]

The end of enclosure has also freed Dominican sisters to travel much more freely. In 1962 Irish sisters were allowed to visit home. From 1969 home visits were extended to at least three months, and from 1975 sisters born overseas were allowed to visit their families at least every 10 years.[61] These visits had a profound impact on sisters and their families. In April 1972 Mai Duignan wrote from Kilbeggan, County Westmeath, to thank New Zealand's prioress general for her 'goodness in allowing my sister to come home to see her mother'.[62] In 1989 Sister Catherine Laboure visited Ireland after more than four decades in New Zealand. Her letter of thanks to the Leadership Team is heartfelt in its restraint, speaking of her joy in the fulfilment of a long-held wish to return to her native land.[63]

In 1978 Sister Susan Logan wrote to Mother Constance asking permission to return home to Ireland for an extended period. 'For some time I have had

In 1985 S Dominic Swindale, S Maureen O'Hanlon and S Louise Timpany attended the Catholic Deaf Conference in Brisbane, and took the opportunity to relax at the beach while they were away. F14B/5/1, DA.

In May 2001 S Judith Anne O'Sullivan visited the New Zealand Dominicans in Dublin. S Maureen O'Hanlon, S Anne O'Neill, S Judith Anne O'Sullivan, S Barbara Dwyer. P10/2/2, DA.

a strong urge to live with my own troubled people,' she wrote. 'I realise that there are at present other forces in life driving me: change of place and in a way change of ministry, my love for my family, time of life, and all other sensible and silly things that make me me.' The Leadership Team consented to her request and Susie left for Ireland in January 1979.[64] She later made several more visits home.

Maureen O'Hanlon was born in New York City and grew up in Ireland. She came to New Zealand to join the Dominicans as a teenager, and made her first profession in September 1956. On the fourth Sunday of each month when New Zealand-born novices received visitors in the parlour, Maureen and other women whose families lived at a distance wrote letters home. 'I always felt very lonely when I was writing to my parents and family,' she recalls. In December 1970 after 16 years away from home, Maureen visited her family in New York. 'I missed them so much and I was aware of how much they had missed me … Stepping off the plane at Kennedy Airport and seeing them waiting for me is a memory I will always hold dear.' It was a great joy to be able to stay at home, spend time with her brothers and their families and enjoy meals together at the family table.[65]

In the late 1990s three Irish New Zealand Dominican sisters – Anne O'Neill, Barbara Dwyer and Maureen O'Hanlon – requested permission to return home permanently. They wished to remain part of the New Zealand Congregation, however Anne understood that, as with her first call, she would be leaving grieving ones behind', but she felt that just as the faith and love of her parents and friends had helped her to remain committed to her original call, the trust and support of her Dominican sisters would give her the courage 'to search out new needs and directions' in Ireland. She had no interest in transferring to the Irish Dominican Congregation: 'I love my New Zealand Dominican Family … You are my sisters in whose midst I have grown spiritually and personally, sharing friendships, experiences, strug-

In the late twentieth century large convents were sold and some were remodelled to suit smaller communities. S Rose Marie Lyons and S Basil Geoffrey in Flat 1/42 Bolton Street, remodelled from the old Siena Convent, 1993.
F16/6/11, DA.

gles and mission, and I'd wish it to remain this way.'[66] After a comprehensive process involving meetings with the Leadership Team and consultation with the wider congregation, Anne, Barbara and Maureen returned to Ireland in November 2000. Maureen went back to New Zealand at the start of 2002, but Anne and Barbara stayed in Ireland and established a mission at the Hampton Hermitage – a Carmelite retreat centre in Dublin. Both women took great delight in their opportunities for closer contact with family and old friends.[67] 'We have carried our New Zealand Dominican torch to Ireland,' they wrote to the wider congregation, 'and we will joyfully continue to walk with you in Dominic's footsteps.'[68]

Inevitably there have been occasions when these changes have given rise to tension. Before the 1960s sisters were moved from one convent to another by a formal written notice from the prioress general; they had no input into their yearly appointments, nor any right to resist. By the end of the twentieth century sisters had become active participants in the process of forming local communities and determining their individual living arrangements. At times this model made the process of settling communities long and complicated.[69] Sisters were still vowed to obedience, and the Leadership Team still took ultimate responsibility for balancing personal needs with community interests, all within very real financial limits. It

S Judith Anne O'Sullivan with Helen, a Malaysian neighbour who visits the Scotland Street community for English lessons, 2015 DA.

was not always possible for a sister to live in the place or in the way that she believed God was calling her, and this was sometimes difficult.

The physical move out of closed convents and into local neighbourhoods also raised basic challenges. In the years before Vatican II convent life was uniformly ordered to reflect the vows of poverty, chastity and obedience. Sisters slept in small, plain cells. As they moved into houses and created their own living spaces, each sister took increased responsibility for interpreting religious poverty in her own context. As individuals and as a congregation, the New Zealand Dominicans have sought to live in the world in a simple way that reflects their commitment to the poor and oppressed. It has not always been easy to find a balance between the traditional austerity of the past and the elevated expectations of middle-class comfort in Western society today.

Ultimately, the shift from convent to wider community has been driven by apostolic motivations and ministerial obligations. Until the mid-twentieth century the Dominican mission in New Zealand was focused exclusively on Catholic education. The apostolate was well served with large communities of teachers living adjacent to their schools, dedicated solely to their students. At its best, the pre-Vatican II model of large enclosed convents stimulated vibrant community life and a powerful experience of corporate religious devotion. But it also cut women off from their families and the communities they wished to serve. With the end of enclosure, New Zealand Dominican sisters are now spread from Invercargill to Ireland, living a range of lifestyles and engaged in a variety of missions. In 1998 Sister Mary Leonie described the Dominican community at Glen Road, Auckland, as 'the pivot for my life. As I think of the prayer, humour and support I experience I realise more than ever the privilege that is mine in being a Dominican woman today.'[70] Although they enjoy far greater freedom than sisters of previous generations, the Dominican sisters of the twenty-first century are bound by a shared commitment to each other. 'We've got that unity. We know who we are.'[71]

Salve procession, St Dominic's Priory chapel. P5/8/3, DA.

5. 'Beauteous order'

The rule

This holy Rule serves as a ministering angel to summon us each morning to rise and bless the Lord, and as a lamp to guide our feet in every step to be taken that day through the whole range of our duties, whether of prayer, obedience, employment, spiritual enclosure, instruction, humility, peace, or love . . .[1]

THE DOMINICAN SISTERS WHO came to New Zealand in 1871 followed the Rule of St Augustine and lived in community according to pontifically approved constitutions and ordinations. Together, St Augustine's Rule, the constitutions and ordinations and the congregational customary comprised the 'rule', referring to all the rituals, regulations and routines of Dominican life in New Zealand. St Augustine's Rule has remained unchanged since the turn of the fifth century when it was first laid down. During their first 100 years in New Zealand the Dominicans adapted Irish constitutions and ordinations and the Irish customary to meet local needs, though they actually changed very little. The rule was a practical expression of the ideals and purpose of the Congregation, prescribing the structure of community interactions and proscribing certain behaviours. As Bishop Moran wrote to the sisters, '[A] Nun who has kept her vows and her Rule is as secure in her convent as I am on my throne in the cathedral.'[2]

In the years before the Second Vatican Council the rule governed every detail of life in the convent. It was a strict syllabus of conduct that included instructions for observing the vows of poverty, chastity and obedience, as well as strategies for detachment from the world, maintaining appropriate relationships within the convent and achieving conformity with approved religious devotions. In subjugating self to the rigours of the rule Dominican women aspired to praise, bless and preach through community religious life. The rule required sacrifice – of independence and personal freedom – but it also liberated. Convent regulations created a safe space in which women were free of the constraints imposed by social expectations. They provided a regime designed to unfetter the spirit and allow individuals to draw close to God. This highly structured existence also offered Dominican women a framework for engaging in mission opportunities with the outside world through the students they taught in Dominican schools.

Monastic horarium

From their beginnings in New Zealand until the late 1960s the Dominican sisters followed the same pattern of daily life as their nineteenth-century Irish forebears, and their medieval ancestors before them. Convent life operated on two complementary and interwoven timetables – one for the choir sisters who taught in the schools, and one for the lay sisters who managed their community's domestic arrangements. St Dominic's principle of dispensation allowed for some flexibility, but it was a busy life.

Every moment of a choir sister's day was accounted for. The horarium prioritised prayer time and allowed time for meals, teaching and preparation, study, and a small amount of recreation and rest. Life in the convent began at 5.30 each morning and finished when the lights went out at 10pm. As well as corporate worship, the timetable allowed for personal spiritual exercises. For choir sisters, most of the rest of the day was spent teaching. Sisters made confession once a week and received communion on Sundays and other holy days during the year. The purpose of this rigid life was twofold: the strict discipline of regular spiritual exercise was designed to aid contemplation and to equip followers for the apostolate.[3]

The 10 Irish founding sisters who came to Dunedin in 1871 brought with them the constitutions they had followed at Sion Hill in Dublin. Like their Irish sisters they observed the Little Office of the Blessed Virgin Mary, a condensed version of the full Divine Office. The Irish Dominicans had first been dispensed from the full Office in penal times. The full Divine Office was designed for strictly enclosed monastic life, whereas the Irish sisters, and the New Zealanders, were only semi-enclosed. The smaller Office allowed them more time in the day for teaching and school preparation. Yet the sisters still yearned for the full Divine Office. The smaller Office set the New Zealanders and the Cabra branch of Irish sisters apart; Dominicans everywhere else in the world said the full Divine Office.

At the end of the nineteenth century the New Zealand Dominicans applied to Rome for their own constitutions. They also applied for permission to return to the full Divine Office. There was some concern that the full Office would take too long to chant (about 15 minutes longer than the Office of the Blessed Virgin Mary), but most sisters were eager to align themselves more closely with the order as a whole.[4] The process took more than 30 years – as Sister Mary Cecily wrote in 1912, 'Rome is always so slow.' The thought of having to wait for their applications to pass through the various necessary stages 'would deter many a stout heart', but they persisted,[5] and in the meantime they depended on a few printed copies of the Sion Hill constitutions. In June 1910 Sister Mary Louis wrote home to Sion Hill: 'Mother darling it is all very well for you at home – you are as it were the body surrounded by living examples of the Rule, while we here are scattered and most untrained in every way. I don't know how we keep together at all.' In some houses there was not even a typed copy of the constitutions; communities had to place their trust in common memory. 'Oh Mother it is pitiable,' wrote Sister Mary Louis, 'this is not holy Ireland where the faith is so strong and traditions so sacred. If you only knew …'[6]

In 1933, when the Pope finally recognised the New Zealand Dominicans as a distinct congregation he also authorised their return to the full Divine Office. The New Zealand Congregation of Dominican Sisters first printed their own Rule and Constitutions in 1939. The constitutions were essentially the same as those approved for Sion Hill, since the 'aim, origin and spirit' of both groups was the same, but New Zealand's new constitutions marked an important turning point in the development of an independent local identity.

The new constitutions identified the special end for which the Dominican Order was created as 'the salvation of souls by the ministry of teaching and preaching'. The special means it employed to achieve this end were 'the solemn Choral Office, and the maintenance of observances designed to support regular life and to render the members of the Order efficient preachers of the Gospel'. The new constitu-

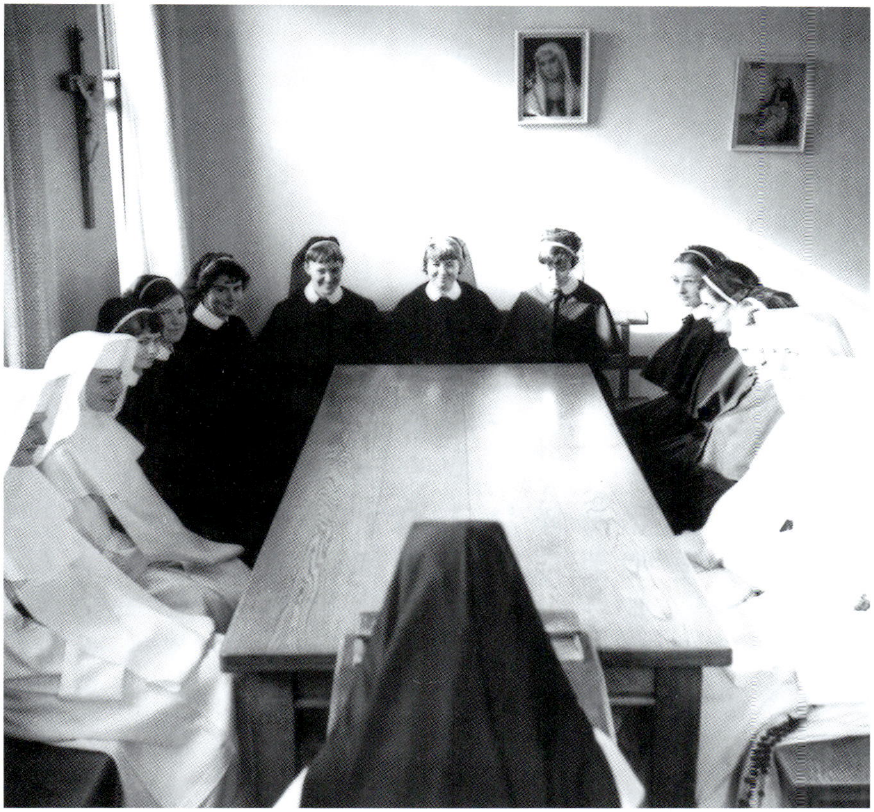

Lecture in the novitiate with MM Jordan McCormick at the head of the table, mid-1960s. P6/12/11.

tions celebrated the sisters' right to the full Divine Office. 'Both because of its intrinsic excellence and because zeal for its devout recitation is, as it were, an heirloom from our holy Father St Dominic, the sisters must cherish their privilege of being associated with the official prayer of the Church.'[7] In circumstances where sisters' capabilities or teaching pressures rendered the full Divine Office 'gravely difficult', the constitutions allowed the prioress general to permit substitution of the Little Office of the Blessed Virgin Mary.[8]

The Divine Office was accompanied by a complex ceremonial. It was not just every moment of the day that was accounted for in the Dominican horarium; it was every gesture, every glance, every attitude of mind and heart.

> *Reverence for God is the first reason for the observance of choral etiquette, but it must not be forgotten that it helps personal devotion also and contributes very much to the edification of the neighbour. Speaking generally, recollectedness of mien should characterise every action and attitude in Choir. One should walk without haste or lagging, stand with dignity, sit with modesty, kneel with reverence: so that one's deliberate bearing may be praise.*[9]

The Customary of the New Zealand Dominican Sisters included detailed instructions for entering and leaving choir, and described the correct words and inclinations to be used at each stage of the day's various rituals. Sisters were warned to keep a 'strict

Sisters in procession at Teschemakers. F8/1/5, DA.

guard' over their eyes and to avoid any violation of religious silence. While the community was in choir, prayer beads were not to be rattled or handkerchiefs used audibly.[10] The New Zealand Dominicans also referred to Cabra's 'Ceremonial', which included additional instructions for the Office that covered everything from the percentage of beeswax to be contained in the candles, to the quantity of candles and the order in which they were lit and extinguished, to the correct occasions for using incense, as well as more directions for inclinations and prostrations.

Processions were regular rituals. The community made the Salve procession every day after Compline, and the Libera procession weekly. On the fourth Sunday of each month they processed in honour of St Dominic. On the first Sunday of the month they processed in honour of the Holy Rosary, and on the second Sunday in honour of the Most Holy Name of Jesus. Other processions took place at Christmas and Easter and at various other times of the year. In procession, sisters had to walk directly behind each other and directly in line with their partners. They were given specific instructions on how to 'wheel' around corners, and were expected to maintain a regular distance from each other at all times.[11]

For the uninitiated the physicality of religious observance could be quite strange, even shocking. In the late 1920s Catherine Mary Nolan travelled out from Ireland with nine other young women intending to join the New Zealand Dominicans. On their way to Dunedin the group stopped in Oamaru where they attended Mass at Holy Rosary Convent. When the sisters prostrated on the floor Catherine Mary thought they had all fainted. By the time she got to the Priory she was better prepared for the other strange rituals that would soon become part of her everyday life.[12]

The complex rites of the choir were attended to by an equally complex team of officials and assistants. The chantress was responsible for all aspects of the ceremonial: she looked after the music and the choral books, arranged practices and prepared the Congregation for special celebrations. She was also responsible for filling out the weekly choral tablet, assigning sisters to various roles in the choir and refectory. Each Saturday the reader at table read out the list for the week. The most important job each week was that of the hebdomadarian, who officiated in choir and led other community exercises. Other weekly roles included the cross bearer, holy water bearer, versicularians, acolytes, readers, the responsorian and the sacristan.[13]

The horarium was demanding, but the New Zealand Dominicans treasured the Divine Office. Cecily Sheehy loved singing the prayer of the church, especially when it was her turn to take the solo parts. Daily practice made the nuns' voices 'very sweet and beautiful'.[14] Sister Judith Anne also appreciated the Divine Office in Latin. Although the busy timetable and spiritual exercises were challenging, the prayerful rhythm of daily life gave 'a sense of belonging, commitment and intimacy with God'.[15] Maureen Connolly remembers an overwhelming sense that 'every minute of every day was totally organised and controlled'.[16] As Carmel Walsh put it, the day 'was all broken up into bits'. There was very little time for study or school preparation, but 'everyone was doing it. You got into the swing of it.'[17] Patricia Hannan experienced daily life in the convent in the years before the Second Vatican Council as 'simple, regular, prayerful and generally satisfying'.[18]

Just as each day had its rhythm, each year in the convent followed a set pattern. School holidays broke the year into terms and, when the children went on holiday, the sisters also took a break from their normal routines. Sometimes they visited other Dominican convents: the Queenstown convent, set amidst the mountains, was a favourite holiday destination. The main holiday each year took place at Christmas time. On the feast day of St Stephen, 26 December 1872, Sister Mary Catherine wrote to Sion Hill describing Christmas in New Zealand. 'We are now on our vacation, enjoying the most delicious weather you can imagine. It seems difficult to realise Christmas times in the midst of scorching sun.'[19] In 1899 the sisters holidayed at Holy Cross College in Mosgiel. The seminary did not open to seminarians until May 1900, so the sisters were in effect its first inhabitants. A Catholic man in Mosgiel owned an 'Irish jaunting car' that he used to take passengers to and from the train. The sisters were 'so delighted with it' that he brought it to Holy Cross several times during their visit and gave rides around the grounds.[20] The following year the sisters holidayed at Larnach's Castle on the Otago Peninsula. The furniture and bedding were sent on horse-drawn lorries and the sisters travelled by bus. They used the billiard room at the back of the house as a refectory and the ballroom as a chapel.[21]

Retreats were another important time for renewal. These were conceived as 'holy days' during which sisters were 'left alone with God and his holy angels'.[22] Usually Dominican retreats were preached, most often by a priest. They were sometimes very brief – just a day taken for spiritual reflection and rejuvenation – and the longest retreat each year was held in December, leading up to Christmas Day. Sister Mary Leonie Parry treasures the memory of her first Christmas in the convent: sisters arrived from all around the country, filling the Priory with energy as they practised together for the Christmas liturgy. 'I will never forget the experience of taking part in that singing of the Divine Office and Mass on Christmas Eve and Christmas morning. I thought that I was in heaven!'[23]

Sisters on holiday at Larnach's Castle, January 1891. P1/13/2, DA.

Sisters after retreat with Father Hingston OP at Teschemakers, 7 July 1960. P16/16/2, DA.

Celebrating the Golden Jubilee of SM Benvenuta (Mary) Carclan, SM Bonaventure (Ruth) Wakelin, SM Gabriel (Teresa) Gaynor and S Zedislava (Annie) Bonisch, 1966. The sisters wear wreaths of flowers on their heads and carry staffs decorated with ribbons and lilies. P11/4/18, D[illegible].

The calendar was also broken up by feast days and jubilees. Once a woman received her religious name she celebrated the feast day of her saint instead of her own birthday. Depending on her position in the community and her age in religious life, the occasion might be marked by a special Mass or a special meal.

Sisters also observed the annual anniversaries of their profession as nuns. On important anniversaries the whole Congregation came together to honour individuals and to celebrate their commitment and persistence in religious life. In 1955, for example, Mother Mary Philomena McCarthy celebrated 50 years as a Dominican sister. The Congregation presented her with a 'spiritual bouquet' consisting of holy Masses, holy communions, the Divine Office and rosaries.[24]

Diamond Jubilee, 1992. SM Declan (Brigid) [illegible] and SM Bridget (Brigid) Cribbin celebrating [illegible] years as Dominican sisters. P11/9/18, D[illegible].

Lay sisters

Lay sisters lived a parallel life in the Dominican community: they followed a briefer version of the choir sisters' horarium to allow them more time for manual work. Lay members had been a part of the Dominican Order from its earliest days. Domestic labour was dignified in theory as a holy path to God, but it was perhaps inevitable that in practice the separation of manual and academic work acquired a strong class distinction. Men and women from wealthy, educated families entered Dominican congregations as choir members, and those from working-class homes nearly always entered as lay members.

Two members of New Zealand's first Dominican community were lay sisters: Sisters Lucy Tracy and Peter Jordan. There is very little written record of lay sisters' lives in the early years, despite the fact that they made up between 20 and 30 per cent of the Congregation. In 1893 the First General Chapter of the New Zealand Dominican Sisters resolved to include lay sisters in their constitutions, and in 1894 when the New Zealanders amended and reprinted the Sion Hill Rule as the 'Holy Rules and Constitutions of the Dominican Nuns, Diocese of Dunedin', they included a whole new chapter dedicated to lay sisters.[25] Lay sisters were clearly ancillary to the community's main purpose – they were accepted into the convent only when it was 'expedient to assist the other sisters' – yet the new constitutions acknowledged them as vital members of the Dominican community: 'It is indeed very certain that the piety and regularity of the lay sisters greatly contribute to the good order and sanctity of the Convent of which they are members.' Though their labours were humble in nature, they were 'not, on that account, less meritorious in the eyes of Him who, being God, annihilated Himself taking the form of a slave'.[26] The constitutions exhorted the prioress and other sisters to 'treat this humble and precious class of sisters with the utmost charity and tenderness'. Care was to be taken that each woman was assigned work suited to her strength and ability, and time was always to be made for the 'essential duties of religion'.

Lay sisters observed the same fasts and the same physical austerities as choir sisters, but said much briefer prayers. Between 1871 and 1933, when the choir sisters recited the Little Office of the Blessed Virgin Mary, the lay sisters recited a short series of Paters (The Lord's Prayer) and Aves (Hail Mary). In 1933 when the choir sisters returned to the full Divine Office the lay sisters retained the Office of Paters and Aves.[27] They were expected to attend Mass daily, say grace before and after meals and, where possible, recite the Office together.

The mistress of lay sisters was responsible for the lay sisters' religious instruction, the welfare of their souls and their material labour. They were accountable for their daily tasks to the procuratrix, or household manager. The constitutions urged lay sisters to perform all their tasks 'cheerfully and exactly', 'to practise strict economy, to preserve from injury the goods of the Convent, also to take the greatest care in preparing the food so that there may be no cause for complaint'.[28] All these daily labours were sanctified by constant prayer and an attitude of active contemplation.

> *To render your daily occupations agreeable and meritorious: 1. Do not fail to offer your work to God in the morning. 2. Unite yourself to the intention and dispositions of our Saviour … 3. Love labour … 4. Do, with constancy, care, activity, and in the spirit of obedience, penance and prayer, everything that is commanded of you.*[29]

New Zealand's first fully independent constitutions, printed in 1939, described choir sisters and lay sisters as complementary roles. Choir sisters

'Nazareth'. The la[illegible] with Mistress of [illegible] Sisters MM Bert[illegible] McLaughlin, St Dominic's Pri[illegible], 1904. Jubilee Album [illegible].

performed the governmental, administrative and scholastic work of the Congregation, and lay sisters performed the manual and material work. Together they formed one community, 'so they contribute to a single work for God, and in its performance they ought to be actuated by the same spirit of faith'.[30] Although their roles may have been conceived as complementary they were certainly not equal. Each sister occupied a designated place in the community hierarchy according to her position and her date of profession. The prioress was at the top and the most recently professed lay sister at the bottom. Lay sisters were not allowed to occupy any positions of responsibility in the community; even the most junior choir novice ranked above the eldest lay sisters. When the community processed together the lay sisters came last. They were never present at congregational chapter meetings. In larger convents lay sisters had their own designated recreation room. Each week they had their own Chapter of Faults. Lay sisters were distinguished from choir sisters by their black scapulars.

The voices of lay sisters are noticeably missing from the congregational records. They usually performed their daily tasks faithfully and unobtrusively, and played no part in congregational affairs or community decision-making. Their names are recorded in the Book of Professions and their deaths are described in the community annals; the years between are largely empty – yet many lay sisters are remembered with particular affection by other community members and by school students.

Congregational visitations and community reports written by local superiors offer brief glimpses of lay sisters at work. In 1936 Mother Mary Reginald Quilter performed her official visitation of all the Congregation's branch convents. At Bluff, she reported, the single lay sister sometimes suffered from loneliness.[31] At Milton the lay sister was 'quite contented and happy', but she was not 'over tidy', nor 'generous'. Her deafness sometimes caused inconvenience and she was sometimes 'pert' in answering her superior.[32] At Lawrence the lay sister was a model of piety: 'Sister Mary Clement seems very happy and has no complaints to make. She … gives the sisters good hot meals, is most economical and tidy about her kitchen which is neat and bright. She is devoted to her prayers.'[33] The lay sisters at St Catherine's Priory in Invercargill were a happy group. A new range in the kitchen had proved 'a great labour saver'. Sister Emily found it 'most delightful' and the other sisters observed that she looked much better since her heavy work had been lightened.[34] Five years later, when Prioress General Mother Mary Dominica McKay visited St Catherine's Priory, she found that the work of the three lay sisters was far too heavy. They had help from a secular woman from 9am to 5pm each day, and much of the laundry was sent out, but two of the sisters were 'no longer young' and the third was 'delicate'. The prioress judged that extra help was 'truly needed' to manage the domestic labour required in such a large household.[35] Sister Mary Paul was the lay sister at Northcote in the mid-twentieth century. Her duties included cooking for six sisters and 22 children, providing tea or dinner for visiting priests and parlour trays for visitors, attending to the laundry (including the boarders' clothes, the sisters' habits and the Dominican fathers' habits), tending to the altar linen for the church, ordering the meat, bread, vegetables and groceries, tending the chickens and acting as the nuns' infirmarian. In 1950 Mother Mary Philomena praised Sister Mary Paul's contribution to the community – she had 'given satisfaction in every way'.[36] However, in 1956 when Mother Mary Philomena visited Northcote again she found Sister Mary Paul terribly overworked. Her oven was entirely inadequate, and in order to get the week's laundry done she had to wash every night after night prayers.[37]

Lay sisters were usually not as well educated as choir sisters, but they were often accomplished in a wide range of skills. Bridie Butterly was born in Dublin in 1907; she travelled to New Zealand to join the Dominican sisters in 1928, and received the name Sister Mary Declan and the habit of a lay sister on 4 September 1929. She lived and worked in many of the Congregation's communities in Otago and Southland, as well as in Auckland and Feilding, usually as community cook and sometimes as infirmarian. 'She could produce single handedly a main meal for the boarding school and the sisters, and also manage to get a meal for a family in need.'[38] Sister Mary Declan was also a talented and creative artist. She knitted beautiful baby garments, made handcrafted toys and loved painting. She also made rosary beads, religious habits and church vestments.

Left: Eileen McCaughan before entering the convent. S, DA.

Above: SM Alban McCaughan, Sacred Heart Home, c. 2010. S, DA.

Decky, as she was known, 'belonged to the Dominican tradition of strong individuals who refuse to conform to any type. In her long life she had been for herself and for the sisters a source of joy and pain, of growth, of challenge and of life.'[39]

Sister Alban (Eileen Margaret) McCaughan made her first profession in September 1936. From the very beginning there was 'plenty of work'. As an elderly woman Sister Alban recalled her mother's horror when she visited her daughter at the convent: 'My hands were so hard, and she was crying. She wanted me to come home.'[40] Sister Alban enjoyed working in the infirmary; at times she slept on the floor beside older sisters who were prone to night wandering. She also enjoyed her time at St Thomas's in Oamaru, where she looked after the little boys, getting them up in the morning and settling them to bed in the evenings. Sister Alban also worked in the Congregation's kitchens. Her recipe books are a tribute to domestic organisation. Fruit sponge for Teschemakers called for 150 servings: 6lb butter, [illegible] sugar, 24 eggs, 24 cups flour, 12 cups milk, 24 [illegible] baking power. Recipes were often annotated with alternative quantities for different communities. Sister Alban's Chocolate Pie recipe was colour-coded. Her base recipe allowed for 24 servings requiring 18 eggs and 2 cups of sugar. Teschemakers was green: 50 servings required 36 eggs and 4 cups of sugar. Henderson was pink: 60 servings required 24 eggs and 48oz sugar. Her recipes included many old favourites such as rhubarb meringue pie, chocolate fudge pudding and 'apple angel'. Sister Alban's recipe for 'Husband's Favourite' – a kind of apple shortcake – included ingredients for 6, 24 or 60 servings – a lot of husbands for a convent!

Lay sisters were often remembered for their kindness – for feeding the indigent at the back door or passing an apple to a lonely child. In some ways their lives were less pressured than those of their teaching colleagues. They were always occupied but they were not rushing between classroom and chapel and trying to fit in study in between. Many of their daily tasks were simple and repetitive, allowing space for prayer and contemplation as they worked.

As technology reduced the physical work involved in running convents, and living standards rose in wider society, fewer women aspired to join the Dominicans as lay sisters. In 1955 their traditional black scapular was replaced with a white scapular; this was less practical for physical work but it served to reduce the distinction between choir and lay sisters. In 1963 the Congregation abolished the term 'lay sister'; from then on all sisters took their place in the Congregation according to their order of profession. Community members shared kitchen and laundry duties, and many communities employed secular women to help with cleaning and gardening. Sisters were free to volunteer for domestic roles but they were no longer confined or defined by their work. They enjoyed full sisterhood with all the other members of the Dominican Congregation.

Sister Nola Gleeson joined the Dominican sisters in 1960 when lay sisters were being phased out. Nola became a 'house sister'. She performed the traditional tasks of service performed by lay sisters, but enjoyed all the same rights and responsibilities as the teaching sisters. 'It's wonderful to be needed … It was important for me that I could do something for somebody. It really boils down to that I suppose … You were there to help, and I think that's what it's all about.'[41] Her first assignment on leaving the novitiate was Teschemakers, where there were 136 boarders. Nola was responsible for the dining room and the dishes, and also helped with the junior boarders – some as young as five – putting them to bed and getting them up in the morning. In North Invercargill she did the housework and managed the kitchen, and at Santa Sabina she looked after the Congregation's elderly sisters. Nola also spent time at St Dominic's School for the Deaf in Feilding, where she worked in the kitchen and helped with bathing the children, putting them to bed and getting them up in the morning. In the 1990s, when teaching sisters moved sideways into new educational roles and established other ministries, Nola moved from domestic work within the Congregation into pastoral work in the wider community. In 1990 she spent a year working in the Mt Tabor community in Auckland: together with Sister Dominic and several other secular caregivers, she lived with and cared for disabled people in a home-based environment. She later lived in Milton with two older Dominican sisters and together they provided a parish-based ministry, visiting the sick and elderly in their homes. Nola now lives on her own in Oamaru, where she continues her parish work.[42]

Rituals and regulations

Every aspect of life in the convent was ordered and monitored, ritualised and regulated. The New Zealand Dominican sisters of the nineteenth and early twentieth centuries saw the rule as God's will revealed.

> *Fidelity to Rule fixes every member of the community at her post, and diffuses over all, that peace and beauteous order which reflects an image of God's own dwelling – determines the time, the place, the manner of our duties, with as much certainty and security, as if God himself visibly*

appeared and spoke. Whenever the Rule calls me, I will think I hear God speak; disregarding the cry of nature, I shall instantly listen to His voice and obey.[43]

Life in the convent was conducted in silence, punctuated at regular intervals by prayer and plainsong. Choir and lay sisters maintained a strict religious silence during all tasks that did not require speech or singing. Silence was understood as a necessary precursor of contemplation, the foundation of Dominican life. Profound silence was observed from nine o'clock in the evening until nine the next morning. During this time it was unlawful for any sister to speak, 'unless from urgent necessity'.[44] By the mid-twentieth century the Congregation's approach to silence was slightly more relaxed, particularly in the smaller convents. In 1959, for example, the Queenstown sisters reported their attempts to honour the rule 'as far as our circumstances permit'; they kept the silence at breakfast but spoke at other meals.[45]

Conversation was kept to an absolute minimum for most of the day, yet the Priory rang with bells. Nola Gleeson remembers that 'bells seemed to be ringing all the time for different things … You lived by bells really.'[46] The bell was used to wake the sisters in the morning, to signal the start of the profound silence at 9pm, and to summon the sisters. Each sister was given a number according to her date of profession. A typed list near the bell set out the number for each sister. An ascending scale of single peals signified the digits from one to nine, and a jangle marked each decade: 'Too bad if number 39 was wanted!'[47]

When Maureen O'Hanlon entered the convent she found the silence a big change from the noisiness of family life and school.[48] And when Sister Mary St Joan (Clare) Terry was told that the sisters never spoke during the day she did not believe it could be true: 'No one could live without talking.'[49] Roxane Parkinson found that the quietness suited her well: 'I'm not a great talker. It was probably an escape.'[50] For many sisters, silence was an aid to contemplation. For others, maintaining religious silence was a difficult, sometimes damaging challenge.[51] Joan Hardiman acknowledges that the quietness made for 'a calm, prayerful environment' but thinks, in retrospect, that the silence was 'less than good' for her own self.[52]

Each sister had her own bedroom or cell. It was expected to be kept perfectly neat, devoid of all 'superfluities and vain ornaments, everything precious in a word, everything that does not savour of religious poverty'.[53] The only adornments permitted on the walls were religious pictures. Sisters were never allowed to enter each other's cells, and knocking at cell doors was strictly prohibited.

The Congregation as a whole depended on the relationships between its individual members. The rule required a careful balancing act – sisters were expected to be kind and considerate to one another, but were warned against friendships that became too familiar. Whenever they passed each other in the corridors they were required to keep religious silence, acknowledging each other only with an inclination of the head. They were instructed to avoid 'short, smart or witty' speech with each other.[54] Nicknames, warned Mother David in a 1958 memorandum, were 'not to be tolerated'.[55] A decade later Mother Jordan reminded her Congregation of the need for formal forms of address: sisters were to call each other by the full religious names bequeathed to them at reception into the convent. 'The use of abbreviations and nicknames is not conducive to the reverence and respect we need to have for one another.'[56] Fear of over-familiarity between sisters was underlain by a nervous horror of lesbian relationships, coded in the convent as 'particular friendships'.

Sister's cell, St Dominic's Priory. F2/6/13, DA.

Mealtimes were formal occasions. Dinner was announced by five strokes of the large bell. If a sister arrived in the refectory after the blessing she had to make the venia (extending the whole body on the ground, lying on the right side with the left knee and foot over the right) in the middle of the refectory until the senior sister present signalled for her to rise. If a sister had to leave the refectory before the rest of the community she asked permission by turning towards the superior and kissing her scapular; the superior granted permission by inclining her head. Ancient custom decreed that the junior sisters were served first, and plates were cleared in the reverse order, beginning with the prioress's table. Before eating, each sister thumbed a small sign of the cross over her food. Sisters were exhorted to 'avoid squeamishness and fastidiousness at the table' and to remember 'how glad the poor would be if they had such things'.[57] During the meal an appointed reader read from the Bible, the congregational constitutions or other religious texts. At the conclusion of the meal the reader said 'Tu autem' and rang the bell. Anyone at fault in reading or serving, or in any other way, then made penance by making the venia.

The horarium allowed a small amount of time for recreation, but even this period of the day was regulated – as Sister Mary Reginald reminded the sisters at Queenstown in 1939, their 'free time' was 'to be spent in study, in works for the good of the community, and in mending their clothes'.[58] Before recreation began, sisters prepared for it with a few minutes' reflection. On entering they uttered the salutation 'Praise be to Jesus.' They were not allowed to do schoolwork or clerical work during recreation, so they usually did mending or embroidery. This was the only time in the day when sisters were free to engage in conversation. The customary, however, decreed strict limits on topic and guidelines on

Community room, Siena Convent, Blockhouse Bay, early 1960s. F16/5, DA.

tone. Sisters were not permitted to discuss confession, nor meals, matters of discipline or the faults of their pupils. They were expected to speak of visitors, priests and relations 'only with great charity and prudence'. They were not allowed to interrupt each other or monopolise the conversation, and they were instructed to avoid any conflict, any obstinacy, any 'assumption of authority in voice or manner', 'immoderate laughter, vulgar and worldly expressions and all familiarity whether of word or manner'. At the same time the customary insisted that all sisters participate in recreation; they were not to appear 'silent, unamiable or abstracted'.[59]

The congregational constitutions and ordinations, the customary and the Dominican ceremonial governed even the smallest details of daily life. Sisters had to ask permission to give or receive, lend or borrow anything among themselves. They had to ask permission to wash any items of personal clothing themselves, use the sewing machine or the iron, take a drink before retiring for the night, cut their hair, answer the phone or receive visitors. They had to ask permission to read newspapers, periodicals or library books, even in the course of classroom preparation. They had to ask permission to send notes to children's parents or to read notes received from parents. Small rituals filled the day. Every time the clock struck the hour each sister made the sign of the cross and said a short, silent prayer. When the Angelus bell was rung the senior sister in the room led the prayer out loud. When receiving something for use from another, sisters were expected to say 'Benedictus Deus in donis suis', and when a superior entered the room sisters were expected to stand.[60]

Every element of the holy rule was performed in full religious habit. The habit itself was a matter of rule. Postulants wore a black dress and black shoes. Novices and professed sisters wore the same habit: a

Novices with their habits tucked up to play tennis, St Dominic's Priory, 1930. P3/1/2, DA.

Novices enjoying recreation time in St Joseph's School playground, 1954. P5/7/14, DA.

white tunic and black cappa, with a white scapular for choir sisters and a black scapular for lay sisters. The tunic was gathered at the waist with a cincture, to which was attached a rosary of 15 decades. The headdress consisted of a veil, a coif, a guimpe and a forehead band. During the first year of the novitiate, sisters wore a white veil and were known as 'white novices', and after first profession they adopted a black veil and were known as 'black novices'. As far as possible, sisters' undergarments were expected to be white, and their shoes were always black. They slept in a tunic and night coif.

Patricia Hannan found the rules and rituals governing everyday life 'far stranger' than she had imagined possible. The Dominican fathers, who taught philosophy, theology, spirituality and scripture in the novitiate, helped her to adapt: 'They all seemed to have a good sense of humour and made practices that seemed peculiar, quite tolerable.'[61] Sister Mary Francis Lister did not always cooperate with all the regulations – the rigidity of religious life made her sometimes feel like 'a caged lion'.[62] Cecily Sheehy thought all the 'silly things' they had to do were 'a bit crazy – stupid'; but she found that wearing a towel on your head to go from your cell to the bathroom, and kneeling in pardon and penance, became normal after a while. She recognised that the rituals and routines of religious life were essentially 'superficial, so it didn't matter'. What really mattered to her was the prayer and religious devotion that lay at the heart of Dominican life.[63] Sister Madeleine McAleese understood that rules provided a clear structure and safe boundaries for religious women. In a way, she believed, life was easier when all your decisions were made for you.[64] Bernie Cheyne joined the order in the early 1960s. 'It was all very strange – the things we had to do – AND NOT DO. However I thought that things would surely change!! They did – with the renewal following Vatican II.'[65]

Dispensation

Notwithstanding the rituals and regulations that covered even the minutiae of daily life, Dominican custom allowed for some flexibility. The Dominican principle of dispensation applied equally to both choir and lay sisters. The Dominican Rule was strict, but not rigid.[66] St Dominic linked the contemplative and apostolic traditions in a way that had not been done before. He understood the monastic horarium and canonical observances of religious life as the bedrock of evangelical action, but he also understood that there would always be 'practical conflicts' in reconciling the daily demands of religious discipline with the realities of apostolic engagement.[67] He addressed these conflicts by empowering superiors to dispense either communities or individuals from particular rules or observances that hindered their ability to study or preach. Simon Tugwell insists that dispensations from observances of rule were not intended as concessions to human frailty; rather, they were a mechanism for promoting more effective preaching.[68] The principle of dispensation placed the monastic horarium in perspective: the choir sisters' observances and the lay sisters' work were a means to an end. From the very beginning Dominicans have been first and foremost preachers tasked with praising God and saving souls.

The Irish sisters who came to New Zealand at the end of the nineteenth century understood the value and intermittent necessity of dispensation. When their teaching workloads grew too heavy they applied for and received dispensation from the full daily Office. When small branch communities with only two or three members found it difficult to observe the Office properly they also applied for and received dispensation. In order to avoid abuses, dispensations were always granted to specific individuals and communities, and usually related to specific situations. The rule was the standard, and exemption from aspects of observance was always the exception.

The New Zealand Congregation's first formally approved independent constitutions, printed in 1939, described dispensation as a valuable mechanism for managing communities. In cases where a sister's health, convalescence or constitutional delicacy was affected by the demands of the rule, or when the efficiency of her work was affected, superiors had 'not only a right but a duty' to grant dispensation from any 'onerous prescriptions' of the constitutions. Dispensation was never granted lightly. Superiors were expected to exercise their power of dispensation 'with great discretion, weighing in each case, the circumstances of persons and matter, and avoiding both the too great facility which never withholds and the too zealous severity which never grants a dispensation which is sought or needed'.[69]

Discipline

The regimented life laid down in the Dominican Rule was carefully designed to lead each sister closer to perfection and closer to God. Although dispensation allowed for an element of flexibility, the Congregation maintained order through the strict exercise of internal and community discipline.

Every day each sister made two personal 'examens' of conscience, taking time to reflect on her faults and pray for forgiveness. Once a week each sister attended confession with a priest. The examen and confession were private.

The community chapter, held once a week, was a public forum for acknowledging fault and receiving correction. Chapter was usually held in a special chapter room. Sisters sat by rank in designated seats. The chapter began with prayer and a short discourse from the prioress then, after any postulants had left the room, the ritual began. The prioress addressed the community: 'Does anyone wish to proclaim the novices?' Any member of the community who had witnessed a novice breaking the rule could make an accusation. Once accused, a novice was not permitted to object or reply. While the prioress imposed a penance the novice made the venia, waiting for the signal to rise. When the novices had all been proclaimed they retired from the chapter. The same procedure was then applied to lay sisters and, after they had been proclaimed, they also left the room.

The choir sisters then took their turn, following a slightly different formula. The prioress said: 'Let those who find themselves guilty of a fault make the venia.' If a sister believed herself to be at fault she came to the middle of the chapter room, made an inclination to the head of the crucifix and, standing erect, voiced her transgressions against the holy rule and constitutions. She asked for pardon and a penance and then made the venia. While she was in the venia, the prioress asked if any other sisters wished to proclaim the prostrated sister for additional faults. When the proclamation had concluded the prioress added her own observations and gave a reprimand and a penance, before signalling the sister to rise and return to her place. All were subject to the same process except for the prioress, the sub-prioress and the councillors, who could only be proclaimed for major breaches of the rule.

Faults against the rule were many and varied. They ranged from 'light faults' such as letting a cloth fall to the ground, breaking a candlestick or giving slow responses in choir, to 'middle faults' such as entering another sister's cell or calling another sister by her birth name, to 'grievous faults' such as breaking silence, disobedience or impertinence to superiors, sending or receiving clandestine letters or revealing community secrets to outsiders.[70]

At a broader congregational level, discipline was exercised through visitation: every three years the

Divine Office in the chapel at St Dominic's Priory, 1959. P5/7/1, DA.

prioress general visited all the local branch convents and spoke with every member of the congregation. Mother Mary David Stark described visitation as 'an opportunity to make known any irregularities or abuses that have perhaps crept into our lives in community'.[71] It was also a means of maintaining centralised control over the dispersed Congregation and ensuring consistency between local convents. The prioress general used her annual visit to monitor observance of the rule and to correct and punish any individual or communal transgressions. Visitation reports highlight variations in tone between the Congregation's various convents: community life may have been structured by rules and regulations, but it was formed by personalities and relationships.

Community cohesion

From 1871 when the sisters first arrived in New Zealand until the early 1960s when Vatican II rocked the established Catholic order, the Dominican Congregation lived in a world of their own construction. They were separated from the secular world not just by the law of enclosure, but by a thousand small rituals and regulations. Collectively, all the rules and routines that governed everyday life were designed to foster harmonious internal relationships and reify a sense of community identity. The 'beauteous order' of the rule was a means to holy ends, cultivating an atmosphere conducive to contemplation and enabling the Congregation to engage in its apostolic teaching mission.

6. Freedom

Community life since the Second Vatican Council

Jesus said, 'If you hold to my teaching, you are really my disciples. Then you will know the truth, and the truth will set you free.' – John 8:31–32

IN THE WAKE OF Vatican II the Dominican Rule became gradually more relaxed. St Augustine's Rule was interpreted for modern times and the New Zealand Constitutions and Ordinations were adapted to reflect contemporary theological developments, and to meet the exigencies of community reality. The regulations governing Dominican life in New Zealand in the twenty-first century are few and, for the most part, very open and flexible. The laws around membership and leadership, and the vows of poverty, chastity and obedience, remain immutable. The laws covering the minutiae of daily life – the identification of sisters by bells, authorised procedures for maintaining hygiene and laundering habits, specifically sanctioned forms of exercise and entertainment, punishments and penances for incursions of the rule, and so many other little rules – have all disappeared. Some of the principal elements of pre-Vatican II religious life were impracticable to sustain in the smaller communities of the late twentieth century. The New Zealand Dominican sisters no longer sing the Divine Office, a previously distinguishing feature of Dominican community life. External markers of religious life such as the habit and use of religious names are no longer matters of rule but of practicality and personal preference.

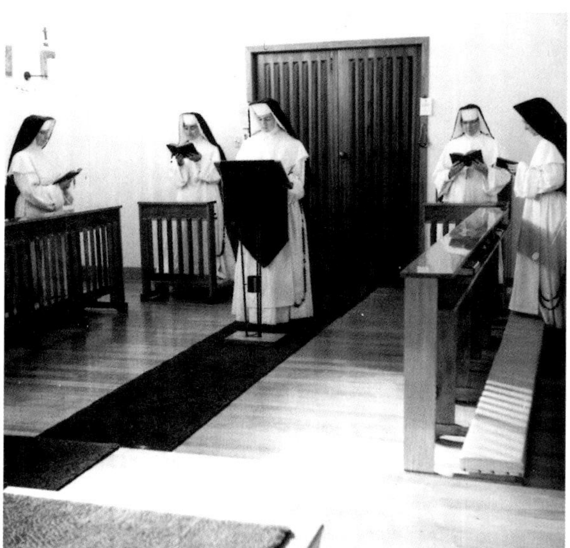

Divine Office, Siena Convent, Blockhouse Bay, early 1960s. F16/5, DA.

Some of the changes made in the wake of the Second Vatican Council have been incremental and experimental. Others have been more radical. Despite all these changes, and possibly because of them, Dominican life in New Zealand is still cohesive and distinctive. Dominican women continue to serve God through prayer and preaching. Sisters

Divine Office at Siena Convent, Blockhouse Bay, 1971. **Left**: SM Patrick Finnigan, SM Josepha Reilly, SM Joseph Mercer. **Right**: SM Brenda Fitzgerald, SM Bernadette Fox, SM Teresita Dunne F15/37, [illegible]

work in different settings and live in different ways, but prayer, community, study and mission remain the unifying elements of Dominican community life, just as they were for the founding sisters in 1871.

Experimentation in the 1960s and 1970s

The early 1960s were exciting years in the Catholic Church. The Second Vatican Council met from October 1962 until December 1965 and passed 16 ground-breaking theological documents covering liturgy, ecumenism, the laity, the priesthood, religious life, divine revelation, religious freedom and mission. The New Zealand Dominican sisters were ready for change, and welcomed the Council's invitation to return to their roots and engage with the world. Despite their geographical distance from Council proceedings, they were eager to engage with the latest developments.

Dunedin's Bishop Kavanagh provided the sisters with copies of all the relevant Council documents. Patricia Hannan recalls the thrill of gathering together to study and discuss each new document. 'We studied these avidly. They challenged many of the things some of us had been secretly challenging and restated the Gospel in current language applying scripture to the issues of the day. Those days were exciting and freeing.'[1] Judith McGinley remembers Dominican scripture teacher Father Paul Jackson arriving at the Priory with 'some scrabby bits of paper that some friend had sent him from Rome. "Just listen to this," he would say, and it was so freeing and liberating for our minds and our hearts, and even though the lives were a straitjacket … this part of us was free.'[2] In Auckland, Bishops Liston and Delargey kept the sisters up to date with the latest developments. Mary Horn remembers Bishop Delargey visiting the Northcote convent and talking to the sisters about Vatican II: 'You'll have your Bible in one hand, and you'll have your Vatican documents in the other hand, and they will be of equal weight.' For Mary, 'it was vibrant, it was exciting, it was new, it was different. We began to think differently.'[3]

Sisters Jordan and Genevieve and other sisters who studied at Regina Mundi in the 1960s formed personal links between Rome and New Zealand. Sister Denise (Roxane) was present in Rome for the promulgation of the Document on Religious Life and for the closing of the Council in 1965. She spent the next three years studying at Regina Mundi and returned to New Zealand empowered with new ideas and new resources.[4] Sister Loreto's time in Rome was cut short by ill health but she still absorbed the excitement in the air, and returned with a deep sense of wonder at God's continued revelation in her life and in the world. Fifty years later she described it as 'a Pentecost time'.[5] The sisters' letters home conveyed the excitement of the moment, and when they returned home in person, these sisters served as agents and conduits of change.

The conciliar documents from Rome and stories from sisters who had been there generated a widespread sense of communal anticipation. To start with, however, change was slow. Mother Mary David Stark, prioress general from 1956 until 1969, was a strict disciplinarian, devoted to the rule under which she had been trained. By 1964 she could feel change blowing:

> *With all that at the present time is being written about adaptation, some of us may be inclined to think that we should curtail our prayers and take a more active part in the apostolate – as if there is not enough activity in our lives already – but we must ever bear in mind our Dominican motto, 'Contemplari et contemplata aliis tradere.'*[6]

Sisters on a roof in Rome, 1966. SM Loreto Meehan and SM Denise Parkinson from New Zealand with friends from Regina Mundi, SM Paul and SM Claude. P5/7/3B, DA.

In 1967 Mother David issued a list of trial adaptations to community religious life. When necessary, sisters were permitted to speak out of silence time. They were allowed to study in their free time and read notes from children's parents. They were allowed to wash small articles of clothing, use the sewing machine and iron, and cut their hair without asking permission. They were given freer access to small personal items like soap, toothpaste, shoelaces and cotton. When members of their families came to visit, sisters were allowed to take a cup of tea with them. If they wished to do so they were allowed to receive Holy Communion when they accompanied the school children to Mass. The word 'cell' was replaced with 'room'.[7] Each of these adaptations of the rule, though small, represented a gradual shift towards increasing respect for personal dignity and individual freedom.

MM David Stark. P5/5/1, DA.

Mother David encouraged her Congregation to study all the Council documents, especially the Decree on the Religious Life.[8] Yet she also continued to insist on respect for traditional forms of institutionalised religious life. She repeatedly warned her sisters against 'discontent and grumbling', calling them to iron out 'any irregularities or abuses' that might have 'crept into' their lives in community. But she was pushing against the wind: after granting permission for Friday, Saturday and Sunday nights to be free, and for speaking on Saturday and Sunday afternoons, the prioress was disappointed that the 'clamouring' for more free nights continued. 'One important factor of religious life is living in community,' she reminded the sisters, 'and if we try to escape from the community whenever we can, something is lacking in our religious life.'[9] The clamouring continued. Some sisters felt, as Mother David did, that community life was under threat. Others strained towards a new model of community life that would free them to follow Dominic's spirit in the modern world.

Responding to *Perfectae Caritatis*, the Second Vatican Council's Decree on the Renewal of Religious Life (1965), the New Zealand Dominican sisters held a Special General Chapter to update their constitutions and customaries in the light of contemporary social conditions. The chapter took place during two sessions, on 26 December 1968–18 January 1969 and 31 December 1969–11 January 1970. The first act of the Special General Chapter was the election of congregational officials. Sister Jordan McCormick was elected as prioress general – she was a progressive leader well suited to the challenge of moving the Congregation forward. The four councillors elected to guide and support Mother Jordan were all older and far more conservative than their new prioress general. They provided a counterbalance to her progressive impetus, reflecting something of the tension between change and tradition in the wider congregation.

Early 1900s: Order of the exercises of the day

5.30am	*Rise*
6.00am	*Prayer and meditation*
6.40am	*Prime, Tierce, Sext and None*
7.00am	*Mass*
8.00am	*Breakfast*
12.15pm	*Visit to the Blessed Sacrament and Examen*
12.30pm	*Dinner*
5.00pm	*Recreation*
5.45pm	*Spiritual lecture in common*
6.00pm	*Vespers and Compline. Rosary*
7.00pm	*Supper*
7.15pm	*Rosary of the Most Holy Name and Novenas*
7.30pm	*Matins and Lauds*
8.00pm	*Recreation*
9.00pm	*Meditation and examination of conscience*
10.00pm	*Lights extinguished*[71]

The Second Vatican Council's Dogmatic Constitution on the Church (*Lumen Gentium*) had recognised all Catholics – priests, religious and laypeople – as 'the People of God', and called all members of the Church to ministry and mission. Mother Jordan understood that religious life could no longer be defined by works of the apostolate. Laypeople as well as religious could serve God as teachers in Catholic schools. Mother Jordan discerned a new vision of

Relaxing at the beach, December 1966. **Standing**: S Marie de Chantal Heath, SM Madeleine McAleese, S Paula Mary Winders. **Seated**: SM Albert Walsh, S Marie de Montfort Murphy, SM Elizabeth Mackie. P6/1/18, DA.

religious life for Dominican women in New Zealand in the later twentieth century. In the wake of Vatican II, religious congregations would be identified not by their particular forms of service to the Church, but by evidence of a radical commitment to following Christ in community life. With a personal commitment to renewal, Mother Jordan led the New Zealand Dominicans through the most dramatic period of change since Mother Gabriel and her sisters had first arrived in Dunedin.

The Special General Chapter of 1968–69 passed a wide range of experimental changes to the rule. The Divine Office remained the main structuring feature of everyday life, but the chapter relaxed the regulations around its recitation. Communities with fewer than three sisters could be temporarily dispensed from the full seven hours. When travelling, sisters were expected to say the Office and perform their customary devotional practices only as far as possible'. The chapter also gave permission for local communities to adapt the horarium according to local circumstances, so that as many sisters as possible could be present for the Office.

The day was lengthened: sisters were expected to be in their rooms by 10pm, and lights were extinguished one hour later than previously, at 11pm. Silence was maintained, but relaxed.[16] The chapter abolished the ceremonial washing of fingers before dinner, and simplified the form of grace before meals. Visiting sisters of other orders were allowed to have meals in Dominican refectories. Superiors were allowed to give permission for sisters to have morning tea with lay staff and meals with other visitors. The Chapter of Faults was now held monthly rather than weekly. Sisters were no longer allowed to accuse one another. The order of accusations was reversed: senior community members went first and juniors last. Some of the harsher forms of discipline were modified.[11] Other changes reinforced the shift towards personal responsibility and greater individual freedom. Each sister was given a free night each month when she was not required to conform with the community horarium. Finally, professed sisters were given two free days in the Christmas holidays, and were allowed to seal their own mail.

On 30 January 1969 Mother Jordan issued a directive to local superiors with a reminder that those in authority should begin to use their powers of dispensation 'more widely and wisely' than before.[12] By March 1969 several smaller Dominican convents were experimenting with their daily timetables, and over the next few years the range of timetable variations between different convents in New Zealand grew more and more broad.

Although it made many changes, the Special General Chapter also affirmed and restated many of the traditional boundaries of Dominican life.[13] The habit stayed the same as it had for centuries. The form of the novitiate stayed the same, too. In recognition of the loosening of many other regulations, the General Chapter passed an ordination reminding sisters that the established forms of authority remained in place. There was no such thing as 'automatic exemption'. Enclosure had been loosened to allow for greater contact with families and to facilitate school trips and conferences, but these cases were regarded as exceptions to the rule. The limits of enclosure had been shifted, not removed.

Each Dominican community responded to change in a slightly different way. By 1971 the Teschemakers sisters were enjoying community discussions on 'a fairly wide range of topics' and had trialled several suggestions for the daily horarium and several different forms of chapter.[14] The Feilding community had also experimented with community discussions and with chapter, and found that both had become more meaningful.[15] The community had made changes to recreation times and to meals: in the weekends sisters were allowed to prepare their own meals when and as they wished. In 1974 St Catherine's Priory in Invercargill recorded several major changes. Tables in the refectory were moved out of the traditional monastic U-shaped formation to create small groups. The refectory was regarded less and less as a place of silence. Occasionally clerical visitors joined the community for meals in the refectory. During recreation time many sisters enjoyed the television and radio, and the convent boasted a good record library. Several sisters had joined the public library and also made use of the college library. Community get-togethers were less frequent than previously, but the sisters from St Catherine's enjoyed regular visits with the Dominican sisters from St Albert's and St Bertrand's, and they enjoyed companionship with other religious women in the newly formed local Association of Religious.[16]

Individual sisters in each Dominican community responded to change with differing degrees of reluctance and enthusiasm. Some sisters stretched the boundaries even further than the new regulations allowed. There were times when Mother Jordan had to warn against violations of enclosure and other laxities of rule. In June 1970 she encouraged the sisters of Santa Sabina convent to take more care in their community prayer, and a few weeks later she was compelled to remind the Northcote sisters of the value of silence.[17] Other communities resisted modern alterations to religious life. The Feilding community, for example, was slow to accept changes in the Mass. The Feilding chapel had been altered to allow the priest to face the Congregation, in accord-

Left: Feilding community, 1974. S Judith Robinson, SM Gemma Finlay, S Maureen O'Hanlon, S Emmanuel Vallis, SM De Montfort Murphy, SM Regina (Philomena) O'Connell (seated).
F14B/5/1A, DA.

Below: Opening of new chapel at St Catherine's, Invercargill, 1 July 1967.
F3A/13/4, DA.

ance with international change since the Second Vatican Council. In June 1970 Mother Jordan issued the Feilding sisters with a strict reprimand: 'I would remark that the sisters lack an understanding of the work and cost entailed in transforming the sanctuary if they continue to ignore the priest who is facing them for the celebration of the Mass.'[18]

No matter how hard it might be, Mother Jordan believed that change was imperative: 'renewal is not an option for us – it is an act of obedience which we owe to the Church'. She constantly encouraged her Congregation to reassess 'those structures of religious life which prevent sisters from radiating spirituality and which distort our image to the world we are called to sanctify'.[19] Difficult though they might be, Mother Jordan believed that all these changes in lifestyle and liturgy would help to forge a Christ-like community in which individuals were valued above the institution.[20]

In 1973 Mother Jordan invited sisters to consider the positive and negative effects of community change since the Second Vatican Council. Reported positives included profitable experiments in community chapter, a growth of trust within communities, a growth of personal responsibility, integration of the novitiate with the community, the benefits of family visits and educational visits outside the convent, and the balance achieved between convent community needs and wider community work in the parish and church. Negatives included the loss of silence in Dominican convents and the impact this had on prayer and spiritual life, some abuse of trust and misuse of personal responsibility, misunderstanding of the delegation of authority, the loss of dignity in casual living, the intrusion of worldly values, the abuse of television in the community room and the abuse of egress.[21]

Cecily Sheehy loved Vatican II and 'all the freshness it brought into the Church'. Even when change was welcome, however, it could still be unsettling. Cecily felt she had her Dominican life 'in control sort of, in inverted commas' before the Council. Then 'this would come in, that would happen, this would be in English, and then we were allowed to wear something else …' Cecily remembers the day when she 'just said "Woosh! – look, let's go for it then! I'm sick of trying to hold it back"… I just wanted the doors to open and get out there and live – but it still crept along bit by bit.'[22]

Despite inevitable challenges, change continued. The General Chapter held from 26 December 1974

The Salve, St Dominic's Convent, Feilding, 1974. Versicularians S Virginia (Judith) Robinson and S Ligouri (Maureen) O'Hanlon. F14A/5/23, DA.

to 15 January 1975 reflected an ongoing commitment to 'answer the call of the Church to renewal of our religious life'. Sister Mary Constance Quinn was elected as prioress general, and continued to lead the Congregation in the spirit of Vatican II. The chapter did not pass many ordinations or declarations, but issued a lengthy statement on evangelical witness in community religious life, emphasising freedom and responsibility. The chapter was concerned that each sister in the Congregation 'be given the opportunity to develop as an individual while contributing to the growth and welfare of the community'. At the same time, it called each sister to examine herself 'and ask whether the image she presents is that of a person whose standards conform to her chosen life of poverty, chastity and obedience'. The chapter explicitly addressed internal community tension. In the decade since Vatican II, increasing freedom and opportunities for individual expression had led some communities into conflict and had strained some personal relationships. The chapter warned that 'lack of charity' was 'acting as a canker to our religious life and preventing our apostolic endeavours from bearing full fruit'. 'Spiteful, hurtful remarks, caustic criticism, envious comparisons and a refusal to see good in what others do … cause endless suffering to others and destroy the unity of mind and heart which should characterise our communities.' All sisters had 'a right to expect support and sympathy from their religious family'.[23]

Informed by these themes, the Interim Constitutions of 1976 became more than a collection of rules and regulations. The Constitutions were written in committee and the final document was drawn up by Sister Mary Elizabeth Mackie. It encapsulated a prophetic vision of Dominican life, inspiring communities to a greater recognition of relationships and valuing of individuals.

> *If the community life is to be a life lived with the Trinity the qualities required of us are truth and charity: truth, by which we can recognise the worth and dignity of all our sisters and in which we should strive to act with unfailing tact openness and sincerity; charity, with which we should accept all lovingly, undertake even the humblest community tasks gladly, and react compassionately to the suffering and to those who are burdened. We are each responsible for creating and maintaining conditions in which each sister is free to use her gifts in the service of the community and in the work of the apostolate.*[24]

The 1976 Constitutions were promulgated as Interim Constitutions and were understood as temporary though binding. Mother Constance urged sisters to obey the rule in its present form. Individuals and communities were not entitled to anticipate further change. The purpose of the Interim Constitutions was to provide a period of time when they could live with these regulations 'in their entirety', to discuss them in community, and to work toward a final document.[25]

The Ninth General Chapter, 1980–81, affirmed the same principles of freedom and responsibility as the 1976 Constitutions, updating the Constitutions to reflect the evolving reality of Dominican community life. The new Constitutions, issued in 1981, were written by Elizabeth Mackie but shaped by the whole community. Every member of the Congregation had had input into each chapter of the new Constitutions. Individual and community comments and suggestions were taken into account and revisions submitted to the whole Congregation for repeated revision. The Constitutions were 'in a very real sense, the work of the whole Congregation'.[26] The democratic nature of this process was itself a marker of changes that had transformed the Congregation in less than two decades.

From white robes to coloured cardigans

The white Dominican habit had been the Congregation's most obvious external marker since the order first arrived in New Zealand. The habit was a matter of strict rule, representing the sisters' commitment to religious poverty. The Second Vatican Council affirmed the religious habit as an outward mark of consecration to God. It was expected to be 'simple and modest, poor and at the same time becoming, to meet the requirements of health and be suited to the circumstances of time and place and to the needs of the ministry involved'.[27] The full-length white serge garb worn by New Zealand Dominicans since 1871 was not suited to life in a temperate climate in the late twentieth century, nor to life as a school teacher. But the process of adapting the habit was slow and gradual.

The New Zealanders made their first experimental changes with dress at the first session of the Special General Chapter held in the summer of 1968–69. Sisters were given permission to wear wristwatches, which had previously been banned. Sisters who required new night attire were allowed pyjamas instead of the traditional night tunic. At night-time in their own rooms, sisters were permitted to abandon the night coif.[28]

In 1969 several sisters began trialling new forms of headdress. The Congregation was making wide-sweeping changes in its traditional community life and religious observances, yet sisters seem to have been cautious about even minor changes in dress. Mother Jordan warned those experimenting with headdresses that the great majority of sisters wished their hair not to be shown. In the same directive she reminded sisters that the Dominican travelling cloak was always to be worn when travelling on public transport, and that only lace-up shoes were permitted outside the convent precincts.[29] Traditionally the habit was required to reach 'at least to the top of the shoe'.[30] In 1970 Mother Jordan issued careful new guidelines. At its maximum length the habit was to clear the shoes, and at minimum length it was allowed to be four inches (10cm) from the ground (in bare feet), and five inches (12cm) for those who had to travel in the course of their daily life.

Experiments continued with various forms of headdress. In June 1970 Mother Jordan asked superiors to indicate how many sisters wished to trial a new model that would come only to the bottom of the ears. Another model that would cover the chin was still in the process of design.[31] From 22 August 1970 some sisters began wearing the experimental headdress,[32] and by the time of the Congregation's centennial celebrations in 1971 the new headdress was the norm.

Sisters negotiated other small changes in dress, too. In July 1970 Mother Jordan gave permission for the Northcote sisters to wear an overall instead of the habit for holidays or work,[33] and in June 1972 she gave permission for the travelling cloak to be replaced with a coat. Sisters were allowed to replace the capuce with a small collar attached to the scapular. Where it was hard to buy white stockings, and for sisters who travelled regularly, they were allowed to wear flesh-coloured stockings. But any sister who wished to wear secular clothes or a swimming costume still had to obtain specific permission from the mother prioress general.[34]

The General Chapter (1974–75) gave no specific instructions for dress but emphasised the habit as a mark of personal dedication. In her dress, and in all her encounters with secular society, each sister was expected to reflect religious values. 'We shall remember that the habit we wear is a sign of our consecration, and is intended to assist us in our life of personal dedication. It will be simple and modest, becoming, and different from dress that is clearly secular.'[35]

'The new look': on 28 August 1957 the New Zealand Dominican Congregation adopted a softer, less structured headdress. **Back**: SM Goretti, SM Cecilia, SM Teresa, SM Genevieve, SM Kevin, SM Adrienne, SM Dolores, SM Elizabeth, SM Augustine, SM Barbara, SM Pauline, SM Jacinta, SM Perpetua, SM Evangelist, SM Rosalie **Middle**: MM Tarcisius, SM de Ricci, SM Gonzales, SM Felicitas, SM Zedislava, SM Margarita, SM Bertrand and MM Brigid, SM Attracta, SM Magdalen, SM Veronica, MM Laurence, SM Hofbauer, SM Sebastian, SM de Lourdes. **Front**: MM Callista, MM Assisi, MM Celestine, MM St Joan, MM Borromeo, MM Bonaventure, MM David, MM Patricia, MM John, SM Borgia, SM Frigidian, SM Xavier, SM Lucy, SM Hyacinth, M Marie Therese. F14A/7A, DA.

In 1975 one of Sister Constance Quinn's first acts as prioress general was to delegate to local superiors the right to give permission for sisters to wear secular dress. Permissions were to be given only for specific occasions; they could not be given for school (except for school camps or fieldtrips), for chapel or for formal occasions.[36] Sister Constance believed that the habit isolated Dominicans from laypeople – 'that's not what we were meant to be as Dominicans – we were meant to be in the forefront of things'.[37]

Barbara Menzies joined the Dominicans in 1973 when things were already changing. She spent her year as a postulant at St Dominic's in Henderson so that she could commute to Epsom Teachers' College. Before she left Henderson to join the other postulants at the Priory in Dunedin Barbara went to say goodbye to Sister Mary Benvenuta in the community room. She recalls, 'She hooted with laughter at me, made me do a full turn and kept laughing. Someone said, "They're not going to know what hit them!" As far as I was concerned, I was dressed like an ordinary 22-year-old.' When she arrived in Dunedin and met the other novices they all wanted to know how she got away with wearing a mini skirt and knee-length boots. 'They had been obliged to let down their hems on arrival and expected to

In the early 1980s some sisters retained the Dominican habit while others moved into cream or white skirts and shirts. SM David Stark, S Frances Scully, S Marie Twomey, S Judith Anne O'Sullivan, S Roxane Parkinson, S Lorraine Challis, S Nola Gleeson and SM Imelda Windle on the front lawn at Teschemakers. F9/17, DA.

wear flat, quiet shoes.'[38] Barbara describes the habit as 'a battleground of choice for some'. On one notable occasion she incurred the wrath of one of the older sisters by removing her veil and scapular in order to drive a carload of sisters from Invercargill to Dunedin for the commissioning Mass for the first community to work in Vanuatu. 'My thinking was that when we reached the Priory I would resume both items, rather than turn up looking as if I had been dragged through a bush backwards. The irate one accused me of disrespecting the holy habit and refused to travel with me.' In the aftermath Barbara and the older sister negotiated 'a lasting peace' based on 'better understanding and mutual support'. Barbara identified a 'great need among many of us to be more relaxed in our communities and make them homes where we know we are accepted and loved for who we are and not what we are'.[39]

In 1977, in a letter to the Prioress and Council, Sister Kathleen Thomson advocated ongoing experimentation with secular dress. At a time when religious women were being asked to show 'womanly responsibility in all aspects of their personal consecration to Christ', Kath believed they should also be given individual responsibility for their style of dress, without having to ask permission of the prioress general and without having to defend themselves against accusations of abandoning their religious ideals.[40]

Many agreed with Barbara and Kathleen, but others opposed change. In September 1978 Sister Marie Eugene expressed her distress over the Congregation's preoccupation with matters of dress. She was concerned with sisters wasting time over dress, with unnecessary expenditure of congregational funds and, most importantly, with the impact on laypeo-

Silver Jubilee, 1984. Brenda Fitzgerald, Lorraine Challis, Bernie Cheyne and Mary Horn. Each sister wears a different form of dress, though most are still in white or cream. All four wear the Dominican cross on either a chain or a pin. P11/8/1, DA.

ple. Sister Marie Eugene believed it was 'a nonsense' to suggest that sisters were more approachable in secular dress; rather, she contended, laypeople were disappointed with religious moving out of the habit. Sister Marie Eugene believed that experiments in dress were 'doing no more than pandering to feminine vanity', and were damaging the Congregation's 'witness to poverty'. One sister was observed to have worn seven different cardigans in a week, many of which were coloured. Another was noted to have changed 'outfits' three times in one day. Sister Marie Eugene urged the council to refocus on religious poverty – to be guided in matters of dress 'by Christ who was poor and was not afraid to tell His followers to be the same'.[41]

Within only a few years, however, more and more sisters were wearing secular dress on regular occasions. The Chapter of 1980–81 recognised this shift and endorsed sisters' right to choose their own dress. The Chapter allowed for three options: sisters could retain the traditional habit of a cream tunic and scapular with cincture and rosary beads and a black veil; they could wear a white or cream dress, with or without a veil; or they could wear contemporary dress.[42] The Congregation's most recent Constitutions, promulgated in 1989, mention dress only briefly: 'As a sign of our consecration and as witness to poverty the sisters will dress simply. Our traditional dress is white or cream.'[43]

Most sisters were happy to move out of the full Dominican habit. Sister Mary Alban spent much of her adult life doing heavy domestic work. The habit was terribly awkward for physical work. By a custom known as 'curtilling' the skirt was hoisted up and tucked out of the way, but the volume of fabric still restricted easy movement. In addition the

S St Roch Rogers in her traditional Dominican habit celebrates 60 years of vowed Dominican life with S Helen Bergin in contemporary dress, 1983.
P11/10/14, DA.

white fabric was utterly impractical – 'my word they were hard to wash and iron!'[44] Sister Alban was very happy to move into less restrictive clothes, but she always retained the veil.

When Sister Dominic Swindale first joined the community at Feilding she found the serge habit unbearably hot: out in the sunny playground on lunch duty, the heat could make you quite sick. One day she had been for a swim to cool off before rushing back to the chapel for choir. Another sister came up behind her and whispered 'Sister, you are not wearing stockings!' If only she knew, Sister Dominic laughed to herself, there was something much more important than stockings missing. Sister Dominic adapted her dress very gradually, in line with most of the rest of the Congregation. Her sister had a drapery shop in Papakura and gave her a nice cream suit. She kept wearing cream, with perhaps the addition of a coloured scarf, for quite some time.[45]

Sandra Winton was never comfortable in the habit, but she accepted the 'funny clothes' as 'part of the role that you took on'. She felt that the clothes were not just restrictive and confining, they also separated the sisters from other people – 'you were kind of set apart and you felt odd'. Sandra was very glad to be rid of the habit. 'Being able to be a person again – I mean you can put up with the discomforts of the dress, but it was great to be freer and more real. That's what it felt like to me.'[46]

Janice Ogilvy had always been an untidy person and, for her, the white habit was a dreadful pain. 'I couldn't stand it. It was terrible.' Her rosary beads were always flying around the school playground. Taking the children swimming at Moana Pool in full habit was a ridiculously comical endeavour. When Jan moved to Palmerston North to work as university chaplain she wore a cream skirt and cream shirt. She didn't have to wear the veil, but students used to joke: 'Keep your veil in the tool kit. If you break down, flick it on and people will stop and help!' Gradually Jan moved from cream into more colour, and now she is comfortable in secular dress.[47]

For Raewyn Benzie the practicalities of shifting into secular dress were quite awkward: 'I didn't know how you got the money to go and get these clothes.' Patricia Hannan helped her get a cheque from the bursar and took her shopping. 'She wouldn't let me out of the dressing room until I had the outfit. It was great. It was very freeing.' For a long time Raewyn continued to teach in a cream skirt and jersey, but without the veil. It wasn't until she returned to teach in the state school system in the 1990s that she wore 'civvies' at school.[48]

Sister Mary Gertrude Fox was reluctant to lose the traditional form of dress. She retained an adapted form of the Dominican habit, with a cream skirt and shirt and a simple black veil. She liked being easily identifiable as a nun – people knew immediately who she was and what she stood for. Initially she found it difficult to understand other sisters' reasons for shifting out of the habit, but once she understood their sincerity in wanting to be closer to normal people she accepted and respected their individual right to choose their own dress.[49]

Sister Maria McDonald believed that Pope John XXIII opened the doors of the Church to change too quickly and too wide, but even he, she observed, never suggested that religious women abandon the habit. Before Vatican II, 'we all wore our habits and felt privileged to do so – as we had to work hard to be accounted worthy to wear it'. Sister Maria looked with hope to growing numbers of young religious women in the United States returning to the habit and to more traditional forms of religious life.[50]

As a postulant, Sister Mary Columba McHugh 'longed to receive the habit'. She saw the changes since Vatican II as detrimental to religious life: 'World wide, there seemed in many religious a desire to "revolt" – not an adaptation to modernising religious life but a complete freedom to do their own thing.'[51] Like Sister Maria, she saw the habit as a profound means of witness to religious identity.

What's in a name?

In the years before the Second Vatican Council sisters left behind all worldly possessions at profession, including their names. They took on new identities, accepting the title 'Sister' to connote their membership of a new family, 'Mary' to connect them with the Mother of Christ, and the name of a saint whose values they would emulate in religious life. They no longer celebrated their own birthdays, but marked the feast day of their patron saint. In the years since Vatican II names have not been subject to chapter discussions or constitutional amendments. There has been no standard approach or community directive. Rather, individual sisters have responded to the spirit of increasing freedom that has characterised community life since the 1970s.

The first record of a sister requesting permission to revert to her baptismal name was in May [illegible]. Mother Mary Jordan granted Sister Mary [illegible]'s request and informed the rest of the Congregation that she would henceforward be known as Sister Maureen.[52] In August 1976 Mother Mary Constance gave permission for 10 sisters to revert to their baptismal names.[53] Some sisters changed their names gradually over the next few years and some retained their religious names.

Mother Mary Constance was prioress general during the period when most sisters who wished to, changed their names. In 1980 she herself stopped using the title 'Mother',[54] and in May 198[illegible] she informed the Congregation of her intention to revert to her baptismal name, Margaret Quinn.[55] She had had no choice at all in her religious name and had always disliked 'Constance'. For a while she answered to both names, but she has enjoyed reclaiming her own name.[56]

Sister Mary Joachim Benzie changed her name back to Raewyn as soon as she was able. In the late 1960s when she made profession, sisters were allowed to nominate several different names that they favoured, and the prioress general usually gave one of these names. Joachim was the [illegible] on Raewyn's list; his feast day was 16 August, [illegible] her's birthday. After the reception ceremony Raewyn asked her friends what they thought of her new name. 'Well I like the "Kim" part', one observed. Raewyn was one of the first sisters to revert to her birth name: 'That gave a whole new sense of being myself … to be able to use my surname as well … that was a significant change.'[57]

Sister Mary Monica Butler went back to her baptismal name, Margaret, later than many other sisters. Like wearing her own clothes, reclaiming her own name was about independence and identity. Margaret remembers 'a really strange sensation': 'Instead of "the sister", "the nun", I became myself again.'[58]

As a keen musician Cecily Sheehy wanted to be Sister Mary Cecilia after the patron saint of music, but there was already a Cecilia in the Congregation. She tried to go back to her birth name, Annette, when she travelled to the United States for study. 'It nearly worked,' she says, but by this stage only her most intimate family still used this name. To hear new acquaintances drawl her name in an unfamiliar accent was very strange, and when one of the Americans commented on her preference for 'Cecily' as a far more musical name she abandoned the change. She has been Cecily to most people ever since.

Sister Dominic was baptised in the Anglican Church in Wairoa as Janet Aston Swindale and was brought up in the Church of England. She attended a Dominican convent secondary school in England and, as a 15-year-old in 1950, she travelled to Rome for the Holy Year celebrations with a small group of other students. There, in St Dominic's Chapel she prayed and hoped that she would one day become a Dominican sister. At 21 she converted to Catholicism, and at 26 she joined the New Zealand Dominicans. She identifies strongly with St Dominic and has chosen to retain her religious name.[59]

When Phyllis Fox entered the convent the prioress general told her that Phyllis was a pagan name. During her year of postulancy she was known as Elizabeth, after her aunt. Phyllis had no choice in her religious name, Sister Mary Gertrude. She respected the right of others to return to their birth names and birthdays, however she herself was content with her religious name.[60]

Changes in clothing and nomenclature are much less important than the deeper changes that occurred in religious life in the 1960s and 1970s, but they are external markers of that process, and they are deeply symbolic of the New Zealand Dominican Congregation's shift towards increasing personal freedom and increasing connection with the outside world.

Contemporary forms of community prayer

Dominican communities have changed radically from the large structured institutions of the nineteenth and early twentieth century. Sisters now live in small groups or alone. The ancient features of religious life – a rigid horarium, the seven hours of the Divine Office, the Chapter of Faults – have been replaced by a wide range of contemporary forms of prayer and devotion.

The current Congregational Constitutions, promulgated in 1989, open with a statement of Dominican identity:

> *A New Zealand Dominican sister lives a life consecrated to God, in a religious community, based on liturgical and contemplative prayer, formed by the study of Divine Truth, and dedicated to making the Lord known and loved. The balance of all these elements is characteristic of the Dominican inspiration and is expressed in our motto: Contemplari et contemplata aliis tradere.*[61]

The Congregation has shifted away from the formal structures of corporate devotion, but prayer is still at the heart of Dominican life. The sisters honour St Dominic as a man 'totally absorbed in God: he spoke continually to God or of God'. 'We too are invited by Christ to become women of prayer, with his love permeating our life and work. It is the responsibility of every community to be the setting within which each sister may grow in prayer.'[62]

S Judith Anne O'Sullivan and S Danielle Melton dancing in the foreground at the 19[illegible] Dominican Chapter. P9/2BBBBE, DA.

Prayer time, Auckland 1990s. SM Thomas Dunn, SM Frances L[illegible], S Maureen Connolly, S Dominic Sw[illegible], S Leonie Parry. [illegible]

In 1990 the Congregation compiled a statistical snapshot of Dominican sisters at prayer. Of 21 communities, most prayed together every day. One community met for prayer three times a week, another once a week, and another irregularly. In two communities sisters only prayed in private. Seven communities celebrated the eucharist in the house regularly. Two communities said the rosary in common.

The form of community prayer also varied between Dominican houses. Some communities followed the Prayer of the Church, others used the scripture of the day as inspiration for their prayers, and others prayed more informally.[3] Today the range of communities and forms of prayer in the New Zealand Dominican Congregation are more diverse than ever.

Raewyn Benzie lives alone in Invercargill. She is in a slower phase of life and enjoys having time to pause and reflect. She listens to reflective CDs and meditates on Jungian thought, seeking to 'enter more deeply really into the divinity within us'. Raewyn treasures the opportunity to live on her own, and at the same time appreciates close contact with the other Dominican sisters in Invercargill. 'As we lose more and more of our sisters, it becomes more and more precious that connectedness that we have with one another … we are really a family …'[64]

For Janice Ogilvy, who also lives alone, each day is different. She likes having more control over her daily timetable than in years gone by, but still keeps to a pattern of prayer, study and mission. The rhythm of community life is the same, but its expression and timing is very different now from the formal community life that existed before Vatican II. Each day she makes time for private prayer, scripture study and meditation – 'the heart of Dominican life is there'. She is also closely connected to the regional Dominican community and to the prayer network in her local parish.[65]

Mary Horn lives, paints and prays in the farmhouse attached to Teschemakers. She did not choose to live by herself, 'But I realise now this is what God wanted. It was meant to be … I'm comfortable now.' She leads a contemplative life, moving between the garden and the studio. 'I don't say the prayers any more. I pray the prayers in doing.' Mary travels in to Oamaru several times a week to visit the sisters there. Once a month all the sisters in the region meet at Sister Adrienne's place for prayer and sharing, and Mary stays in close contact with the wider congregation by phone and email. 'So community life is different. Before … you had to live together. And now … it's still a common life, we're living a common Dominican life, but you don't have to live in the same place.'[66]

Mary Anna Baird describes prayer as 'the essence' of her life. She lives alone in Arrowtown and has a commitment to private prayer and community prayer. Every Monday morning around a dozen people gather at her home to pray and share the scriptures for the coming Sunday. Mary Anna is part of the local Catholic parish and meets regularly with an ecumenical women's group. Once a month she spends a whole day in prayer by herself. Prayer for Mary Anna means asking God to help her take 'a long loving look' at a particular situation or person.[67]

In Blockhouse Bay, Auckland, seven elderly sisters live in four adjoining flats. Sister Dominic Swindale is the youngest; she looks after Sister Genevieve in their shared flat and helps the other sisters as well: 'I've got the energy and I like doing it.' Despite their different styles of praying Sisters Dominic and Genevieve pray together every day. Sister Genevieve likes to use the breviary for morning prayer and evening prayer, and Sister Dominic joins her. They also make time to share thoughts, meditations and informal prayers – and this form of shared contemplative time is more meaningful for Sister Dominic. She also makes time for a daily walk down to Blockhouse Bay beach – an important part of her routine for maintaining personal equilibrium. Sister Dominic is committed to her Dominican sisters and her Dominican vows – 'it's a deep part of me'.[68]

Sister Loreto and Sister Bernadette live together in another of the Blockhouse Bay flats. Sister Loreto finds community life much more meaningful now than before Vatican II. Before the Council, 'you lived in a kind of bonded way to the community but you didn't have to be close to them … You prayed together and you ate together. There wasn't much play.' Vatican II led Sister Loreto to a profound sense of God's presence in her life. 'Now we know that God is revealing himself in every little moment of our lives.' She and Sister Bernadette pray together once a day. Sister Loreto's most meaningful prayer time

Scotland Street community, 2012. **STANDING**: Mike Noonan, Father Kevin Toomey. **SEATED**: Maria Noonan, S Joan Bennett, S Judith Anne O'Sullivan. DA.

is private. She uses tapes and commentaries as aids to contemplation. Often she will meditate on a passage from the Gospel, and sometimes she maps her thoughts on paper. 'I like to just think and be quiet and take a word and just tease it out … not that it's easy, but I find that I must do it.'[69]

The Dominican Family Community based at Scotland Street in Dunedin is composed of six members living in two households: Dominican sisters Judith Anne O'Sullivan and Joan Bennett, Dominican father Kevin Toomey, Mercy Sister Mary Hepburn and lay couple Maria and Mike Noonan. Together they maintain a regular community life structured around a daily liturgy that is open to the wider community and local neighbourhood. Community members rise around 5.30am, as the sisters would have before Vatican II. They meet in the prayer room in silence at 6.45am and share a time of private meditation until 7.15am. After a 15-minute break they reconvene for half an hour of Gospel reading and reflection. In the evening they come together again for prayer and meditation from 5.30 to 6pm. This rhythm of prayer and meditation holds the Family Community together. As Mike Noonan says, contemplation 'forms our community, informs our study, and is the bedrock of our various ministries … Prayer together builds a subterranean space of belonging together which is beyond words and beyond psychology. It is the gift of the Kingdom to discover ourselves as brothers and sisters, and as members of the family that is Trinity.'[70]

Sandra Winton lives on her own in Dunedin but maintains close contact with her Dominican sisters: 'This is my family, these are my people, this is a commitment I've made, and I live with that at the same time as I try to live freely with it and maintain my own life and the integrity of my own life.' She has her own quiet times each morning, and once or twice a week she prays with the Family Community at Scotland Street and often shares a meal there. She enjoys her regular visits with the elderly sisters living in rest homes, and takes an active part in regional Dominican meetings and congregational affairs. 'It's an independent life in the Congregation, which isn't contradictory as I see it ... it's a self-organised and self-generated life in lots of ways rather than time-tabled and programmed in that rigid way that it was in the past.' For Sandra the freedom of this new way of life is 'kind of like living the Dominican vision or dream'.[71] She describes the Church as an institution as 'quite peripheral' to her life in lots of ways, but her identity as a Dominican sister is fundamentally important.

> *The joy for me is in belonging to a group of women that I love and respect and with whom we try to have some common sense of direction and commitment and purpose in the world, and with whom there's a common spiritual understanding or respect for the spiritual dimension of the life journey.*[72]

Helen Bergin and Carmel Walsh live in community in Mt Albert, Auckland. They spend time in prayer together most evenings, and one morning a week they are joined by a lay Dominican woman for morning prayer and scriptural reflection.[73] Helen describes prayer as an honest engagement with God and His Word, and a loving attendance to God, self, others and mission. Before the Second Vatican Council the New Zealand Dominican Sisters gathered together early each morning to meditate on the Word of God. In the twenty-first century the form of each sister's daily meditation varies. 'As Dominic strode European roads reflecting on God's Word, so Dominic's followers now choose time, place and posture which best fosters daily contemplation.' So much has changed since the first sisters arrived in New Zealand, but praying with the Word of God remains central to Dominican life.[74]

'My gang'

The changes in Dominican life since the Second Vatican Council have been wide ranging and deep reaching. The diversity of lifestyles has encouraged many sisters to engage in creative missions and enjoy meaningful prayer life, but it has also created inevitable tensions. In Patricia Hannan's words, 'Prayer life, commitment to apostolic ministry, to working for justice in its many forms, and a healthier lifestyle for everyone, were all obvious consequences of the changes. The witness given by a praying community dedicated to truth and justice became less clear.[75] Removing the formal boundaries and structures has meant that sisters sometimes have to work harder to maintain their connections with each other. They can no longer rely on the rule to hold them together; they must rely on prayer and a shared commitment to St Dominic's special charism.

As in any family or intentional community there have been inevitable tensions. In the years before Vatican II there were situations in which personality differences were exacerbated by the stress of the rigorous rule and the demands of the sisters' teaching apostolate. In the years after the Council some sisters struggled to reconcile dissimilar expectations of each other and of religious life, and to cope with the challenges of ageing. Community life – whether in large enclosed convents or in small connected households – has had moments of strain and conflict, but major problems have been rare in the New Zealand Dominican Congregation.

Roxane Parkinson found it terribly hard returning to New Zealand after three years in Rome absorbing the atmosphere of the Second Vatican Council: 'It broke my heart really.' But she remembers arriving home to St Dominic's Priory in Dunedin during the annual retreat before Christmas. Crowds of sisters were walking in silence down the hall to the refectory. 'I remember having this absolutely wonderful

SM Augustine McCarthy with S Mary Horn, Teschemakers farm house, early 2000s.
P10/17/2, DA.

experience … It was kind of an overwhelming feeling of joy … *These are my sisters*.' Roxane still feels powerfully connected to her Dominican sisters. 'Because, all right. Who've we got? We've got our families, but they've got a life of their own too, and we're all kind of in a way part of it. But if we haven't got one another … We need one another, especially in these days when we're not big numbers.'[76] For Roxane, the greatest joy of Dominican life is just belonging. In Sister Dominic's words, 'Everyone has got their own gang.' 'That was my gang,' she says, 'I chose to join that gang.'[77]

7. Money, men and power

The New Zealand Dominican sisters as part of a worldwide web

God has combined the members of the body and has given greater honour to the parts that lacked it, so that there should be no division in the body, but that its parts should have equal concern for each other.

– 1 Corinthians 12:24–25

The New Zealand Congregation of Dominican Sisters is part of the Roman Catholic Church, connecting it to an international web of overlapping networks based on politics, prayer and power. The Congregation is an institute of pontifical right, approved by the Church and accountable to the Pope. The New Zealand Dominican Sisters are also members of the Dominican Order, a worldwide organisation of brothers, sisters, nuns and laity. At a more local level, the Dominican sisters live and work within four of New Zealand's six regional dioceses. Within the diocese most sisters relate to their own particular neighbourhood parish. All these different networks serve to weave the sisters into the Church. They are strong enough to provide structure, meaning, institutionalised authority and support, yet loose enough to be tolerable at the worst of times and life-giving at the best.

In the early years the sisters relied heavily on Bishop Moran: he was the instigator of their mission and its chief support. Mother Gabriel's correspondence with Moran – her 'dearest Father' – reveals two strong personalities engaged in a productive working partnership. In the nineteenth and early twentieth centuries the New Zealand sisters continued to rely on their Mother House. Correspondence with Sion Hill reveals ongoing practical, financial, spiritual and emotional support for the mission to New Zealand. When the Irish Dominicans moved towards amalgamation in the 1920s the New Zealanders sought to join them. An international controversy over the legal religious status of Dominican nuns brought matters to a head, and in 1934 the New Zealanders established their own Congregation. They retained their independence but also secured recognition as part of the Dominican Order.

Vatican II added impetus to developing connections between male and female branches of the order. By the 1980s the New Zealand sisters and brothers were engaged in a variety of joint local projects and took an active part in regional meetings in Asia and the Pacific. The sisters also developed relationships with other Dominican sisters around the world and with other congregations of women religious. At home they drew strength from their involvement in local Catholic churches and from ecumenical groups in the places where they lived. As in the mission's early years, their relationships with male clerics, with other religious women and with the Church bureaucracy are multilayered and multipurpose. They provide the vital context, both then and now, for understanding the fulfilment of the Congregation's preaching mission in Aotearoa New Zealand.

Bishop Patrick Moran, friend and father to the New Zealand Dominican sisters.

P1/16/1, DA.

'Dearest Father ...'

The first New Zealand Dominican sisters had no formal connection with the Dominican Order. They identified themselves as Dominicans, looked to St Dominic as their founder and followed Dominican rites, but their primary pastoral relationship was diocesan rather than Dominican.

This was not always the case. The first Dominican nuns in Dublin had been directly connected to the Dominican Order, but by the early nineteenth century the sisters' numbers were dwindling and Dublin's Dominican fathers were also struggling. Relations between the sisters and the friars were strained. In 1829 the nuns applied to Rome to have their Congregation transferred from the authority of the Dominican superior to the immediate jurisdiction of the local ordinary (bishop or archbishop) of the diocese. Dr Cullen, Rector of the Irish College in Rome, interceded on their behalf, and in January 1832 the nuns received a special brief from Pope Gregory XVI constituting the Archbishop of Dublin as ecclesiastical superior of the convent. The brief decreed that the sisters should enjoy all the same privileges and indulgences as before the transfer. The new arrangement was highly satisfactory.

By the mid-nineteenth century the Cabra nuns were thriving and looking to expand. In 1862 they asked permission from the Prefect of the Sacred Congregation of Propaganda for the same rules to apply if any of the sisters were to move into other dioceses. The prefect granted his permission; any nuns who shifted out of Dublin would also come under the authority of the local ordinary rather than the Dominican superior.[1] As a foundation made from Sion Hill, which was itself a foundation of Cabra, the New Zealand Dominican mission came under the authority of the local bishop.

Patrick Moran was the first Bishop of the Diocese of Dunedin, established on 26 November 1869, just two weeks before the opening of the First Vatican Council. It was a time of general insecurity in Europe, with the Franco–Prussian War unsettling the established balance of power and rationalist philosophers questioning past certainties. The First Vatican Council issued just two documents, both designed to reinforce Church authority: the Dogmatic Constitution on the Catholic Faith defined the Roman Catholic Church's teaching on God, revelation, faith and reason. The First Dogmatic Constitution on the Church of Christ articulated the doctrine of papal infallibility and affirmed the episcopal jurisdiction of local bishops. As successors to the apostles, bishops were empowered to 'tend and govern' the flocks assigned to them, supported and defended in their power by St Peter's successor, the 'Supreme and Universal Pastor'.[2]

At the time of the Council, Moran was content in his role as Bishop of South Africa and tried to refuse the new appointment. The Prefect of the Sacred Congregation of Propaganda summoned him to Rome, where Moran took his place at the Council as a strong advocate for the doctrine of papal infallibility. He met with the Pope and tried to decline the See. Pius XI was direct: 'My son, will you not obey?' Moran knelt and asked to be blessed: 'Holy Father, I go willingly.'[3] He went straight to Ireland to get help for the mission.

Subject to papal authority, Bishop Moran had no real choice in his career path. The Dominican sisters, by contrast, came to New Zealand through the exercise of collective democracy and individual choice. When Moran approached Sion Hill with his request for nuns, the Congregation discussed the matter at length and the choir sisters voted unanimously in favour. Individuals volunteered for the mission, and once again every choir sister had a say in the make-up of the mission.

The bishop presented the sisters with a clear contract: they would send out 10 nuns to teach a primary school and a high school at their own expense and he would provide a suitable house and school rooms. He further promised that 'in reference to the Rules of the community' there would be 'no interference whatever on his part'.[4] Within the parameters of this formal legal agreement the nuns and their bishop established a close working relationship. The success of his educational policy depended on their schools, and the success of their schools depended on his support.

The first few months in New Zealand were difficult for them all, but Moran made the sisters' welfare his main priority. On 17 March, after only a month in Dunedin, Sister Mary Francis Sullivan wrote home to Mother Clare at Sion Hill:

> *We do not repine in the least nor with such a Bishop have we any reason. All the complaints we could notice is that we are too much cared for, and that he worries himself too much about us. We have begged him to think first of building a suitable Church … but he will hear of nothing but providing us first with what he calls a suitable house and schools … the poor Bishop seems so perplexed at the weight of his responsibilities, and we cannot help feeling that we are the heaviest of them …*[5]

The Dominican sisters acknowledged Bishop Moran as their spiritual father from the start, couching their relationship in the typically sentimental prose of Victorian paternalism. 'Nothing can exceed his fatherly care of us,' wrote Sister Mary Francis, 'it is only too great and too tender, and we all love and revere him.'[6] More than two decades later, Moran's 'obedient children' expressed their thanks for his ongoing support, praying that their 'dearly beloved Father' would 'be spared for many years' to continue his 'wise guidance of our nuns and their work'.[7]

Moran's contract with the nuns stipulated an expectation of financial independence, but the realities of establishing a new congregation in a distant colony were complicated. The Dominicans' earliest accounts with the Bank of New Zealand were held in trust by the bishop. He received and banked monies on their behalf for general community purposes and for the convent building fund, to which he himself was one of the most generous contributors.[8] The Dominicans depended on Moran not only for the practicalities of their banking arrangements, but also for financial advice. As the sisters' trustee he was very aware of their debt. In 1893 he wrote to Mother Gabriel instructing her to begin preparations for a 'Grand Bazaar and Art Union'. He was 'most anxious that the sisters should reduce the capital sum of their debt with the Bank of New Zealand in order to lessen the burden of annual interest. As bishop, Moran was struggling to balance the range of fundraising causes in his diocese. So that charitable events would not clash and the faithful would not be too often harassed for money, he informed the sisters that all future bazaars and art unions should be held in the order and at the time of his prescription.[9]

Moran's original contract with the sisters also promised autonomous government. He assured the sisters that he would not interfere with the rules of their community. In fact, he was closely involved in convent life, both at a daily operational level and at a broader level guiding principles and policy. Mother Gabriel sought Moran's advice on a regular basis. As the community's ecclesiastical superior, he was responsible for sanctioning exceptions and adaptations of the rule. Among other permissions granted, in 1894 he approved Mother Gabriel's request that St Dominic's Priory be free to offer hospitality to other nuns; that four or five nuns from the Priory should visit Sacred Heart Church in North East Valley every Sunday for catechetical classes; and that sisters traelling to and from Queenstown be allowed to walk between the convent and the steamer.[10] Moran usually approved Mother Gabriel's arrangements, but he did not take his oversight lightly. At the end of 1894 he wrote to the council regarding the appointment of local superiors for the following year. He wished the matter to be gone into 'very carefully' and reminded the sisters that no decision could be finalised until he himself had 'opportunity of giving grave consideration to the contemplated appointments'.[11] Earlier that year Mother Gabriel had approached Moran regarding the convent in Oamaru, where the heavily overworked community had asked for additional assistance. Moran was loath to endorse unnecessary changes or travel between convents in the middle of the year: 'If there be any inconvenience there, the Nuns ought to try and bear with it, and make the best of it as they do in other places ...' Moran was firm in his opinions, but generally he used his authority to support Mother Gabriel's governance of her community. 'With regard to Oamaru,' he wrote, 'I only wish you to do what your judgement considers best under the circumstances ... I have no desire whatever to interfere with your discretion.'[12] In this case, as in most others, Mother Gabriel followed his advice.

There were times, however, when Bishop Moran used his power to overrule the nuns. In 1893 Dr Luck, Bishop of Auckland, approached the Dominicans to establish a foundation in Gisborne. The council considered the proposal in great detail and agreed to proceed, but eventually Bishop Moran refused his permission.[13] As Bishop of Dunedin it was his responsibility to consider the welfare of his diocese as a whole, and it seems most likely that he refused the Gisborne foundation in order to protect the interests of Catholic schools in Otago and Southland.

The sisters' first General Chapter in New Zealand (1893–94) relied on the bishop's authority and expertise to shape a new rule and constitutions for colonial conditions. It was Moran who convened the chapter and, although he was unwell for most of its duration, he exerted a strong influence on proceedings through Father Lynch, who presided in his stead, and through letters sent from his bed.[14] The formal minutes documenting chapter business are interspersed with expressions of concern for Moran's health. At one point the sisters gathered at an upper window to receive Moran's blessing from his bedroom window.[15] Moran's 'Concluding Words and Last Advice' to the first General Chapter included an exhortation to the nuns to 'keep their own business to themselves'. 'Let no one lay or cleric be the wiser of their domestic affairs if the sisters want to be respected and live in peace ...'[16] Moran assured the Dominicans that 'so long as the sisters are loyal to the Prioress and the Bishop unity will prevail, charity will flourish, peace will reign, and the blessing of heaven will descend peacefully upon all'.[17]

The sisters were indeed loyal to their bishop. The line between independence and interference was not entirely straightforward, but Bishop Moran remained the sisters' main supporter and advisor throughout his episcopacy. In fact, his close relationship with the nuns was a source of gossip, particularly among Moran's political opponents. In July 1876 the *Evening Star* published an article (copied from the *Tuapeka Times*) which implied that one of Dunedin's Catholic priests had forsaken his vows to marry one of the city's nuns. Moran erupted: he unsuccessfully sued the *Evening Star* for 'false, scandalous and malicious libel'. If it had been only his own reputation at stake, he assured the court, he would have treated the allegations with the contempt they deserved, but he could not tolerate such aspersions being cast unchecked against the nuns.[18]

The Diocese of Dunedin was founded on the formal legal and financial relationship between Moran and Mother Gabriel's Dominican sisters. The bishop and his clergy ministered to the pastoral needs of the Catholic settlers, while the sisters tended to the education of their children. In practical terms it was a mutually beneficial working relationship, with both parties striving for the same cause. At a personal level, bishop and sisters relied on each other for friendship and support.

Mother Gabriel and Moran worked hand in hand for nearly 25 years. They journeyed out to New Zealand together, faced the strain and difficulties of the early years together, and celebrated together as Otago's Catholic community and schools grew and flourished. When Mother Gabriel suffered several months of illness after first arriving in New Zealand, Moran sent bouquets of flowers to her bedside.[19] He himself was ill for several years before he died in May 1895 Mother Gabriel was bereft. Father Lynch, who supervised the funeral, accorded her family rights. She recorded her final moments with the bishop in movingly intimate detail:

> *Father Lynch, may the Sacred Heart reward him for his charity, called out my name, and I was taken, from a corner in which I was crouching, by him through the Sanctuary into the aisle and up the steps of the magnificent catafalque to gaze on that too-well loved face so sadly still and serious in death … My right hand was the last object that rested on that saintly brow before he had the two lids fastened over him before the funeral started. The cathedral being closed I accidentally lingered with a piece of lace which I wanted to place on the dear face, and Father Lynch again in charity let me place it there myself. That boon I shall never forget.*[20]

Mother Gabriel's relationship with Bishop Moran was unique. No other subsequent Bishop of Dunedin has been so heavily involved with the sisters, nor so well loved.

Father Patrick Lynch. P_/16.4, DA.

Though the first New Zealand Dominican sisters lived a semi-enclosed life in one of the Church's most far-flung provinces, they remained connected to the Vatican – just as St Catherine of Siena had done – through letters. The New Zealand sisters enjoyed a close relationship with Archbishop Kirby, Rector of the Irish College in Rome and uncle of Sister Mary de Ricci Kirby. Mother Gabriel and Sister Mary de Ricci both corresponded with Kirby on familial terms. He was not only their 'dearest Uncle' but also 'the chain that connects with the Eternal City'.[21] Sister de Ricci's letters to her uncle are warmly affectionate. She clearly valued the familial connection, often resorting to teasing reproach when the correspondence lagged.

> *I am afraid you have made up your mind never to write to me again now. I don't think this is fair. You know I want a blowing up now as well as formerly so I shall expect a long letter soon …*
>
> *I remain dearest Uncle*
> *Your faithful niece*[22]

It was Kirby who interceded with the Pope on Mother Gabriel's behalf for permission to proceed with a New Zealand novitiate in Ireland.[23] He was also a source of practical support, sending rosary beads, crosses, holy pictures, vestments and altar linen to New Zealand.[24] Most importantly, he was a source of spiritual support, giving the sisters access to the Pope – Holy Father of them all – and procuring spiritual favours and blessings for his niece and her congregation.[25]

Bishop Moran's five successors have all worked with the sisters to further the interests of Catholic education in Otago. There have been occasional periods of tension, but in general the diocese has been supportive of the sisters and their schools.

Michael Verdon was Bishop of Dunedin from 1896 until 1918. Historians have generally characterised him as a milder figure than his predecessor, but Verdon's relationship with the Dominicans was somewhat strained in the first few years of his episcopate. Almost as soon as he arrived in Dunedin, Verdon invited Australian Mercy sisters to join the diocese. He was only too aware of Dominican opposition. After 25 years in Dunedin the sisters had established a strong position in the city but they still laboured under a heavy burden of debt,[26] and they saw a second order of teaching nuns competing for students and resources as a serious threat. Verdon, however, believed they would complement each other: the Dominicans would focus their energies in North Dunedin and the unenclosed Mercy sisters would serve the poorer suburbs of South Dunedin. As 'visiting nuns', the 'Mercies' were free to venture out into the streets and homes of their students and to meet social as well as educational needs. 'I know, indeed, that you do not wish this change,' Verdon wrote to the Dominicans, 'but what we dislike is often for our good.' As bishop it was his job to balance the needs of diocese, parishioners and nuns. He promised to take all precautions to protect Dominican interests 'and prevent any unpleasant collision' with the Mercies.[27] When the Mercy nuns arrived in Dunedin at the end of the year the Dominicans relinquished St Patrick's School in South Dunedin and the income that went with it. Mother St Peter Slattery encouraged her sisters in the need for extra economy. She also reminded them of their duty to welcome the Mercy sisters, 'who doubtless will be able to reach the haunts of sin and sorrow from which by enclosure we will be barred'.[28]

Verdon's invitation to the Mercy sisters was a long-sighted administrative decision taken in the interests of the diocese as a whole, yet it left the Dominican sisters vulnerable, underscoring their dependence on episcopal authority. The Dominican Council responded strategically. If Verdon was giving St Patrick's School in South Dunedin to the Mercies, the Dominicans reasoned that he also planned to transfer Sacred Heart School in North East Valley to the new nuns. They asked permission to surrender the Valley school immediately, 'as there would seem to be an inconsistency in our driving through the city to teach one out-door school, when the other has been taken from us'. The sisters were willing to give up the North East Valley school but not St Joseph's School, which was adjacent to the Priory. They asked for Verdon's assurance that this school would be secured to their care. The council also looked for Verdon's support in recouping their lost income, and asked for permission to establish a new foundation in one of the 'richer country districts' or in another diocese.[29] The bishop responded with repeated reassurances of support. Both Sacred Heart and St Joseph's would continue permanently under Dominican administration and the sisters were free to make another

Sister Mary de Ricci Kirby. P2/3/7, DA.

Bishop Michael Verdon. P1/16/2, DA.

foundation either in Otago or in another diocese, so long as they could do so without weakening any of their existing foundations.[30] The council used the opportunity to push for a convent at North East Valley: they would be happy to maintain the valley school, they assured the bishop, but the school fees barely covered the expense of cabs to and from the Priory. What they really needed was a house near to the school.[31] They had a compelling case but funds were short. Eventually the sisters bought land in North East Valley themselves.

In the meantime, the Dominicans wrote to the Archbishop of Melbourne, offering to send out nuns for a new foundation in one of the wealthier districts of Victoria. Disappointingly, the archbishop turned them down.[32] Not long afterwards a new opportunity opened up in Western Australia. Verdon was not impressed. Having made his promises earlier, he gave unwilling consent to the new foundation at Geraldton, but only after repeating the condition that the teaching staff of Otago's schools not be compromised, and on the understanding that the mission would not be a branch house tied to the Priory in Dunedin; it would be an entirely separate, financially independent foundation with its own prioress.[33] Verdon was concerned that Geraldton should not drain Dunedin's resources. Even if it had been wealthy (which it was not), the bishop's conditions ensured that the new foundation was never going to serve its original purpose of replacing income lost on the arrival of the Mercy sisters. The Dominicans were undeterred. Their response to the bishop's introduction of Mercy sisters to Dunedin was as much about power as it was about money. What they really wanted was security and a greater sense of control over their own affairs. They went to Geraldton with no expectations of financial return, just 'happy to do a good work for God … and in one small way to help the spread of holy religion'.[34]

The relationship between Verdon and the sisters may never have been as close as with Moran, but over time they adjusted to his style. On Easter Monday 1903 Sister Mary Louis wrote home to Sion Hill that the bishop had paid an Easter visit at the Priory. 'He chattered away for about an hour surrounded by us all and sipping a fragrant coffee. He is really extremely kind and fatherly. The sisters are growing to like him better each day.'[35]

In 1920 Bishop Verdon was succeeded by Bishop James Whyte who, like both Moran and Verdon, was Irish. 'His Lordship is everything to us that we can desire,' wrote Mother Cecily in 1924, and in a separate letter, 'he has been a true father to us and kindness itself'.[36]

The New Zealand Dominican Sisters' first independent constitutions, approved in 1933, accorded local bishops an active role in congregational affairs. The sisters were required to consult the local bishop before establishing any new foundations or closing existing houses. The bishop himself examined all candidates for profession, whether first, temporary or perpetual. The bishop had the right to choose the community's confessors and chaplains. Bishops were not, however, permitted to interfere in the congregational constitutions, nor were they entitled to enquire into financial affairs or to interfere in matters of internal discipline.[37]

Within these terms of reference the New Zealand bishops were generally supportive, but in 1955 they joined forces to prevent the New Zealand Dominicans from extending into the Pacific. The Australian Dominican sisters had invited the New Zealanders to cooperate on a mission to the Solomon Islands. At a time of limited interaction between Pākehā and Māori in New Zealand, the Dominican sisters professed themselves eager to evangelise 'the poor dark races' of the Pacific. At the start of March 1955 any sister interested in working on the 'Foreign Mission' was urged to forward her name to the council without delay.[38]

By the end of the month the project had been quashed. A large number of sisters had volunteered for the mission but the bishops decided that it was 'most unsatisfactory to all concerned': a composite mission so far away from the mother houses was bound to face vaguely 'unsurpassable difficulties'.[39] The bishops were protecting the interests of their schools: class sizes in Catholic schools were huge in New Zealand at the time, and they argued that the Church could ill afford to sacrifice valuable teaching staff to untested mission work.

Bishop Whyte was succeeded by John Kavanagh who, as bishop from the 1960s until the early 1980s, led the diocese through a period of major change in the Church and orchestrated a massive reorganisation of diocesan schools, both to meet changing social needs and to satisfy the bureaucratic requirements of integration with the state school system. In the early 1970s Dunedin's Catholic school enrolments burgeoned. St Dominic's was under pressure at both ends of the school, with large new entrant enrolments and more pupils staying on in the senior forms. In July 1975, when enrolments closed for the following year, the bishop was informed that there was literally no room for new pupils: having occupied every available space in the school buildings and in the convent itself, St Dominic's had nowhere else to spread. Something had to change.[40]

Bishop Kavanagh's eventual decision to amalgamate St Dominic's and St Philomena's halfway through 1976 was made without formally consulting either the Dominican leadership or the Mercy sisters. In private, the Dominicans expressed embarrassment and concern over the lack of communication, but Mother Constance persuaded the council not to write to Kavanagh.[41] Perhaps she felt he had enough

Catholic Education Conference, Dunedin, 1939. Dominican sisters at the back; Sisters of Mercy, Christian Brothers and clergy in front. P3/13, DA.

to deal with? When the bishops of Dunedin and Auckland asked the Dominicans to join the same programme of phased integration as the diocesan schools the sisters agreed.[42]

Despite occasional failures of communication and tensions between individuals, the New Zealand bishops have always recognised the Dominican sisters as an independent Congregation and valued their contribution to Catholic education and, increasingly, to other forms of pastoral care. During the course of the 1980s the school system continued to develop, the Congregation aged and the focus of mission widened. The Dominican sisters gradually moved out of diocesan primary schools and relinquished their secondary schools to diocesan management. Although some sisters moved into diocesan and parish administration and into other areas of Catholic education, the Congregation enjoyed a greater degree of independence from the Catholic bureaucracy than ever before.

Sisters and clergy celebrating together at the Golden Jubilee of the Dominican sisters' arrival in New Zealand, 1921. P3/4/2, DA.

'Loving Mother ...'

In their early years in New Zealand the Dominican sisters looked to Bishop Moran for immediate guidance and encouragement, and to Sion Hill for ongoing leadership and assistance from afar. The Mother House continued to provide periodic infusions of Irish personnel as well as financial, emotional and spiritual support well into the twentieth century.

The initial mission to New Zealand was financed entirely by the Dominican Sisters of St Catherine's Priory at Sion Hill. Sion Hill paid for the passage of the first sisters from Dublin to Dunedin, and for the cost of outfitting the new foundation. The founding sisters travelled to New Zealand on the understanding that the new diocese would provide them with a suitable home and furniture, so they brought very little with them apart from a piano and several framed religious pictures.[43] At such a distance from the Mother House the new foundation was expected to be completely independent: the New Zealanders would generate their own income and fund any branch houses from their own resources. If they required additional members from the Mother House they were expected to defray all costs.

The reality of mission was never so clear-cut. The New Zealand community worked tirelessly to support themselves and expanded beyond the bounds of Dunedin rapidly, but it was decades before their income was adequate to meet most expenses. They relied on Sion Hill for large loans at low interest. Even so, by 1892 the New Zealanders had paid nearly £500 in interest to the Mother House.[44] They struggled to meet their repayments and asked, over a series of years, for extensions and interest reductions that they knew would not be conceded for their larger loans with the Bank of New Zealand.[45] 'Interest swamps us and eats up every gain,' wrote Mother Mary St Peter to Sion Hill in 1908, and a year later, 'Oh money difficulties are very heavy. You yourselves have your own burdens but have ever so much more help and less opposition than we …'[46] The New Zealand foundation did not clear its debt with Sion Hill until 1920, 50 years after the first sisters had left the Mother House.

The New Zealanders also relied on Sion Hill for practical help. It was difficult to procure educational and liturgical resources so far from the centre of empire, and sometimes even 'basic necessaries' were hard to come by. Sion Hill sisters served as remote shopping assistants, purchasing schoolbooks, religious medals and rosary beads on the New Zealanders' behalf.[47] In 1903 Sister Mary Louis wrote to Sion Hill asking for two good flannel nightdresses. 'It is awfully hard, in fact impossible, to get good white flannel out here, and it is very cold in the winter.' She also asked for Teneriffe lace wheels. 'When one sees how expensive everything is here, one would be inclined to bring a whole cargo of goods out from home … The little ribbon they pay 10p a doz for at home, is 2p a yard in the colonies!'[48]

One of the most valuable consignments from Ireland was a parcel containing 200 copies of the freshly reprinted Rule of Sion Hill, which arrived in February 1913.[49] There could be no stronger connection between the two houses than their shared customs and rule. In 1924 the New Zealanders received a revised copy of the Holy Rule and Constitutions along with a collection of other books. 'It was indeed most thoughtful and sisterly of you,' wrote Sister Mary Cecily Mulcahy to Mother Mary Gonzales. 'The links that bind us to our loved ones in the dear old land are strengthened by the mutual kind remembrance.'[50]

For many years the Dunedin Dominicans produced all the altar breads for the diocese. Once again, their distance from Ireland sometimes caused problems and their sisters at Sion helped span the divide. In 1882 Sister Mary Catherine wrote to Sion's Mother Clare for help with the altar bread machine. 'It is not working satisfactorily. We find the breads get scorched and stick to the top, sometimes to the bottom. We have spent three or four hours some days without anything for our trouble …'[51] Sister Mary Catherine asked Mother Clare to make 'minute inquiries' regarding the parts of the machine and its operation, and to relay the required information back to the sisters in Dunedin.

Just as important as the financial and practical assistance was the emotional and spiritual support afforded by the Mother House to its daughters in the mission. Though only a portion of the correspondence survives intact, archived letters from the early New Zealand Dominicans to their Dublin sisters provide an expressive, often moving sense of personal relationships. In the late nineteenth century mail took months to travel from Ireland to New Zealand via Australia and the New Zealanders received every parcel and letter as a precious gift. 'We are anxiously looking out for news from Melbourne,' wrote Sister Mary Francis to Mother Clare, 'but I fear we shall not have any before the mail closes, it has been so stormy the vessels could not put out.' In 1872 Mother Gabriel returned thanks for the arrival of a double packet of letters evidence of Sion's 'unwearied fidelity'. 'Six large sheets closely written and crossed – two of them also in German, in addition to about 25 or 30 others … gave me reading and recreation for more than 10 days.'[52]

All the New Zealand sisters were pressed for time, but Sister Mary Francis made correspondence a priority. After the final meal of the day on the fifth centenary of St Catherine of Siena in 1880 she devoted a brief window of time before the children's recreation and prayers to her 'darlings' at Sion Hill. A new building had just gone up at Sion. 'I should so much like to see it,' she wrote, 'I don't like to feel there is any part of old Sion (my more than home since my tenth year) that I do not know.'[53] Any news of Sion Hill was interesting to Sister Mary Francis, but she sometimes felt that her rushed letters were a bore to those at home. Even so, she knew that the post would 'show my dear ones at least that I think of them oftener than I write to them, being all day in school between hammer and tongs it quite unfits one for writing anything like a reasonable letter'.[54] She depended on her connection with the sisters at Sion Hill, and berated them with gentle wit in an effort to elicit more mail from Ireland:

> *You see I am taking the earliest opportunity of putting myself in your debt, an obligation I hope you will discharge by return of post by sending me a regular Sion Gazette of all the doings since you last wrote … Tell Sister M Patrick we are expecting a true and full account of the grand May proceedings in her own handwriting which we have not seen for a considerable time… In fine where are all the silent voices and lazy pens that should find time to have a little chat with us poor exiles in a foreign land, from time to time.*[55]

This ongoing bond with home was not a weakness or a distraction. It was their sense of connection with Sion Hill that gave the New Zealand founding sisters the strength and courage to establish a new life in a foreign land. Sion provided the networks of financial, physical, psychological and spiritual support to enable the missioners to transition from Ireland to New Zealand. As Sister Mary Agnes wrote in 1872: 'I rely dearest sisters on your charity in praying and procuring prayers for our Mission which is becoming dearer to us each day.'[56]

The strongest links between Dublin and Dunedin were people. The New Zealand Dominicans continued to depend on Sion Hill for extra choir and lay sisters well into the twentieth century. For many decades, letters from New Zealand were liberally peppered with requests for more nuns. Sister Mary Francis's approach was typically droll:

> *I am beginning to think you do not care how we are since you refuse to help us in what you know as our most urgent needs. Well if I meet an untimely death and go mount my fast steed in the Gully there will be an inquest and the verdict will be for me and my fellow travellers who like me will fall down dead at the same time, but who have no horses to mount hereafter as I have, 'Died of hard work' imposed by Mother Mary Clare in as much as she peremptorily refused to hold out the hand of fellowship to these poor sufferers in the Lord's vineyard in Dunedin and let them sink under their labours when she could but would not help them.*[57]

Notwithstanding Sister Mary Francis's fussing and fuming, Sion Hill did send irregular reinforcements of postulants, novices and professed sisters to New Zealand right up until the mid-twentieth century. With their Irish accents, training and customs, these women helped to maintain the relationship between Dublin and Dunedin.

Some Irish sisters found it hard to adjust to life in New Zealand. A couple of years after arriving in New Zealand Sister Mary St Evangelist's allegiance remained with Sion Hill; she felt her separation from

Mother Clare deeply; she described herself half jokingly as a spiritual orphan, and devoted every spare minute to correspondence 'Home'. Sister Mary Louis Keighron, who arrived in New Zealand in 1902, kept her eyes firmly fixed homeward. Her letters convey a sense of dislocation as she struggled to adjust to life in the Antipodes. 'It seems so strange to be sending you my greeting from the other side of the world,' she wrote a few months after her arrival. 'Even yet I can hardly realise that I am here.'[58] Several years later she was still eager for news from Sion Hill and Ireland. 'You might send me a paper occasionally – we long for home news here and rarely get it. The news is stale by the time the New Zealand geniuses dish it up for us.'[59] Writing home was her 'biggest earthly consolation'. In 1911 she threatened that if she had not soon heard back from Sister Mary Benedict she would 'hire an airship and take a run across the Pacific to see what is the matter with her!'[60] Sister Mary Louis' focus on Ireland was reflected in her disdain for colonial standards. 'No doubt about it,' she wrote home to Sion Hill, 'the future of our Order in the Colonies, spiritual and temporal, depends on our home-trained Irish sisters'. Understanding that the Dublin Dominicans also needed working members at home, Sister Mary Louis and the other 'home-birds' felt uneasy about their future prospects in New Zealand.

> *The colonials are excellent in many ways but I should never like to see them predominating in the Community … a good many little relaxations have crept in and unfortunately it is now very hard to put them out – The tendency in the colonies is to make life as easy and pleasant as can be. Everyone lives as comfortably as possible – there are no very poor people – one never sees a real beggar going about as at home. This desire of ease and having a good time of it has found its way inside the convent walls too and even some of the home sisters have caught the infection – Most of them have got very uneasy of late and are longing for something to be done to check matters before they are past remedying.*[61]

MM Teresa Lynch, SM Agatha Lynch and SM Bertrand McLaughlin in Teneriffe en route to Ireland to procure more vocations for New Zealand. The woman in the hat is Mrs [illegible] who accompanied the sisters from Dunedin to Dublin and home again. GH2/1/31, DA.

Father Finbar Ryan OP at Teschemakers.
F8/9/1, DA.

In 1920 Mother Mary Raymond accompanied her request for more Irish nuns with an assurance that they would 'always be sure of a warm welcome and a happy home in New Zealand'. Homesickness could be a problem for nuns like Sister Mary Louis who left Ireland later in life, but in the prioress's experience 'most quickly get over that to become more enthusiastic New Zealanders than the native born themselves'.[62]

Sister Mary Louis' loyal correspondence home was remarkable. As Mother Mary Raymond observed, most other sisters got swiftly caught up in the busyness of life in New Zealand. 'I have nearly lost my link with home as far as correspondence goes,' wrote Mother Mary St Peter Slattery in 1908, 'I cannot find time for letters … I have not had energy for anything that was not a positive and present duty, so that will have to be my excuse.'[63] She signed herself 'your grateful old child in Jesus Christ'. The immediacy, not the underlying strength of the relationship, was all that had changed over time. In 1920 Sister Margaret Mary Coffey professed herself as keenly interested 'with all the happenings of Sion Hill' as the day she left Ireland. Like Sister Mary St Peter she wrote apologetically after a long lapse: 'I am really ashamed of myself and don't know how to begin …' With so little time at her disposal between religious and teaching duties she tended to rely on Sister Mary Louis for news of the sisters at Sion.[64]

In 1921 the Dominicans celebrated 50 years in New Zealand. They chose a photograph of Sion Hill for the cover of the jubilee magazine. As a statement of identity it could hardly have been more simple or more powerful. A printed address of congratulations from the Mother House affirmed the two communities' shared Dominican identity and recognised the importance of personal connection. Mother Bertrand was the one surviving founding sister.

> *Thank God for these living links, and if even these be broken, as in the order of nature they one day must, let us not lose courage. Let us rather take comfort in the thought that there still remains the closest bond of all – the ever-living spirit of Our Holy Father St Dominic. Let us go on bravely, strengthened by the hope that in the future, as in the past, in the homeland as in the Antipodes, Our Holy Patriarch, with fatherly care, will lead us, his sea-divided children, ever safely onwards, till we reach the heavenly Sion, where united under Mary's protecting mantle we shall sing the praises of her Divine Son for all eternity.*[65]

It was indeed their ongoing bond with Sion Hill that connected the New Zealand Dominicans with the broader order. Coming, as they did, under diocesan rather than Dominican authority, their regular infusions of Irish personnel and their correspondence with the Mother House kept the New Zealanders aligned with the traditions of St Dominic.

Dominican identity, amalgamation and independence

The Irish Dominicans' nineteenth-century dispensation from Dominican control and Dominican rites freed them to serve the needs of their teaching apostolate more fully, but it also placed their identity as Dominicans into doubt. The New Zealand community was never embroiled in the worst of the 'status controversy', but the resultant push towards amalgamation of Cabra foundations affected them deeply. In the end New Zealand retained its independent identity, maintaining an ongoing affiliation with Sion Hill and the other Irish houses while making formal application for autonomous recognition as a distinct Dominican congregation.

In 1832, when the Pope placed the Irish Dominicans under diocesan control and commuted their religious obligations from the full Divine Office to the Little Office of the Blessed Virgin Mary, questions began circulating immediately. How could these nuns be true Dominicans when they did not follow Dominican religious rites? If they did not answer to the Dominican Master General, what right had they to be called Dominicans? Were they in fact even nuns?[66]

The controversy simmered for years.[67] In 1897 Dominican Master General Andreas Frühwirth visited the Dominican convents at Cabra and Sion Hill. He assured them definitively of their position as true daughters of St Dominic whether they were under his own jurisdiction or that of the local archbishop. He failed, however, to resolve ongoing concerns around the nature of their religious vows. Were they enclosed nuns of the second order of St Dominic, or sisters of simple vows belonging to the third order?

At the turn of the century Australia's Cardinal Moran took up the Dominican case in Rome. In September 1903 Pope Pius X issued a formal decree of recognition acknowledging the Cabra Dominicans and all their foundations, and granting them all the privileges, indulgences and spiritual favours belonging to nuns of the second order of St Dominic.[68] The decree further recognised the Cabra sisters' Rule and Constitutions and their canonical submission to diocesan rather than Dominican authority. It was received as a triumph in Ireland, America, South Africa, Australia and New Zealand. Though it did not technically acknowledge the Cabra sisters as members of the second order, it promised them all the rights of such status.[69]

In 1917 the Vatican promulgated a new Code of Canon Law requiring religious congregations and orders to revise their existing constitutions. This process sparked renewed debate over the canonical status of Cabra Dominicans and prompted a push toward amalgamation. The Sacred Congregation for Propaganda and the Dominican Master General actively promoted amalgamation in the interest of centralisation and improved efficiency. The nuns themselves were eager to strengthen their connections, pool resources and bring a collective approach to their ongoing quest for acknowledgement as second order Dominicans.

The New Zealanders played an active part in amalgamation negotiations. In December 19[illegible] Prioress Mother Mary Raymond McGrath responded to recent news from Sion Hill:

> *That is glorious news re: the adjusting and fixing up of things Dominican. The idea of amalgamation with our home houses has been hailed with great satisfaction by all here and we hope and pray that nothing may stop the progress of events till they reach a satisfactory conclusion. Our sisters [illegible]*

be home for Retreat and holidays in a few weeks time and I shall formally submit the project for their consideration. Don't expect there will be one dissenting voice.[70]

Inspired by the spirit of amalgamation, the West Australian Dominican foundation made from Dunedin at the end of the nineteenth century asked to rejoin the New Zealand Dominicans. The New Zealanders hoped for amalgamation on broader lines; they were holding out 'for such a measure of central Government as will bring us into closer touch with our religious Brothers and Sisters in Australia, and consequently with the Spirit and traditions of the Order'.[71] Eventually in 1928 all the Dominican convents in Dublin were amalgamated into a pontifical congregation affiliated to the Dominican Order, with Cabra designated as the Mother House. The Galway Dominicans were not included; they chose to maintain their independence in the hope of one day restoring full enclosure.[72]

Nor were the colonial foundations included. Despite the New Zealanders' early enthusiasm, the impetus for a broad amalgamation of Irish and colonial Dominican houses seems to have dissipated over the course of the 1920s. A collective of houses within the same country made eminent sense, while a disparate collection of foundations spread over several continents may have seemed too much to manage. In 1925 the General Chapter of the Dominican Order decided that the term 'second order' had no real sanction in law. Dominican nuns and sisters were free to use the letters OP (Order of Preachers) after their name in the same way as Dominican priests.[73] This decision clarified the vexed status question once and for all. It did not matter if the New Zealand sisters were strictly enclosed or semi-enclosed. It did not matter if they recited the full Divine Office or the Little Office of the Blessed Virgin Mary. With their Dominican identity assured, the urgency for union with other Dominican foundations died away.

By 1930 the New Zealand Dominicans had begun independent correspondence with Rome in order to bring their constitutions into line with the new Code of Canon Law.[74] In 1931 Father Finbar Ryan, Dominican Provincial of Ireland, visited New Zealand. He toured all the branch houses, spending at least a week in each place and lecturing on average seven hours a day. His main purpose, however, was to help the New Zealanders adapt their rule to meet the new requirements of canon law. He urged them to form their own congregation with a modified version of the rule already approved for Cabra.[75] Having planted the seeds in person, Ryan continued to advise the New Zealanders from Ireland. In August 1932 he sent out forms for presenting a petition to the Holy See, with specific instructions for ensuring an expeditious consent to their new constitutions. Ryan had also visited the Australian Dominicans and guided them through the same process. In encouraging the New Zealand and Australian communities to adopt the Cabra Constitutions he believed the sisters might 'strike a blow for the assertion of their moral unity with the parent Irish stock'. If, in the future, the possibility of amalgamating these 'far-flung congregations' arose again, the process would be facilitated by their having the same fundamental organisational structures and law.[76]

The New Zealanders lost no time in compiling their petition. They sought papal permission to adopt the Irish Constitutions and to constitute their 12 convents as one distinct congregation. The Sacred Congregation for Religious granted formal consent on 21 April 1933.[77] The New Zealand Dominicans became 'The Congregation of the New

SM Louis Keighron, 1900s. P2/3/6, DA.

Zealand Dominican Sisters, under the protection of Our Lady of the Most Holy Rosary and of St Catherine of Siena', affiliated to the Order of Preachers and under the ecclesiastical authority of the local ordinary, with the right to return immediately to the recitation of the full Divine Office.

It was almost exactly 100 years since the Cabra Dominicans had replaced the full Office with the smaller Office of the Blessed Virgin Mary in order to meet the demands of their busy teaching apostolate. Their twentieth-century successors were busier than ever, but the status conferred by the full Office, and the link it affirmed with the larger order, held huge significance. The New Zealanders had failed to achieve amalgamation with Ireland, but the drawn-out process of responding to Rome's new Code of Canon Law had fostered a growing sense of cohesiveness in the worldwide Dominican family. The New Zealand Dominicans had established themselves as an independent congregation and tightened connections with the order as a whole.

Dominican fathers and Dominican family

The New Zealand Dominican sisters' relationship with the wider Dominican family continued to develop over the course of the twentieth century. They forged strong links with the Dominican fathers in New Zealand and, towards the end of the century, focused increasing attention on relationships with Dominican women around the world and with other Dominican congregations in Asia and the Pacific.

The first Dominican priest to visit New Zealand came in 1769 on French Admiral Jules Dumont d'Urville's voyage of exploration. The first Dominican priest to settle in Australasia arrived in Australia in 1831, but the first foundation was not made there until 1898 in North Adelaide. Visiting priests occasionally reached New Zealand and the sisters counted themselves blessed to receive a Dominican retreat. In 1949 the Australians set up two foundations in New Zealand – one in Auckland and one in Dunedin.

The Dominican sisters welcomed the priests eagerly. In Dunedin the sisters gave the friars a donation of land from their convent grounds in North East Valley, and it was here that the friars established Aquinas Hall as a hall of residence for men attending Otago University and Dunedin Teachers' College. The sisters at St Dominic's Priory benefited from the friars' superior theological training; they received regular lectures in theology and spirituality. In the 1950s the friars also provided regular lectures and spiritual services to the sisters' foundation in Auckland. In 1960 the friars took control of the newly formed parish of Blockhouse Bay, and in 1962 the sisters joined them there to establish a Dominican school. Until 1976, when the friars moved out of the parish, Blockhouse Bay functioned as a uniquely Dominican parish.

MM David Stark, Master General Aniceto Fernandez Alonso and Father Hilary Carpenter OP, 11 March 1967.
P6/20/2, DA.

The Second Vatican Council encouraged a growing sense of cohesion within the order at an international level. As Dominican houses around the world refocused on St Dominic and his unique spirituality, they drew closer together in a shared effort to revitalise their unique charism in the modern world. Dominican Master General Father Aniceto Fernandez Alonso led the way, emphasising the strong links between the order's brothers and sisters. In 1967 he visited New Zealand. Sisters from Invercargill, Oamaru, Teschemakers, Milton, Lawrence, Cromwell and Queenstown all gathered in Dunedin for the occasion. Alonso celebrated Mass with the sisters as a 'family banquet'. 'The Dominican vocation is a special bond of unity which draws us together more closely than any ordinary family,' he told them.[78]

At a 1969 address to the Dominican mothers general in Rome Alonso again affirmed their place in 'the great Dominican family'.[79] He encouraged the brothers and sisters to continue exploring practical forms of spiritual and pastoral collaboration as they worked together in the service of the Church. 'Nowadays women are taking their rightful place in the church's work; so too the sisters must have their proper place in the Order's apostolate.'[80]

The General Chapter held in Naples in 1974 witnessed several momentous developments. A decision was made to include the order's nuns in the next General Chapter. In the interests of greater unity among the branches of the Dominican family the terms first order, second order and third order were finally set aside as unsuitable for the present and lacking in historical authenticity. Over the next few years, with Father Vincent de Couesnongle as master general, the order strove to integrate its different branches on a footing of true equality.[81]

The New Zealand sisters played an active part in the move towards equality and the ongoing evolution of the Dominican Family as a formally organised entity. The first Basic Charter of the Dominican Family was sent to all the order's constituent foundations around the world. The New Zealanders studied the document in their communities. They responded as a congregation, with general praise accompanied by a constructively robust critique objecting to the use of sexist language and persistently hierarchical attitudes.[82] They also took the opportunity to reflect on the reality of Dominican relationships in local context.

> *We have restricted our interaction as a family by casting the friars into a giving role. We have thereby prevented dialogue among the three branches. We have tended to emphasise the intellectual expertise of the friars and have maintained the expectation that they be the leaders most of the time. We need DIALOGUE.*[83]

In 1983 the Dominican General Chapter approved 'The Bologna Document on the Dominican Family', calling Dominic's heirs to 'the task of manifesting the equality and complementarity of men and women'.[84] Joined together on a basis of true equality, Dominican priests, Dominican nuns, Dominican sisters and Dominican laity would care for each other, cooperate with each other and serve the Church as collaborative preachers of the Word.

In the late 1970s and early 80s New Zealand Dominican priests and sisters sought active opportunities for interaction and engagement. They shared liturgical celebrations of the Feast of St Dominic, held prayer days together, attended study days and began to work together on directed and preached retreats. The three branches of the New Zealand Dominican Family also began meeting together for social occasions such as shared meals, jubilee celebrations and Dominican feast days. In May 1984 the friars and sisters held their first combined council meeting.[85]

The broadening apostolate created more opportunities for shared ministry. Fathers and sisters worked alongside each other in Auckland in hospital chaplaincy and visitation. In Dunedin and Auckland they worked together in university chaplaincy. It was at Teschemakers, however, that the various branches of the Dominican Family engaged with most intensity and effectiveness. By the mid-1980s Teschemakers was a truly shared venture, with fathers, sisters and laity not only ministering to each other but reaching out to the Church and the wider community. As sisters, friars and laity prayed, studied, socialised and ministered together, their sense of group identity and purpose gathered strength.

> *There is a division of labour into complementary tasks, with a strengthening of confidence in our vocation by the sharing of our ideal with the rest of the Family. The Family does create the freedom for each to serve in their own way. This works through a spirit of trust and sharing of concerns that we find. Also through a sense of contact with the whole a Family …*[86]

The New Zealand Dominican sisters have continued to embrace and encourage the evolving reality of the Dominican Family. The connection between fathers, sisters and laity remains loose and open. The Dominican Family includes 'those women and men whom we recognise as belonging with us in some way that goes beyond friendship or the status of past pupil'. They are people who want to share in Dominican prayer, mission and community. By 20[illegible] the sisters had compiled a mailing list of over [illegible]0 people wishing to receive ongoing information on Dominican issues and events.

Two distinct groups within this loose arrangement have special significance to the sisters. First, some of the women who have lived as Dominican sisters and left the Congregation have sought to renew a connection with Dominican life as Dominican Family members. Second, the Catholic deaf community remains tightly woven into the fabric of Dominican life in New Zealand: the Dominican Family provides a framework for these men and women to maintain an ongoing connection with the Dominican legacy of their years at St Dominic's School for the Deaf.[87] As the number of vowed Dominicans in New Zea-

Shared leadership meeting, Teschemakers, 1984. P8/13/1, DA.

New Zealand friars and sisters with Master General Damian Byrne, 1988. **Back**: Father David Halstead, Father Ambrose Loughnan, Master General Damian Byrne, Fr Kevin Toomey, S Janice Ogilvy. **Front**: S Mary Horn, Fr Michael Sherris, S Susan Logan, S Judith Anne O'Sullivan, S Carmel Walsh. P8/10/3, DA.

land gradually decreases, the sisters see Dominican Family members as a source of hope for the future. At an international level the New Zealanders played an increasingly active role in Dominican affairs in the later twentieth century, particularly in meetings of women Dominicans and in regional meetings in Asia and the Pacific.

In 1965, in response to *Perfectae Caritatis*, the Sacred Congregation for Religious inaugurated the International Union of Superiors General (UISG) to provide for contact between religious women on a world scale. The first general assembly took place in 1967, and in 1970 Mother Jordan was elected to represent the New Zealand superiors general.[88] Mother Constance attended the UISG assembly in November 1975. She described the meeting with nearly 500 superiors general as 'a unique occasion during which we experienced the universality of the Church and the love that is the binding force irrespective of race or culture'.[89]

In the 1980s Dominican superiors general began using their presence at UISG gatherings to hold informal multilingual meetings with the Dominican master general. In May 1995 Judith McGinley and Susan Logan joined others from around the world at the first formal meeting of Dominican Sisters International (DSI).[90] Six years later Sister Judith Anne O'Sullivan represented New Zealand at the DSI's Third General Assembly in Caleruega in Spain. Master General Timothy Radcliffe told the 123 assembled women, representing 32,000 Dominican sisters in over 100 countries, that the foundation of DSI was the most important event of his term of office. As Judith Anne observed in her report to the New Zealand Congregation, 'OP men have been international from the beginning. We as OP women need to be more intentional about being international.'[91]

The New Zealanders were certainly intentional, prioritising DSI and fostering local links with Dominican sisters in Australia, Asia and the Pacific. In 1996 Judith McGinley attended a meeting of Dominican superiors in Hong Kong. Judith Anne and Hazel McDonald organised a small Asia-Pacific meeting in Perth, and a regional meeting of Asian sisters as part of a larger regional Dominican Family gathering in Multan, Pakistan. Later that year Judith Anne and Jacqui Ryan attended the regional Justice Peace and Creation gathering of Dominican Family in Taiwan. Judith Anne preached at a Dominican retreat in the Solomon Islands and spent time with

In 1970 MM Jordan McCormick attended the Major Superiors Conference in Rome. F7/11/3A, DA

In February 2011 Jacqui Ryan travelled from New Zealand to New York to take up a short-term position as volunteer intern at the Dominican NGO office at the United Nations. Her appointment represented an opportunity for the New Zealand Dominican sisters to contribute to the worldwide community of Dominican women and to play a meaningful role in international mechanisms for promoting peace. Private collection.

the Dominican sisters in Indonesia. Judith Robinson represented the Pacific at an international DSI workshop on eco-justice. Helen Bergin contributed a chapter in a DSI publication on theology and theologians. Two women from Timor Leste attended the New Zealand Dominican Sisters' Summer School, where their presence was valued as 'a gift and a joy'. In their distribution of financial support overseas in 1996 the New Zealand Dominicans made grants to the Dominican sisters in Iraq, Pakistan, Timor Leste, Indonesia and the Solomons, to DSI, and to the Prouille Dominican Family Project.[92] In 1996 the New Zealand Dominican Sisters also initiated a newsletter designed to connect Dominican women in the Asia–Pacific region.

In 1987 the Seventh Annual Asia Pacific Regional Dominican Conference was held at Teschemakers. It was the first time the meeting had been held in New Zealand and the first time that fathers and sisters had all attended. Forty people from 11 countries, representing 3000–4000 Dominican religious, experienced a 'glorious family reunion'. For Mary Horn the sense of connectedness was inspiring:

> *As Dominican women in the South Pacific we have experienced isolation, and the bringing together of so many diverse members of our international order was indeed a rich experience. It signified for me the power we have in our 'multinational' organization that is as yet untapped for the good of our sisters and brothers struggling for justice in their own areas.*[93]

The experience helped Mary see herself as part of a wider family bound by a 'mutual love of Dominic', and a 'commitment to finding and spreading the truth'.

The sisters continued to play an active part in regional Dominican meetings. In 1988 Sister Margaret Quinn represented New Zealand in Hong Kong at the Dominican Conference on Justice and Peace for the Asia–Pacific region.[94] In 1991 Judith McGinley attended the first joint Conference of Dominican Superiors and Formators in the Philippines.[95] That same year Sandra Winton and Raewyn Benzie represented New Zealand at the Asia Pacific Dominican Family Conference on the Rights of Women and Children in Hong Kong.[96] In 1998 Maureen Connolly spent three months at the Dominican Retreat Centre in Caleruega in the Philippines, and Carmel Walsh spent time at the centre in 2005. In 1998 Mary Anna Baird and Father Peter Murnane were appointed Dominican Co-Promoters for Justice and Peace in the Asia–Pacific Region, and spent four weeks in the Philippines at the end of that year.[97] In 2003 Sister Judith Anne was appointed as the Asia–Pacific regional executive member for DSI; she attended the general assembly in Spain as well as DSI executive meetings in Rome and Prouille. In 2006 Jacqui Ryan represented New Zealand at the Dominican Family Asia Pacific Justice, Peace and Care of Creation Conference in Taiwan.[98]

The New Zealand Dominican sisters have always maintained a particularly close relationship with the Australian Dominican congregations, but until recently their association was fairly loose. In the early years Dominican sisters bound for New Zealand would stop off in Australia and would often stay with the Dominican sisters at Maitland, New South Wales. Maitland had been founded from Cabra so the two antipodean missions shared a common cultural heritage. The New Zealanders shared an even closer connection with the West Australian Dominican Congregation, which originated as a mission from Dunedin. In the 1920s it seemed a real possibility that New Zealand, West Australia, South Australia and East Australia would join together to form one congregation, but the impetus died away as each group concentrated on securing its own constitutions. In the late 1940s the Dominican Sisters of Eastern Australia initiated a new push toward union. The New Zealand sisters took part in early negotiations, but when the Australian congregations eventually established a generalate and a joint novitiate in 1957 the New Zealand sisters were not included.[99]

The Second Vatican Council refocused attention on the common roots of the Australasian Dominican sisters. Over the next several decades the New Zealand Congregation continued to develop informal links with the Australian congregations based on membership of larger groups like DSI, participation in regional affairs through Dominican conferences in Asia and the Pacific, and personal friendships.

S Elizabeth Mackie and S Judy Lawson, prioresses of the Dominican Sisters of East Australia, at the Federation of Dominican Sisters in Oceania, 9 March 2014. Author's collection

In 2011 the New Zealand Leadership Team asked the congregation to consider the possibility of formal federation with the Australian Dominicans:

> *It would mean that we commit to building stronger relationships with the Dominican Sisters in Australia, for our good and for the good of Dominican life in our part of the world. The day may come when we need one another more than we do at present … Belonging to the Federation would mean that mutual cooperation, development and promoting of the Dominican charism and regular communication on shared vision and mission are deliberately built into the rhythm of our lives.*[100]

The Leadership Team emphasised that all this was already happening but in an 'unplanned, ad hoc way'. Federation would underpin the existing relationship with a strong structural foundation. The great major-

New Zealand and Australian Dominicans in St Dominic's Chapel, Dunedin, for a formal ceremony marking the Federation of Dominican Sisters in Oceania, 9 March 2014. Author's collection.

ity of sisters were enthusiastically in favour, but even so the process took time to unfold. In March 2014 representatives from the four Dominican congregations in Australia – the Dominican Sisters of Eastern Australia (including the Solomon Islands sisters), the Holy Cross Congregation of Dominican Sisters in Adelaide, the Congregation of Dominican Sisters of North Adelaide and the Congregation of Dominican Sisters of Western Australia – travelled to Dunedin to meet with the Leadership Team of the New Zealand Congregation of Dominican Sisters. On 8 March the sisters held a formal liturgy of federation, acknowledging and celebrating the legacy of their shared origins and committing to work together and support each other in the future.[101] The New Zealand Congregation retains its independence – highly prized by many of its members – and it gains formal acknowledgement and status as part of a local network of like-minded sisters who share similar challenges and concerns. Like the evolution of the Dominican Family, the Federation has been a source of hope and inspiration as the sisters face the future – with all its possibilities and uncertainties – hand in hand.

Pope and parish

As a congregation, the New Zealand Dominican Sisters are irrevocably bound to the Roman Catholic Church. They acknowledge the primacy of the Pope and the authority of diocesan bishops. Yet the congregation's fierce commitment to peace and justice and to women's rights has sometimes strained relations with the local Church. After the joyful libera-

S Maureen O'Hanlon and S Judith Anne O'Sullivan with Pope John Paul II, Rome, 1981. DA

tion of the 1960s, the Vatican at the start of the new millennium seemed to be gradually returning to a clerical conservatism that many of the New Zealand sisters struggled to accept. Pope Francis, with his emphasis on simplicity and his active commitment to justice, represents a new direction that is more closely aligned with the New Zealand Congregation's hopes for the Church and their vision for God's people. Each sister has her own approach to the Church, her own relationship with her local parish priest and her own feelings about the Pope and the Vatican, but the group as a whole has always maintained an independent stance balanced by a formal commitment to established Church authority.

The congregation's most recent Constitutions, promulgated in 1989, frame obedience in reference to Christ 'whose perfect fulfilling of the Father's will brought life to the world'. They also draw on the example of the congregation's founding sisters – women who 'left us the heritage of an obedience which is creative, responsible and prepared to accept the risks that faith requires'. Local bishops play a less active role than they have in the past, notwithstanding the fact that the Constitutions still acknowledge them as legitimate ecclesiastical superiors:

> *By our vow of obedience we make a total dedication of our will to God and to his service, and sacrifice of ourselves to him. We are subject in the first place to the Pope whom we are bound to obey in virtue of our vow. We also owe obedience to our legitimate superiors according to the Rule of Saint Augustine and the Constitutions of our Congregation.*[102]

The Congregation is governed by the common law of the Church and by decrees of the Holy See relating to religious institutions. It is subject to the diocesan bishop only in matters 'which come within his jurisdiction' – a fairly vague prescription that is open to interpretation. As a congregation of pontifical right the sisters are not subject to the authority of the Dominican master general, but they are guided 'by those ordinations of general chapters of the Order which interpret for our times the authentic spirit of Saint Dominic'.[103]

The Constitutions reflect a loosening of the sisters' relationship with established clerical authority. In the nineteenth century and the first half of the twentieth century the New Zealand Dominican sisters' involvement in Catholic schools – running parish primary schools and operating their own private secondary schools – placed them in constant contact with the bishops who supervised the Catholic education system. They were engaged in productive, generally harmonious working relationships that nonetheless tied them in to the hierarchical structure of the Church. The Second Vatican Council's call to religious institutes to return to the spirit of their founders liberated the sisters to move beyond their traditional teaching roles and expand into new apostolates, reclaiming their place in the charismatic structure of the Church. Though many sisters continued to work in the field of education, they often occupied new roles and related with diocesan authority in an increasingly professionalised environment. In the present day the New Zealand bishops are more inclined to relate to the Dominican Sisters through the language of invitation rather than instruction.

Most sisters relate to the 'Church' at a local level through meaningful personal relationships and participation in parish affairs and activities. Roxane Parkinson, who lives in Johnsonville, still attends morning Mass at Sts Peter and Paul Church most days. She experiences the parish as 'a lovely praying community' led by Father Peter Fitzgibbon, 'a very gifted human being'. Roxane is involved with music in the church.[104]

The sisters living in North Otago are very involved in the life of their local parish. Sister Madeleine McAleese and Sister Catherine Laboure served for many years on the board of St Kevin's College. Sister Madeleine organises the Saturday liturgies at St Patrick's Basilica, and when the priest is away, also takes care of Sunday liturgies. She is an active member of the Oamaru Catholic Women's League. Sister Nola Gleeson opens and closes the church each day, takes communion to the sick, visits the elderly and volunteers for the Society of St Vincent de Paul. Mary Horn runs the scripture group and serves as a reader in church. She is involved with the liturgy group and facilitates a Walk by Faith group. Like many of the sisters Mary has struggled with the conservative direction of the Roman Catholic Church in recent years. 'The Catholic Church is out there. And I'm here … I get very upset about what's happening out there sometimes, but that's not the Church, that's the institutional Church. There's another Church happening.'[105]

S Lorraine Challis, Fr Mark Chamberlain of Holy Name Parish, Dunedin, and S Judith Anne O'Sullivan, March 2014. Author's collection.

Along with many of the Dominican sisters who live in Dunedin, Margaret Quinn attends Holy Name Church in North Dunedin. Holy Name is a vibrant faith community led by Father Mark Chamberlain, whose mother Margaret was a pupil at Teschemakers. Margaret Quinn is uncomfortable with the new liturgy and with the Roman Church's attitude toward

Celebrating 800 years of Dominicanism at St Benedict's Catholic Church, Auckland, 2006. S Maria McDonald, S Columba McHugh, Bishop Patrick Dunn. P10/16/14, DA.

women, but she is very happy in her local church. Father Mark values and celebrates the Dominican presence in his parish and is supportive of the sisters as individuals and as a group.[106]

In Invercargill Raewyn Benzie is involved in St Patrick's parish and enjoys her connection with the people there. In the years that her mother lived at Calvary Rest Home Raewyn led the liturgy there and Calvary became her parish. Raewyn finds the swing toward conservatism in the wider Catholic Church disturbing; she identifies more strongly with Dominican values and philosophies.[107]

Cecily Sheehy, who lives in Auckland, is tightly connected to her Dominican sisters, but her journey into creation spirituality 'kind of put the Church in a new perspective'. She found herself asking why the earth wasn't in every sermon and every prayer of the Church. She lives a Dominican spirituality – 'the contemplation is there, and the veritas – the search for truth – is there ... seeing the divine in all beings'.[108]

Sarah's circle

In 1980 New Zealand Dominican Sister Bernadette Cheyne completed an MA at Fordham University, New York, on the psychological and spiritual development of women in mid-life. She drew on the work of Matthew Fox, a former Dominican and an influential exponent of creation spirituality, who has argued for the global necessity of moving from the competitive, hierarchical paradigm of patriarchal Church authority – symbolised by Jacob's ladder – to a creative, interdependent paradigm – symbolised by Sarah's circle.[109] Bernadette's thesis encouraged women 'to come off "Jacob's ladder" and dance "Sarah's circle"'.[110]

The New Zealand Dominican sisters are already dancing Sarah's circle. They resisted Jacob's ladder from the start, forming layers of interconnected relationships with clergy at home and abroad that enhanced their ability to serve the Church and to exercise feminine power in a colonial setting. Over time they have developed formalised institutional support structures such as DSI, USG and the Federation of Dominican Sisters in Oceania, engaging with other Dominicans and religious women in creative processes designed to illuminate truth, spread peace and foster justice. These overlapping networks form a web that is strong enough to connect the New Zealanders securely into the Roman Catholic Church, yet flexible enough to allow them to generate new shapes and patterns in the web – to listen to God's voice and follow His lead. The New Zealand Dominicans are part of the charismata older than the hierarchical structure of the Church: they claim their authenticity as preachers from their vows as Dominican sisters.

8. A women's world

Internal structures of authority

Sisters leading and serving together. We have a dream …
We will hold to the vision of the leadership of each one of us.
– General Chapter of New Zealand Dominican Sisters, 2011[1]

The New Zealand Congregation of Dominican Sisters is a unique community of women. The sisters live and work within the framework of the Catholic Church and the Dominican Order, but most identify first and foremost as Dominican women of Aotearoa New Zealand. They are held together by shared lives and a common call to preach the Word of God, and by a mutual understanding of equality and obedience that is reflected in the Congregation's organisation and management. Leadership roles and governance processes are designed to serve a corporate vision, protecting, supporting and empowering sisters as individuals and as a community.

In the early years the Dominican sisters were organised according to rigidly hierarchical principles. The mother prioress dominated the congregation, and each sister occupied a fixed position in the community. This model, although it confined many to subservient lives, offered the nuns an escape from contemporary cultural expectations and social mores. Clergy provided external guidance and support, but the nuns governed themselves. The privileged few who rose to a position of power exercised authority over a large group of other women, and held responsibility for the congregation's schools, and property and other assets.

The Second Vatican Council initiated a radical reorganisation of the congregation's structures of authority. By the end of the twentieth century the New Zealand Dominicans had adopted a highly democratic form of government and had fine tuned a team approach to leadership.

At an individual level, sisters in the late twentieth century made similar vows to those a century earlier. Their continued commitment to each other – sharing the intimacy of daily life and spiritual experience, their work and their material wealth – is a powerful countercultural witness. In an age of individualism and sexualised materialism the New Zealand Dominican Sisters connect to each other as women committed to the earth, to peace and to justice.

Power and position in the priory

For nearly a century after arriving in New Zealand, the Dominican sisters maintained the structures of governance inherited from Sion Hill. Power was centralised and concentrated, with the prioress and council ruling the Congregation from the Mother House in Dunedin. The sisters took their place in the

St Bertrand's community, Invercargill, 1960s. SM Helena, S Peter Julian, SM Ignatius. F13/10/4. DA.

community according to a strict order of precedence that determined their status in the Congregation and their position in choir, refectory, chapter and processions:

1. *The Mother Prioress General*
2. *The Vicaress General*
3. *The Conventual Prioress of her own convent*
4. *The Councillors General in order of election*
5. *Ex-Prioresses General*
6. *The Conventual Prioresses out of their own convents, who, if there be more than one, rank among themselves, according to the time of their first profession*
7. *The Vicaress of a House not yet erected into a Priory*
8. *Sub-Prioress in her own Convent*
9. *Mistress of Novices everywhere*
10. *Choir sisters professed, according to the time of their profession*
11. *Choir novices, according to the time of their reception of the habit*
12. *Choir postulants*
13. *Lay sisters professed, according to the time of their profession*
14. *Lay novices, according to the time of their reception of the habit*
15. *Lay postulants*[2]

Sisters at the 1995 Congregational Chapter.
P9/2R, DA.

Hailed by subsequent generations as 'Mother of the Missions', New Zealand's first prioress, Mother Gabriel Gill, led the Dominican founding sisters from Dublin to Dunedin, managed the initial process of settlement and supervised the first stages of expansion. Each new mission began with three or four sisters (two or three choir sisters and one lay sister to care for the practical needs of the new community). The mother prioress usually accompanied the sisters to their new home and helped them set up, leaving the most senior sister in charge as the local superior. Once established, branch houses functioned as satellites of the Mother House – St Dominic's Priory in Dunedin. Sister Mary de Ricci Kirby was appointed as the first superior in Invercargill; technically she was in charge of the house and its inhabitants, but ultimate responsibility still sat with Mother Gabriel. 'We are not an independent house,' wrote Sister Mary de Ricci, 'our dear Mother lays down our regulations which we have only to follow, and should anything of any importance occur I apply to her for directions.'[3]

In terms of policy and practice, branch house superiors answered directly to the mother prioress. In terms of finance, the missions were expected to be independent. The bishop approved only new foundations that promised to be self-supporting. Local Catholic communities rallied together to provide homes for the nuns and buildings for schools. Sister Mary Francis, the first superior at the Convent of the Holy Rosary in Oamaru, wrote to Mother Clare at Sion Hill:

> *You have now five decades of the Rosary in Maoriland, namely two in Dunedin, one in Invercargill and one in Queenstown and one in the White Stone City … How I wish you could all see it. Such a lovely view as we have, and such trees, fruit and flowers, all like the old country, but more luxuriant, and the more broad Pacific at our feet, for here we are situated on such a pretty hill …*[4]

Oamaru's Archdeacon Coleman had raised the funds for a 'splendid stone building' to use as school and chapel, and the sisters moved in 'without a penny owing'. The local parishioners were not wealthy but they supported the ideal of religious education – 'they are all struggling, but are good Catholics true to their faith'.[5]

In Oamaru and in the other mission regions, local Catholic families provided the nuns with ongoing support. Farming families delivered regular supplies of produce, meat and eggs. Men provided labour and performed odd jobs, and women baked and organised fêtes. In 1904 when Sister Mary Louis shifted from the Priory to Oamaru, she was most impressed. 'The people are so good to us! They are constantly sending us presents of one kind or another.' Over the course of the year the convent had bought no potatoes, grain or fowl – 'All supplied by the generosity of our neighbours and much more besides.'[6] The nuns' most important source of supplementary income was music and speech lessons that were attended by both Catholic and Protestant children.

Each year the sisters in the mission houses returned to the Priory for the Christmas retreat, where the community reconnected and recharged for the year ahead. At the end of the Christmas holiday each sister received a printed card with her assignment for the year ahead. Some would return to their previous posts, others would be sent somewhere new. Even in the middle of the year there were sometimes unexpected changes due to ill health or staffing needs. Sisters had no say in their appointments; the mother prioress, in consultation with her general council, had full control – and full responsibility – for all appointments. This was not a responsibility held lightly. Council minutes suggest that the prioress and her advisors considered annual placements very carefully and sought not only to meet school staffing needs, but to balance personalities within each community. Many sisters found shifting between convents stressful. Sister Mary Louis described New Zealand as 'a dreadful place for changes':

SM St Peter Slattery and MM Gabriel Gill. P/2.3, DA

> *One is never sure of her quarters – everyone seems to live on just from day to day, always in expectation of a change. This may be very good for promoting the spirit of detachment, but I fear it is rather detrimental to the religious spirit.*[7]

The prioress was in charge of the whole congregation, with the bishop as her ecclesiastic backstop. She was aided by four general councillors including a designated vicaress who acted as her deputy. Each prioress had her own manner and methods.

Mother Gabriel was a strongly independent leader. The council minutes book records only two formal meetings in 1871, one in 1872, two in 1873 and none in 1874. The prioress dictated the agenda. After 'suitable discussion' each matter in question passed to 'secret scrutiny', with councillors invariably voting to support Mother Gabriel's recommendations.[8] In contrast, Mother Peter Slattery, prioress from 1895 until 1901 and then again from 1907 until 1910, called regular council meetings and appeared to consult on a range of issues and asked her councillors for advice on new foundations, financial affairs and personnel.[9]

Each prioress developed her own style of leadership with the wider congregation, too. Mother Gabriel addressed the sisters in the maternal language typical of the times – 'My own dear children' – and signed off with 'your unworthy but devoted Mother'.[10] She was an active manager who rose early to say the Office with the sisters and often worked late into the night when the rest of the community was asleep. There were times when Mother Gabriel seems to have felt her responsibilities heavily. In the middle of 1882, for example, she was pushing ahead with the new convent at Oamaru while still trying to secure funding for school rooms in Invercargill. Invercargill's parishioners had not given as generously to the building fund as she had hoped. She went ahead with plans for extensive new buildings 'in fear and trembling' lest the bishop disapprove.[11] If her fear and trembling had been real rather than metaphorical she would have written to the bishop or waited to consult him in person. Mother Gabriel was not, however, slow to action: she was a bold, decisive leader. For more than a quarter of a century it was she who held the dispersed community of New Zealand Dominicans together. She wrote frequent letters of encouragement and instruction to the branch convents, visited whenever necessary and enforced consistent standards of spiritual discipline through sheer force of personality.

The position of prioress entailed not only power and authority but service and commitment. Sister Lucy Tracy and Sister Mary Francis Sullivan both died at the start of 1894, and Mother Gabriel sat with both until the very end. Her description of Sister Lucy's last hours is testament to the prioress's fortitude and her devotion to the community. Through the long hours of the night she knelt beside Sister Lucy's bed, praying and sprinkling her over and over again with holy water.

> *My poor child grasped my hand and kept it strongly pressed to her side, as if to ease her pain … Then followed a sleep disturbed by moans. Often did the sufferer look around to see if I was still beside her. Then closing her eyes she would moan, say 'mother' and gently doze – indeed she was always a faithful child to me!*[12]

Within the framework of enclosure, visitations provided a formal mechanism for monitoring communal religious observances, inspecting student progress in the schools, checking on individual sisters and assessing community dynamics. Mother Mary Philomena McCarthy visited Helensville in September 1947. Her summation was brief: 'Essentials of Religious Life. One sister is especially wanting in deference to Superior. Plainer food should be used for lunch. Too much cake.'[13] In October 1953 she made her visitation of the Lawrence convent and used the opportunity to guide the local superior, Mother Damian, in her exercise of delegated authority. 'Mother should be more gentle and less dictatorial as a Superior. She is somewhat harsh in exacting obedience. One sister gives trouble in the manner of food. She needs careful consideration, but firmness.'[14] On her 1964 visitation of Teschemakers Mother David Stark found 'a great deal of destructive criticism of authority' and 'an atmosphere of suspicion and mistrust'. She urged sisters to be 'humble and gracious … It is a case of "give and take" with "giving" to the fore. Don't be petty – be Dominicans!'[15]

In the wake of Vatican II the Dominicans set aside many of the traditional customs of religious life, but visitation remained an important feature of the calendar. It served the same function in the 1970s as it had in the 1870s, connecting individual communities as a single congregation and providing the leadership with a formal means of oversight.[16] By the turn of the twenty-first century the emphasis

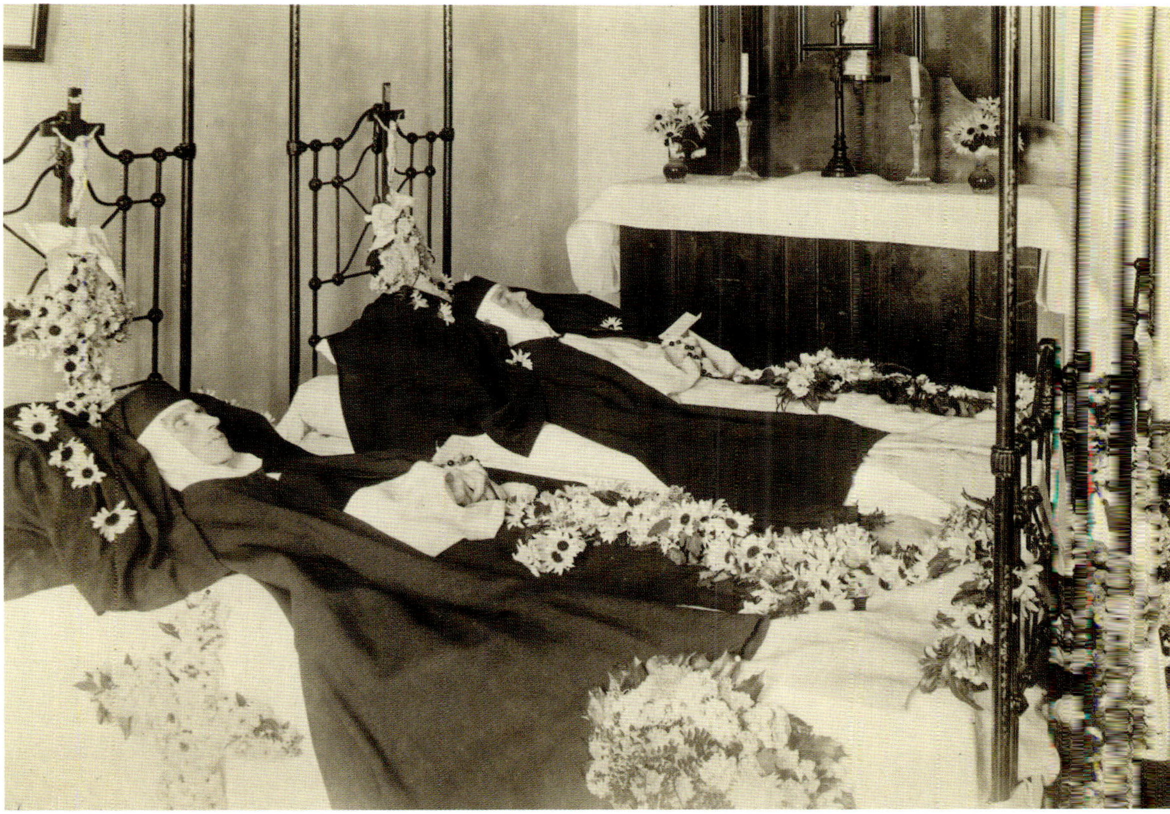

SM Francis Sullivan and S Lucy Tracy on their deathbeds, 1894. P1/8/1, DA.

had shifted away from discipline. Visitation was an increasingly reflective process aimed at identifying strengths and weaknesses – going in close to understand individual experience and stepping out wide to survey the Congregation as a whole.[17]

The other main calendar process still used for connecting convents and communities as a whole is the General Chapter. For most of the twentieth century the General Chapter was held every six years. The New Zealand Dominican Sisters' first General Chapter opened on 27 December 1893 with the purpose of adapting Sion Hill's Rule and Constitutions for local conditions. All the choir sisters were present. Within the chapter all sisters participated 'on a footing of perfect equality', being 'perfectly free to express their opinions'.[18] The chapter was, however, a restricted democracy – none of the community's lay sisters was entitled to attend.

The first General Chapter, held in two sessions between December 1893 and January 1894, made a series of important decisions about internal community arrangements. On 5 January 'a very animated and protracted discussion' took place regarding leadership elections.

> *Father Lynch several times reminded all present to express their opinions in writing. These he read aloud to the sisters, so that each nun learned the different views of all the others, without [illegible]*

being aware of who precisely held the particular opinion: thus the most complete freedom in expressing their views was given on most important points. There was besides no lack of speaking, and when the final vote at the meeting was taken all felt pleased that while so much had been said, and such important work transacted, the greatest harmony had characterised the proceedings.[19]

The chapter decided that all sisters 25 years and older who had been professed for four or more years would be entitled to vote for the prioress. They also looked to the future, anticipating a time when the Congregation would be too large for all entitled sisters to participate in elections. The chapter agreed on a system of election by delegate, to be implemented at the bishop's discretion. Discussions around leadership continued for several days. On 6 January 1894 the chapter passed a resolution limiting the power of individual personality: no prioress would be allowed to stay in office for more than six consecutive years, and two successive terms of three years each had to be followed by an interstice of three years. (Mother Gabriel had ruled as prioress from 1870 until 1886, and then again from 1889 until 1895.)

The Constitutions created by the first General Chapter remained largely unchanged until after the Second Vatican Council. Even the Congregation's first independent constitutions, passed in 1933, maintained the same general structures of authority as those originally adopted from Sion Hill. A change in nomenclature meant the prioress became the prioress general and local superiors became known as prioresses.

As anticipated, the Congregation soon grew too large for all eligible nuns to participate in chapter. Each convent sent an elected delegate and the larger houses also sent the local prioress. Previous prioresses general were entitled to take part, as well as those currently in office. The first and most important task at each chapter was the election of major officials: prioress general, councillors and procuratrix. The chapter also provided a regular opportunity to clarify questions of rule, establish consistency between the various convents and connect the branch houses to the Mother House as a single unified congregation. Delegates passed ordinations and made recommendations regarding community customs and practices, but the chapter did not have the power to make constitutions or alter fundamental structures of authority.

Though none of her successors was perhaps as dominant as Mother Gabriel Gill, each of the prioresses and then prioresses general who followed her exerted a huge amount of power within the congregation. Regular general chapters gave the select a voice in choosing the women who would lead them. The four elected councillors wielded a degree of influence and the bishop was involved in any very serious matters, but this was a tightly closed community: ultimately, the woman elected as prioress general was the one in control.

Shared responsibility

As they responded to the 'signs of the times' the sisters moved into new fields of mission and gradually developed looser forms of prayer and community life. Hierarchical relationships inherited from Ireland and maintained for nearly a century no longer fitted the New Zealand Congregation's evolving understanding of its true Dominican legacy. Returning to Dominic's concept of 'first among equals', the New Zealanders joined other Dominican congregations around the world in developing their own model of democratic government. Over several decades the New Zealand sisters moved toward shared leadership, inclusive government and a participative style of management and organisation.

The Special General Chapter, held in two sessions between December 1968 and January 1970, signalled the shift when it elected Sister Mary Jordan McCormick as mother prioress general. The structures of authority remained essentially the same during her term of office, and her four conservative councillors served as a counterbalance to change, but Mother Jordan exercised a new style of leadership. Her predecessors had been charged with maintaining the status quo, providing security and preserving stability. Under the terms of the Second Vatican Council's directives to religious, Mother Jordan was responsible for unsettling her Congregation; for challenging, inspiring and engaging them. 'Change is a condition of life,' she warned them, 'sometimes a condition of survival.'[20]

Mother Jordan supervised the team responsible for updating the New Zealand Constitutions to meet the requirements of Vatican II. The Interim Constitutions, printed in 1976 but never formally authorised by Rome, confirmed existing structures of authority but also reflected new priorities. The General Chapter was described as 'the highest legislative authority in the Congregation': 'Its work is to elect the Prioress General and other major officials, to reflect upon the nature and purpose of the Congregation and to make decisions which will intensify the spiritual and apostolic vitality of the sisters.'[21] A new system of delegation was proposed whereby chapter representatives were elected not from different convents but from different groups of sisters, ordered according to profession. The arrangements were complicated, but the intention was clearly to provide for a greater range of perspectives to be represented at congregational level.

Mother Jordan was followed as prioress general by Mother Constance Quinn (Sister Margaret), who led the Congregation through ongoing change in the late 1970s and early 1980s. Looking back at her time in office, Sister Margaret described the role as 'an opportunity', but reflected that 'it wasn't easy'. Sister Loreto Meehan was on the general council in the early 1980s. She, too, found the work challenging but satisfying – 'we initiated a lot'.[22] Though she worked very closely with her council, final responsibility always rested with the prioress general. Sister Margaret was based in Dunedin but in reality she lived and worked out of a suitcase, moving up and down the country as she helped different convents work through changes in observance, community life and mission.[23]

MM Mary Jordan McCormick. P6/12/1F

The Special General Chapter had passed several resolutions regarding finance. The medieval role of 'procuratrix' was replaced with the modern term 'bursar', and the chapter approved the adoption of modern bookkeeping methods throughout the Congregation.[24] In 1981 the General Chapter moved to centralise congregational finances. After more than a century working within a decentralised model, the change was significant: it reflected an effort to set aside outdated structures and develop systems that served ministerial priorities. As Sister Margaret explained to the wider congregation, 'We are looking for a financial system that will free us to proclaim the Word more effectively and at the same time help us to live a deeper poverty as a result of responsible community budgeting.'[25]

As bursar, Sister Ann Keogh implemented the change to a centralised financial administration. She had to develop a system that allowed for communities with uncertain and irregular income, for property maintenance, charitable donations and the variable cost of personal study.[26]

The new system also had to allow for the financial implications of integration of Catholic schools with the state system. In the early days the sisters had received no pay – school fees went to the convent to be used according to the discretion of the prioress, council and procuratrix. Integration with the state education system meant that Catholic schools received state funding for teachers. This was the realisation of a dream long hoped for by Bishop Moran and others. Religious teachers, however, had taken vows of poverty. They needed a way to accept their salaries, which could then be used for congregational purposes. The New Zealand Dominicans joined with other New Zealand religious congregations to consult a panel of lawyers, who advised that religious men and women receiving salaries needed to sign a legal declaration transferring that salary to their congregation.[27] Under the new system all income went straight into the Congregation's central fund and was dispersed according to estimates drawn up by each community. Centralised funding was part of a larger shift in the Congregation towards personal responsibility. Shifting budgeting responsibility away from the bursar and prioress was intended to empower individuals and communities to manage their own money.

In the early 1980s the Congregation made its first experiments in shared leadership. At the start of 1980 the Teschemakers community – Sisters Imelda, Anthony, Loreto, Denise and Gregory – chose not to elect a superior. The model worked well: each sister contributed her own unique gifts to the group, and the community responded together 'to what we each see as the will of God, searched through in dialogue and prayer and seen as a collegial form of obedience'.[28] Sister Margaret and the council encouraged other communities to look at issues of leadership. In 1983 each convent completed a detailed study considering how members might 'take greater responsibility for the life of the group and that of individuals'.[29] Most communities preferred that the prioress general continue to appoint the local superior, but Siena Convent in Blockhouse Bay chose to follow the Teschemakers model.[30]

In 1986 Sisters Susan, Ambrose, Winefride and Kay asked permission to live without a superior at St Brigid's Convent in Tainui:[31] 'We own and we experience that each sister is a responsible community member. We meet daily for prayer and a shared meal. Situations are dealt with as they arise or at community meetings …'[32] At Henderson the sisters took a more structured approach – they shared roles within the community according to a calendared roster. Each sister acted as the community coordinator for a month at a time, as bursar for three months, annalist for two months and liturgist for a week.[33] They spent some time experimenting with different arrangements and, like other communities, eventually developed a free-form model adapted to the strengths and preferences of individual members.

The devolution of responsibility within local communities mirrored changes that were occurring simultaneously in religious observance, community life and mission. Vatican II sparked a shift away from the restrictive conformity of traditional religious

Leadership Team, 1986. S Carmel Walsh, S Susan Logan, S Judith Anne O'Sullivan, S Mary Horn, S Janice Ogilvy. P8/11/1, DA.

life towards new models of community and leadership, which recognised the value of individuals and emphasised the principle of freedom.

At the General Chapter of 1986 the Congregation explored and affirmed the concept of consensus decision-making. The chapter itself was rather more directive than previously legislative chapters: 'there was a growing sense of confidence in our freedom to do what we considered best for us, using law as a guide and preserver of rights rather than as a constriction that would stop the movement of the group'.[34] The chapter confirmed a move away from 'a pyramid-type structure with the Prioress General at the top'. Sisters wanted to share responsibility and work collegially, but they still wanted a designated leader: 'The leader is the centre – focus – servant of a team, all of whom exercise collegial responsibility'.[35] After lengthy discussion the chapter agreed to reduce the term of office from six years to four. Five Leadership Team members would be elected in no hierarchical order. Once the team was confirmed the chapter would elect one of these sisters as prioress. The election process involved small group discussions, full group reflections and time for prayer.

The chapter elected Sister Judith Anne O'Sullivan, Sister Mary Horn, Sister Carmel Walsh, Sister Susan Logan and Sister Margaret Mary Ogilvy to the team, with Sister Mary Horn as leader.[36] Mary made a conscious decision that she would make no decisions on her own. Some of the other sisters still wanted 'Mother' to take charge, but she insisted on consultation.[37]

Most of the team lived in Dunedin, and for the first year of their term they lived in the same community. They faced complicated challenges within the Congregation and with the ongoing process of integration, but they held themselves together as a group, articulating a sophisticated understanding of responsible authority:

> *The authority invested in the Congregation is the power of Christ given to each sister at her Baptism and throughout her Christian pilgrimage. It is the power of Christ invested in His Church and given to this Dominican Congregation through His Church. In the local community and at regional level each sister invests personal authority. The Congregation at the Chapter invested authority in the Leadership Team and in the Prioress. This giving, receiving and exercising of authority is part of our obedience, a gift and a responsibility accepted at Baptism and ratified at Profession.*[38]

Although the Leadership Team and the prioress could issue directives and impose a formal obedience, the model was collegial.

Some sisters found the new model frustrating. Without a single clear leader the process of decision-making was often time-consuming:[39] 'We are not yet sure about shared responsibility. Is it who's in charge and organises (who does what?) or who is taking responsibility for our life as Dominican women (how will we live?)?'[40] There was a general sense, however, that the team approach was the best means of representing and expressing the Congregation's priorities and values. Successive teams have followed the same model. The Leadership Team elected in 2007 – Jacqui Ryan, Maureen O'Hanlon, Joan Hardiman, Elizabeth Mackie and Mary Anna Baird – confirmed that the team model of collective decision-making had become 'firmly entrenched' within the Congregation: 'It is an enriching model, which calls on all the gifts of each person and requires a willingness to debate, discuss and be silent and reflect before decisions are made.' The members of the team had to trust each other and be willing to have their ideas accepted or rejected, tweaked or transformed.[41]

Shared responsibility applies not just to the Leadership Team – it is an active principle that applies to the whole New Zealand Congregation of Dominican Sisters. Each individual member takes personal responsibility for herself, for her relationships with her spiritual sisters, and for her involvement in congregational affairs.

Committees devoted to specific issues that affect Dominican life have played an increasingly important role in supporting the team and engaging the wider congregation in aspects of governance. Each successive chapter has adapted the committee structure to meet evolving needs. Membership has shifted over time according to skills, needs and availability, and the Leadership Team has approached and appointed members as required. By the turn of the twenty-first century the finance committee and the mission formation committee had evolved as the two most important groups. They functioned as creative think-tanks and worked with the Leadership Team throughout the year to shape vision and direction and to address practical issues of management. From 2011 the mission formation committee was replaced by the Dominican Family Mission and Justice Group in which sisters, friars and laity worked together.

The finance committee is responsible for managing the Congregation's material assets, allocating community budgets and overseeing overall income and expenditure. They work in close regular contact with the Leadership Team, and present a full report to the whole Congregation at every chapter. In 2003 the Congregation employed Angela McMorran as a financial assistant. Initially she worked in close collaboration with Sister Paddy McCann, the congregational bursar. Paddy saw a future need for increasing lay involvement in the congrega-

Mission formation committee, 1998. **Back**: Joan Bennett, Jane Rutherford, Helen Bergin, Margaret Butler, Cecily Sheehy, Leonie Parry. **Front**: Judith McGinley, Mary Anna Baird, Judith Anne O'Sullivan, Danielle Melton. P9/5/…, DA.

tional administration and, over time, Angela's role expanded – she now functions as the Congregation's financial administrator. Angela works from the Congregation's administrative centre in London Street, Dunedin. She deals with the practical details of banking, buildings and insurance, takes part in finance committee meetings and assists the Leadership Team. Anne Haines works with Angela on a part-time basis and provides administrative support during Leadership Team meetings.

The Dominican Sisters Trust Board is the legal entity that administers the Congregation's material goods. The board is made up of members of the Leadership Team and the bursar, and they are free to appoint additional members. The board has two regular meetings each year, and additional meetings as required. It approves the annual budget, including annual community allocations, oversees the

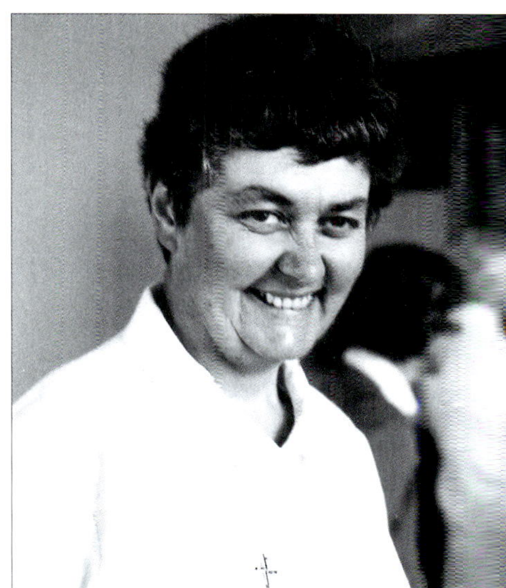

S Paddy McCann, early 1970s. DA.

Regional meeting, North Otago, 1992. S Jacqui Ryan, S Lorraine Challis, S Margaret Quinn, S Anne O'Neill, SM Augustine McCarthy. P9/12/3A, DA.

Group discussion at Chapter, St Margaret's College, Dunedin, 1998. 10/12/24, DA.

accounts, monitors investments and makes decisions on any major financial matters.[42]

The Congregation's collaborative style of governance goes much deeper than the Leadership Team and consultative committees. It is underpinned by a strong structure of regional networks. The concept of 'regions' evolved in the 1980s with natural groupings of sisters meeting regularly on the basis of geographical proximity. Regional meetings have provided a space for individuals and small communities to share Dominican prayer, study together, address specific issues affecting the wider Congregation and enjoy family time. Each region developed its own style, and some have functioned more cohesively than others. The regional meetings held in Dunedin in 1988 were hugely successful – 'bonding and connecting within the region and a sense of ministering to each other'.[43]

The regions function independently, but they are also connected to each other and to the Leadership Team. In 1998 the five regions spent time preparing for the chapter at the end of the year. They considered the legislation passed at the previous chapter and developed themes to be explored at the next. Dunedin's theme was 'Live life now! Carry forth the fire with justice and compassion and hope', and Southland's was 'Moving into mystery: compassion and relationship'. Auckland also focused on relationship: 'With the world, with one another, with God'. North Otago/Christchurch developed the concept of 'Panning for gold – seeking the essence – persisting – hoping – rediscovering PURE GOLD'. The Manawatu sisters called for attention to 'Our spirituality as New Zealand Dominican women'.

With much of the 'business' of chapter attended to in the regions and standing committees, chapters have become less legislative and more focused on community, providing a mechanism for shaping and expressing congregational values and identity, and empowering those in positions of authority. The earliest general chapters were held every three years, and for most of the twentieth century they were held every six years. They are now held every four years. All sisters are invited to attend and all have an active voice. Planning for the first session of the seventeenth General Chapter in September 2014 involved the whole Congregation.

> *As we continue our journey to the Chapter and beyond this is a wonderful opportunity to remember that we are all reaping the fruit of those who have gone before us. Some of us will be able to attend the chapter physically but all of us are part of the process through prayer, reflection, discussion or in any other way we are able. The lives of each of us have contributed to who we are together – we have been commissioned – all of us – to go out and bear fruit that will last.*[44]

The management processes and leadership structures of the New Zealand Congregation of Dominican Sisters are now intentionally collective and collaborative.

Whether they are serving as members of the Leadership Team, participating in regional meetings or caring for each other at the local level, sisters engage in a model of leadership as a gift shared and exercised by all.

Obedience and independence

The radical restructuring of leadership has been part of a broader shift in understandings of authority. A growing recognition of individual identity and increased emphasis on personal responsibility have paralleled and reinforced the Congregation's shift towards collective responsibility. Yet the vow of obedience that all Dominican sisters make at profession remains fundamentally important: it signals the depth of their commitment to God, to the Order and to each other. Even as they have moved out of enclosure and into suburban neighbourhoods, engaged in new missions and begun praying in new ways, the shared vow holds the Dominican sisters together as a group and apart from the world.

In the nineteenth and early twentieth centuries the most significant exercise of personal responsibility in the convent occurred when a woman chose to enter. The mother prioress and novice mistress took care to ascertain the suitability of each applicant and to make sure that she was under no undue pressure. Each woman who offered herself as a postulant had to do so of her own free will and take personal responsibility for her decision and its consequences. The nuanced factors affecting that decision might be multilayered and complex, but the intention of the regulations was clear: on entering the convent every woman had to reassure the mother prioress of her freedom of choice, and at every stage of profession she made a public avowal of free will.

Golden Jubilee: the New Zealand Dominican sisters celebrated 50 years in New Zealand in 1921. P3/4/1, DA.

Following the same formula as at Sion Hill, the New Zealand Dominican sisters made a single representative vow at profession, promising obedience to the mother prioress. The form of vows spoken at profession ceremonies has remained roughly the same since the nineteenth century:

I, Sister N., make profession and I promise obedience to God and to Blessed Mary and to Blessed Dominic and to you, Sister N., Prioress of the New Zealand Dominican Sisters under the protection of Our Lady of the Most Holy Rosary and of Saint Catherine of Siena, according to the Rule of Saint Augustine and the Constitutions of this Congregation; that I will be obedient to you and to my other prioresses until death [or for three years or for the period for which temporary profession is being made].

Obedience was understood to cover the other traditional religious vows of poverty and chastity. It was an all-encompassing promise of submission to God's will as expressed through religious superiors. The sisters relinquished any form of independence as soon as they entered the convent. The prioress decided where they would live and what work they would do; their community superior directed day-to-day tasks; and the rule dictated everything from how they would pray to when they could talk.

From the mid-1930s until the mid-1970s the prioress general made a formal declaration at each sister's profession:

> *We make protestation to you that by your profession you will be obliged to the three vows, viz: poverty, chastity and obedience; and you will be bound to observe the Rule of St Augustine, and the Constitutions of our Congregation, to the letter, in such manner that should you at any time be constrained by your Superiors to the exact observance of them you would be bound to simply obey. We also make protestation to you that your profession will be null if you have craftily concealed any hidden infirmity or other impediment of which you would according to the common law or by the Constitutions of our Congregation be rejected.*[45]

Wider cultural values reinforced the convent's approach to authority. In nineteenth- and early twentieth-century New Zealand, young single women were not expected to live independently, whether or not they entered religious life. Dominant domestic structures of authority were simple: the father was the head of the family; the mother was his support, caring for the household and children. Children owed their parents respect and obedience. Unmarried women remained the responsibility of their fathers. Young women who joined the convent escaped the control of fathers and husbands, accepting instead the authority of religious superiors.

By the late 1950s Prioress General Mother Mary David was aware of a shift in modern culture. 'The spirit of the age is one of independence,' she warned her sisters, 'and we must be careful not to allow it to creep into our individual lives and into the convent.'[46] In the mid-1960s when the Second Vatican Council called religious to respond to the signs of the times, the New Zealand Dominican sisters responded wholeheartedly, adapting their rule to allow all sisters a far greater degree of personal independence. Mother Mary Jordan, who led the Congregation through the first phase of change, conceived religious obedience as spiritual liberation. 'In the matter of Christian liberty and religious obedience liberty for the religious is the freedom to commit herself to God and to her apostolate, to live entirely in the will of God in communities which are led by the Spirit of Love.'[47]

The Congregation's current constitutions describe the public vows of chastity, poverty and obedience as 'a free response' and a 'gift of ourselves'.[48] Consecrated chastity is understood as a gift from God 'enabling us to find in the Lord himself the love and companionship that will fill our lives and enable us to share his love with others'. Living in a culture that often undervalues love, the New Zealand Dominican sisters believe their chastity is a 'powerful and attractive witness'. It frees them 'to love with spontaneous warmth, to delight in friendship and to appreciate each individual unconditionally.'[49]

Many of the Dominican sisters of New Zealand identify themselves as feminists. The women's liberation movement of the 1970s resonated with Dominican principles of justice and with many sisters' experience of strength and ability in the women they lived and worked with. Chastity, conceived of historically as a form of denial, has become a form of freedom in the twenty-first century. Dominican women are liberated by their vows from the gendered expectations of modern society, and are freed from the constraints of family life to preach to the world they serve.

In poverty, as in chastity, the sisters seek to imitate Christ. Their vows commit them to living simply and to accepting a life of work. They hold all material

St Catherine's, 1967. F14A/7E.

wealth and goods in common, and live in 'a spirit of dependence'. Any income they generate belongs to the Congregation (although inheritances are treated separately).[50]

Before she makes profession, each sister is required to sign a series of legal documents: a will, a statement of cession of administration of personal property, an assignment of income and/or benefits in favour of the New Zealand Dominican Sisters Trust Board, and a waiver of the right to claim remuneration compensation for services rendered.[51] In responding to the signs of the times and loosening the rule, the Dominican sisters have become far more individuated than their predecessors: they dress differently from each other; they often pray differently; they work differently and perhaps hold different theological perspectives and political convictions. Yet their common vow of poverty holds the sisters together as a family. It is a profoundly countercultural witness. 'Poverty involves us in the life of the poor. For us as New Zealand Dominicans, this means that we must affirm the dignity and rights of those under-privileged because of race, social conditions or deprived family background.' In their lives and their ministries the sisters seek to 'deepen awareness of the needs and rights of others'. In the midst of Western materialism, their religious poverty testifies 'to the beauty and goodness of creation and to the fact that our true treasure is in heaven'.[52] Their financial interdependence also testifies to the sisters' commitment to each other.

The vow of obedience is the single vow made in public. According to the congregational constitutions, religious obedience draws each sister 'into union with Christ whose perfect fulfilling of the Father's will brought life to the world'. The New Zealand Dominicans base their understanding of obedience on the spiritual legacy of St Dominic and the 10 Irish foundresses who came to Dunedin in 1871.

> *The deep desire to carry out God's saving will that burned in Dominic made him exceptionally free for his preaching mission. He saw obedience in terms of mission and he wanted it to be for his order a liberating and unifying force … The dynamic response of our foundresses to the needs*

of early New Zealand has left us the heritage of an obedience which is creative, responsible and prepared to accept the risks that faith requires.[53]

The vow of obedience is a 'total dedication of our will to God', and a 'sacrifice of ourselves to him'. Sisters are subject by their vow to the Pope, to legitimate ecclesiastical superiors as specified in the Constitutions, and to the Leadership Team.

Our vow commits us as individuals and as a community to search for the will of God and unites us in the task we do for the Church. In our personal and community struggles to find and realise God's will we enter both into the mystery of our own lives and into the mystery of Christ's passion, death and resurrection. If we are faithful to this commitment, we witness that it is only in submission to God's will that people become truly free and truly themselves.[54]

This nuanced understanding of obedience is far more open and perhaps more challenging in its complexity than the simple exercise of authority and performance of compliance acted out in the years before Vatican II. In the 1970s and 1980s some sisters struggled to adjust to the evolving model of responsible obedience; they clung to old patterns and relationships. As Mother Antoninus observed, 'many sisters had exchanged the authority of their parents and their school principal for that of their novice mistress and then their prioress'. It was understandably challenging 'to take responsibility for themselves as autonomous adult women of faith'.[55]

The Congregation's changing understanding of obedience has had major practical implications. Formerly, the mother prioress and her council made yearly convent and job assignations. Sisters were given little or no warning of new appointments and, once assigned to a new post, they had no right of refusal or even of explanation – they had to be prepared to gather their belongings, leave their communities and their pupils and re-establish themselves wherever they were sent. For some of those who had spent their whole lives in the deep south, being sent suddenly to Auckland, which was so culturally, socially and climatically different, was very difficult.

By the end of the twentieth century annual assignations were a thing of the past. Each sister was encouraged to take responsibility for expressing her living preferences, so that the Leadership Team could try and make arrangements that met individual needs. An expanded understanding of mission and preaching and the integration of Dominican schools also freed sisters to start making their own decisions about how and where they might work. Before integration in the 1970s schools depended on religious teachers, and sisters had continued to work into their seventies and eighties. A few decades later there were very few sisters still working as teachers, although most still worked within education developing new professional pathways. In consultation with the Leadership Team they responded to career opportunities within the church and created new roles in the wider community. Others retired – they left active employment but continued to work, offering their prayers, their relationships and their volunteer efforts as an important contribution to Dominican preaching in New Zealand.

Ageing raises particular issues of independence and responsibility within the current Congregation. As women who have committed to each other as family, the sisters look to each other for care and advice as they age. The Leadership Team and the wider congregation take responsibility for unwell and aged sisters in a deliberate and comprehensive manner. They attend to practical considerations such as medical insurance, living wills and rest-home placements. In 2009 the Leadership Team broached the question of driving; they observed that 'often families are best placed to advise their older family members when they have concerns about that person's ability to continue driving'. The team encouraged sisters to act as family to each other and to talk about driving and other such issues in community, 'difficult though it may be'.[56] As they have always done, the sisters treat their most elderly with sensitivity and respect. They honour their dead in a particularly beautiful way, as individual women who have contributed to something much bigger than themselves.

The post-Vatican II model of responsible obedience has freed Dominican women to engage in contemporary social and political issues. In 1981 Sister Barbara Menzies was living at St Catherine's Priory in Invercargill when she chose to participate in the small Southland protest against the Springbok Tour. The Priory community supported her decision, despite the fact that several sisters were dedicated rugby fans. On other marches Barbara had worn civilian dress, but the game against Southland was played on the Feast of St Dominic and so, as she explained to the community, she felt obliged to don her habit on this occasion.[57]

A number of other sisters also marched against the Springbok Tour in Dunedin and other centres. For these sisters, as for many New Zealanders in general, the tour was a moment of awakening. They began to make links between apartheid in South Africa and colonisation and the position of Māori in New Zealand.

In the 1980s and 1990s Dominican sisters took an active role in the anti-racism movement in New Zealand. Some joined the Dunedin Anti-Racism Coalition, which was working for recognition of the rights of tāngata whenua. Jan Ogilvy and Sandra Winton worked with a group called Pakeha Women Against Racism. The sisters participated in anti-racism workshops and some helped deliver training programmes designed to combat institutional racism. In 1986 the Congregation seconded Barbara Menzie (at her request) to the National Council of Churches Programme on Racism. From 1988 until 1993, when she left the Congregation, Barbara worked for the Kia Mohio Kia Marama Trust on a major research project for the 1990 sesquicentenary of the signing of the Treaty of Waitangi.[58] Susan Healy, who has since left the Congregation, was also involved in the fight against racism. In 1988, supported by the Leadership Team, she completed a master's degree at the University of Auckland that focused on institutional racism in New Zealand theological colleges. Susan still identifies as a Dominican laywoman, and works as a Treaty educator.[59]

'Pakeha repentance nun in the media hot seat', trumpeted the *Dominion* in September 1993 after controversy erupted in the midst of a women's suffrage church service. Elizabeth Mackie was the 'repentance nun'. Together with a group of 17 other women of various ages, races and churches she had planned a service in the Christchurch Cathedral to celebrate the centennial of women's suffrage in New Zealand. Over 1000 people attended, taking part in what Elizabeth described as 'an exhilarating, moving and joyful celebration with evocative music and vibrant gymnastic dance'. A prayer at the beginning of the service called white women to stand and repent for sins committed against their Māori sisters. A handful of people took offence and walked out. The organisers were stunned and disappointed; they used the resultant media attention to protest against the 'thinly disguised and easily exposed' racism that the occasion had brought to the fore. Elizabeth explained to reporters that she had first been struck by racism in the mid-1960s while working as a

Sisters at the 1995 Congregational Chapter. **Back**: S Bernadette Fox, S Raphael Gallien, S Louise Timpany, S Loreto Meehan. **Front**: S Anne O'Neill, S Clare Timpany, S Barbara Dwyer. P9/2O, DA.

Sisters at the 1995 Chapter. **Back**: S Madeleine McAleese, S Peter Higgins, S Frances Lister, S Winefride Morris, S Margaret Fahey, S Basil Geoffrey. **Front**: S Gemma Finlay, S Catherine Tither. P9/2DDD, DA.

young religious teacher in Auckland. When a Māori pupil from Northland failed to return to school after the Easter holidays, Elizabeth rang the parish priest. The priest explained that the community had made great sacrifices for this child to be educated, but that the climate of the school had alienated her to such an extent that she could not return. Elizabeth began to see that 'the school was run in a way that only catered to pakehas'. She and her colleagues had come to see the world 'through a highly sensitised consciousness of Maori–Pakeha relationships'. In the women's suffrage service they wanted to ask what 100 years of vote for women really meant. 'We Pakeha women had to face the painful reality that even though we've had the vote for that long we haven't succeeded in making a difference in the way this country is governed and organized, to honour the Treaty of Waitangi.' Elizabeth was unapologetic for the service's remembrance of wrongs against Māori. She believed there was an ongoing necessity to keep calling the community to repentance 'till real reconciliation based on justice can happen'.[60]

Other sisters involved themselves in other protest movements. On St Patrick's Day 1991 Sister Mary Basil was arrested along with 11 other members of 'Operation Rescue' for trespassing outside the Epsom Abortion Clinic. For over a year Sister Basil had been a member of the prayer support group for Operation Rescue. Convinced of the need for a more positive witness to the cause, Sister Basil prayed and wrote to the Leadership Team asking permission to commit herself further, not as a member of the Congregation but as an ordinary person. 'This was a very difficult decision for me to make,' she explained. 'Any public demonstration of this nature was so alien to me.'[61] The Leadership Team supported her.

In the early 2000s Mary Horn was propelled into local politics by her love for the local landscape and her Dominican passion for justice. Mary lives and works in North Otago, where she draws inspiration from the environment. In 2005 she joined other Oamaru artists in an art protest, 'Artists Against Aqua', at the Forrester Gallery to protest against Meridian Energy's plans for diverting the lower Waitaki River. The lower Waitaki group for protecting the river worked in conjunction with the local Waitaha Māori, who also opposed development. When the Environment Court met to consider the case Mary presented one of her paintings as a representation of her opposition.[62]

The New Zealand Dominican sisters also engage with social and political issues as a collective group of women. They make regular submissions to government, particularly on issues of peace and justice. In 2004 the sisters made strong submissions against the Labour Government's controversial Foreshore and Seabed legislation, and in 2007 the New Zealand Dominican sisters and friars wrote to Prime Minister Helen Clark in opposition to the anti-terror raids conducted in the Urewera.[63] In 2009 the Congregation made a collective stand in support of Catholic peace activists Peter Murnane, Adi Leason and Sam Land in their trial for deflating the dome at the Waihopai spy base. The sisters supported the trio in prayer and provided moral support in the courtroom, and they celebrated together when the men were found not guilty.[64] The New Zealand Dominican Family has used its website to focus attention on a range of environmental and social justice issues ranging from fracking to child poverty to human trafficking.[65]

Among equals

Obedience still lies at the heart of religious life, but it is now exacted differently. Each woman who belongs to the Congregation of New Zealand Dominican Sisters understands herself as an equal, regardless of

Leadership Team [illegible]94.
S Teresa Rough[illegible]
S Lorraine Chal[illegible]
S Judith McGin[illegible]
S Sandra Winto[illegible]
S Susan Logan. [illegible]

her role in the Congregation, her length of service in religious life or her education. In the twenty-first century the New Zealand Dominican sisters live as individuals or pairs in suburban neighbourhoods, they attend church and pray according to their own patterns and they engage with the wider world on issues of social and political conscience. In comparison with the sisters of Vatican I, these post-Vatican II sisters 'do their own thing'. Yet their vow of obedience holds them together at the centre of a series of interconnected webs of authority. Regional groups gather regularly for fellowship; the Leadership Team takes responsibility for congregational management issues and vision; local diocesan clergy and Dominican friars work with the sisters in collaborative dialogue; and international networks of religious women and Dominican Family provide ongoing support and inspiration. Ultimately, individual sisters dance their own way along the same path, balancing personal identity and self with responsibility to the Congregation and the wider spiritual family.

S Helen Bergin and S Bernie Cheyne a[illegible]
Congregational Chapter, 1995. P9/2Y, [illegible]

9. Love of learning

Dominican sisters as students and teachers

The wood of the cross for a Dominican is the wood of the desk.
– Fifteenth General Chapter, 2006–2007[1]

What an honour to be permitted to train little souls for heaven!
– Sister Mary de Ricci Kirby to Uncle Kirby, November 1882[2]

Education was the raison d'être of the Dominican sisters' mission to colonial New Zealand, and study, teaching and preaching through other forms of education continue to energise Dominican life in New Zealand today.

Dominican theology understands study as the search for truth, and teaching as a means of sharing the fruits of that search. Together with contemplation, mission and community, study is one of the four fundamental pillars of Dominican life. It informs the New Zealand Congregation's practice of contemplation, their approach to mission and their expression of community.

Teaching was the main form of mission for the New Zealand Dominican sisters for more than a century. During that time changes in teaching practice and school management have reflected the developing relationship between the Catholic Church and the state. The Private Schools Conditional Integration Act (1975) marked a major watershed in religious education. In the context of declining numbers and aging congregations, integration set religious teachers free from the classroom. With access to government funding, Catholic schools could afford to employ lay teachers. In the wake of Vatican II the New Zealand Dominicans were already exploring new opportunities for mission. They gradually moved out of their schools and into the community, often continuing to minister through alternative forms of education.

Perpetual students: The Dominican commitment to study

Study was always integral to Dominican theology, but in the earliest days of the New Zealand mission it was not a high priority – there was simply too much to do, preparing for lessons, observing the rule and settling into a new home in a new country. Yet study, however limited, was the philosophical and practical basis for Dominican teaching. Even after the sisters had adjusted to life in New Zealand they focused their attention on their work in schools and on meeting the demands of the horarium. Enclosure meant that study was conducted within the convent walls. The mistress of novices gave lectures on religious life and directed her charges in their religious reading. Professed sisters read books on the lives of the saints and other spiritual texts that were assigned in the daily timetable at the time.

In these early years teacher training depended on the student teacher system, whereby capable older

School students at prayer in the chapel at Teschemakers. F8/1/7, DA.

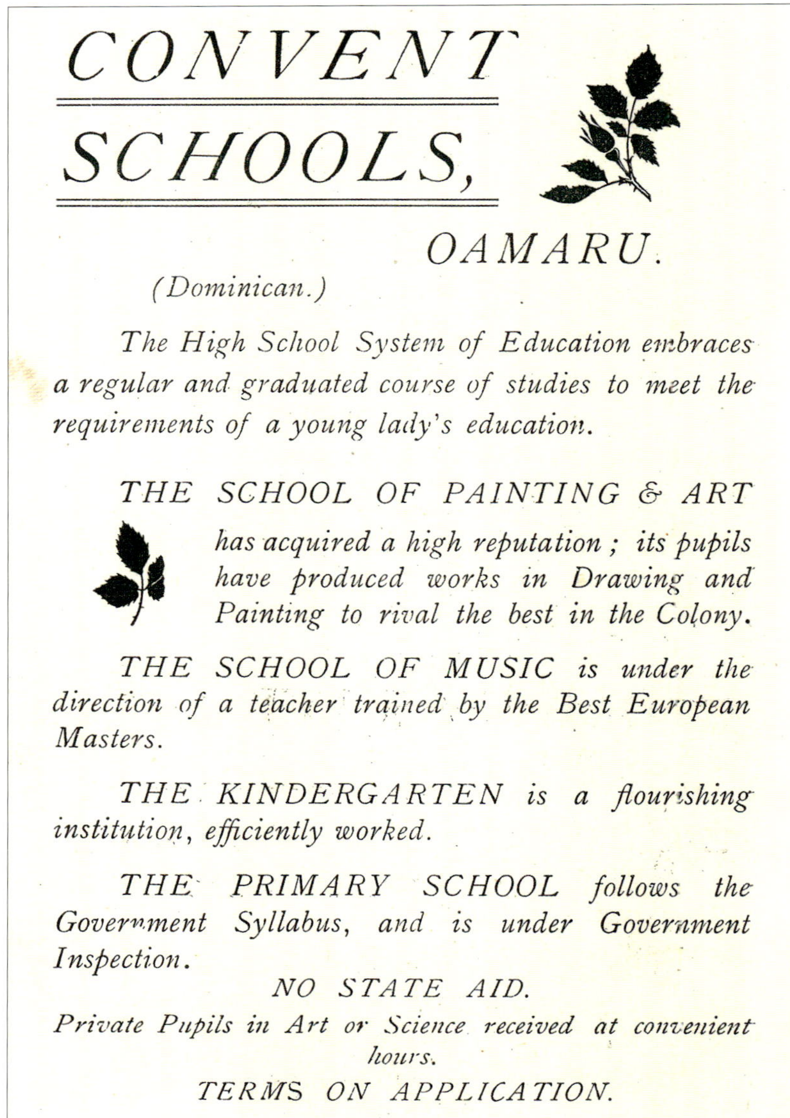

Advertisement for Oamaru convent schools, 1899. M2, DA.

students learnt to teach on the job. Student teachers who went on to enter the convent continued to learn their craft under the supervision of older sisters. In essence it was a system of apprenticeship rather than a professional education. Sister Mary Francis, who had trained under this system in Sion Hill, was very aware of her limitations. 'A child so ignorant I was sent to teach the highest class the day after I entered the Convent and since then, what injustices lie at my door! My only refuge is that I never sought any duty so I trust I may be sheltered under obedience.'[3]

In the 1890s the imminent threat of government

inspection prompted the Dominican sisters to refocus their attention on study. The Catholic bishops required all new teachers to obtain a certificate of competency approved by the local bishop (though professed religious already teaching in schools were exempt).[4] Bishop Moran was eager that the nuns in his diocese should be qualified in 'the department of high studies'. In 1895 he arranged for a Mr J.A. Scott MA BLL to give a few 'lecturettes' to the Dominican sisters 'with a view of their thoroughly understanding the trend of Dunedin University studies'.[5]

The New Zealand Dominicans' first external teacher training came from a young Irish woman based in Australia. Barbara Bell had been a student at Sion Hill and went on to tertiary study in England, becoming a 'specialist educationalist'. In 1895 she accepted an appointment training teachers for the Loreto sisters in Australia, and in 1904 she visited New Zealand. Barbara stayed with the Dominicans for a year, during which she visited all the branch convents and established the same methods in every school. Her methods focused on thorough preparation for lessons, timetabling and good weekly records. Barbara insisted on high standards and demanded strong leadership, and despite some sisters finding the extra work and new methods challenging, they generally responded with enthusiasm.[6]

In the early twentieth century the impetus to study was still based very much on the demands of the sisters' teaching apostolate. In 1907 Bishop Verdon granted permission for sisters from Lawrence and Milton to travel to Dunedin for a few days at Easter for the purpose of receiving lessons in dancing and painting from the sisters at the Priory.[7] By 1911 several sisters were taking extramural courses at the University of Otago and working towards undergraduate degrees.[8] In 1930 the New Zealand Dominicans adopted the Montessori method for their infant rooms in Dunedin and Oamaru; Sisters Mary Aquin and Mary St Joan were sent off to train, and Sister Mary Aquin then took charge of the class in Oamaru and Sister Mary St Joan in Dunedin. Sister Mary St Joan trained several other teachers in the method, and the Montessori room continued in Dunedin until the 1970s.[9]

The Congregation celebrates Sister Mary Reginald Quilter as the first Dominican woman in New Zealand to obtain a university degree. Born at Waitahuna, near Lawrence, in 1872, Margaret Ann Quilter made her first profession as Sister Mary Reginald on 27 December 1891. She graduated from Otago University with a BA in 1914 and then with an MA in 1915. She served as prioress general from 19[illegible] until 1939, and used her position to encourage others to study.

> *It is consoling to find that the younger sisters are throwing themselves very whole-heartedly into their studies; please God, the spirit of study and the love of learning will sink deeply into their minds and hearts of all. We belong to the great Order of Preachers and our share of the preaching consists in instructing the children confided in our care. As we cannot instruct others efficiently unless our own minds are permeated with this love of learning, the great thing is for each sister to equip herself thoroughly for this great work for souls ...*[10]

Sister Mary Gertrude Fox made her profession into Mother Mary Reginald's hands in September 1939. Originally it was planned that Sister Gertrude should do further language studies at the University of Otago to prepare herself for teaching secondary school Latin and French. As it transpired, the commercial teacher at St Dominic's in Dunedin fell ill and Sister Gertrude, still a teenager herself, filled the gap, teaching shorthand and typing. She was told that the class was up to exercise 89, so by the end of

Montessori classroom for junior children, St Dominic's, Dunedin. F2/1/10A, DA.

the holidays she had to get herself up to exercise 90 and be ready to take them on.[11]

Professional development continued to function as the principal motivation to study from the 1930s to the 1950s. In 1931 the first conference for Catholic teachers was held in Wellington. Sister Mary Reginald Quilter and Sister Mary Dominica McKay travelled to the conference and presented papers.[12] Over the next few decades Catholic education conferences provided sisters with opportunities for networking and personal development, and served as a way to keep the wider congregation up to date with modern educational developments.

The first General Chapter of the New Zealand Dominicans as an independent Congregation, held in the summer of 1933–34, paid particular attention to teacher training. An injunction was laid on junior and intermediate sisters 'to regard it as duty to prepare themselves by examinations for the work of teaching'. Superiors were instructed to see that those under their supervision had time for study and for the preparation of schoolwork. A system of specialisation was to be established in the Congregation's secondary schools, and the mother prioress general and directress general of studies were commissioned to visit Maitland in New South Wales, to study the organisation of the Australian Dominicans' new Teacher Training School with a view to establishing a similar school in New Zealand.[13]

In practice, most training still happened on the job. In 1942 sisters at St Dominic's in Dunedin and St Catherine's in Invercargill used the May school holidays to run in-house conferences, during which sisters could exchange methods and ideas. Prioress General Mother Mary Dominica McKay (who had earlier served as directress of studies) encouraged the Congregation toward more of this kind of interchange.[14] From 1950 the New Zealand bishops insisted that all Catholic school teachers be qualified with their 'Teachers' C' certificate.[15] Sisters began to attend 'refresher courses' held in conjunction with other religious teaching orders.

Sister Christopher (Brenda) Fitzgerald had worked as a nurse before entering the convent in the late 1950s. She spent her novitiate helping in the infirmary. When the date for her profession grew close she was sent to Dunedin to spend some time observing in one of the classrooms at St Dominic's. The supervising teacher taught her how to take the class roll, 'but as for teaching … You had to sort of learn on the spot really.' After profession Sister Christopher was sent to North East Valley and placed in charge of the new entrants class: 'I didn't have a clue.' She knew she could tell stories so that's what she did – 'we had stories and stories and stories' – but by lunchtime on the first day she wasn't sure she could keep going. One of the older sisters who had trained in the state system eventually helped her sort out a work plan and a timetable and once she 'got the hang of it', she 'really quite enjoyed it'.[16]

Training for teachers of the deaf provided some sisters with specialised study opportunities and higher education. In September 1954 Sister Mary Conrad, then superior at St Dominic's School for the Deaf in Feilding, was the first to attend a conference in Australia. In 1956 Sister Mary Mercedes (Molly) Griffin travelled to England to study at Manchester University. She was the first New Zealand Dominican sister to complete an academic qualification in the teaching of deaf children. After a year in Manchester studying for the Certificate for Teachers of the Deaf, Sister Mercedes spent time teaching deaf children in Birmingham and visiting schools for the deaf in England, Ireland and Europe. From that time on many of the sisters at the School for the Deaf worked towards a formal qualification. Most completed a diploma from the National Council of Teachers of the Deaf in London, studying by correspondence. In 1961 Sisters Mary Conrad and Jacinta completed a special course for teaching deaf children at Christchurch Teachers' College – the first sisters to become students at any teachers' college in New Zealand.[17] Dominican sisters continued to train in specialised deaf teaching courses at Christchurch Teachers' College throughout the 1960s

Loreto Hall Catholic Teachers' College opened in Remuera, Auckland, in 1950. Previously, religious had studied for university degrees extramurally but had not been given access to external teacher training. Loreto played an important role in professionalising Catholic teaching staff. In the early 1960s Sister Virginia (Judith) Robinson did her teacher training in the novitiate by correspondence and, after she had spent a few years teaching in schools in Kaikorai, Oamaru and Bluff, Mother Jordan sent her and several others to Loreto Hall in Auckland. She recalls it as a great experience.[18]

From the 1950s sisters were increasingly permitted to break enclosure to attend university lectures in person. In 1951 Sisters Mary Louis and Josephine attended classes at the University of Otago, and later the Congregation sent sisters to the Dunedin School of Commerce to train as commercial teachers, and to the School of Art at King Edward Technical College.[19] Sisters Mary Augustine McCarthy and Madeleine McAleese were sent to chemistry classes at the University of Otago in order to equip them for the classroom. The two sisters became great friends:

> *We were sent together to the university to gain expertise in Chemistry, a new experience for me to be a university student and for her, whose field was rather in classics than in science. I remember that we were late for lectures on one occasion – Sister was never very quick on her feet and I'm not sure if that was why we were late – but the custom in the Medical Intermediate classes of about 130 students was for all to stamp their feet from the time the latecomers entered until they reached their places. Imagine two young Dominican Sisters, fully garbed in the habit making their way to their places. We went through the whole experience. I can tell you it only happened the once.*[20]

The Dominican fathers' arrival in Dunedin in the 1950s gave the sisters unprecedented access to regular spiritual and theological teaching. During her canonical year in the novitiate Mary Horn relished the fathers' lectures, but looking back she wishes she could have deepened her understanding by making notes and writing assignments on the topics they covered. 'You were supposed to bring your sewing and do stitchery … You were supposed to just soak it up.'[21] When Margaret Butler entered the convent in 1966 she went along to her first novitiate lecture armed with pencil and paper, only to find the novice mistress reading aloud from a holy book. Having been to university and teachers' college and taught for a year already, Margaret found this limited approach to study very difficult.[22]

On the cusp of the Second Vatican Council, Mother David sent Sisters Mary Jordan McCormick and Genevieve O'Rourke to study at Regina Mundi in Rome.[23] They were the first of many. While they were there the two sisters travelled in Europe and spent time teaching Christian doctrine in Germany. Study was the main purpose of the trip, but they also valued their experience of other cultures: 'it was wonderful to see how other religious and other people lived'.[24] In 1964 Sister Mary Josephine was awarded a scholarship to study at the Sorbonne in Paris. Sister Mary St Anne accompanied her and followed the same course of study,[25] and both sisters also attended a summer school in linguistics.

In 1959, after completing her MA, Elizabeth Mackie was appointed to the teaching staff of the Classics Department at the University of Otago, and two years later she took up a postgraduate scholarship at Oxford University. She visited Sion Hill and reported to the New Zealand sisters her impression of 'immense vitality' there. She noted there was a marked emphasis on study and professional training: two hours were set aside each day for obligatory study, and the well stocked library facilitated genuine learning.[26] As these first sisters returned to New Zealand and shared their experiences and the fruits of their study, they energised those around them. At the same time, the Second Vatican Council's injunction to return to the spirit of St Dominic called the New Zealand Congregation to greater intent in their study. 'We had always paid lip service to the ideal of study,' Sister Judith McGinley remarked. 'Now we welcomed it as being very Dominican and the key to renewal.'[27]

It was still hard, however, to find adequate study time in the full horarium. In 1966 Sandra Winton lived at St Dominic's Priory as a postulant and attended lectures at the University of Otago in civilian clothes. She made her first profession in January 1968 and the following year she completed an MA in English. Sister Jordan, her novice mistress, tried to help Sandra find time to study: '"Don't tell me what time you put your light out," she said, "and

SM Marie Eugene (USA), Fr Vincent Ryan OP and SM Mercedes Griffin in Rome, 1958.
F14A/9B, DA.

SM Bede (Sandra) Winton, S Paula Mary (Suzanne) Winders and SM Albert (Carmel) Walsh at the Otago University graduation ceremony in December 1968. Dominican women had been graduating from the university since the early twentieth century, but this was the first time Dominican sisters had been capped in a public ceremony.
F6/17/1, DA.

then when I'm asked by Mother David (who was the prioress), I won't know."' Sandra, Carmel Walsh and Suzanne Winders were the first members of the order to have their degrees conferred in a public graduation ceremony.[28]

On 28 February 1965, the same day she entered the convent, Sister Judith McGinley was told she would be studying at Otago Polytechnic to prepare her for high school science teaching. The next morning she and Sister Susan attended their first physics class. On Monday, Wednesday and Thursday evenings they returned to the Polytech for chemistry and maths classes. Over the next few years the needs of the Congregation changed. In 1968, after making first profession, Judith began teaching primary school classes and studying by correspondence for her 'Teachers C'.[29]

In 1971 the Congregation established an Education Trust Fund for sisters. Quoting from *Perfectae Caritatis*, promotional material for the trust stated that 'suitable renewal for religious communities depends very largely on the training of their members … No one simply teaches. Teachers must also learn, and this advanced learning is a continuous process.'[30] The fund was to enable sisters to further their studies in New Zealand and overseas, and to help bring overseas experts to New Zealand.

The Congregation's Interim Constitutions described study as a vital instrument of the apostolate: 'Through study we ponder the manifold wisdom of God and prepare ourselves to proclaim it to others.' Their study was expected to be grounded in Divine Revelation as expressed through the Word of God and illuminated by theologians, but it was also expected to range broadly, covering the writings 'of those outstanding witnesses to the mind of Christ, who through diverse cultures and philosophies, make the work of God better known'. They were also encouraged to 'reflect upon contemporary discoveries and questions, recognizing the truth wherever it is to be found'. Whether or not sisters were actively engaged in the apostolate of teaching, study was seen as an essential element of Dominican life. 'Constant study by its discipline of all our powers is a valuable ascetical observance; it also provides rich nourishment for our life of contemplation.'[31]

In 1971 the Roman Catholic Church came to an agreement with the Education Board that each state teachers' college would accept up to five members of religious orders. Until then, religious teachers had been excluded from state teacher training colleges; the state education system and the Catholic system were entirely separate (apart from the occasional refresher course held in the holidays). Since religious students would be teaching in religious schools they were not entitled to the benefits of state training. In 1973 Sister Patrice (Helen) Bolger was the first Dominican sister to attend Dunedin Teachers' College. Her attendance there was not without controversy: when the principal of the college wrote to welcome her as a religious quota student he stated that college council policy required all members of religious orders to wear civilian dress to classes.[32] A month later the council changed its policy and allowed Sister Patrice to attend classes in the habit, but she was required to wear civilian clothing for all school visits.[33] Other Dominican sisters attended Dunedin Teachers' College during the 1970s, and maintained an active involvement with the college through Sister Jan Ogilvy's work preparing students for teaching in Catholic schools.

Mother Mary Constance made study a conscious priority during her period of office as prioress: she encouraged sisters to study for personal as well as professional development. As a young sister, she had had her own university studies interrupted when she was shifted from Dunedin to Teschemakers to meet the needs of the wider congregation; and now, as prioress she was eager to make sure that others had opportunities for study.[34]

In the 1970s and 80s a steady stream of sisters travelled overseas to Australia, Europe and North America to attend courses on Dominican spirituality, specialised deaf education, campus ministry, scripture and theology, and other areas of particular individual interest. In September 1976 Sister Marie Therese went to Chicago to attend a new programme on Dominican spirituality and to study specialised deaf education and campus ministry; Sister Patricia Hannan completed a Diploma in Religious Education at the National Pastoral Institute in Melbourne. In 1983 Sister Mary Concannon travelled to Rome

S Mary Horn and S Elizabeth Mackie with the first graduates of the Catechetical Studies Diploma, 1982. P8/18/2, DA.

to attend lectures at the Gregorian and Angelicum, and Sister Helen Bergin took up postgraduate study in theology at the Catholic University of Washington. In September 1986 Sister Patricia Hannan travelled to Ottawa where she spent the next three years studying canon law.

In New Zealand the Congregation ran a series of summer schools and brought in visiting lecturers from overseas. In January 1978, 78 sisters attended a series of seminars at Teschemakers led by two Dominican academics from the Aquinas Institute of Theology in Iowa: Professor Tom McGonigle specialised in the history of theology and Professor Tom O'Meara taught contemporary systematic theology. The following year Sister Dianne Kennedy and Father J.F. Taylor from the Aquinas Institute led a study focused on collaborative pastoral ministry between men and women.[35]

The sisters' 1992–93 summer school at Mosgiel was open to the wider community. It was billed as a chance to reflect on women's experience and to reclaim the feminine heritage of the scriptures: 'Women Explore: Who is God for us today? An opportunity for women to do theology together.' A total of 140 women attended, including four Dominican sisters from Australia, two from Pakistan and two from the Philippines. Twenty-one other religious came from around New Zealand, and numerous laywomen also attended. Course facilitators included Dunedin GP Anna Holmes, who presented a session on life stages; Margaret Schrader, a Presbyterian minister who looked at sexuality and spirituality; Joy Cowley, poet and writer, who led a session on 'story as gospel'; Marie Grunke, a Blessed Sacrament sister from Australia who spoke on land and creation; and Jo Ayres, a teacher of liturgy and ritual at the Catholic Institute of Theology.[36]

The Congregation has continued to invest in sisters' spiritual, personal and professional development and, increasingly, to support other women's access to educational and growth opportunities. Accepting their declining membership, the Congregation was determined to focus on creating 'life-giving communities where there is a genuine commitment to the poor, a felt spirit of love and enlivening prayer'. 'We need to extend these things to other women,' the Leadership Team decided, 'working with them, praying with them, or even living with them according to our capacities.'[37] They committed to spending some of the annual study/renewal budget for other women, by either involving other women in their own programmes, sponsoring programmes for women, or donating to individual women.[38] The Congregation still makes generous donations to educational causes, and in recent years they have identified the rich congregational archives as a potential resource for research and study in the wider community.[39]

A Catholic education

For more than 100 years Catholic schools were the focus of Dominican mission in New Zealand: the sisters sought to impart a holistic education with distinctly Dominican values. Over time teaching styles and school structures developed in response to changing educational theories and government policies, but the Dominican charism continued to animate their schools and to influence their pupils.

The Dominican sisters came to New Zealand to meet a need in the colonial Catholic community. Church teaching on education in the nineteenth century was firm: Catholic children should attend Catholic schools. Bishop Moran was controversially aggressive in his support for Catholic schools: 'I hold that all education should be based on religion, am opposed to mixed education, and there is nothing I am more thoroughly opposed to than secular education.'[40]

Before the sisters came and set up schools, Catholic children either stayed at home or attended government schools. In 1875 the Catholic residents of Oamaru wrote to Bishop Moran to plead the cause of education in their town: 51 Catholic children between the ages of four and 12 were currently attending state schools and 31 were not in school at all.[41] The main hindrance to establishing Catholic schools was cost. Religious orders whose members had taken the vow of poverty provided cost-effective staff. The Dominican sisters eventually established a mission at Oamaru in 1882.

As soon as local Catholic schools opened, Bishop Moran made it a point of discipline that Catholic parents should remove their children from government schools; those who failed to do so were threatened with excommunication. Moran was vilified in the press, but he remained a fierce advocate for Catholic education throughout his episcopacy. He lobbied government ministers, campaigned locally and nationally, and gave unstinting support to the religious women and men who staffed the colony's Catholic schools. He encouraged the Dominican sisters to 'exert themselves to the highest degree possible for the meritorious and glorious office of teaching children in the schools'.

> *I pray God to bless you abundantly in every way, to give you an ever increasing measure of faith, hope and charity and sisterly benevolence, to bestow upon you a high resolve a love for your High Institution & an enthusiasm for the glorious work of a true child of Saint Dominic: Ever remember the inspired words 'they who instruct others unto justice shall shine like stars for all eternity'.*[42]

His exhortation became a touchstone for the Dominican sisters. Successive prioresses have laid claim to Moran's reference from the Book of Daniel, and Sister Mary Augustine McCarthy adopted it for the title of her centennial history *Star in the South*.

St. Dominic's College

Established 1871

Tennyson Street,
DUNEDIN.

Registered Primary and Secondary Schools, conducted by the Dominican Nuns, under the patronage of the Right Rev. James Whyte, D.D., Bishop of Dunedin.

The Course of Instruction embraces a thorough knowledge of Christian Doctrine, all the branches of a high-class English education, modern languages, Latin, Mathematics, and Science, and is arranged to prepare pupils for the various local examinations—Public Service, Teachers' Certificates, Matriculation, and University Scholarships.

The School of Music attached to the College is well known through the pupils it has sent forth, whose brilliant attainments would do credit to a Continental Conservatoire. Pupils are prepared for the various theoretical and practical examinations of the Associated Board and Trinity College, London. They are also provided with opportunities of hearing the best performers and of being present at high-class concerts.

Moral and Religious Training.—The system of moral training adopted in the College is a happy blending of mind and heart culture with its external expression, ladylike modesty and gentleness. On account of the proximity to St. Joseph's Cathedral, resident pupils have very special religious advantages and abundant opportunities of hearing sermons and instructions, and of being present at the solemn ceremonies of Holy Church.

The Health and Physical Development of the pupils are maternally watched and tended. Long walks into the country and to the seaside, picnics, excursions, games of tennis, net-ball, and other outdoor amusements obviate the too great strain of study.

Reports.—Notes for work and conduct are given each week. Written examinations are held at the end of each term, and the result of the term's progress is forwarded to the parents.

Terms and Fees.—The year is divided into three terms. The first term commences in the first week of February, the second about May 25th, the third about September 14th.

Boarders	50 guineas per annum
Laundry	4 guineas per annum
Entrance Fee	3 pounds (paid once)
Piano, Violin, Singing, Painting (Junior Grade)	9 guineas each per annum
Piano, etc. (Intermediate and Senior Grades)	12 guineas each per annum
DAY SCHOOL—	
Seniors	12 guineas per annum
Intermediate	8 guineas per annum
Juniors	6 guineas per annum
Preparatory	3 guineas per annum
Kindergarten	2 guineas per annum
EXTERN STUDENTS—	
Piano, Harp, Violin, Singing	4 guineas per term
Harmony, Painting, Languages, Needlework	3 guineas per term

For Further Particulars Apply to the Rev. Mother Prioress.

Advertisement for St Dominic's College, Dunedin, 1921. M2, DA.

Dominican school pupils behind the new priory building, 1880s. P1/9/1, DA.

The sisters arrived in New Zealand with a strong legacy of educational involvement in Ireland. As discussed in earlier chapters, the Cabra nuns had adapted their observance of Dominican rites to meet the exigencies of their demanding teaching apostolate. Teaching was not only a source of income for the Irish nuns who came to New Zealand; it was a holy call. In Mother Gabriel's words, the New Zealand Dominican sisters were called to 'the high office of spiritual maternity'.[43] Mother Gabriel looked for prudence, zeal, self-control, concentration, clearness and sound judgement in her teachers – and she also looked for genuine humility, patience, candour, honour and purity, generosity and unselfishness, and a natural affection for children. She encouraged her sisters to look for God in their pupils:

Enter the study hall with a deep sense of your responsibility, treat every child with respect, regard in each the image of the Deity and remembering that your influence for good or for evil will last for ever and that when you appear before your Judge at the hour of death you will have to answer for those young souls redeemed at no less a cost than the Precious Blood of the Divine Saviour our Lord Jesus Christ. Pray then daily, and before each duty with the children, that you may cooperate with His designs on their souls.[44]

The New Zealand Dominicans' first printed Constitutions celebrated teaching as an 'exalted' work:

Our labours, our prayers, acquirements, and talents, are devoted to save souls, for whom He

> *shed His blood. We are called to tread in His blessed footsteps, to suffer and invite the little children to come unto us, that we may preserve their robes of innocence, unspotted to mould their tender hearts by the beneficent hand of religion; and by prayer, example and instruction, to instill into their souls those precepts and principles of faith, hope and love, which are the foundation of Christian life … Let us therefore study and pray that we may walk worthy of the vocation in which we are called.*[45]

The Dominican Sisters believed in the value of educating women: a woman in 'the higher ranks of life' influenced not only her domestic sphere but the 'tone of society' and, through her husband, 'the politics of the Nation'. The sisters also believed in educating those of humble origins. Inspired by St Dominic's example, the order valued learning as an end in itself and as a path to religious truth.[46]

The social structure of colonial New Zealand was less rigid than the Old World, but class-based distinctions still prevailed. The New Zealand Dominican Congregation was structured on class lines, with lay sisters providing for the physical needs of teaching sisters. Sister Mary Francis's initial impressions of Dunedin settler society were not favourable: although the Dominican sisters had met 'some very good kind of people' and all dressed 'quite in the fashion', she did not believe they had seen a single 'lady' 'in the general acceptation of the word' since their arrival. Indeed, she suspected there was 'scarcely one in the Colony'. As to religion, she reported that it was at 'the very lowest'. Even the most well-brought-up children had no Christian teaching: 'the name of God seems a strange sound to them, and as to the Blessed Virgin and the Saints, if they were all protestants they could not know less about them and what is worse they seem to take so little interest in such topics …'[47]

In Dunedin both St Joseph's, the 'free' primary school for poorer children, and St Dominic's, for fee-paying pupils, followed the same general curriculum. The main difference was that children at St Dominic's learned some French and had extra music lessons.[48] Mother Mary Gabriel herself made teaching notes for every class, with instructions for textbooks and for expectations of the standard expected in each subject.[49]

The Dominican Convent High School catered for well-bred young ladies and aimed to equip the students with 'all that is required for a refined high class education'. The course of instruction included classics, modern languages (French, German, Spanish and Italian), mathematics and natural science, as well as music, art, needlework, lacework and wood carving in relief.[50] During class hours teachers and students conversed in French.

Life in the boarding school was modelled on life in the convent. The regulations were strict. Each morning, pupils were woken by a bell (at 5.[illegible]am in summer and 6.30am in winter). The dormitory sister went around each bed sprinkling holy water. While the girls dressed she led them in their morning prayers. Before the girls left for class they presented their brushes, combs and fingers for inspection. Hair was worn simply brushed back, 'no curling or frizzing allowed'. Dressing-room sisters would examine the contents of girls' pockets regularly 'to see that no sweets, money, jewellery, postage stamps, etc be kept there'. Noisiness, lateness and personal untidiness were not tolerated. Pupils were expected to be gentle and polite', to stand up when addressed by a sister, to salute when entering or leaving a room and to close doors as gently as possible.[51] When they moved about within the school, the girls walked silently in assigned pairs at 'a respectable, moderate pace'. On stairs they were expected to pause at each landing and wait for a signal from the supervising sister

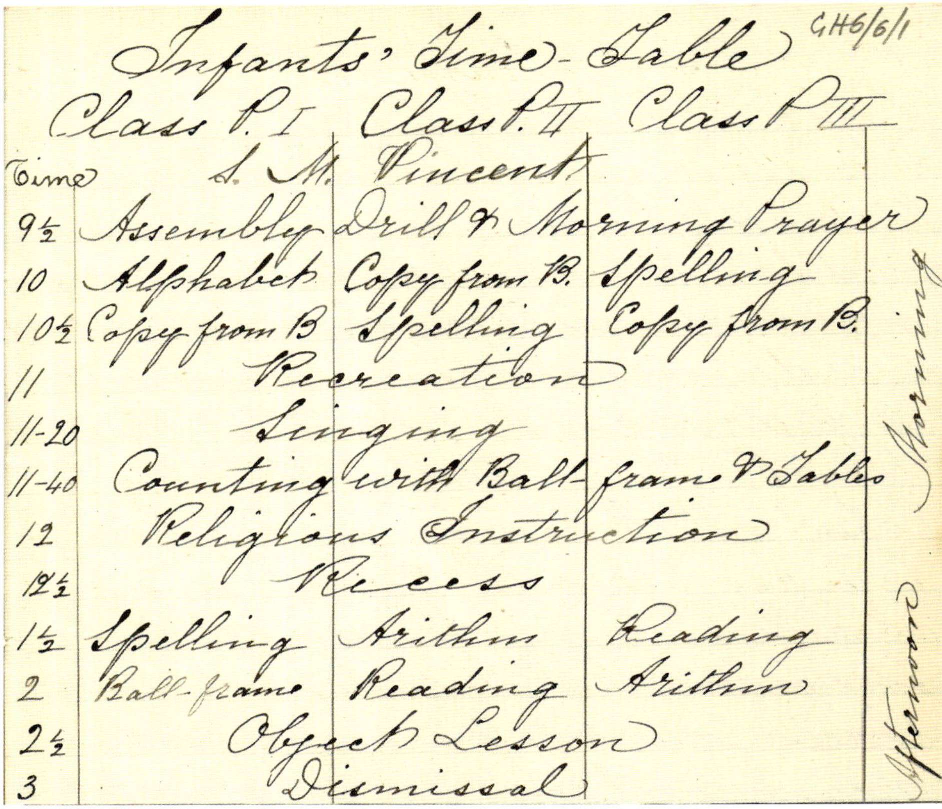

Infants' Time-Table GH6/6/1

Time	Class P. I	Class P. II	Class P. III	
	S. M. Vincent			
9½	Assembly Drill & Morning Prayer			Morning
10	Alphabet	Copy from B.	Spelling	
10½	Copy from B	Spelling	Copy from B.	
11	Recreation			
11-20	Singing			
11-40	Counting with Ball-frame & Tables			
12	Religious Instruction			
12½	Recess			
1½	Spelling	Arithm	Reading	Afternoon
2	Ball-frame	Reading	Arithm	
2½	Object Lesson			
3	Dismissal			

Infant timetable laid out by MM Gabriel Gill. GH6/6/1, DA.

before proceeding – 'no holding of hands, or linking allowed in rank, neither should hands be put on banisters'.[52] Pupils were expressly forbidden to talk unnecessarily during piano lessons, or to linger in music rooms. Sisters were expected to monitor the girls during recreation hours, guard against unduly intimate relationships and guide conversation away from dangerous topics such as 'balls, theatres, dress, young gentlemen, family arrangements, criticism whether of school rules, or of the nuns or of each other'. 'Screaming and rough play' were certainly not tolerated.[53] Every effort was made to cultivate in the children 'that genuine politeness that grows out of charity, giving place to others, guarding against any kind of uncharitable word or criticism, or the least allusion to the faults of another'. Many of these rules were enforced from the sisters' earliest years in New Zealand right up until the early 1960s.[54]

Life as a Dominican teacher was unceasingly busy. Early letters home to Ireland are littered with references to the New Zealanders' extreme workload. Sister Mary Francis wrote that she '[lived] so much in the school' that she could only think of 'history, grammar or geography'.[55] In September 1882 Bishop Moran wrote to Mother Clare at Sion Hill to tell her that the New Zealand Dominicans had

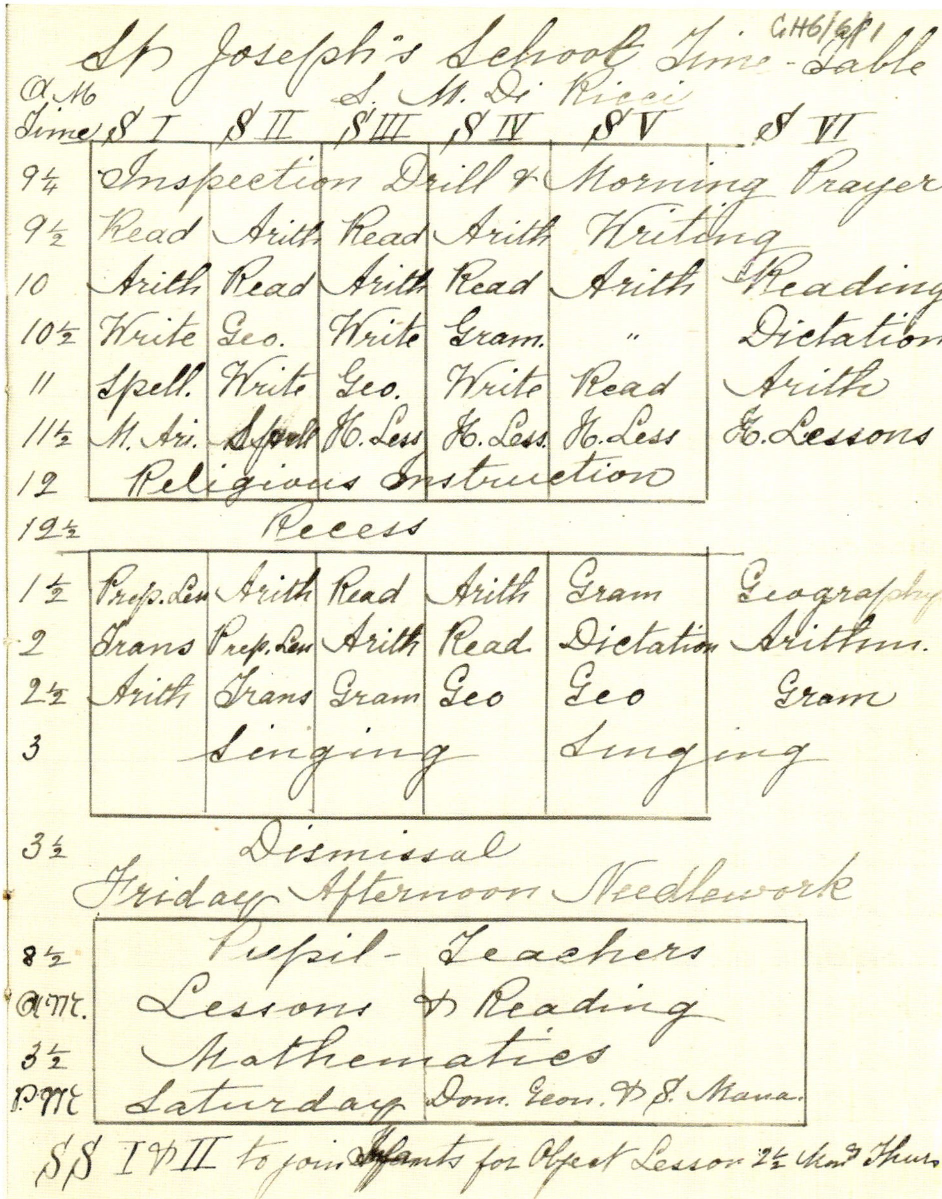

School timetable, St Joseph's School, 1870s. GH6/6/1, DA

recently taken charge of St Patrick's School in South Dunedin: two sisters, assisted by a lay teacher, had responsibility for 110 children, 'so you see the nuns are not idle'. He reported that the sisters were all in good health; indeed, he quipped, 'they have no time to be sick'.[56] Writing from St Catherine's in Invercargill, Sister Mary de Ricci Kirby described the pressures of teaching in a letter to her uncle in Rome:

> *Help is badly needed in the mission Houses. Here for instance there are only two sisters and myself to do the work of two large schools, every branch has to be taught and the Sisters have to study hard to prepare for their classes. The Sisters teach from 8.30 am to 6 pm except for one half hour of dinner time. This leaves them not much time for spirituality.*[57]

Referring to the Carmelite sisters, who were a strictly enclosed contemplative order, Sister Mary de Ricci expressed her struggle to reconcile apostolic mission with religious enclosure – a struggle that lay at the heart of the New Zealand Dominican sisters' pre-Vatican II teaching lifestyle. 'I sometimes regret that I did not carry out my first intention of being a Carmelite. There would then be no necessity of trying to cope with studies of world knowledge of the present day, and where there would be more time devoted to one's spiritual duties.'[58]

The other main constraint on Dominican schools, apart from time, was finance. Bishop Moran had expected that the educational and religious reserves set aside at the foundation of Otago would be divided equally among the colony's denominational schools. When he arrived in Dunedin and found that the money was used only for public schools, he decried the system's unfairness with continuous and vociferous passion. 'I shall never cease till I make the history of the injustice here ring throughout the world,' he declared in May 1871. 'I will try to let the world see how the boasted cry of religious liberty here means only license for one class to do as it pleases, and the denial of even-handed justice to all others.'[59] When the colonial government passed the 1877 Education Act establishing a nationwide system of compulsory free, secular education, Moran was outraged even further. Catholic citizens were denied support for their own schools while subsidising government schools through their taxes. Moran spent much of his time as bishop campaigning for government funding, but it would be another 100 years before Catholic schools began receiving state aid.

As Mother Francis bemoaned to the sisters at Sion Hill, 'the government schools have every advantage to offer the children and it is very hard to compete with them'.[60] The Dominican sisters supplemented school fees and their income from private music and speech pupils with revenue generated by ladies' art and catechism classes. The genteel accomplishments taught in the sisters' fee-paying schools attracted wealthy Protestant as well as Catholic families. The sisters were wary of accepting too many Protestant students but could not afford to turn them down. In 1872 the Feast of St Catherine was lived as an ordinary school day in Dunedin's Dominican schools, as Mother Gabriel feared that Protestant pupils' parents might take offence and withdraw their children and their money.

> *To speak of a saint's feast in this mixed or rather heretical and anti-Catholic society would be a crime, which would be punished by the withdrawal of some pupils. You can form no idea of the difficulty we encounter daily in our efforts to do our duty to our Catholic pupils in religious matters, without offending our protestant, Jewish or Presbyterian disciples.*[61]

In later years the Dominicans depended less on Protestant pupils. Private Protestant schools established around the turn of the century catered specifi-

Clothing class, St Dominic's College, Dunedin. DA.

cally for Anglican and Presbyterian girls, and by this time the Catholic roll was sufficient to fill Dominican schools.

As part of his campaign for state funding, Bishop Moran insisted that Catholic schools provide a level of education comparative with the best public schools. He himself took daily religious education lessons at St Joseph's School.[62] In the early 1890s the New Zealand bishops prepared for government inspection. 'In view of the obligations of justice to parents and their children, and in anticipation of government inspection of our schools at no very distant date', they asked teaching orders to take 'immediate measures to secure efficient teaching in all our Catholic schools'. Only sufficiently qualified teachers should be placed in charge of classes, and all teachers should be given adequate preparation time for lessons.[63]

By 1895 when the first inspections took place, the Dominicans were ready. An internal memorandum explained that it was 'of the utmost importance that teachers present children in the last full standard completed so that they had the best possible chance to pass; students were not to be presented for examination in standards they had not fully completed. If they were partway through the year, then teachers should 'quietly have them revise the previous standard's work and sit that'.[64]

St Catherine's College, Invercargill. F3B/1/30, DA.

Dominican schools performed strongly in their first government inspections. The inspector's first report for Queenstown Convent School was glowing: 'The pupils of this school have attained a very creditable standard of proficiency. Their oral answers were ready and intelligent and their written exercises were models of neatness and careful arrangement. Conduct and manners entirely pleasing.'[65]

Inspector William Fitzgerald and several of his colleagues attended the annual St Dominic's College prizegiving in December 1899. Addressing the assembled pupils, parents and clergy, Fitzgerald observed that government inspectors visiting Dominican schools expected 'to find thorough work, good order, good manners, and a nice tone pervading all'. The schools 'did not disappoint them'.[66]

The New Zealand Dominican Sisters' first independent Constitutions, promulgated in 1939, emphasised the dignity of teaching as a vocation. 'Of teachers it may be said that they occupy a position intermediate between God and their pupils: directly, when they impart religious instruction; indirectly, when they bring aid to the pupil's God-given intelligence.'[67] The Constitutions reminded sisters of their 'quasi-parental responsibility'; those 'animated by worldly ideas' might regard physical and civil education as the chief lessons taught in school, but the sisters' primary focus was on religious and moral training. The Constitutions insisted on strong disci-

Senior classroom, St Dominic's College, Dunedin. DA.

pline, but they also emphasised respect for the individual child:

> *The sisters must respect the personal dignity of the child, and, consequently, preserve the right order of relations between their pupils and themselves. The teacher's function is to stimulate the child's God-given intelligence, to aid her to acquire and assimilate knowledge; she is, therefore, definitely a coadjutor, and relatively, subordinate to the pupil … the teacher must realise that her training of the child is to prepare her to independent life, not only by ensuring her possession of suitable knowledge, but, especially, by leading her to an intelligent use of liberty.*[68]

As the Catholic population boomed in the mid-twentieth century, classes swelled. In 1944 Sister Mary Placid had charge of 35 students in the infant room at St Mary's in Kaikorai. She also took school music, served as the community procuratrix, led the Children of Mary and took 18 external music pupils.[69] Government inspectors complained repeatedly about the number of children in the infant room at St Joseph's primary school in Invercargill.[70] The sisters of St Catherine's Priory in Invercargill staffed three schools: in 1950 five sisters taught 173 children at St Joseph's primary school, four sisters taught 144 children at St Catherine's primary school and three sisters taught 76 girls at St Catherine's secondary school. The sisters also took 192 students for

The first teachers at St Dominic's College, Blockhouse Bay, 1962: SM Rose, Mrs Watt, SM Gemma. F16/4, DA.

private music and elocution lessons.[71] In 1958 the senior inspector of the Auckland Education Board wrote to the Dominican General Council to request that, where possible, classes should not exceed more than 50 students.[72]

Classrooms were still crowded in the early 1960s. In 1962 – the Dominicans' first year at Blockhouse Bay – four teachers taught 185 pupils at St Dominic's Primary School. Sister Mary Gemma had 45 pupils in her junior class, including 25 new entrants, and Miss Watt, a lay teacher, had 51 pupils in the standard one and two class.[73]

When Sister Mary Regis (Joan) Hardiman went to Northcote in 1960 the Dominicans had charge of the local parish school and a small secondary school with 60 boarders. The Auckland harbour bridge had opened in 1959 and large tracts of farmland had been sold for urban development. Within a couple of years the schools were overflowing. Sister Mary Regis took a class of 65 children. Between teaching, cleaning duties, cooking lunch for the parish priest, playground duties, bus duties, and music and speech lessons before and after school, not to mention community religious observances, 'we barely had time in the day to blow our noses, let alone go to the loo'. The parish priest held the purse strings: he gave the nuns one box of chalk for the term. The convent and the school were both in dire poverty.[74]

Music and speech lessons were still vital to the sisters' economic survival. In the early 1940s there were around 60 children on the roll of St Mary's School in Milton, and an average of 30 to 35 in the music school. Each year the parish contributed £100 towards the sisters' maintenance and a small

Left: SM Ceslaus Fox with piano students Teschemakers, 1960. Waitaki District Archive P0011.1069.121.

Below: S Jacinta with twins Cherie and Vickie Smith, St Dominic's School for the Deaf Feilding, 1958. [illegible] DA.

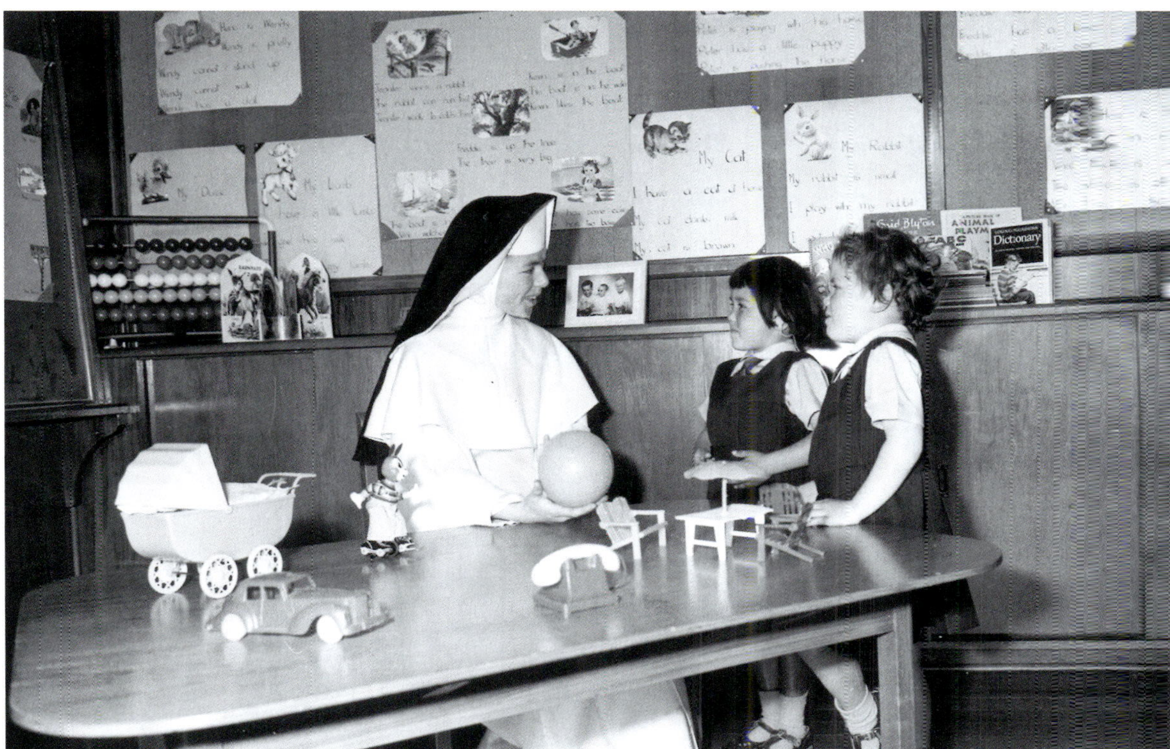

S Marie Therese Smith taught in Dominican primary and secondary schools for over 60 years. She also served on the general council and as the directress general of studies. S Sandra Winton, a past pupil, gave the eulogy at S Marie Therese's funeral. 'I believe that she epitomised all that was best of the great years of Catholic girls' secondary schools. She prepared women who would lead, study, achieve, influence – and who knew how to polish the back stairs till they shone.' DA.

amount more was received from the quarterly collection taken up at the church door. School fees were minimal, so the chief source of income was private fee-paying music students.[75] In 1947 the sisters of St Dominic's Convent in Helensville had 42 pupils on the school roll and 55 private piano students, two violin students, four singing and three elocution students. They received £106 9s in school fees and £568 13s 6d from music students, with total income almost meeting expenditure.[76] In 1950 St Catherine's Priory in Invercargill received £2100 in fees from their primary schools and boarding school and a total of £3660 from piano, elocution, singing and violin student fees.[77] As in the early days, the extracurricular tuition offered at Dominican schools signalled the type of cultured education the sisters endeavoured to provide.[78] Ultimately, however, speech and music lessons were a financial imperative. Even so, the sisters kept music fees as low as possible, and if a talented child was from a family that could not afford the fees, the sisters often waived payment.[79]

Even in the midst of balancing school duties and music lessons with religious observances, Dominican teachers aspired to high ideals. In the late 1950s Prioress General Mother Mary David Stark reminded her sisters that teaching should be an outcome of prayer; a Dominican sister should combine 'the highly competent teacher and the ideal mother'.

> *She must before all else, love the child and make it realise that it is loved. If she is to lead it in the way of truth and virtue, she must first establish a relationship of confidence and trust. Her function is not just about the communication of knowledge and the stimulation of intelligence, but also the imparting of the concept and practice of Christian living, so as to fit the child to be a citizen of heaven.*[80]

Mother David insisted that children be treated with respect and patience, emphasising each child's individuality.[81] She reminded her sisters that corporal punishment was a last resort: 'our sisters must try other methods which are more effective'. The prioress was aware that some ex-pupils of Dominican schools refused to send their children to Catholic schools because of the severe corporal punishment they had experienced during their own schooling. 'This is a very serious matter,' she warned. 'Cruelty in any shape or form should be foreign to a Dominican nun.'[82] In 1970 Mother Jordan banned corporal punishment in all Dominican schools.[83]

As the Congregation responded to the Second Vatican Council, the New Zealand Dominicans reaffirmed their commitment to the teaching apostolate. The Special General Chapter of 1968–69 paid particular attention to the quality of teaching in Dominican schools and provided for the establishment of a Scholastic Council.[84]

The Chapter of 1974 asked sisters to look at their teaching practice closely and take care that they approached their students with respect.[85] The 1976 Interim Constitutions called sisters to an example of integrity in their own lives as they sought to establish relationships of mutual love, respect and trust with their students:

> *In all our educational work, both in schools and in parishes, our inspiration is the great ideal Saint Dominic set before his Order, Truth. It is our task to help our pupils to begin and to continue enthusiastically their life-long search for infinite Truth and to accept generously and positively whatever the God of Truth reveals to them or requires of them … Our aim is to develop minds that are enquiring, open and eager in the pursuit of wisdom.*[86]

The changes instigated by the Second Vatican Council led Dominican teachers to apply new methods and adapt their delivery: 'the Christian message if it is to have any meaning must be relevant to the present age and speak to our students as they are in the environment in which they live.'[87]

Yet the combined demands of their teaching apostolate and religious duties placed many Dominican teachers under a lot of pressure. Cecily Sheehy felt her lack of training from the start. Together with others in her novitiate she completed papers on education and spent time in senior teachers' classes, but she was never taught how to teach. Cecily loved taking music and teaching creative subjects but found teaching life stressful and pressured.[88] It was a difficult system, but Cecily, like many others, developed her own style and became a highly successful teacher. [illegible] Benzie had trained in the state system before entering the convent, and had taught in government schools; she was shocked at the Dominican sisters' lack of preparation time.[89] Roxane Parkinson had also trained as a teacher in the state system before she joined the convent, and found the Catholic system very different – classes were much bigger and the system was not as supportive.[90] Mary H[illegible], who had attended Dunedin Teachers' College and taught for a year before joining the Dominicans, also found the Catholic system difficult to adjust to. The schools were poorly organised, there were no staff meetings and, as a postulant, she was not allowed to talk with the community sisters, so there was limited support. Because she was a trained teacher she was given two other postulants to train up in her classroom. That first year was difficult but Mary came to love teaching in Dominican schools. 'I think Dominicans have that sort of emphasis on really good quality education, and every child, not just those who were academic, deserved the best education we could give them.'[91] Mary acknowledges that the sisters have not always been able to achieve this ideal; nevertheless, their underlying sense of each child's fundamental worth has functioned as a consistent theme in the Dominican sisters' history of teaching in New Zealand.

Crisis, closure and integration

By the early 1970s New Zealand's Catholic education system was in crisis. Changes in wider society and within religious orders exposed the inherent structural limitations of a system that relied on free staff. Later in the decade several Dominican schools were forced to amalgamate with other Catholic schools, and some had to close. By 1985 the remaining Dominican schools had been integrated into the state system. They received state funding for operational costs, and the diocese and student fees covered capital works. Within another decade the schools founded by Dominicans sisters were staffed mostly by lay teachers. Despite these radical changes the new system allowed Catholic schools to retain their special religious character.

The postwar baby boom of the late 1940s and early 1950s accentuated an existing trend in New Zealand's Catholic population. Between 1900 and 1965 Catholic school rolls multiplied by six and a half times. During the same period the Catholic proportion of the national school roll rose from 7 to 10 per cent. In 1944 the school leaving age was raised to 15, and in 1964 the compulsory starting age was lowered to six.[92] Private religious schools struggled to cope with their burgeoning rolls.

Until the 1960s Catholic schools were staffed almost exclusively by unpaid religious teachers. The Dominican sisters employed lay staff to teach dancing and physical education and, very occasionally, to meet a gap in the academic staff. By the late 1960s the teaching population of religious men and women in New Zealand was ageing and declining and the Dominicans, like other orders, had to employ more and more lay staff. The proportion of lay teachers working in Catholic schools increased from 5 per cent in 1956 to 38 per cent in 1972, and in 1974 the Dominican sisters appointed their first lay principal and first lay director of religious studies.[93] As they struggled with increasing salary costs, Catholic schools also battled to compete with the state system's drive towards smaller class sizes and improved facilities. Some schools accrued large debts in their efforts to survive; many cut maintenance costs and let their buildings get run-down. The whole system was close to collapse.

In 1972 Norman Kirk's Labour Party came to power and sought an immediate solution to the crisis facing Catholic school funding. Over the next few years the Education Department worked together with the Catholic bishops, in consultation with the religious orders, to develop a feasible framework. As president of the Dominican Education Committee, Sister Marie Therese led the Dominican response: she attended meetings in Wellington, liaised with the Dunedin Catholic Education Office, made submissions to the Education Department and kept the wider congregation informed of unfolding developments.[94]

In January 1974 Sister Elizabeth Mackie, who was also a member of the Dominican Education Committee, addressed the Congregation on the challenges facing their schools. 'The effort to "stretch" existing personnel to continue the work that the sisters were able to do in the past, would clearly be unjust both to the sisters and to the schools,' she told them. Foreshadowing the sisters' later shift into new spheres of educational work, she encouraged 'a courageous response and a readiness to change'. 'While we remain faithful to our commitment to the work in the schools, we must offer just support to the total educational work of the Church.' As teachers the Dominicans were familiar with change and were practised in the 'art of updating'. They were already prepared for changes in curricula, textbooks and methods, Sister Elizabeth said, but they also needed to be ready 'for some deeper and more lasting changes'.

We have a certainty that our work will always be needed, provided we are prepared to work in loyal service to the Church. For Christ's call to reach all nations is a never-ending challenge. If we remember and appreciate the past, and stand ready – with a free spirit – to meet the future, we shall continue to meet that challenge.[95]

In 1975 the Labour Government passed the Private Schools Conditional Integration Act, which provided for the integration of Catholic schools into the public system. Under the Act, proprietors retain ownership of school land and buildings and ensure that the special character of their schools is maintained. In all other regards integrated schools operate in the same way as public schools: they receive state funding for salaries and comply with the government's administration guidelines and testing requirements. Integrated schools are permitted to give preferential entrance to students who identify with their special character, but they may also accept non-preference students up to the school's maximum roll. To provide for capital costs, integrated schools are permitted to charge attendance dues in order to keep their facilities up to the standard of state schools. They may also seek voluntary donations to supplement attendance dues and government funding.

Sister Mary Gertrude Fox, who was on the general council in the mid-1970s, describes integration as a 'tremendous relief' for the Dominican sisters.[96] They were able to staff and resource their schools properly while still maintaining the unique charism of their Dominican founding sisters. The process of integration, however, was often very stressful.

Before being accepted for integration, Catholic schools had to be brought up to state standards. Some schools had been left to deteriorate for too long: several were forced to close, and others to amalgamate. Some sisters struggled to accept the 'loss' of schools that had formed the heart of the Dominican mission in New Zealand for so many years. The congregational leadership encouraged sisters to see that they were not really losing their schools – rather, they were 'making room for dedicated laypeople to help shoulder the burden of diocesan education, laypeople whom we have prepared for the responsibility.'[97]

In 1979 St Patrick's primary school in Lawrence began to prepare for integration. At the start of 1980 the Dominican General Council decided that the sisters would withdraw from the school at the end of the year to focus their resources in other areas, and St Patrick's would be passed over to lay teachers. But in July the school received notice from the Ministry of Works that it did not qualify for integration: the 54-year-old buildings were 'structurally unsatisfactory'. The cost of rebuilding to the standard required was beyond diocesan resources, so Bishop Kavanagh decided to close the school at the end of the year. The Dominicans retained a presence in Lawrence for the next few years, and the sisters often visited their old students at Lawrence Area School.[98]

Whereas the diocese had always owned Catholic primary schools, most secondary schools were owned and operated by the orders themselves. Moreau College, created in 1976 by amalgamating St Dominic's with the Mercy sisters' school, St Philomena's, was owned by the diocese and was eventually integrated into the state system. By 1977 there were only four Dominican sisters teaching at Moreau. There were four sisters teaching at St Thomas's in Oamaru, which was owned by the parish. There were eight sisters teaching at St Dominic's, Henderson, 11 at St Catherine's, Invercargill, and nine at Teschemakers; these last three schools were all owned by the Dominicans.[99]

Teschemakers, which had occupied a special place in the Congregation's history and had served Otago's rural families for almost seven decades, had been losing students since the early 1970s and struggling to maintain its buildings. In May 1977 Mother Constance and the general council met with members of the education committee to consider the school's future. After prayerful discernment they resolved to close the school: 'to retain Teschemakers as a boarding school was not in the best interests of the girls, nor was it enabling us to use our resources of personnel in areas that the Church considered most urgent'.[100] The school community was appalled. The Parent Teacher Association and the school's Board of Governors appealed for the decision to be revoked, and the controversy spilled into the media. Mother Constance insisted that the decision to close Teschemakers was private – 'the decision had to come from us'.[101] The school closed at the end of the year.[102]

For the next few years Teschemakers' pupils boarded at St Thomas's in Oamaru, but it was also very run-down. By the early 1980s it was clear that the school would need a complete rebuild to meet the requirements of integration. This was not a cost that the Dominicans or the diocese could afford, so in 1983 St Thomas's was amalgamated with St Kevin's College to form a state-integrated, coeducational Catholic secondary school.

The cost of bringing buildings at St Catherine's College in Invercargill up to the required standard was similarly unfeasible. At the end of 1980 Bishop Kavanagh approved a plan for the amalgamation of St Catherine's with Marist College. Prioress Sister Mary Constance kept her Congregation informed as the process evolved. 'A situation such as this is a further reminder to us that as a Congregation of Dominican women we are at the service of the Church and that at times this demands the sacrifice of what we hold dear.'[103] Senior St Catherine's students began attending classes at Marist College in 1981. By the third term of 1982 the progressive amalgamation was complete. The new school was known as Verdon College.[104]

The Board of St Dominic's College in Henderson took some time to negotiate terms of integration with the Education Department. Before the school could be integrated the proprietors had to upgrade the electrical wiring and lighting, instal fire protection, replace incinerators, attend to paintwork and instal gates; the full schedule of works to be planned, executed and paid for by the Dominicans was 17 pages long.[105] The school was eventually integrated in 1982. On 18 March 1998 the Dominican Congregation transferred ownership of the buildings and grounds of St Dominic's to the Diocese of Auckland.[106] The community marked the occasion with a beautiful liturgy, and the school continues to honour the sisters and their charism today.

An expanded apostolate

Beginning in the early 1970s, the Dominican sisters began expanding into other forms of educational mission outside their schools. As Mother Constance explained to the parents who were disappointed at the closure of Teschemakers, one of the aims of the Second Vatican Council was to make people more aware of the total needs of the Church. Religious were asked to appraise their lives in the light of contemporary culture and to 'make adjustments in their activities according to the needs of the time and place and in favour of what would benefit the universal Church and any particular diocese'.[107]

The first major development outside of schools was the 'motor mission' in the South Island. As smaller Catholic schools in rural areas became unsustainable they gradually closed, leaving Catholic families without access to religious education. The Catholic Education Office in Dunedin established the motor mission to provide catechetical classes for Catholic children and support for their families. The Dominicans worked together with the Sisters of

Students singing Compline at Dominican Hall with Father Ambrose Loughnan, 1956. F15/8/2, DA.

St Joseph (the 'Brown Joes'), travelling around the countryside in pairs.

The sisters also moved into other new roles: they became diocesan education advisers, led sacramental programmes in local parishes and ran adult education courses in Christian living. As Sister Mary Elizabeth said: 'Our commitment is not just to the Catholic school system. We are at the service of the Church in all her educational work.'[108]

Several sisters who had worked with deaf children at St Dominic's in Feilding went on to work with the adult deaf community. Sister Mary Louise became a strong advocate for the needs of the adult deaf, and in 1975 she lobbied candidates before the general election.[109] In 1978 four sisters left school posts to work with deaf people in the Catholic community. Sisters Gemma Finlay and Molly Griffin went to Wellington to work as members of the Religious Education Team in the Archdiocese of Wellington, and Sisters Dominic Swindale and Kathleen Thomson worked with the Religious Education Team in Auckland. The sisters helped coordinate liturgies, camps, retreats, youth groups and a quarterly journal for deaf people. In 1982 Sister Louise was appointed director of the National Training and Resource Centre for the Ministry to the Deaf (established at St Dominic's, Feilding in 1977). She was available to help with scripture studies, adult literacy and sacramental programmes and also supervised a lending library. Father David Molloy, the first deaf priest in New Zealand, moved into the Catholic ministry to the deaf in 1984, and after he left the priesthood he continued to work as a lay chaplain. The sisters gradually moved out of deaf adult ministry and education as they reached retirement, but many of those who worked in Feilding still have a strong connection with the deaf community.[110] Maureen O'Hanlon began working at St Dominic's School for the Deaf in 1972, and apart from time spent studying in Rome and a brief stint in Henderson, she has been based in Feilding and then Palmerston North ever since. She has continued in voluntary ministry with the deaf community and has formed strong personal relationships: 'I feel like a grandmother sometimes.'[111] In June 2014 Molly Griffin, Dominic Swindale, Judith McGinley, Roxane Parkinson and Margaret Butler returned to Feilding to join the deaf community's celebration of 70 years since St Dominic's School for the Deaf was first opened.

Another natural field of expansion for the sisters was into tertiary education. In 1945 they had opened Dominican Hall to provide accommodation for Catholic girls attending Otago University and Dunedin Teachers' Training College; however, with declining student enrolments and a preference for flatting, and the increasing cost of compliance with council regulations, the Hall closed at the end of 1978. But the sisters were keen to continue their involvement with students on campus.[112] Sister Judith McGinley was appointed tertiary chaplain at the University of Otago – a role she shared with fellow Dominican Father Kevin Toomey.

In 1981 Bishop Peter Cullinane of Palmerston North extended an invitation for the Dominican sisters to set up a community to witness to the students at Massey University, Palmerston North Teachers' College and Technical Institute. Jan Ogilvy and Michelle Wheatley were the first of several Dominicans to work as a tertiary chaplain in Palmerston North. Jan loved her work with the students, and went on to work at the Dunedin College of Education, where she continues to supervise the training of teachers preparing to work in Catholic schools. She values the Catholic school's ability to teach the whole child. Being a Dominican informs her teaching in a fundamental way – 'that spiritual side ... that you are preaching the truth of the Gospel, that those are the values, every day I'm trying to live them more deeply, and that's who I am, its what I bring.'[113]

In the 1970s and 80s several sisters studied at Holy Cross College, the national seminary then based in Dunedin. Sister Helen Bergin completed a theology degree at Holy Cross in the 1970s before she went to work as a teacher in Dominican high schools. At the end of 1981 the dean of studies at Holy Cross wrote to ask if she would be interested in studying overseas, with a view to teaching at the seminary. Helen was thrilled – 'just the whole idea that they wanted women to be teaching future priests!' In January 1983 she moved into residence at the college and did some further study and some teaching. In August she went the United States, and she returned to Holy Cross two and a half years later to teach theology. She lived at the college from 1986 until 1991.[114]

After completing a master's degree in the United States, Sister Bernadette Cheyne joined the formation staff at Holy Cross in 1985 and worked there for nearly a decade. Sister Carmel Walsh joined the staff in 1994 to teach New Zealand church history. In 1998 Carmel moved with the seminary from Dunedin to Auckland. She is still teaching at Good Shepherd College, New Zealand's Catholic theological college.

Raewyn Benzie moved from teaching in Catholic schools to a specialised educational advisory role in Catholic and state schools. After working as a teacher and principal for several decades she felt burnt out. She spent a year at Kairos Spirituality School in Sydney and when she came home she was asked to return to the principal's position at St Joseph's School in Queenstown. She turned the position down and spent the next 10 years as an itinerant religious educator for the diocese, working with parents and children in rural areas. In the 1990s she moved into guidance and learning support work in Invercargill, and eventually trained as a resource teacher of learning and behaviour.[115]

Judith McGinley also moved from a career as a Dominican teacher and principal into specialised educational roles. In 1977 she was appointed to the tertiary chaplaincy team, serving Otago University, Otago Polytechnic and Dunedin Teachers' Training College. In 1985 she studied at the Pacific Mission Institute in Sydney for six months before joining the Congregation's mission to Vanuatu, where she taught English and science (and whatever else was needed each day) and helped develop a new school curriculum. The Dominicans in Vanuatu worked alongside the local women as companions and friends – mutually learning, teaching and encouraging. They taught practical skills to young women at the Training Centre, and provided older women with opportunities for spiritual development, leadership and service through the Legion of Mary. The Dominicans also took catechetical classes and bible studies for local women. In 2000 Judith joined Challenge 2000, a Wellington-based organisation involved in youth development and family social work.[116] 'Sister Jude', as she is known at Challenge 2000, initially ran a small school for students whose needs were not being met in the mainstream system. She now works as a volunteer community worker and mentor.

> *What I love most of all is to encourage people to recognise their gifts and to believe they are called to be people of compassion and hope, makers of justice and peace – to keep going on the hard days. For me Challenge 2000 is more than a workplace – it is a Gospel place of hope, real life and growth, of family and community, of faith and commitment.*[117]

Sister Paddy McCann loved her work teaching small children in Dominican schools and then teaching the deaf in Feilding. In the early 2000s she worked in the Catholic Education Office in Dunedin, rewriting the new religious education programme and designing school workbooks and music resources. In 2005 she took up a role as congregational bursar. Paddy brought all her skills to the finance role – she not only managed the Congregation's financial resources, but served as a central point of connection for many of the sisters and providing practical care for the unwell and elderly. In 2015 Paddy and Bernie Cheyne were appointed as health care coordinators for the congregation. Paddy is still involved with children as leader of the sacramental programme at Sacred Heart Church in North East Valley.[118]

Helen Bergin gave an address on the changes since Vatican II at the Congregation's fourteenth General Chapter in 2003. She described love of learning and education as 'a principal motivation in the New Zealand Dominican story'. One of the main challenges of the later twentieth century was 'adapting this thrust from the ways in which it was previously handed down'. The Integration Act had effectively released the Dominican sisters from the classroom. Many had moved into related fields of education, and others into totally new spheres of activity, but all continued to be informed by the educational tradition at the heart of Dominican life in New Zealand. 'This is being a Dominican,' Helen maintained, 'involving ourselves in study, learning, teaching, enquiring, exploring, in seeking the truth that often lies somewhere deep down.'[119]

A Dominican legacy

The Dominican sisters no longer own or manage schools. Some work in an expanded educational apostolate, and others work in different fields of mission. The sisters and their schools have had a profound impact on individual students, and on the

Prayer at the Dominican Summer School held at Mosgiel 1992/93. P9/15/14, DA.

development of Catholic education in New Zealand. The Dominican charism – the search for truth – continues to enliven Dominican-founded schools and inspire Dominican-educated men and women.

Strong alumni associations in many Dominican schools are an indication of the importance of their school years for many past pupils. Some old girls, and some ex-pupils of St Dominic's School for the Deaf in Feilding, have become lay associates or Dominican Family members – a sign of the strength of their commitment to the Dominican charism.

Some alumni have spoken of the impact of their Dominican education. Marian Hobbs attended St Dominic's College in Dunedin and went on to a teaching career, before she became a Labour Member of Parliament from 1996 until 2008. Marian felt that the 'intellect of women was treasured' in the convent school. She was encouraged 'to be an intellectual, a person who could stand on her own, a person who could think for herself. Independent. That's the gift they've given me, that gift of confidence, the belief I could do anything, and being able to stand alone.'[120]

Paula Ryan attended Teschemakers in the 1960s and went on to a highly successfully career in modelling, fashion and publishing. Though she found the convent regime repressive, she came to appreciate the self-discipline and self-esteem that it fostered. She was 'something of a rebel', but the sisters encouraged her creativity. 'They believed, and encouraged me to believe, that I could do anything I wanted to do.' The sisters organised a correspondence course in art and a tutor in town – 'they had the imagination to encourage me to do something they had no provision for'. Paula also acknowledges the sisters as role models of women's managerial ability. 'Here were all these women running this quite complex community, and doing it with consummate skill and competence. After living in that community any negative stuff about women in business was bound to fall on stony ground.' Dominican schoolgirls had 'seen women working effectively. We knew women could do anything.'[121]

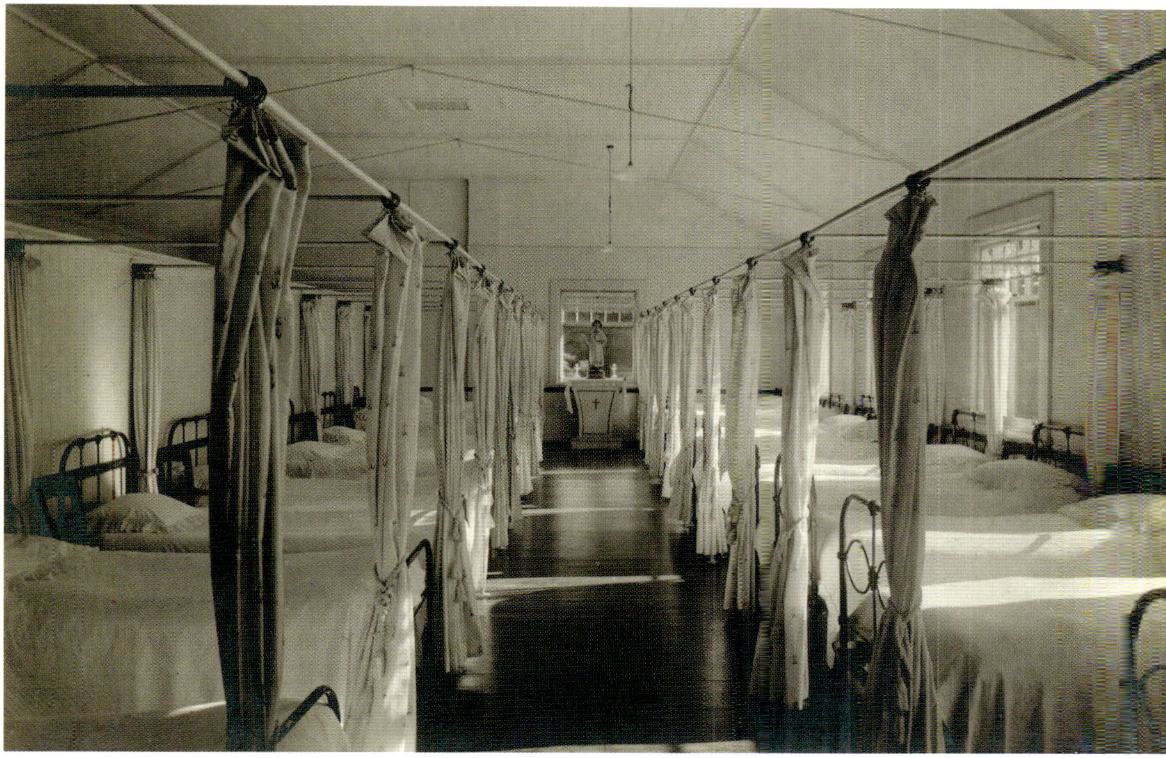

Blessed Virgin Mary dormitory above the dining room, Teschemakers. F8/8/5, DA.

Not all students enjoyed their schooling with the sisters, and some found certain aspects of the rigid structure difficult to accept. Some students encountered individual teachers whose harsh imposition of discipline affected their trust in the Church. Paddy McCann was scared of the nuns at St Teresa's primary school in Invercargill, but her years at St Catherine's high school were much happier.[122] Barbara Menzies attended St Joseph's primary school in Dunedin and then St Dominic's College.

> *We all knew that some of our teachers, while clever women in their own right, had little ability to light the fire of discovery in their pupils – a weakness thrown into sharp relief by the contrast with their gifted and inspiring colleagues, both religious and lay.*[123]

Teaching has shaped the story of the Dominican Order in New Zealand and has been central to most sisters' lives. Involvement in study and support for education are still important elements of personal identity for many sisters. Sister Paddy acknowledges her time spent teaching religious education in schools as an important part of her own personal spiritual journey. As she has spent time talking to children about the loving person of Jesus, her own relationship with Him has developed – a process she describes as an 'absolute gift, and truly remarkable'.[124] In a similar way, teaching has helped Mary Anna discover just how much God loves her. Appreciating each of the children she taught as special and unique gradually led to an understanding of her own

Infants classroom. DA.

value to God – 'thank you God for making me, me'.[125]

Schools founded by the Dominican sisters acknowledge their religious heritage and honour the Dominican charism still today. Verdon College has embraced both Dominican and Marist principles: it lists its core school values as:

> *truth (living in a genuine and honest way), presence (being there for others in our community), passion for work (enjoying the fruits of our hard work), living our lives in the example of Mary, family spirit and community, diligent study, simplicity, witness and prayer (expressing our faith through spiritual practice)*[126]

St Dominic's College in West Auckland lays proud claim to the Dominicans' 800-year tradition of service to education. Their religious education classes emphasise the ethos of the Dominican Order, and the school's motto is 'Veritas'.[127] In Sister Loreto's words, 'what we've taught over the years since 1871, and the pupils we've had over the years, they are carrying on in a sense what we were doing, but they're doing it as a layperson, and I think that's marvellous'.[128]

Through the Dominican Sisters' Faith Education Fund the Congregation offers financial support to people involved in religious education. Funding is available for final-year high school students, for ter-

S Janice Ogilvy speaking at the Federation of Dominican Sisters in Oceania, 9 March 2014, Kavanagh College. Jan is standing in front of a photo board memorialising the school's Dominican heritage. Authors collection.

tiary students preparing to teach in Catholic schools, for teachers in schools with a Dominican history, for attendance at Dominican Education Conferences and for people supplying faith education in areas without Catholic schools.[129]

From the 1870s until the present, Dominican schools have sought to provide students with a well rounded, good quality education underlain by a sense of their own dignity and of God's presence in their lives. In 1931 Irish Dominican priest Father Finbar Ryan wrote to Mother Mary Teresa Lynch to tell her of a conversation he had had with Bishop Liston about the Dominican sisters' proposed foundations at Northcote and Helensville:

> *It gave me a so deep satisfaction to hear him assert (as it is a joy to repeat to you) that it was a commonly recognized fact that there is 'a something' about the children from the Dominican schools that gives them a 'quality' brand. How proud of you that little remark made me and how it made hope and confidence more strong for your future!*[130]

That certain 'something' that characterises Dominican students is still a source of hope and confidence in the twenty-first century.

Mary Horn, *Wise Woman.* Private collection.

A community of preachers

The Word of God is powerfully preached by young and old, by skilled and unskilled, when persons follow in their own lives the practical wisdom lived and taught by Jesus of Nazareth. Preaching has many forms and innumerable faces. It brings life and it transforms what it touches. It is God's gift and when received it spreads beyond itself. The Word of God is truly alive and active. – Helen Bergin, 2006[1]

Ultimately, truth is lived … There are lives which shine with integrity and authenticity, offering glimpses of truth which can touch us deeply. Perhaps our own lives, in all their uncertainty, offer such shining glimpses to others without our knowing. – Elizabeth Mackie, 2006[2]

Preaching

Preaching is the ultimate purpose of Dominican community life. It is based in study and reflected in education. It is a lived and spoken transfiguration of contemplative prayer. It is both the search for, and the sharing of truth. During their first 100 years in New Zealand the Dominican sisters' main form of preaching was teaching. In the 1960s the Second Vatican Council's dual call to religious congregations to return to the spirit of their founders and to respond to the signs of the times initiated a radical transformation of the ways Dominican women prayed, studied and lived together. In doing so it opened up limitless new opportunities for preaching. In the twenty-first century the Dominican Sisters of Aotearoa New Zealand maintain their commitment to education as a Congregation, and several individuals are actively involved in educational ministries. The Congregation has also strengthened its commitment to issues of social justice and ecological sustainability. Some sisters have developed ministries focused on pastoral care and spirituality; others have followed their creative gifts, using painting, poetry and music to explore and express their relationships with each other, their place in the world and their search for God. Each sister's ministry is uniquely individualised, but they are connected by strong underlying themes. As the Congregation ages and declines, preaching remains a primary priority – it is their spiritual patrimony and their living legacy.

Responding to local conditions in early thirteenth-century Spain and France, St Dominic established an order of preachers to combat the gnostic Cathar heresy that was threatening the Catholic Church. Officially approved in 1216, the Order of Preachers is most commonly referred to as the Dominican Order, although friars and sisters still identify themselves with the letters OP (Order of Preachers or *Ordo Praedicatorum*). The early Dominicans followed the model of the apostles, travelling among the people and preaching the Gospel in the vernacular. Their monasteries were conceived as a vital part of the order's preaching function – centres of prayer, study and contemplation which stood in themselves as witness to their members' religious commitment and provided the spiritual base and support for active engagement with the world.

The Irish Dominican women who travelled out to New Zealand in 1871 were direct descendants of Dominic and his band of itinerant preachers. So [illegible] and cultural constraints kept them largely confined to the cloister, but their identity as preachers impelled them to mission in the farthest corners of the earth, and informed and inspired their work as teachers in Catholic schools. In the mid-twentieth century the New Zealand Dominican sisters lived a highly structured religious life that was often harsh in the severity and strictness of its rule. They still wore medieval robes and followed a medieval horarium. They continued to minister to the children they taught in schools, but the spirit of Dominican preaching had gradually been subordinated to the structures of religious observance.

With roots planted deep in contemplative spirituality, the New Zealand Congregation of Dominican Sisters responded to the promptings of the Second Vatican Council with immediate attention to their lifestyle and their mission in the modern world. Spurred on by feminist discourse and influenced by the ecumenical movement, indigenous rights protests and an evolving environmental consciousness, they reclaimed their preaching purpose.

In July 1961, not long before the Council was convened, Prioress General Mother Mary David Stark addressed the Congregation on the Dominican preaching legacy. Her reference to modern heresies harks directly to the order's original purpose. Her model of preaching infuses every action with a holy purpose, but in this context it also highlights the limits on religious women at the cusp of the Council. Mother David emphasised the significance of preaching by action, because preaching with words (except in the classroom) was not an option for religious women in the 1960s.

> *Our 'preaching', since it is by action, can make a far deeper and more lasting impression on the world than any or all the sermons preached in a great cathedral ... Only thus, by living our lives as St Dominic would have us his children live them, can we hope to save the world from the heresies that are in our midst and especially from Communism that has in its clutches so many countries and peoples.*[3]

In the immediate wake of the Second Vatican Council the New Zealand Dominicans focused their response on revising their Constitutions and updating the Congregation's lifestyle. They continued to understand their mission as a corporate witness to religious commitment. In 1979 Mother Mary Jordan McCormack considered the role of religious in the modern world. 'At the vital centre of the Church at one with and committed to mankind's hopes and problems, they afford a reminder by their vowed life, that the following of Jesus is the foremost priority.'[4] Mother Jordan believed that this reminder 'should be not in words but in living'. 'The religious community should be not only a Christian community of believers, but a community whose heart is the exemplar of Christian faith lived in the religious, as Jesus lived His Father's life among His disciples.'[5]

In the 1980s the New Zealand Dominicans began moving out of their convents and, at the same time, into new ministries. As a group they continued to witness collectively to religious ideals, but as individuals they gradually developed more independent living arrangements and careers. Along with many other congregations of women religious they abandoned the uniformity of their pre-Vatican II lives for the freedom to respond, as St Dominic had, to local need and the Spirit's lead.

By 1986 the New Zealand Dominicans were working not only in schools but in adult education, chaplaincy, pastoral roles and spirituality. Sister Margaret Quinn reflected on the sisters' breadth of apostolic engagement: 'I find the degree and variety of activity quite overwhelming and appreciate the generosity of time and energy involved.' Referring to

S Helen Bergin reading while an interpreter signs below at the 800th Jubilee of Dominican life celebrated in St Benedict's Church, Auckland, 2006. P10/16/12, DA.

Evangelii Nuntiandi, Pope Paul VI's exhortation on evangelisation in the modern world, Sister Margaret observed that the New Zealand Dominicans were deeply involved in the process of 'bringing Good News into all the strata of humanity and through its influence transforming humanity'.[6]

The diversification of ministry sprang from and reinforced a shared understanding of preaching as the Congregation's fundamental purpose. It mirrored changes occurring in Dominican congregations around the world. In an era of ever-increasing mobility and communication, sisters from New Zealand, Africa, the United States and Europe shared ideas, experiences and resources as they laid collective claim to their identity and power as preachers. In the words of Mary Ann Wiesemann-Mills, a Dominican sister from Ohio: 'As a Dominican woman, I have discovered I am a Somebody. I am a preacher! I am a living word of praise as is every member of the Dominican family.'[7]

In 2003 the General Chapter of the New Zealand Dominican Sisters articulated a mission statement centred on preaching:

> *As women of faith, committed to prayer together in community, we are called to live the Gospel.*
>
> *We are preachers of the Word.*
>
> *We understand that this commits us to uncertainty and risk.*
>
> *We support and trust one another in all that we are doing and in the directions we may yet take.*

We see our commitment and planning less in terms of specific works and institutions than in our individual and collective response to the call we are hearing today.

The Congregation makes a deliberate choice to stand with the poor and oppressed and to work for justice.

As a group of Dominican women in this country, we recognise that to do justice we must face the truth that we belong to a colonizing people, and are called to address in ourselves, our Church and our society, the basic injustice that deprives Māori people of their rights.

We honour the way our sisters have stood with the poor and worked for justice in the past, and build on that in responding to the needs of this time and place.

We recognise that it will be necessary to continue to develop a new understanding of our world in the light of justice.

There are many ways of responding according to the gifts of each person and each community.

We support and encourage the diverse expressions this response takes, whether this be in new initiatives or in a new understanding of existing works.

We will express this commitment to ministry from the basis of our educational tradition.[8]

The theme of the 2006–07 Chapter was 'Dominicans: A Family of Preachers'. The sisters, along with Dominican friars, Dominican laity and others who identified as part of the wider Dominican family, explored preaching as 'the place where the scriptures enter into the world – where truth enters into the world'. The Leadership Team called the Congregation to claim the right to preach as daughters of Dominic – to 'seize every opportunity for preaching'. 'Let us live as communities of holy preaching, in contemplative silence, in community and in mission … We are called to listen to reality – our own and society's – and to respond with joy, pain, love and God-given freedom.'[9]

In preparation for the 2011 General Chapter the mission formation committee articulated a succinct statement of congregational identity in the twenty-first century: 'We are preachers and teachers, God seekers and hope-makers.'[10]

Social justice

For the New Zealand Dominican sisters, listening to society's reality and responding to the needs of the modern world in the spirit of Vatican II has led to an increasing focus on issues of social justice. The Congregation has made a deliberate decision to stand with the poor and oppressed and to work for peace and justice.

As ever, the Dominican commitment to justice is grounded in prayer and study. Helen Bergin is a Dominican academic whose research has focused on the Belgian Dominican priest Edward Schillebeeckx and the development of his theology of liberation. For Schillebeeckx, writes Helen, 'God is continually offering liberation'. 'This God has self-identified with injustice through the Son's solidarity with victims. This God continues to identify with suffering through the Spirit's activity in the Christian community.'[11] Helen teaches theology at the University of Auckland and in her research and writing she continues to explore the Christian search for truth as a path to liberation.

Margaret Quinn was prioress general in the late 1970s and early 1980s when the Congregation clarified and articulated its commitment to social justice. After finishing her role in active leadership she established a ministry in Christchurch, standing alongside those in need in her local community. Over 25 years in the eastern suburb of Linwood she volunteered for Women's Refuge, worked with teenage mothers and intellectually disabled people, helped at the Linwood Community House and maintained a prayerful Dominican presence in her neighbourhood. She saw her ministry as part of St Dominic's call: 'What would Dominic be doing if he were here today?' For Margaret, 'it's not just the truth of what religion is, it's the truth of what we should be living in the world, and the importance of justice in the world … that's what we should be doing – looking at the justice system and seeing what we can do to change that, change the world really …'[12] Margaret's deep sense of justice stems from her Dominican grounding in study and prayer.

> *To work for justice I think is important. Justice comes really from the person whom you are yourself. So you've got to look at your own life … justice in your own life. And that must come from a deep study, of prayer and contemplation. But it's not just for yourself, it's for what you're able to give to other people, from the person that you are.*

Joan Hardiman was 16 years old when she joined the Dominicans in 1954. Like others of her generation she worked for several decades as a Dominican teacher before moving into other fields. After several years in Vanuatu in the 1980s she became increasingly involved in issues of social justice. She spent a year in Brussels working in the office of Pax Christi International, where she focused particularly on the troubles in East Timor. As a member of the New Zealand Council of Christian Social Services she has been involved in calling politicians to account on the growing gap between rich and poor in Aotearoa New Zealand. She has done volunteer work for the Tenants Protection Association in Auckland, providing support to disempowered and underprivileged tenants, and she is a volunteer visitor at Wiri women's prison.[13]

Jacqui Ryan and Elizabeth Mackie have both focused their vision on international issues of peace and justice in their work with Christian World Service (CWS). Elizabeth spent 21 years with CWS, which functions as the development, aid and justice agency of the New Zealand churches. She worked on an ecumenical basis to provide humanitarian relief and support struggling communities in many parts of the world, particularly in Asia and the Pacific. When Elizabeth and Margaret shifted from Christchurch in 2011 a lawyer colleague expressed amazement that there had been only two Dominican sisters living in the city – 'My God. You feel like a hundred!' Elizabeth's passion for truth and justice continues to drive her forward: 'I want to be one of the two that feels like we are a hundred until there are no more of us.'[14]

Jacqui Ryan came from a Catholic family with a high level of social awareness and political involvement. The Dominican commitment to social justice was a natural fit, but her time in the novitiate, when she was not allowed to talk or read about politics, was extremely difficult. Jacqui worked as a commercial teacher in secondary schools in the 1980s before spending several years in chaplaincy – in schools, workplaces and at Auckland's Mercy Hospital. After a sabbatical at the Dominican Spirituality Center at Long Island, New York, she returned to New Zealand to work as an education fieldworker with CWS in an itinerant role, promoting a greater understanding of the work of CWS in local parishes often by preaching from the pulpit. She has preached hundreds of times in various churches – Anglican, Presbyterian, Methodist and others – but tellingly, as she notes, only once in a Catholic church. Social justice remains her motivating passion. Dominican values of truth, peace and justice dominate her work, her relationships and her life in community as a Dominican sister.

> *We have to strive to see things differently from the way society necessarily sees them. Because that's what we are, we're supposed to be a counter-witness to all the things that society takes for granted – wealth, pleasure, sensualness – all that kind of thing. Showing that there's a life that can point to more than that – not necessarily better than, but it can be more than …*[15]

As a group, the New Zealand Congregation of Dominican Sisters has taken a proactive stance in support of Treaty of Waitangi principles and justice for Māori. Based as they were in Otago and Southland, the early Dominican sisters had very little contact with Māori, and even until the 1970s there were not many Māori students in their schools. The sisters were, however, increasingly aware of the impact of colonisation on Māori social, cultural, political and economic aspirations. At the Congregation's eighth General Chapter from December 1974 to January 1975 the sisters committed to investigate 'practical ways of extending the apostolate to working among the Maori and Polynesian peoples'. They also pledged financial assistance for Māori education.[16] From this time onwards they engaged with Māori issues: they held seminars, devoted personal study time to racial issues, discussed biculturalism in communities and set aside a portion of congregational income for Māori groups.

The Dominicans remain committed to seeking out opportunities for increasing their understanding of issues around biculturalism and asserting their collective voice in support of Māori rights. Susan Healy, who was professed as a Dominican sister in 1967 and dispensed from her vows in 2000, maintains an ongoing connection with the Congregation as part of the wider Dominican Family. In 2010 she and Elizabeth Mackie led workshops in Auckland, Palmerston North and Dunedin, examining Treaty of Waitangi concepts through the lens of the Dominican charism.

Judith Robinson has a family connection with Ngāti Porou through her brother-in-law. Through her family, and through her students at St Dominic's School for the Deaf in Feilding and St Joseph's in Invercargill, she became increasingly immersed in Māori culture during the 1980s. As principal at St Joseph's she was involved with several different Māori groups who used the school buildings. St Joseph's eventually employed a teacher who was bilingual in Māori and English, and it later established a full Māori language immersion class. Judith does not attend mainstream church; she has found a supportive faith community at Toimairangi marae, where a priest takes the service every first and third Sunday of the month. Judith serves as kaikaranga, making the ceremonial call to visitors on the marae. She sees her role as 'both an honour and challenge', and a means of 'gently keeping alive indigenous hospitality and practice'.[17]

In 2014 the Dominican Family Mission and Justice Group sent letters to the leaders of all political parties encouraging them to replace Guy Fawkes Day with Parihaka Day in commemoration of 5 November 1881 when government troops marched on Parihaka marae, which had become a centre for peaceful resistance to Pākehā land purchases in Taranaki. The committee also commissioned a PhD student to compile a short piece about Parihaka for the Dominican Family website.[18]

The Dominican sisters have honoured their commitment to the Treaty through their use of te reo Māori, too. The mission formation committee has worked with Rangi Davis, a lecturer in Māori spirituality, to translate some traditional Dominican

Dominican sisters at the Hikoi of Hope, 1999. P9/16/1, DA.

hymns and prayers into Māori. Together they produced a small book of simple waiata and karakia that could be sung and prayed together in communities and regions.[19]

Wherever possible the Congregation provides financial support for Māori groups. In 1992, for example, they gave $5000 to St Joseph's School in Invercargill for their bilingual unit, and $5000 to the Maori Pastoral Care Team to be used for the religious formation of Māori women. The Dominicans are committed to supporting other peace and justice initiatives, too; they donate regularly to CWS, Caritas, the St Vincent de Paul Society and Pax Christi and contribute to disaster relief funds and other causes. The Congregation's commitment to social justice is grounded in study and contemplation, and expressed through ecumenical connections. Dominican sisters work with a range of Christian, interfaith and secular groups, both locally and internationally. As a Congregation they are open and willing 'to respond to new needs, to discover new talents and to do whatever we can'.[20]

Ecology

The Dominican sisters' commitment to protecting the earth is a natural extension of their involvement in issues of social justice. In the late twentieth century they responded to the increasing awareness of environmental issues in wider society. As a Congregation they have committed themselves to protecting the earth as a matter of natural justice.

Cecily Sheehy and Judith Robinson have been particularly involved in sharing the insights of creation-centred spirituality with the wider congregation. The creation spirituality movement recognises the universe as a blessing; acknowledging God as both immanent and transcendent, its proponents assert the imperative of ecological justice in order to protect the earth for future generations.

Korimako Farm is a Dominican initiative in Invercargill. Established in 1999 by Judith Robinson with support from Sister Dominic Swindale, it is an ecology and spirituality centre set on a two-hectare farmlet. It is conceived as 'a place of hope where care for the earth and its inhabitants is honoured'.[21] Judith runs workshops on permaculture and organic gardening and makes Korimako available to those wanting time out from their busy lives. The centre responds to the needs of the surrounding community: it hosts creation spirituality and Māori spirituality groups, runs retreats for students and seminars for teachers, and offers locals the opportunity to take part in the community gardens. Korimako incorporates a peace garden for quiet reflection, a harmony sanctuary, a food forest and community gardens. A 'cosmic walk' provides a space for children and adults to take a meditative journey through the story of the evolving universe, where they can 'recognise the sacred, diverse, interconnectedness in the universe story, earth story and our place as kaitiaki (guardians) of our precious planet'.[22] Korimako is a base for Judith's involvement in a range of other eco-justice projects, including biodynamic farming, organic farming and permaculture. She is also a member of Transition Towns Invercargill, a group interested in increasing local communities' resilience to the challenges and opportunities of peak oil, climate change and economic uncertainty. She has been instrumental in spreading the Earth Charter through New Zealand – an ethical framework for addressing environmental protection, human rights and peace as interdependent and indivisible issues. 'I can't change the world,' she says, 'but I can live in my little corner of the bio-region … be a responsible guardian.'[23]

The New Zealand Dominicans are proactively committed to care of the earth: they support Korimako, commit to ethically sound and environmentally conscious investments and seek new ways to honour and protect the environment. 'Care of the earth has become an urgent question within the Congregation as in the wider community. Several sisters are guiding us through this period of education, showing initiative and patience as they help us raise our awareness.' Working with other interfaith and multicultural groups engaged in ecological issues, the sisters acknowledge that although they have much to offer, they have even more to learn.[24]

Pastoral care

Pastoral care has always been a significant ministry within the New Zealand Dominican Congregation as sisters have cared for and supported each other through illness, ageing and death. In the 1930s the sisters in Invercargill and other smaller convents where there were no 'visiting sisters' were dispensed from enclosure for the purpose of visiting the local hospitals.[25] In the wake of Vatican II some sisters moved into ministries of pastoral care in the wider community. Some have worked in local parishes,

Students from St Thomas Aquinas Primary School on the Cosmic Walk in the sanctuary at Korimako, 2014. Private collection.

providing care for church members in need and a prayerful presence in the local community.

By the 1990s there was no parish priest at St Mary's Star of the Sea in Bluff, so Margaret Butler ran the parish.[26] Nola Gleeson lives just across the road from the Catholic basilica in Oamaru. Before Mass each morning she meets with a group of others from the parish to say the prayer of the day together. She is very involved with the St Vincent de Paul Society and spends much of her time in pastoral work, visiting the sick and elderly in the parish and taking communion to those who cannot get to Mass. People are always asking her for prayer – 'that's what I can give … they know they can talk to me'[27]

Maureen Connolly works as a parish assistant in a multicultural parish in Auckland. She has made strong connections with parishioners from different backgrounds, including refugees, asylum seekers and new immigrants, all striving to make a new life for themselves in New Zealand. 'Their stories and their obvious faith and trust in God made a deep impression on me, taking me to a new level of consciousness of the working of the Spirit in our lives and the power of the Spirit to heal and transform.'[28] Maureen has been involved in a range of projects to support people in need in the parish: she has propagated plants to sell at affordable prices, with the proceeds going back into school uniforms; she has taken part in a knitting group that produces affordable warm children's clothing; and she has been involved in a Young People's Choir that gives children and their families a sense of belonging in the parish and an opportunity to build confidence in participating in the liturgy. She brings a contemplative approach to her practical work:

> *In the midst of all the form-filling, constant dealing with government departments, house-hunting, plants, knitting and 'emergencies' I try to keep in mind our diverse cultures and traditions, rooted in our common humanity, knowing that if we open ourselves to the gift of conversion from the Spirit of the Creator and Redeemer of us all, the face of the earth will be renewed.*[29]

Paddy McCann has been very involved in caring for the Congregation's sick and elderly sisters. It is a ministry that is grounded in her morning prayer time. On Ash Wednesday 2011 Paddy wanted to be at Mass, but instead found herself waiting in Accident and Emergency at Dunedin Hospital with Sister Louise. At the end of the day Paddy said to Louise, 'We're eucharist for each other here: you're my daily bread and I'm yours.'[30]

In the 1980s more sisters moved into chaplaincy positions in tertiary education and, not long afterwards, into hospital chaplaincy. Brenda Fitzgerald had trained and worked as a nurse before she joined the Dominicans as a 'late vocation' and began a new career as a teacher. After nearly 20 years teaching new entrants she travelled to Sydney in 1980 for a spiritual renewal course and returned to take up a position as Catholic chaplain at Auckland Children's Hospital alongside Father Ambrose Loughnan. The position was totally outside Dominican tradition but Father Ambrose persuaded the Leadership Council of its merit, and Brenda loved her return to hospital work. When the old hospital was demolished Brenda became chaplain at the new Starship Children's Hospital. At times she struggled with the limits imposed on her role by the Catholic hierarchy, but she felt she was very much supported by her Dominican sisters and by the other Christian chaplains at the hospital. She developed her own rule of thumb: 'If Jesus was here, what would he do?' After a year in retirement, Brenda returned to Starship in the late 1990s as a 'hospital grandma'. She spent the next few years as a volunteer, providing a comforting presence for children undergoing treatment in hospital, and ongoing care and support for their families.[31]

Bernie Cheyne also served as a hospital chaplain, working at North Shore Hospital from 2001 until 2009 and then at the North Shore Hospice until 2014. Bernie saw herself as 'a companion' on the journey, supporting patients in any way she could, helping them to come to terms with their fears and giving them hope.

> *I never ask a patient what religion they are. That is immaterial. The kinds of questions I ask are, 'Are you at peace?', or 'Is there anything I can do to help you get through this day?' ... I'm not a medic. I'm a chaplain and while doctors and nurses care for patients' physical needs, I have*

the privilege of caring for their spiritual needs. The work I do here is very gentle. I am here to support not only patients and their families, but also staff and volunteers. I've learnt that every person is different, but that everyone responds to a compassionate presence.[32]

When Bernie left the hospice in 2014, Jacqui Ryan took over her position, continuing a Dominican ministry in end of life care.

Sandra Winton works as a psychotherapist. After teaching in Dominican schools in the late 1960s and 70s she took up tertiary chaplaincy at the University of Otago in the 1980s. In 1990 she began working as a therapist at Dunedin Catholic Social Services, and completed several psychotherapy diplomas while she worked. In 2002 she established her own private practice, offering psychotherapy for children and adults in the Dunedin community. One morning a week she works at the prison, offering psychotherapy services for inmates. 'To walk alongside people as they move through very important times in their lives, to be part of their finding healing and often liberation is a privilege and a blessing,' she says. Her Dominican family provides her with support: 'When the work is difficult or I feel discouraged I feel sustained by the Congregation's mission commitment and by my community.'[33]

Though they have moved into new fields of pastoral care, the Dominican sisters also continue to exercise a ministerial compassion in their relationships with each other, taking time and care to honour the oldest among them and to walk beside those at the end of their life with patient tenderness and love.

Spirituality

In many ways, ministries of pastoral care overlap with ministries focused on spirituality. Spiritual direction and prayerful ministries of presence and companionship have their roots in the spiritual formation processes of the novitiate, and the spiritual guidance Dominican teachers gave their school pupils.

In the early 1990s when the Leadership Team considered withdrawing from Milton, the locals pleaded with the Dominicans to stay; the sisters were no longer teaching in the local parish school but the community and the parish priest valued their presence in the neighbourhood. Members of the parish appreciated the sisters' house as 'a place of welcome and comfort … where they can drop in to the kitchen for a cup of tea and talk, and feel AT HOME.'[34] Lorraine Challis maintained an ongoing Dominican presence in Milton in the late 1990s. She offered one-to-one spiritual direction, personal accompaniment and retreats, supporting people on their journeys of personal and spiritual growth.[35]

Retired sisters living in the community and in rest homes are committed to a prayerful way of life reflecting Dominican values. In 2011 Sister Mary Gertrude lived in Calvary Residential Home in Invercargill. Prayer has always been her 'great love'. 'I feel my vocation is as it always has been: it's been a personal relationship between God and myself, and that you can take with you anywhere …'[36] For her the rest home was a mission field, and despite restricted mobility she looked further into the community: she volunteered for many years as a phone operator for Lifeline.

Sister Judith Anne O'Sullivan trained as a spiritual director at the Dominican International House of Studies in Rome. After several years working there she returned to New Zealand in 1984 to run retreats

Anne O'Neill and Barbara Dwyer, New Zealand Dominican sisters living in Dublin, October 2011.
Author's collection.

at Teschemakers. As well as formally structured, guided liturgical retreats, Teschemakers provided a relaxed space where people could be part of a praying community and have time 'to "BE" or to share and receive assurance about their relationship with the Lord'.[37] For Judith Anne herself, running the retreats and providing spiritual direction at Teschemakers was a source of 'inspiration, challenge, stimulation, awe and above all gratitude for the privilege of witnessing what God is doing in the lives of so many'.[38] She has also worked in an ecumenical setting, offering spiritual direction at Still Point Women's Centre in Palmerston North in the 1990s. In 2008 her vision for a Dominican family community came to life in Scotland Street, Dunedin, where she continues to base her ministry.

Creativity

For some sisters, Dominican spirituality finds expression in creative form. Art and music have always been valued in the Dominican school curriculum, not only as markers of cultural sophistication but, more fundamentally, for their ability to touch the soul – to provide a means and focus for contemplation and a form for expressing the fruits of contemplation.

The New Zealand Dominicans take pride in their sisters' artistic accomplishments. The congregational archives include a significant collection of sacred and secular embroidery and lacework, including Sister Aloysius Moylan's needlework. The large stations of the cross at Teschemakers were painted by Sister Mary St Peter Slattery, Sister Mary Paul Lyons, Sister Mary Raphael Martin and Sister Mary Philomena McCarthy. Sister Mary Dominic Swindale designed the stained glass windows in St Catherine's Chapel in Invercargill.

Mary Horn continues a long tradition of Dominican artists who have shared their truth and preached through paint.[39] She is a self-taught artist whose work is grounded in her local Oamaru community and the surrounding environment; her subjects are often local women and local scenes. Mary's art – and her writing, which often accompanies her drawings and paintings – is contemplative in nature, 'a still wilderness where God's I am and my I am are one'.[40] It is also profoundly political, as discussed in previous chapters: 'We desire in our time to hear a WORD SPOKEN in HOPE, but we long for more than a spoken word, we look for a WORD of ACTION.'[41] Ultimately, Mary's art is a quest for truth.

Like Mary, Margaret Butler also worked for many years in Dominican schools, and it is only in recent years that she has found the time and space to develop her gift for writing.[42] Margaret prays and preaches with the Bible in one hand and the newspaper in the other: 'My understanding of the gospels is enriched

Needlework by Sister Mary Aloysius Moylan. Moylan Collection, DA.

Liturgy of closure of St Catherine's Convent, 12 December 2004. S Frances Scully and SM Gertrude Fox in the foreground, with Bishop Colin Campbell sitting to the right. The abstract stained glass windows in St Catherine's chapel were designed by SM Dominic Swindale.
F3A/10, DA.

Music and lyrics by Cecily Sheehy, from 'Beautiful Blue-Green Planet and other songs of cosmic connection', 1992, DA.

Mary Horn.
Love Songs for the Land.
Private collection.

by my reflection of the events around me, and my understanding of the events is definitely enriched by praying about them in the light of the gospels.'[43] Her writing entwines personal, local and international concerns with an underlying Dominican spirituality. In 2011 she reflected on recent earthquakes in Christchurch and Japan through a Christian framework that acknowledges tragedy and grief and offers hope for the future:

On a Friday
the earth moved
On the Sunday
the stone was rolled back
This Easter we remember
those whose earth moved
in Christchurch and Japan
We find the risen Christ
in the love of one another
in the truth we share
in the compassion we offer and receive
in the darkness and uncertainty of Good Friday
and in the new life of Easter[44]

Cecily Sheehy expresses her Dominican spirituality through music. She came from a musical family and enjoyed teaching music and leading choirs in Dominican schools. Since moving out of classroom teaching she has followed a creative path: she has trained in therapeutic massage, studied and taught creation spirituality, and gives private music lessons. She is also a prolific composer: her lyrics confront issues of social and environmental justice, set to melodies that invite a heartfelt response. Cecily's songs continue the tradition of sung Dominican praise in New Zealand: they are a means of connecting with the Congregation's mystical legacy – searching for truth, sharing the fruits of contemplation, 'trying to make sense of life given – to see, touch and probe a little of the immense mystery of our experience'.[45]

The word

New Zealand Dominicans preach with the creative word in poetry and song and with the spoken word from the pulpit, the assertive word in letters to government, the reflective word in personal writing and the scholarly word in academic theses and publications. The lines between all of these are well and truly blurred. As Dominicans they are committed to speaking truth, writing truth and providing space for others to share truth.

The Second Vatican Council opened up the world to religious women, but the Catholic hierarchy has continued to exclude them from ordination. Modern theology understands preaching as a sharing of Gospel truth through innumerable vehicles and means, but the traditional platform for preaching – in a homily addressed to the congregation from the pulpit at Mass – is still a sanctified male preserve. Since the 1970s the New Zealand Dominicans have preached in a range of settings – at seminars, adult education classes, workshops, retreats and scripture groups. In 1998 Sister Judith Anne and Mary Eastham preached a shared homily on Mary and Martha in the Palmerston North Cathedral. Sister Susie Logan was part of the Sophia group, which helped the two women research and prepare for the homily and supported them in prayer. Susie shared her excitement in a letter to Brenda Fitzgerald:

> *On the altar they were so good. After both Masses the individual response was humbling. Older women said they had waited a lifetime to hear what they heard. We are hoping for fairly regular opportunities to preach, and have set a good method of procedure. There was the involvement of so many people. So while Rome says we are outside the church if we think women can be ordained, here in this little neck of the woods we may be making some progress towards another form of being OP, the one that for ever the men have had for their own.*[46]

LEFT: S Margaret Butler with her great-nephew Duncan McPhail at the launch of *Living in the Planet Earth*, edited by Neil Darragh. Margaret contributed a chapter entitled 'Korimako Dominican Ecology Centre: A venture in Southland'. Sacred Heart Cathedral, 17 April 2016. Private collection.

BELOW: S Sandra Winton, S Cecily Sheehy and Barbara Menzies singing together at the 2006 regathering of Dominican sisters. DA.

S Joan Hardiman preaching at St Benedict's Church at the 800th Jubilee, 2006. P10/16/10, DA.

In her late seventies, Joan Hardiman proclaims the Word as a preacher in her local parish, at retreats around New Zealand and on the internet through podcasts. She is a regular contributor to word.op.org – a Dominican website that provides daily preaching based on the scripture of the day.[47]

Tui Motu is a preaching initiative shared widely throughout New Zealand. In the late 1990s the New Zealand Dominicans and the Sisters of St Joseph saw a need for an independent Catholic magazine to connect Catholics across the country, share news and views and confront the tough questions and big issues of modern life. The two congregations held consultation meetings and produced the first issue of *Tui Motu* magazine in September 1997. The Dominicans still provide funding for *Tui Motu*. Elizabeth Mackie has been on the board of directors since the magazine's inception and has served as assistant editor since 2011. Other sisters provide articles from time to time, and help secure subscribers. *Tui Motu* covers contemporary developments in theology, reflects on Church history and runs articles on modern spirituality. Each month its pages include articles from a wide range of Catholic and non-Catholic contributors, poetry, art, book and film reviews and 'a mother's journal'. The magazine has a strong commitment to addressing important issues, including suicide, sexual abuse in the Church, poverty and inequality. *Tui Motu* preaches Christian values and sends words of hope, courage and challenge into churches and homes around the country. In a 2006 article Sandra Winton reflected on *veritas*:

> *The divine may be glimpsed in moments of human connection whether in pain, anger or compassion. It flickers through our lives in times when we truly see things – beautiful, incongruous or ugly. It opens us to difference, to humility, to laughter. Eight hundred years on, the human heart thirsts for truth as much as it ever did. This desire is, I believe, God-given and invites us to fuller life.*[48]

Hope for the future

> *It seems to me that what you should be thinking is not how to close the future with definitions which you will henceforth live out, but how to keep the future completely open so that you will be able to liberate yourself and one another in an open community with the help of your love for one another.*
>
> *– Thomas Merton, quoted at the beginning of the Ninth General Chapter of New Zealand Dominican Sisters, 1980–81*[49]

At the same time as Vatican II re-energised and inspired religious congregations around the world, changing cultural conditions and demographic trends were leading to a steady decline in the number of men and women committing to vowed religious life. The New Zealand Congregation of Dominican Sisters reached peak membership in the early 1960s, after which some women left the Congregation and fewer and fewer joined.

In the 1960s declining vocations were a major cause for concern. 'Perhaps our lack of vocations is due entirely to ourselves,' suggested Mother David. 'Can we honestly say that we are living our religious lives as we should?' Mother David feared that a prevalent 'spirit of destructive criticism' as well as 'a want of loyalty' in the Congregation would certainly deter prospective applicants.[50]

In the 1970s and 80s the Congregation struggled with the challenge of contraction. Jacqui Ryan, who made her profession in 1984, was the last to join the New Zealand Congregation and is still the youngest sister. A few other young women spent time in pre-novitiate formation in the 1980s but left before making formal vows. The future for the Congregation seemed uncertain and, for some, that was frightening. Some sisters still hoped and prayed for new vocations; others grieved for a past way of life.

Prioress General Margaret Quinn urged the sisters to focus their attention on the preaching mission: 'The way of the evangelising community that cooperates with God in his plan can only be that of Abraham disposed to go where it knows not, and to hope against all hope,' she told them.[51] At the Tenth General Chapter in 1986 Margaret challenged the Congregation to face the future – 'a future in which the message of the Gospel has to compete with the developments in modern science and high technology'. She described the changes affecting the Congregation as part of 'an ongoing story'. She called on the New Zealand sisters to continue adapting, responding to changing pastoral needs and developing creative new ways to deploy their resources in a changing world. 'Our Dominican charism requires that … we be free to teach and preach TRUTH wherever and however that is possible for us.'[52]

The changes and challenges affecting the New Zealand Dominicans were not unique: Dominicans and other religious orders around the world were struggling to maintain confidence and vision as their membership shrank. Father Vincent de Couesnongle, Master General of the Dominican Order in the late 1970s and early 1980s, called for difficult decisions and necessary sacrifices as the order faced up to its declining membership: 'this must not discourage us. The history of the Order shows that reduced forces, if they are well prepared, can accomplish great things if they are judiciously chosen.'[53]

In an article published in *New Zealand Catholic Newspaper* in 2005, Carmel Walsh described the adaptations that New Zealand religious men and women have made in response to the Second Vatican Council: 'During the past 40 years religious have taken the request of the Council very seriously, sometimes in the face of stinging criticism.' She paid particular attention to the Congregation of New Zealand Dominican Sisters:

> *These religious women aged between 60 and 90 years of age have fulfilled the Vatican Council directive in a simple and wonderful way. They are renewed and they have adapted. Contemplative prayer and study of scripture nourishes their relationships with God and with other people, often in an ecumenical context. The creative ways in which the lives of these women preach and teach enthusiasm for Gospel values and love of God's people speaks to us of hope for the future.*[54]

Raewyn Clark greets S Louise Timpany, 2008. Raewyn was received as Sister Raewyn in December 1971 but left before profession in June 1972. DA.

Though New Zealand could not boast the large numbers of young men and women in formation in other parts of the world, such as the Philippines, Carmel affirmed the spirit of vowed religious in New Zealand as 'both quietly effective and inspiring'.

No sisters have been dispensed from vows for several years, but nor have any new women joined. Only a few in the Congregation still hold hope for new vocations to the same form of vowed Dominican life as they themselves live. Most believe that Dominican life will continue in New Zealand through the schools they have founded, the pupils they have taught and the Dominican Family members they preach and pray with. They recognise the possibility that their Congregation may have served its purpose and come to the end of its life: they may be the last women to minister as vowed Dominican sisters in New Zealand.

Other religious congregations around the world are also faced with declining membership. Sandra Schneiders describes the last few decades for religious women in the United States as a 'dark night', but observes an 'emerging sense of serenity'. Rather than accepting their demise with passive expectation, some congregations have chosen, in Schneiders' words, 'to die into Christ's resurrection, leaving a legacy that will somehow rise in those they have loved and served'.[55]

In 2009 the Leadership Team expressed a willingness to promote a day or a weekend for younger women interested in vowed Dominican life, but in reality they had shifted their focus to the continuation of the Dominican charism in New Zealand through Dominican laity and Dominican family. Looking to the future, the team conceived a vision for the way the New Zealand Congregation of

Dominican Sisters might function in coming years.

> *Every house is open to others for prayer and scripture study and many people join us regularly in silence, study and hospitality. We preach in all the ways available to us, including online. We teach and study. We arrange opportunities for others to experience retreats, experiences of contemplative prayer, scripture and theology and we commit significant resources to this. We keep our eyes on the big picture and are socially, politically and culturally involved. We are wide open to the whole world in our awareness, analysis and prayer. We take care of one another and we are good neighbours. There are strong local mission and justice groups wherever the Dominican family is present, with younger lay Dominicans taking very active roles. We are well connected with people of other Christian denominations and with people of other faiths. We are ageing OP women, sharing our lives, our hopes and our dreams. We are full of hope and joy and we still have great vision. We are wise women, giving evidence of God's presence in our lives and communities.*[56]

The sisters are conscious of just how uncertain the future is for their Congregation, but they 'have ceased to fret and agonise over details'. They 'love one another trustingly', and walk forward together.

In 2014, as the Congregation prepared for its seventeenth General Chapter, the Leadership Team considered the main concerns facing their sisters: security, ageing, declining health and mobility, diminishing numbers, isolation, balancing individual needs with the needs of the community, changing roles and expectations, and the need to engage in ongoing dialogue around the 'hard questions' and 'underlying issues' facing the Congregation. The team believed that the time had come to start a discussion about the long-term future of the Congregation's financial assets. 'What will be our legacy? To whom shall we give it so that our charism of preaching the Good News will continue?'[57] Despite so many uncertainties as they move into the unknown, the sisters face the future with hope. 'We want to reach out in mission in a rapidly changing country, finding a new way of being Dominican in this country in the twenty-first century, open to those who may wish to join us or to form new ways of being Dominican.'

S Mary Anna Baird and S Elizabeth Mackie at the Federation of Dominican Sisters in Oceania, 5 March 2014. Author's collection.

This focus on preparing for the future is not only a venture of faith, but also a continuation of the process of radical transformation begun in the 1960s. The Second Vatican Council was a dramatic turning point for the New Zealand Dominican Sisters, propelling them out of their large convents, out of the constraints of their traditional identity as teachers, out of their black and white habits, and out of the confines imposed by their monastic timetable. Living by themselves and in small communities situated in urban neighbourhoods, the sisters of today con-

S Margaret Quinn, S Judith Anne O'Sullivan and S Carmel Walsh at the Federation of Dominican Sisters in Oceania, 9 March 2014. Author's Collection.

tinue the work of Vatican II, caring for one another in community and responding to the needs they see around them in New Zealand society.

Ngā Whaea Arahi Rongo Pai, the Dominican Sisters of Aotearoa New Zealand, continue to preach truth through ministries of social justice, ecology, art, music, teaching, spiritual guidance and pastoral care. Their most profound preaching is perhaps in the example they provide of a community of women who are committed to living in a countercultural Christian way. They live together as sisters, and stand together on behalf of those in need. Although the Dominican women of today live radically different lives from the 10 Irish women who travelled out to New Zealand in 1871, they are firmly committed to the same Dominican call to praise, to bless and to preach.

The Chapter Call composed at the end of the seventeenth General Chapter of 2014–15 is at once a strong statement of shared identity and an expression of inspiration; both a requiem hymn and a song of hope.

In this time when we are fewer and older
we have unexpectedly found ourselves called to hope.

We have opened ourselves to an invitation to see our lives
as part of the ongoing mystery of the evolving universe
and to place ourselves on the side of its life and protection.

We choose to be part of a turning towards life,
a future we will not see but for which we sow seeds …

We draw on and reaffirm our commitment

to justice, the poor, te tiriti, to women and small Pacific nations,
joined with humanity to cherish our one small planet
and to be part of the turning that will preserve its life
for all beings of land, sea and air …

We treasure the Dominican life we have been given,
which we have expressed in different ways through the years,
and which calls us again today.
Living true to this calling will be the legacy we leave.

Like our ancestors … we too set sail for a land that is both home,
the deep place of our soul, contemplative and compassionate,
and at the same time full of the unknown.
We walk in hope, we walk in truth, we walk together.[58]

Members of the 17th General Chapter of New Zealand Dominican Sisters, Auckland, 2014/2015

Fourth row: S Cecily Sheehy, S Mary Anna Baird, S Jan Ogilvy, S Margaret Butler, S Carmel Walsh, Ann Hayes (secretary), S Judith Anne O'Sullivan, S Judith Robinson.

Third row: Anne Lythgoe (assistant presenter), S Mary Horn, S Maureen O'Hanlon, S Susan Logan, S Frances Lister, S Lorraine Challis, S Raewyn Benzie, S Genevieve O'Rouke, Margaret Mayce (presenter), S Anne Lan[illegible] PBVM (facilitator).

Second row: S Joan Hardiman, S Helen Bergin, S Patricia Hannan, S Maureen Connolly, S Judith McGinley, S Leonie Parry.

Front row: S Roxane Parkinson, S Joan Bennett, S Margaret Fahey, S Jacqui Ryan, S Marie Twomey, S Nola Gleeson, S Madeleine McAleese.

Absent: S Elizabeth Mackie, S Paddy McCann, S Sandra Winton, S Bernie Cheyne, S Dominic Sw[illegible]ale, S Columba McHugh, Angela McMorran (secretary).

Unable to attend Chapter: S Noreen Murphy, S Cecelia Kennedy, S Marie Eugene Nicolson, S Gertrude F[illegible], S Margaret Quinn, S Molly Griffin, S Adrienne White, S Mary Thomas Dunn, S Loreto Meehan, S Anne O'Neill, S Barbara Dwyer. DA.

Dominican sisters singing in the chapel at St Dominic's Priory, 9 March 2014. Author's collection.

Appendix 1: Timeline

1170 Dominic Guzmán born in Spain

1206 Twelve women form religious community at Prouille under Dominic's spiritual direction

1216 Papal approval of the Order of Preachers

1500s First records of Dominican women in Ireland

1539 Suppression of the monasteries under Henry VIII

1814 25 December: first Christian service in New Zealand, led by Anglican missionary Samuel Marsden

1829 Catholic Emancipation Act

1838 10 January: Bishop Pompallier arrives at Hokianga harbour and celebrates the first Catholic Mass in New Zealand on 13 January

1840 6 February: Treaty of Waitangi signed

St Catherine's Dominican Convent established in Sion Hill, Dublin (transferred from Mount Street, the first foundation from the Cabra Dominican Sisters in 1836)

1869 8 December: Opening of First Vatican Council (adjourned 20 October 1870)

1870 9 October: 10 Dominican sisters from St Catherine's Convent, Sion Hill depart from Dublin for New Zealand

1871 18 February: The Irish sisters land at Port Chalmers

20 February: The sisters take charge of Catholic girls' primary school

27 February: The sisters open a girls' high school for day pupils

1876 August: Excavations begin for foundations of new convent

1877 Fierce denominational debate over the introduction of the New Zealand Education Act, which establishes a national system of free education in which state-funded schools must provide secular education

7 October: The sisters move into the newly erected St Dominic's Priory (community moves out 1982, Priory sold 1983)

1882 January: St Catherine's Convent established at Invercargill (closed 2005)

September: Rosary convent established at Oamaru (closed 1992)

1882 February: Our Lady of the Sacred Heart Convent established at Queenstown (closed 2001)

1886 14 February: Official opening of St Joseph's Cathedral, Dunedin

28 April: Mother Gabriel departs from Dunedin to set up Irish novitiate at Beaumont, returning to New Zealand in January 188[illegible]

1890 5 October: Official opening of St Dominic's College (convent boarding school attached to St Dominic's Priory)

1891 January: Our Lady of Perpetual Succour Convent established at Milton (closed [illegible])

1893 February: St Gabriel's Convent established at Lawrence (closed 1985)

December: First General Chapter of Dominican Sisters in New Zealand

1899 24 April: Mother Gabriel leads a group of Dunedin sisters to establish a Dominican convent in Grenough, West Australia

St Joseph's Convent established at Cromwell (closed 1969)

1900 St Teresa's Convent established at Bluff (closed 1969)

1902 West Australian foundation becomes independent

1903 Santa Sabina Convent established at North East Valley (the sisters established a school in North East Valley in 1895 and travelled out each day from the Priory) (closed [illegible])

1912 24 March: St Patrick's Convent established at Teschemakers (closed 1996)

1922 April: St Mary's Convent established at Kaikorai (closed 1971)

1932 January: St Dominic's Convent established at Helensville (closed 1970)

1933 January: St Dominic's Convent established at Northcote (closed 1967)

21 April: Promulgation as a Pontifical Institute: papal recognition of New Zealand houses as a separate congregation, Constitutions of New Zealand Dominican Sisters granted, Divine Office granted

1939 27 August: St Albert's Convent established in North Invercargill (closed 1987)

1944 St Bertrand's Convent established in Invercargill (closed 1988)

5 March: Dominican Convent and St Dominic's School for the Deaf opened at Island Bay

1946 Dominican Hall opened in Dunedin as a hostel for women students at Otago University and Dunedin Training College (closed 1978)

1949 Dominican fathers made foundations in Auckland and Dunedin

1951 Dominican sisters began attending lectures at Otago University

1953 Dominican School for the Deaf moved to Feilding

1955 Lay sisters replace traditional black scapular with white scapular

1963 Siena Convent opened in Blockhouse Bay, Auckland (closed 1993)

1962 11 October: Opening of Second Vatican Council (closed 8 December 1965)

1965 Second Vatican Council publishes *Perfectae Caritatis* calling for renewal of consecrated religious life

1967 First visit of the Master General of the Dominican Order to New Zealand

1969 Santa Rosa Convent opened at Henderson (name changed to Dominican Priory in 1972) (closed 1993)

1970 Publication of *Star in the South* by Sister Mary Augustine McCarthy

1971 Centennial celebrations

1975 Private Schools Conditional Integration Act enables Catholic schools to be incorporated into the state system while preserving their special character

1976 Interim Constitutions of the New Zealand Dominican Sisters (prepared in response to the Second Vatican Council)

1980s Sisters establish smaller communities, including some living alone

1980 New Zealand Dominican Sisters establish a mission to Vanuatu (closed 1988)

1989 Promulgation of revised Constitutions of the New Zealand Dominican Sisters

1995 First meeting of Dominican Sisters International in Rome

1997 Publication of first edition of *Tui Motu*

1999 Establishment of Korimako Farm in Invercargill

2003 Cabra Homecoming Symposium

2014 New Zealand Dominican Sisters join with Australian Dominican Sisters to form the Federation of Dominican Sisters in Oceania

Appendix 2: Leadership

Prioress/Sub-prioress

1871 MM Gabriel Gill/MM Agnes Rooney

1886 MM Agnes Rooney/MM Catherine Hughes

1889 MM Gabriel Gill/MM Raymond McGrath

1892 MM Gabriel Gill/MM St Peter Slattery

1895 MM St Peter Slattery/MM Gabriel Gill

1899 MM St Peter Slattery/MM Raymond McGrath

1901 MM Raymond McGrath/MM Cecily Mulcahy

1904 MM Raymond McGrath/MM Bertrand McLaughlin

1907 MM St Peter Slattery/MM Antonius Mullany

1910 MM Cecily Mulcahy/MM Genevieve Downing

1913 MM Cecily Mulcahy/MM Bertrand McLaughlin

1916 MM Raymond McGrath/MM Bertrand McLaughlin

1921 MM Cecily Mulcahy/MM Bertrand McLaughlin

1927 MM Teresa Lynch/MM Bertrand McLaughlin

Prioress General/Sub-prioress

1933 MM Reginald Quilter/MM Frigidian Butler

1939 MM Dominica McKay/MM Philomena McCarthy

1944 MM Philomena McCarthy/MM Patricia Hynes

1950 MM Philomena McCarthy/MM di Pazzi Gaffaney

1956 MM David Stark/MM Patricia Hynes

1962 MM David Stark/MM Colman O'Sullivan

1969 MM Jordan McCormick/SM Raymund O'Reilly

1975 MM Constance Quinn/SM Louise Tierney

1980 S Margaret Quinn/S Elizabeth Mackie

Leadership Team (Prioress listed first)

1986 S Mary Horn, S Susan Logan, S Judith Anne O'Sullivan, S Carmel Walsh, S Margaret Mary Ogilvy

1991 S Judith McGinley, S Susan Logan, S Sandra Winton, S Clare MacKenzie, S Teresa Roughan

1995 S Judith McGinley, S Roxane Parkinson, S Lorraine Challis, S Mary Anna Baird, S Brenda Fitzgerald

1999 S Judith Anne O'Sullivan, S Brenda Fitzgerald, S Patricia Hannan, S Margaret Butler, S Hazel McDonald

2003 S Judith Anne O'Sullivan, S Elizabeth Mackie, S Joan Hardiman, S Maureen O'Hanlon, S Lorraine Challis

2007 S Elizabeth Mackie, S Maureen O'Hanlon, S Mary Anna Baird, S Joan Hardiman, S Jacqui Ryan

2011 S Carmel Walsh, S Raewyn Benzie, S Mary Anna Baird, S Margaret Butler, S Judith McGinley

2015 S Elizabeth Mackie, S Judith McGinley, S Judith Anne O'Sullivan, S Raewyn Benzie

Appendix 3: New Zealand Congregation of Dominican Sisters

Sister	Family Name	Birth Name	Date of Birth	Date of Profession	Date of Dispensation from Vows	Date of Death
MM Agnes	Rooney	Mary Elizabeth	1811	26/11/1836		10/10/1902
MM Francis	Sullivan	Marie	30/11/1825	11/04/1851		7/03/1894
MM Vincent	Whitty	Margaret	24/11/1831	14/04/1852		8/08/1911
MM Gabriel	Gill	Victoria	22/06/1837	18/08/1854		22/04/1905
MM Catherine	Hughes	Charlotte	7/07/1830	17/02/1857		28/01/1902
SM Lucy	Tracy	Mary	1827	21/07/1858		8/03/1894
MM Gertrude	Dooley	Mary Anne	5/03/1837	24/02/1859		16/11/1919
MM de Ricci	Kirby	Ellen	7/06/1837	24/02/1859		19/05/1915
MM Bertrand	McLaughlin	Helena	5/10/1850	15/10/1869		10/03/1947
SM Peter	Jordan	Anne	04/1849	3/10/1870		20/10/1910
SM Raymond	McGrath	Mary	6/01/1852	14/12/1871		1/11/1920
SM Paul	Lyons	Johanna	25/11/1853	1/09/1874		14/12/1933
SM Alphonsus	Owens	Agnes	26/09/1849	1/09/1874		19/04/1918
SM Joseph	Neylon	Jane	12/04/1854	1/05/1878		27/05/1946
SM Evangelist	Ryan	Mary	12/11/1854	24/09/1878		20/09/1889
SM St Peter	Slattery	Mary	15/11/1857	24/09/1878		16/12/1927
SM Rose	Cantwell	Teresa Anne	25/02/1859	4/08/1879		14/09/1918
SM Dominic	Williamson	Mary	19/10/1853	4/08/1879		3/05/1881
SM Aquinas	Gawne	Henrietta	17/06/1860	28/01/1881		26/01/1919
SM Columba	Fagan	Mary	30/04/1851	31/03/1881		27/05/1886
SM Patrick	Collins	Margaret	3/11/1856	5/08/1881		29/11/1923
SM Albertus	Hall	Jane	5/11/1848	18/03/1882		10/06/1925
SM Magdalen	O'Connor	Julia	4/12/1853	18/03/1882		11/10/1894
SM Louis	Keighron	Agnes	21/01/1860	9/11/1882		2/01/1920
SM Stanislaus	Gough	Ellen	22/07/1854	28/12/1882		9/07/1925
SM Michael	McCarthy	Margaret	4/01/1860	28/12/1882		7/04/1956
SM Aloysius	Gunn	Eliza (Bessie)	1855	4/09/1883		29/04/1939
SM Dominic	Scully	Kate	14/11/1861	4/09/1883		20/05/1959
SM Alacoque	Calvert	Mary Genevieve Saunderson	22/11/1847	16/04/1884		1/06/1934
SM Hyacinth	O'Neill	Mary	23/03/1865	16/04/1884		11/11/1895
SM Gonzales	Wall	Maria	19/07/1865	16/04/1884		16/10/1940

Sister	Family Name	Birth Name	Date of Birth	Date of Profession	Date of Dispensation from Vows	Date of Death
SM di Ricci	Berry	Mary Agnes	7/05/1864	3/10/1884		22/[illegible]
SM Martha	King	Teresa	6/03/1845	4/08/1885		22/[illegible]
SM Imelda	O'Neill	Kate	21/01/1858	21/01/1886		4/[illegible]
SM Anne	Walsh	Ellen	1863	21/01/1886		26/[illegible]
SM Veronica	Creed	Johanna	1849	13/01/1887		8/[illegible]
SM Raphael	Martin	Mary	15/08/1863	13/01/1887		22/[illegible]
SM Bridget	Diamond	Bridget	2/05/1853	4/08/1887		11/[illegible]
SM Bernard	King	Mary Anne	1854	4/08/1887		30/[illegible]
SM Gertrude	Chitty	Mary	24/08/1856	25/01/1888		26/[illegible]
SM Clare	McIntyre	Mary Anne	29/03/1867	25/01/1888		23/[illegible]
SM Augustine	Hanning	Mary	2/09/1869	11/07/1888		2/[illegible]
SM Antoninus	Mullany	Teresa	29/01/1862	16/01/1889		31/[illegible]
SM Jordan	Cosgrove	Fanny	23/07/1863	18/02/1889		22/[illegible]
SM Berchmans	Diamond	Ellen	1860	18/02/1889		6/[illegible]
SM Cecily	Mulcahy	Annie	21/08/1865	11/07/1889		2/[illegible]
SM Pius	Rowe	Mary	15/10/1867	11/07/1889		26/[illegible]
SM Thomas	Crofts	Margaret	20/02/1862	5/02/1890		15/[illegible]
SM Angela	Enright	Kate	1857	5/02/1890		19/[illegible]
SM de Sales	Grennell	Anne	05/1865	5/02/1890		10/[illegible]
SM Dominica	Murphy	Rita	11/07/1866	5/02/1890		24/[illegible]
SM Benignus	O'Connor	Ada	7/08/1863	5/02/1890		19/[illegible]
SM Josepha	Warren	Mary Angela	24/11/1852	5/02/1890		19/[illegible]
SM Malachy	O'Neill	Bridget	1848	25/12/1890		2/[illegible]
SM Ignatius	Ralph	Mary	6/09/1859	25/12/1890		28/[illegible]
SM Scholastica	Eissenhardt	Amelia	25/10/1858	31/03/1891		7/[illegible]
SM Columba	Lowe	Margaret	9/09/1863	31/03/1891		1/[illegible]
SM Frigidian	Butler	Bridget	14/07/1871	15/07/1891		26/[illegible]
SM Agatha	Carroll	Helena	1868	15/07/1891		11/[illegible]
SM Dympna	Connolly	Margaret	19/07/1873	15/07/1891		3/[illegible]
SM Ita	Connolly	Mary	11/12/1870	15/07/1891		19/[illegible]
SM Cataldus	Kavanagh	Bridget	10/12/1871	15/07/1891		3/[illegible]
SM Philomena	McGrath	Kate	13/03/1871	15/07/1891		27/[illegible]
SM Virgilius	Mannion	Kate	1/03/1872	15/07/1891		15/[illegible]
SM Brendan	Murphy	Sarah	17/01/1867	15/07/1891		2/[illegible]
SM Monica	Tobin	Maggie	1857	3/12/1891		14/[illegible]
SM Bonaventure	McIntyre	Ann	29/06/1872	27/12/1891		12/[illegible]

Sister	Family Name	Birth Name	Date of Birth	Date of Profession	Date of Dispensation from Vows	Date of Death
SM Reginald	Quilter	Margaret Ann	26/08/1872	27/12/1891		16/02/1946
SM Philip	Hughes	Julia	5/04/1871	8/07/1892		4/02/1908
SM Teresa	Lynch	Ann	8/01/1872	5/04/1893		31/12/1942
SM Evangelist	Murphy	Kate	10/07/1870	5/04/1893		26/06/1943
SM Baptist	O'Connor	Mary	18/05/1867	5/04/1893		18/08/1943
SM Kevin	Ritchie	Margaret	15/03/1867	27/08/1893		19/04/1943
SM Regis	Houlahan	Annie	18/12/1872	9/07/1894		3/02/1935
SM Genevieve	Downing	Susie	20/02/1855	9/11/1894		19/09/1923
SM Benedict	O'Connor	Nora	4/06/1872	15/08/1895		27/11/1956
SM Ursula	Mintern	Mary	10/03/1875	4/06/1896		16/12/1900
SM Anthony	O'Reilly	Mary Ann	22/10/1877	17/03/1898		7/07/1944
SM Xavier	Hart	Florence Mary	23/12/1874	22/06/1898		8/06/1965
SM di Pazzi	Miscall	Mary Josephine	8/12/1877	16/03/1899		22/01/1915
SM Margaret Mary	Coffey	Nora	28/11/1872	8/09/1899		13/10/1966
SM Cecilia	Dickinson	Katharine Mary Josephine	14/05/1871	15/08/1900		15/11/1945
SM Gerard	Milligan	Kate	10/04/1878	15/08/1900		*Unknown*
SM Sebastian	Burke	Mary	22/08/1878	11/07/1901		16/06/1961
SM Ceslaus	Freed	Alice	4/05/1880	11/07/1901		16/11/1948
SM Magdalen	Morkane	Teresa	13/08/1875	11/07/1901		31/03/1909
SM Alexius	O'Neill	Nellie	25/07/1879	11/07/1901		17/08/1959
SM Francis	Morton	Edith	2/10/1874	1/04/1902		19/08/1946
SM Martina	Sullivan	Lizzie	5/08/1873	1/04/1902		21/08/1948
SM Austin	Coffey	Annie	1/03/1881	3/10/1902		29/01/1963
SM Ambrose	Donnelly	Katherine	30/12/1877	14/04/1903		28/11/1939
SM Chanel	Hughes	Annie	26/07/1878	14/04/1903		18/06/1957
SM Perpetua	McNamee	Eleanor	7/07/1878	14/04/1903		24/11/1952
SM Barbara	Prendergast	Margarita	18/11/1879	14/04/1903		13/06/1949
SM Agnes	Roche	Jane Teresa	20/05/1883	7/07/1903		4/09/1951
SM Bernardine	Cockerell	Mary Jane	1/03/1881	8/09/1903		1/04/1956
SM Anastasia	Boyle	Bridget	27/05/1869	15/07/1904		29/11/1945
SM Cuthbert	Hayes	Jane	17/04/1883	3/07/1905		28/04/1971
SM Felicitas	Plunkett	Annie	22/09/1883	3/07/1905		10/06/1912
SM Agatha	Lynch	Katie	1/04/1873	4/01/1906		13/06/1915
SM Philomena	McCarthy	Anne	7/08/1881	4/01/1906		25/11/1971

Sister	Family Name	Birth Name	Date of Birth	Date of Profession	Date of Dispensation from Vows	Date of Death
SM Lucy	Murdoch	Agnes	19/02/1885	4/01/1906		15/08/[illegible]
SM Catherine	Oakley	Helen	26/06/1878	4/01/1906		4/08/[illegible]
SM Ursula	Collins	Mary Margaret Alice	9/04/1884	17/07/1906		15/[illegible]
SM Aidan	McNamee	Jane	13/10/1880	17/07/1906		8/[illegible]
SM Hyacinth	Oakley	Rachel	13/02/1880	27/01/1908		17/[illegible]
SM Finbarr	Mullin	Annie	26/10/1883	27/06/1908		15/[illegible]
SM Gerard	Culhane	Catherine	9/02/1885	7/07/1908		30/[illegible]
SM Monica	Staunton	Mary	4/10/1879	17/03/1910		29/[illegible]
SM Ceslaus	Corcoran	Ann	7/03/1889	15/08/1910	1928	[illegible]
SM Emily	Mullin	Mary Frances	11/05/1878	27/12/1910		25/0[illegible]
SM Felicitas	Scully	Nora	6/03/1881	15/10/1911		9/0[illegible]
SM Elizabeth	White	Catherine	16/10/1873	15/10/1911		4/0[illegible]
SM Dominica	McKay	Mary Hilda	29/02/1888	3/09/1912		3/0[illegible]
SM Thecla	Forde	Mary	29/06/1884	28/01/1913		16/0[illegible]
SM Winifred	Moran	Irene Constance Imelda	12/11/1889	28/01/1913		24/0[illegible]
SM Clement	Mulholland	Margaret	26/01/1881	28/01/1913		18/0[illegible]
SM Magdalen	Meenan	Alice	4/10/1881	2/07/1913		10/0[illegible]
SM di Pazzi	Gaffaney	Imelda Catherine	26/05/1891	16/07/1914		3/0[illegible]
SM Benignus	McCarthy	Kate	05/1884	16/07/1914		19/12/[illegible]
SM Philip	Burke	Margaret	31/07/1882	8/12/1914		19/0[illegible]
SM Borgia	Crowley	Julia Agnes	25/11/1883	8/12/1914		5/04/[illegible]
SM Patricia	Hynes	Mary	13/04/1894	8/12/1914		21/12/[illegible]
SM Alphonsus	Falconer	Honora Jimima	19/04/1879	16/07/1915		27/04/[illegible]
SM Mechtilde	Mace	Mary Clare	12/02/1891	16/07/1915		13/11/[illegible]
SM Zedislava	Bonisch	Annie Helena	7/06/1888	19/07/1916		20/04/[illegible]
SM Carmel	Butler	Mary	8/11/1886	19/07/1916		30/10/[illegible]
SM Benvenuta	Carolan	Mary Gertrude	29/09/1894	19/07/1916		16/05/[illegible]
SM Gabriel	Gaynor	Teresa	4/05/1888	19/07/1916		22/12/[illegible]
SM Vincent	O'Gorman	Mary	17/09/1879	19/07/1916		27/03/[illegible]
SM John Berchmans	Quigg	Mary	7/01/1887	19/07/1916		3/11/[illegible]
SM Dorothea	Scully	Anna Maria	26/03/1885	19/07/1916		29/08/[illegible]
SM Hofbauer	Spillane	Elizabeth	25/05/1890	19/07/1916		1/07/[illegible]
SM Bonaventure	Wakelin	Ruth Josephine	26/07/1894	19/07/1916		16/03/[illegible]

Sister	Family Name	Birth Name	Date of Birth	Date of Profession	Date of Dispensation from Vows	Date of Death
SM Celestine	Radford	Mary Elizabeth	24/10/1886	9/01/1917		6/09/1966
SM Petronilla	Sloane	Margarita	1/06/1895	9/01/1917		28/05/1982
SM Borromeo	Venning	Mary Anastasia	22/01/1889	9/01/1917		27/07/1961
SM Claver	Dillon	Mary Ellen	1/02/1886	26/09/1917		25/01/1968
SM Gonzaga	Sweeney	Mary Christina	9/06/1893	26/09/1917		20/03/1976
SM Stephena	Duhig	Julia Frances	26/02/1896	27/12/1917		19/02/1978
SM Kieran	O'Donnell	Kate	26/04/1892	27/12/1917		1/12/1957
SM Nicholas	Duggan	Mary Frances	21/10/1893	15/08/1918		3/07/1974
SM John	Carrick	Mary Elizabeth	2/12/1890	11/12/1918		26/10/1969
SM Eithne	Croker	Margaret	24/10/1894	11/12/1918		8/08/1945
SM Cyprian	Dennehy	Kathleen Elizabeth	1/06/1894	11/12/1918		7/07/1941
SM Laurence	Spillane	Gertrude	30/10/1894	11/12/1918		14/03/1976
SM Anselm	Clifford	Margaret	8/01/1899	20/01/1920		17/02/1966
SM Camillus	Coles	Dorothy Mabel	12/03/1896	20/01/1920		7/01/1983
SM Rinaldo	Heffernan	Anne	9/06/1886	20/01/1920		19/10/1969
SM Juliana	O'Donnell	Mary	6/02/1889	20/01/1920		1/03/1957
SM Jarlath	Lee	Mary	22/02/1892	29/03/1921		18/01/1965
SM Casimir	McKone	Martha	26/12/1899	29/03/1921		23/08/1945
SM Callista	Dennehy	Mary Gabrielle	25/05/1896	10/05/1921		13/01/1979
SM Angela	Kaveney	Margaret Teresa	12/02/1900	10/05/1921		5/02/1973
SM Assisi	O'Meara	Margaret Francis	4/10/1901	10/05/1921		1/03/1976
SM Rose	Kaveney	Winifrid	15/04/1895	2/07/1922	27/07/1931	*Unknown*
SM Alvarez	O'Donnell	Teresa Mary	4/05/1901	2/07/1922		8/03/1926
SM Aquin	Lister	Moana Winifred	27/12/1901	8/06/1923		29/09/1969
SM St Roch	Rogers	Ivy	12/06/1899	8/06/1923		11/07/1984
SM Aidan	Wilson	Anne Mary	5/04/1889	8/06/1923		30/12/1963
SM Bernadette	Bourke	Catherine	7/11/1903	11/05/1924	23/04/1936	*Unknown*
SM Jerome	Lynch	Mary Dominica	8/05/1899	27/06/1924		13/09/1977
SM Rita	Rohan	Mary	21/10/1902	27/06/1924		28/06/1994
SM Paschal	Sorenson	Julia Constance	26/12/1894	27/06/1924		12/09/1971
SM Colombière	Ryan	Kathleen	14/02/1904	11/10/1924		11/10/1924
SM Carmel	Dowdall	Mabel	24/07/1903	18/03/1925		2/02/1982
SM Agatha	Hickey	Katherine Julia	14/11/1905	21/01/1927		22/08/1948
SM Christina	Kennedy	Mona Helena	14/09/1905	2/05/1927		5/04/1986
SM Colman	O'Sullivan	Annie	17/07/1902	2/05/1927		2/01/2000

Sister	Family Name	Birth Name	Date of Birth	Date of Profession	Date of Dispensation from Vows	Date of Death
SM Patrick	Finnigan	Alice Mary	10/09/1903	10/10/1927		22/[illegible]7/197[illegible]
SM di Ricci	Bell	Alice Margaret	24/12/1899	19/01/1928		5/[illegible]2/197[illegible]
SM Antoninus	Columb	Brigid	25/12/1907	19/01/1928		4/[illegible]4/195[illegible]
SM Vianney	Knowler	Katherine	10/04/1905	19/01/1928		15/[illegible]2/197[illegible]
SM St Joan	Terry	Clare Agnes	4/12/1900	19/01/1928		17/[illegible]3/199[illegible]
SM Stanislaus	Gavin	Catherine	10/05/1909	2/02/1930		26/[illegible]1/19[illegible]
SM Tarcisius	Toomey	Josephine	29/06/1902	7/09/1930		19/[illegible]6/19[illegible]
SM Bartholomea	Fitzsimmons	Jane	22/09/1900	28/08/1931		1/[illegible]2/197[illegible]
SM St Anne	Brennan	Margaret Mary	6/06/1912	4/01/1932		7/[illegible]9/200[illegible]
SM Ignatius	Cournane	Julia Agnes Mary	9/05/1910	4/01/1932		22/[illegible]7/197[illegible]
S Bridget (Columbanus)	Cribbin	Brigid Veronica	7/02/1906	4/01/1932		21/[illegible]8/199[illegible]
SM Oliver	Dooley	Kathleen Christina	18/12/1911	4/01/1932		7/[illegible]4/199[illegible]
SM Teresita	Dunne	Pauline Mary	26/06/1913	4/01/1932		29/[illegible]9/200[illegible]
SM Peter	Fraser	Kathleen Williamina (Ina)	2/11/1911	4/01/1932	13/04/1939	Unk[illegible]
SM Canice	Lowe	Mary Ann	4/09/1909	4/01/1932		17/[illegible]4/197[illegible]
S Catherine Mary (Amata)	Nolan	Catherine Mary	22/03/1911	4/01/1932		15/[illegible]5/200[illegible]
SM Damian	Sligo	Ada Mary	30/03/1907	4/01/1932		4/[illegible]0/197[illegible]
S Marie Thérèse	Smith	Honor Marcella	30/07/1911	4/01/1932		1/[illegible]9/200[illegible]
SM Enda	Treacy	Catherine Mary	7/02/1906	4/01/1932		27/[illegible]0/197[illegible]
SM Declan	Butterly	Brigid Margaret (Bridie)	30/07/1908	2/04/1932		5/[illegible]5/200[illegible]
SM Claude	Forde	Kathleen	11/07/1907	2/04/1932		23/[illegible]3/19[illegible]
SM Veronica	Kearns	Josephine Mary	17/01/1910	2/04/1932		17/[illegible]8/195[illegible]
SM Louis	Cahill	Julia Mary	26/02/1911	10/12/1932		12/[illegible]1/200[illegible]
SM Raymund	O'Reilly	Lydia Mary Theresa	5/10/1913	7/01/1933		24/[illegible]5/200[illegible]
SM Albertus	Smith	Helen Agnes	18/01/1910	7/01/1933		23/[illegible]2/19[illegible]
SM David	Stark	Mary Georgina	3/11/1907	2/04/1933		5/[illegible]1/19[illegible]
SM Imelda	Windle	Katherine Mary	13/10/1913	2/04/1933		4/[illegible]5/201[illegible]
SM Ceslaus	Fox	Margaret Jane Catherine	30/04/1912	11/09/1933		16/[illegible]4/19[illegible]
SM Mannes	Lister	Gemma Teresa	1/12/1912	11/09/1933		19/[illegible]0/19[illegible]
SM Rose	Noble-Campbell	Cecily Joan Agatha	12/07/1911	11/09/1933		22/[illegible]7/197[illegible]

Sister	Family Name	Birth Name	Date of Birth	Date of Profession	Date of Dispensation from Vows	Date of Death
SM Bernard	McCarthy	Eileen Mary	29/04/1912	2/04/1935		13/11/1988
SM Raphael	Gallien	Madge	11/10/1914	7/01/1936		24/08/2003
SM St James	Vallis	Rose	18/10/1910	7/01/1936		2/01/1990
SM Gerard	Leonard	Catherine Ellen	18/07/1912	2/04/1936		22/09/1970
SM Christopher	Burke	Edna May	6/05/1915	27/04/1936	1952	*Unknown*
SM Alban	McCaughan	Eileen Margaret	18/06/1915	11/09/1936		24/06/2012
SM Fabian	McSoriley	Mary Agnes	21/07/1911	11/09/1936		7/07/1996
SM Conrad	Smith	Eileen Margaret	4/01/1911	11/09/1936		23/12/1991
SM Emmanuel	Vallis	Veronica	18/10/1910	11/09/1936		10/09/1989
SM Hilary	McDonnell	Ellen	10/12/1899	12/04/1937		24/12/1969
SM Theophane	Herron	Theresa	15/06/1917	20/01/1938		15/03/1997
SM Vincent	McCarthy	Mary Clare	4/08/1913	20/01/1938		19/11/2004
SM Winefride	Morris	Veronica Josephine	25/04/1914	20/01/1938		9/01/2015
SM Basil	Geoffrey	Mary Teresa	5/05/1918	2/04/1939		5/11/2011
SM St Luke	Kerin	Mary	15/09/1918	2/04/1939		9/02/1984
SM Alvarez	O'Shea	Sylvia	15/06/1917	2/04/1939		15/07/1988
SM Gertrude	Fox	Phyllis	11/03/1920	11/09/1939		
SM Placid	McRae	Mary Muriel	5/11/1918	2/02/1940		10/11/1962
SM Paul	O'Loughlin	Ellen Philomena	22/11/1915	22/07/1940		5/02/1995
SM Catherine Labouré	McAleese	Annie	7/04/1921	13/01/1941		1/09/2008
SM Josephine	Prisk	Shona Marjorie	4/06/1921	13/01/1941		23/08/1977
SM Aquinas	Munro	Bernice	27/08/1921	30/12/1941		6/09/1973
SM Madeleine	Pavletich	Anne (Nan)	4/12/1919	30/12/1941	28/10/1943	*Unknown*
SM Ambrose	Kerin	Nancy	18/11/1919	14/04/1942		13/09/1997
SM Euphrasia	Rosa	Mary	21/10/1912	22/05/1942	22/05/1945	*Unknown*
SM Columba	McHugh	Sarah Margaret	22/11/1921	12/01/1943		
SM Brigid	Nolan	Gertrude Mary	16/03/1903	12/01/1943		20/09/1990
S Joan Marie (Gonzales)	McCluskey	Joan	10/12/1921	16/05/1943		28/07/2005
S Maria (Attracta)	McDonald	Cecilia Mary	6/01/1922	16/05/1943		21/10/2012
SM Francesca	Moylan	Honor	26/01/1920	16/05/1943		11/06/1993
SM Louise	Timpany	Mary	27/08/1920	24/09/1943		26/06/2011
SM Joanna	Toomey	Maura Teresa Brigid	19/09/1917	24/09/1943		13/01/2002

Sister	Family Name	Birth Name	Date of Birth	Date of Profession	Date of Dispensation from Vows	Date of Death
S Margaret (Constance)	Quinn	Margaret Agnes	19/02/1922	23/03/1944		
SM Jordan	McCormick	Maree	30/06/1922	30/12/1944		29/07/2004
SM Martin	Henderson	Helen Elizabeth	15/09/1905	24/05/1945	5/06/1949	*Unknown*
SM Margarita	O'Connell	Norah	31/01/1923	24/05/1946		27/12/1993
SM Martha	Calnon	Ruby	2/06/1923	28/01/1947		31/10/1973
SM Rosalie	Loan	Marion	24/09/1917	28/01/1947		28/07/1998
SM Cyprian	Marsden	Joy	3/10/1925	28/01/1947	17/10/1967	*Unknown*
SM Clare	Timpany	Monica Bernadette	30/01/1925	28/01/1947		20/08/2011
SM de Sales	Lynch	Mary	6/12/1905	30/01/1948		7/11/1980
S Frances (Anthony)	Scully	Frances Mary	11/11/1924	30/01/1948		30/08/2011
SM Bernadette	Fox	Mary	5/03/1922	31/01/1949		17/01/2015
SM Aloysius	Moylan	Patricia Monica	16/07/1925	31/01/1949		3/05/2008
SM Josepha	Reidy	Mary Ellen	27/06/1927	31/01/1949		23/10/1981
SM Cecilia	Kennedy	Nora Marie	6/12/1926	9/10/1949		
SM Loreto	Meehan	Patricia	12/07/1922	9/10/1949		27/02/2015
SM Teresa	Roughan	Catherine Valda	21/08/1927	9/10/1949		17/10/2002
SM Madeleine	McAleese	Monica Mildred	9/05/1929	28/01/1950		
SM Genevieve	O'Rourke	Margaret Mary (Marjorie)	27/08/1924	28/01/1950		
SM Catherine	Tither	Ellen Teresa	19/12/1929	28/01/1950		14/06/2011
SM Adrienne	White	Millicent Mary	15/05/1927	28/01/1950		
SM Thomas	Dunn	Eileen Mary	13/10/1929	25/10/1950		
SM Augustine	McCarthy	Monica	24/02/1925	9/05/1951		11/06/2010
SM Frances	Lister	Maureen	17/01/1932	21/11/1951		
SM Reginald	Moylan	Margaret Frances	6/06/1928	21/11/1951		18/07/2009
SM Leonie	Parry	Melvis Marion	19/06/1929	21/11/1951		
SM Gemma	Finlay	Noeline Margaret	25/12/1930	31/01/1952		15/11/2011
SM Joseph	Mercer	Eileen	12/07/1930	31/01/1952		18/07/1973
SM Jadwiga	Rombel	Marie	28/05/1928	31/01/1952		30/09/2005
SM Majella	Dennehy	Margaret Teresa	21/06/1928	28/01/1953	14/05/1963	*Unknown*
S Molly (Mercedes)	Griffin	Mary Teresa	23/08/1929	28/01/1953		
SM Peter	Higgins	Edna Mary	1/09/1920	24/09/1953		10/09/1997
SM Agnes	Gavin	Moira	21/06/1927	9/05/1954		29/08/1975
SM Brendan	Hurley	Mary Margaret	17/01/1936	2/07/1954	14/06/1978	

Sister	Family Name	Birth Name	Date of Birth	Date of Profession	Date of Dispensation from Vows	Date of Death
SM Barbara	Magee	Elizabeth Geraldine	27/01/1936	2/07/1954	27/01/1972	
SM Martin	Dolan	R. Louise	31/01/1937	29/09/1954	1955	
SM Evangelist	Downey	Philomena	11/6/1929	29/09/1954	29/09/1960	
SM Pauline	Lynch	Frances	12/04/1927	29/09/1954		12/09/2006
S Rose Maria (Maria Goretti)	Lyons	Rosemarie	3/02/1930	29/09/1954		2/06/2002
S Noreen (Bertrand)	Murphy	Noreen Constance	20/08/1933	29/09/1954		
SM Eithne	Tracey	Bernadette	7/01/1932	29/09/1954	29/09/1957	*Unknown*
SM Kevin	Tracey	Imelda	3/11/1935	29/09/1954	29/09/1960	
S Susan (Dolores)	Logan	Susan Veronica	2/08/1932	24/05/1955		
S Barbara (de Lourdes)	Dwyer	Barbara Catherine	16/07/1938	1/02/1956		
S Kathleen (Marie Grignon)	McAleese	Kathleen	12/08/1927	1/02/1956		15/08/1983
SM Elizabeth	Mackie	Mary Terese	19/08/1934	1/02/1956		
S Anne (Perpetua)	O'Neill	Anne Philomena	23/02/1938	1/02/1956		
SM Jacinta	O'Reilly	Angela	24/01/1938	1/02/1956	1973	
S Maureen (Norbert)	Connolly	Maureen Gertrude	16/12/1938	24/09/1956		
S Maureen (Ligouri)	O'Hanlon	Maureen	8/07/1938	24/09/1956		
S Joan (Regis)	Hardiman	Joan Cecilia	25/04/1938	8/12/1956		
SM Stephen	Hobbs	Judith	4/09/1937	8/12/1956	24/07/1967	
S Hazel (Gregory)	McDonald	Hazel Rose	21/04/1936	8/12/1956		19/09/2005
SM John Baptist	Magee	Gloria Winefride Collette	7/02/1939	8/12/1956	9/09/1986	
S Roxane (Denise)	Parkinson	Roxane Mary	4/09/1933	8/12/1956		
SM Timothy	Rabbitt	Patricia Isla	24/01/1938	8/12/1956	19/06/1959	
SM Gerardine	Collins	Carmelita	22/10/1932	24/10/1957		20/06/1992
SM Agatha	Hurley	Catherine	24/08/1938	24/10/1957	28/11/1976	
S Mary (Michael)	Concannon	Mary Perpetua	16/12/1937	6/01/1958		24/01/2012

Sister	Family Name	Birth Name	Date of Birth	Date of Profession	Date of Dispensation from Vows	[illegible]
S Patricia (Alphonsus)	Hannan	Patricia Mary	31/08/1938	6/01/1958		
SM Peter Julian	Baird	Margaret Judith	6/03/1936	24/05/1958	22/12/1972	
SM Helena	Gibson	Katherine Esther	14/05/1933	22/11/1958	19/12/1995	26/[illegible]
SM Cecily	Sheehy	Annette Margaret	20/07/1938	22/11/1958		
SM Philippa	Crosbie	Mary Cecilia	19/02/1932	22/07/1959	30/08/1977	
S Marie Eugene	Nicolson	Ngaire Joy	3/07/1932	22/07/1959		
S Lorraine (Roberta)	Challis	Margaret Lorraine	12/02/1939	21/10/1959		
S Bernadette (Bernadine)	Cheyne	Bernadette Irene	5/12/1937	21/10/1959		
S Brenda (Christopher)	Fitzgerald	Brenda	18/02/1927	21/10/1959		[illegible]
S Mary (Chanel)	Horn	Mary Dominica	17/10/1937	21/10/1959		
S Danielle (Benedict)	Melton	Mary Danielle	15/11/1938	24/10/1960	22/08/2001	
SM Mark	Rillstone	Jennifer Anne	30/07/1938	24/10/1960	17/04/1974	
S Marie (Assumpta)	Twomey	Mary Elizabeth Angela	20/03/1930	24/10/1960		
SM Anastasia	Boyle	Margaret	3/07/1941	25/05/1961	24/04/1974	
S Kathleen (Andrew)	Thomson	Kathleen Deanna	20/08/1938	25/05/1961	13/03/1987	
S Nola (Martin)	Gleeson	Nola Mary	21/08/1940	3/10/1961		
S Joan (Diana Mary)	Bennett	Joan Veronica	21/01/1941	30/11/1961		
S Valerie (Antoninus)	Dibley	Valerie Marie	30/09/1939	30/11/1961	8/08/1981	
S Judith Anne (Magdalen)	O'Sullivan	Judith Anne	24/09/1941	30/11/1961		
S Margaret (Marie de Chantal)	Heath	Margaret	13/04/1939	22/07/1962		11/[illegible]
SM Dominic	Swindale	Janet Aston	21/07/1934	22/07/1962		
SM Matthew	Kelly	Joan	9/03/1940	30/11/1962	20/07/1971	
S Marie de Montfort	Murphy	Carol Josephine	7/09/1942	30/11/1962	12/05/1977	
S Carmel (Albert)	Walsh	Carmel Anne	24/09/1941	30/11/1962		
S Paula Mary	Winders	Suzanne Therese	18/04/1942	30/11/1962	18/06/1984	

Sister	Family Name	Birth Name	Date of Birth	Date of Profession	Date of Dispensation from Vows	Date of Death
S Judith (Virginia)	Robinson	Judith Ann	17/09/1942	18/05/1963		
SM Luke	Rose	Ursula Jane	1/10/1942	30/11/1963	16/05/1967	
S Marie de Porres	Roughan	Kathleen Wilma	30/09/1943	30/11/1963	7/01/1989	
S Mary Anna	Baird	Mary Winifred	8/07/1940	30/11/1965		
S Benedicta Mary	O'Reilly	Aileen	30/01/1946	30/11/1965	24/12/1965	
SM Philip	Perriam	Mary Margaret	15/03/1946	30/11/1965	1973	
S Ann (Anne Marie)	Keogh	Gwenneth Ann	18/02/1945	11/02/1966	13/03/1987	
SM Patrice	Bolger	Kathleen Helen	19/08/1946	28/10/1966	20/01/1993	
S Patricia (Antonia)	McCann	Patricia Marie	12/11/1946	28/10/1966		
S Marie Michelle	Wheatley	Julianne Elizabeth	29/11/1946	28/10/1966	3/12/1986	
S Susan (Aidan)	Healy	Susan Mary	6/04/1946	6/01/1967	20/12/2000	
SM Judith	McGinley	Denise Frances	14/11/1945	6/01/1967		
SM Regina	O'Connell	Philomena Margaret	22/04/1947	6/01/1967	8/05/1976	
SM Dominica	Neale	Wynsome Margaret	9/09/1946	15/11/1967	15/11/1970	
S Raewyn (Joachim)	Benzie	Raewyn Margaret	18/10/1944	27/01/1968		
S Margaret (Monica)	Butler	Margaret Mary	4/07/1942	27/01/1968		
S Sandra (Bede)	Winton	Sandra Margaret	13/02/1946	27/01/1968		
S Jan (Margaret Mary)	Ogilvy	Janice Margaret	22/08/1944	30/01/1969		
SM Paulette	O'Connell	Erin	4/12/1947	4/10/1969	3/12/1970	
S Margaret (Catherine Marie)	Fahey	Margaret Mary	19/02/1949	6/06/1971		
SM Kenneth	McKenzie	Christina Mary	7/02/1948	6/06/1971	6/02/1972	
S Helen	Bergin	Helen Frances	24/02/1948	2/09/1972		
S Micaela	Dillon	Micaela Mary	7/05/1947	31/03/1975	*Transferred to new congregation*	
S Barbara (John)	Menzies	Barbara Mary	2/2/1951	31/03/1975	12/03/1992	
S Colleen Mary	Young	Colleen Ann	26/09/1952	27/05/1976	1979	
SM Aquinas	Sowienski	Helena Teresa	8/09/1955	24/05/1977	24/05/1980	
S Clare	Mackenzie	Clare Patricia	31/07/1951	20/05/1978	29/11/1994	
S Patricia	Robinson	Patricia Marie	28/10/1955	20/05/1978	2010	
S Jane	Rutherford	Jane Marie	8/12/1955	20/05/1978	2010	
S Jacqui	Ryan	Jacqueline Mary	28/02/1958	19/05/1984		

Notes

Prologue

1 Nineteenth-century sources refer to the building's location as being the corner of Smith and Dowling Streets. The upper part of Dowling Street, after the intersection with Smith Street, is now called Tennyson Street.

2 Being Frank Blog, 16 April 2013: www.beingfrank.co.nz/how-the-mighty-have-fallen

1. Introduction: The fruits of contemplation

1 Sister Mary Joseph Mercer, Speech at Vocation Rally, Gore, 11 September 1966. CL7/4/66, DA.

2 Simon Tugwell, *The Way of the Preacher* (London: Dartman, Longman & Todd, 1979), 2.

3 Constitutions of the Congregation of the New Zealand Dominican Sisters, 1989, 4. Con, DA.

4 M.H. Vicaire, *Saint Dominic and His Times* (London: Darton, Longman & Todd, 1964), 119–29.

5 Translation from Barbara Cahill, *Dominic: The preacher* (London: Darton, Longman & Todd, 1988), 101.

6 Tugwell, *The Way*, 15–19.

7 William A. Hinnebusch, *Dominican Spirituality: Principles and practice* (Washington: The Thomist Press, 1965), 2.

8 Ibid., 39–40.

9 Tugwell, *The Way*, 62–63.

10 Sister Mary Joseph Mercer, Speech, 11 September 1966.

11 Ibid.

12 Rose O'Neil, *A Rich Inheritance: Galway Dominican nuns 1644–1994* (Galway: Dominican Sisters, 1994), 9–23.

13 Cahill, *Dominic*, 38.

14 Daphne D.C. Pochin Mould, *The Irish Dominicans: The friars preachers in the history of Catholic Ireland* (Dublin: Dominican Publications, 1957), 221.

15 Kevin Roach, 'The growth of Roman Catholicism in New Zealand', in Christopher Nichol & James Veitch (eds), *Religion in New Zealand Society* (Wellington: Victoria University Press, 1980), 111–12.

16 Pochin Mould, *The Irish Dominicans*, 221.

17 Margaret Heath, 'Elements of the spiritual patrimony of the New Zealand Dominican Sisters with particular reference to preaching the Word of God', MA thesis, St Paul University, Ottawa, 1992, 4. DA.

18 Ibid., 13.

19 Mary Ann Wiesemann-Mills, 'Standing up straight: A self-reflective resource for United States Dominican women on the charism of preaching', 1996, 20. DA. 'Fidelity to the charism is not fidelity to its structures of expression. These structures are institutional architecture enabling the historical and cultural expression of the charism. Structure is vital, yet charism always transcends structure. When the structures become the important focus, then ossification of the charism has begun; the life-giving breath of the Spirit is choked out of the organism, leaving only a shell.'

20 Sister Mary Joseph Mercer, Speech, 11 September 1966.

21 Report on the Dominican Symposium at Tallaght, Dublin, Ireland, in August 2003. GH11/1, DA.

22 Constitutions of the Congregation of the New Zealand Dominican Sisters, 1989, 4. Con, DA.

23 Geoffrey Troughton & Hugh Morrison (eds), 'Introduction: Perspectives on Christianity and New Zealand history', in *The Spirit of the Past: Essays on Christianity in New Zealand history* (Wellington: Victoria University Press, 2011), 11.

24 Patrick Moran, *History of the Catholic Church in Australasia* (Sydney & Melbourne: Frank Coffee & Co 1896), 984–85.

25 J.J. Wilson, *The Church in New Zealand: Memoirs of the early days* (Dunedin: New Zealand Tablet, 1910) 205–06.

26 Ibid., 4.

27 Mary Augustine McCarthy, *Star in the South: The centennial history of the New Zealand Dominican Sisters* (Dunedin: St Dominic's Priory, 1970).

28 Mary Augustine McCarthy, *Mother of the Missions: Mother Mary Gabriel Gill OSD* (Dunedin: St Dominic's Priory, 1989).

29 Mary Veronica Delaney, *Gracious is the Time: Centenary of the Sisters of Mercy, 1850–1950* (Auckland:

Sisters of Mercy, 1952); Pat Rafter, *Never Let Go: The remarkable story of Mother Aubert* (Wellington: A.H. & A.W. Reed, 1972); Mary Gulley, ed., *Centenary of Sisters of St Joseph of Nazareth, Wanganui, New Zealand* (Whanganui: Sisters of St Joseph, 1980); Phyllis Mary Goulter, *Sowers and Reapers: A short history of the Society of the Sacred Heart in New Zealand* (Auckland: Society of the Sacred Heart, 1982); Anne Marie Power, *Sisters of St Joseph of the Sacred Heart: The New Zealand story, 1883–1983* (Auckland: The Sisters, 1983).

30 Diane Strevens, 'Some issues around writing the histories of Catholic religious congregations for women in Aotearoa New Zealand', in Troughton & Morrison (eds), *The Spirit of the Past*, 70.

31 See, for example, Vicaire, *Saint Dominic and His Times*; Hinnebusch, *Dominican Spirituality*.

32 Simmons, *Brief History*, 107.

33 Michael King, *God's Farthest Outpost: A history of Catholics in New Zealand* (Auckland: Penguin, 1997), 22.

34 Mark Williams (ed.), *The Source of the Song: New Zealand writers on Catholicism* (Wellington: Victoria University Press, 1995).

35 Bernadette Hall, 'The words that get up', in Williams (ed.), *The Source of the Song*, 166.

36 Dominic O'Sullivan, *Faith, Politics and Reconciliation: Catholicism and the politics of indigeneity* (Wellington: Huia, 1995).

37 Jane Tolerton, *Convent Girls: New Zealand women talk to Jane Tolerton* (Auckland: Penguin, 1994), 93.

38 J.M. Collins, 'Hidden lives: The teaching and religious lives of eight Dominican Sisters, 1931–1961', MEd thesis, Massey University, 2001, 7–8.

39 Ibid., 4.

40 Pauline O'Regan, *A Changing Order* (Wellington: Bridget Williams Books, 1995), 65.

41 Jessie Munro, *The Story of Suzanne Aubert* (Auckland: Auckland University Press & Bridget Williams Books, 1996). See also Jessie Munro (ed.), *Letters on the Go: The correspondence of Suzanne Aubert* (Wellington: Bridget Williams Books, 2009).

42 Ann Trotter, *Mary Potter's Little Company of Mary: The New Zealand experience, 1914–2002* (Wellington: Bridget Williams Books & Little Company of Mary, 2003).

43 Diane Strevens, *MacKillop Women: The Sisters of St Joseph of the Sacred Heart Aotearoa New Zealand 1883–2006* (Auckland: David Ling Publishing, 2008).

44 Susan Smith, *Call to Mission: The story of the Mission Sisters of Aotearoa New Zealand and Samoa* (Auckland: David Ling Publishing, 2010), 309–11.

45 See for example O'Neil, *A Rich Inheritance*; Geraldine Smyth (ed.), *Distance Becomes Communion: A Dominican symposium on mission and hope* (Dublin: Dominican Publications, 2004); Stephanie Burley & Katherine Teague, *Chapel, Cloister and Classroom: Reflections on the Dominican Sisters at North Adelaide* (Adelaide: St Dominic's Priory College, 1993); M.R. MacGinley, *Ancient Tradition – New World: Dominican Sisters in Eastern Australia 1867–1958* (Strathfield: St Paul's Publications, 2009); Ruth Marchant James, *Fields of Gold: A history of the Dominican Sisters in Western Australia* (Doubleview: Dominican Sisters of Western Australia, 1999); Honor McCabe, *A Light Undimmed: The story of the Convent of Our Lady of Bom Sucesso, Lisbon, 1639–2006* (Dublin, Dominican Publications, 2007); Kathleen Boner, *Dominican Women: A time to speak* (Pietermaritzburg: Cluster Publications, 2000).

2. Historical overview: The story of a southern star

1 Mary Augustine McCarthy, *Star in the South: The centennial history of the New Zealand Dominican Sisters* (Dunedin: St Dominic's Priory, 1970), 28.

2 After his ordination in 1847, Booterstown had been Moran's first parish, so he knew the Dominican sisters well.

3 *Book of Annals. Sion Hill Convent, Blackroack, Co. Dublin, Golden Jubilee 1854–1904* (Dublin: Browne & Nolan, 1904), 49–51.

4 Related by Mother Mary Michael McCarthy to Sister Mary Augustine McCarthy, in McCarthy, *Star in the South*, 16.

5 *Book of Annals. Sion Hill*, 60–64.

6 Bishop Patrick Moran, Letter of agreement with the Dominican Sisters of Sion Hill, 2 October 1870. GH3/2/1, DA.

7 Congregational Annals, Book 1: 1871–1910. CA1, DA.

8 Ibid.

9 Sister Mary Catherine Hughes to Mother Mary Clare Elliot, October 1870. GH3/2/2, DA. Sister Mary Gabriel Gill to Sisters, 10 October 1870. GH3/2/3, DA.

10 *Book of Annals. Sion Hill*, 64–65. Note: I have relied on the dates and details in the published Annals of Sion Hill. The dates and some details in the unpublished New Zealand Annals are slightly different. This section of the New Zealand Annals was not written until 1931.

11 A niece and two granddaughters of the hosts became Dominican sisters.

12 *Otago Witness*, 25 February 1871, 6.

13 Congregational Annals, Book 1, 1871–1910, 18 February 1871, 32. CA1, DA.

14 Mother Mary Gabriel Gill to the Cardinal Prefect of Propaganda, 3 October 1886. GH1/2/22, DA.

15 Sister Mary Francis Sullivan to Mother Mary Clare Elliot, 17 March 1871. GH3/2/4, DA.

16 *Book of Annals. Sion Hill*, 66.

17 Sister Mary Gabriel Gill to Sion Hill, 7 November 1871. GH3/2/5, DA.

18 Sister Mary Francis Sullivan to Mother Mary Clare Elliot, 17 March 1871.

19 Ibid.

20 Sister Mary Gabriel Gill to Sion Hill, 7 November 1871.

21 Ibid.

22 Sister Mary Francis Sullivan to Mother Mary Clare Elliot, 17 March 1871. GH3/2/4, DA. In *Star in the South* Sister Mary Augustine McCarthy quotes from the Congregational Annals (written in 1931) which relate a similar story: The day after arriving in Dunedin Bishop Moran called Mother Gabriel to see him; he awaited her with a sheaf of bills. Mother Gabriel, 'all spirit and enthusiasm', took them from him cheerily, saying 'Give them to me, my Lord, I will quickly settle them!' She went through the house stripping it of everything but the bare necessities. The story is essentially the same, but I have relied on Sister Mary Francis's firsthand account for the details and the time frame. *Star in the South*, 37.

23 Congregational Annals, Book 1: 1871–1910. CA1, DA.

24 Sister Mary Francis Sullivan to Mother Mary Clare Elliot, 17 March 1871. Some later accounts have three first-day pupils, including *New Zealand Tablet,* 10 October 1890, 3. I have relied on Sister Mary Francis's firsthand account written at the time the school was opened.

25 Sister Mary Francis Sullivan to Mother Mary Clare Elliot, 17 March 1871.

26 Sister Mary Francis Sullivan to Sister Mary [illegible] July 1879.

27 Sister Mary Francis Sullivan to Mother Mary Clare Elliot, 17 March 1871.

28 Ibid.

29 Ibid.

30 *Otago Daily Times*, 25 February 1871, 2.

31 Sister Mary Francis Sullivan to Mother Mary Clare Elliot, 17 March 1871.

32 Bishop Moran, Pastoral Letter, 3 March 187[illegible] quoted in McCarthy, *Star in the South*, 38–39.

33 Sister Mary Gabriel Gill to Sion Hill, 7 November 1871. By October 1871 the convent building fund stood at £1100, well short of Moran's goal of £[illegible]. In early November 1871 the bishop made an offer on the sisters' behalf on a suitable property for a priory, but he was unable to secure a mortgage from the bank.

34 *Otago Daily Times*, 25 November 1871, 1.

35 Art unions were a popular form of fundraising in the nineteenth century: lottery tickets were sold in advance of a public draw, with works of art as prizes.

36 Sister Mary Gabriel Gill to Sion Hill, 7 November 1871.

37 Ibid.

38 Congregational Annals. CA1, DA. McCarthy, *Star in the South,* 44–45.

39 Bishop Moran's Diary, 13 February 1872, 13 October 1872, quoted in McCarthy, *Star in the South*, [illegible]7.

40 Bishop Moran's Diary, November 1872, quoted in McCarthy, *Star in the South*, 48.

41 McCarthy, *Star in the South*, 50–51.

42 Ibid., 56.

43 Bishop Moran's Diary, May 1877, quoted in McCarthy, *Star in the South*, 64. The Jesuits stayed only five years. The Wakari site is now a golf course.

44 Congregational Annals, Book 1: 1871–1910. CA1, DA.

45 *New Zealand Tablet*, 17 November 1876, 11.

46 *New Zealand Tablet*, 31 August 1877, 13.

47 E.J. McCoy, 'Petre Churches', in Francis Porter (ed.), *Historic Buildings of New Zealand: South Island* (Auckland: Methuen, 1983), 150–59.

48 *New Zealand Tablet,* 31 August 1877, 13.

49 Patrick Moran, *History of the Catholic Church in Australasia* (Sydney & Melbourne: Frank Coffee & Co., 1896), 953–55.

50 Sister Mary de Ricci Kirby to Uncle Kirby, [illegible] 187[illegible] GH4/2/1, DA.

51 Sister Mary de Ricci Kirby to Uncle Kirby, 10 January 1880. GH4/2/7, DA.
52 Congregational Annals, Book 1: 1871–1910. CA1, DA.
53 Ibid.
54 McCarthy, *Star in the South*, 88.
55 Sister Mary John the Evangelist Ryan to Mother Mary Clare Elliot, 4 September 1883. GH3/4/19, DA.
56 Sister Mary Alphonsus Owens to Mother Mary Clare Elliot, June 1882. GH3/4/11, DA.
57 Congregational Annals, Book 1: 1871–1910. CA1, DA.
58 Sister Mary Agnes Rooney to Mother Mary Clare Elliot, 12 July 1882. GH3/4/13, DA.
59 Sister Mary Clare Elliot to Archbishop Kirby, 22 April 1885. GH4/2/12, DA.
60 Congregational Annals, Book 1: 1871–1910. Mother Mary Gabriel Gill's Correspondence, Beaumont, 1886–88. GH1/2/1–33, DA.
61 *Otago Witness*, 10 October 1889, 9. Moran returned from Dublin with five new priests for the diocese and 'a number of young women who were determined to devote themselves to the service of God and education in this diocese'. Congregational Annals, Book 1: 1871–1910. CA1, DA.
62 Congregational Records. DA. Sister Mary Brendan Murphy, Sister Mary Evangelist Murphy, Deceased Sisters Files. S4, DA.
63 Sister Joseph Neylon, Deceased Sisters Files. S4, DA.
64 Congregational Records. DA.
65 *Otago Daily Times*, 14 October 1889, 2–3.
66 Congregational Annals, Book 1: 1871–1910. CA1, DA.
67 McCarthy, *Star in the South*, 128.
68 Congregational Annals, Book 1: 1871–1910. CA1, DA.
69 *Dominican Star* (Dunedin: New Zealand Tablet, 1900), 168. M1, DA.
70 Bishop Moran to Mother Mary Gabriel Gill, 22 January 1894. C1/3/5, DA.
71 Congregational Annals, Book 1: 1871–1910. CA1, DA.
72 Ibid.
73 Sister Mary Winefride Morris in 'One hundred years on the hill 1912–2012: St Mary's Catholic Church and School Kaikorai', unpublished book of memories (Dunedin, 2013), 24. DA.
74 Sister Mary St Peter Slattery to Sisters, 7 November 1898. CR1/2/17, DA.
75 Ibid.
76 Ibid.
77 Sisters at St Dominick's to Mothers and Sisters of Sion Hill, 2 January 1894, in Minute Book of the First General Chapter of the Dominican Nuns of the Province of Otago, 1893–94. CH1/1, DA.
78 Congregational Annals, Book 2: 1911–1937. CA1, DA.
79 10 November 1915, Book of Permissions, St Dominic's Priory, Dunedin, 1894–1916. C1/1, DA.
80 Michael King, *God's Farthest Outpost: A history of Catholics in New Zealand* (Auckland: Penguin, 1997), 274–75.
81 Congregational Annals, Book 2: 1911–1937. CA1, DA.
82 Personal communication with sisters, 28 June 2014, Dunedin.
83 McKinnon, *New Zealand Historical Atlas*, plate 70. In the upper South Island and North Island in 1921 Catholics made up 13.6 per cent of the population, with 19.9 per cent Presbyterian and 45.8 per cent Anglican.
84 Ibid.
85 King, *God's Farthest Outpost*, 157. See also Dom Felice Vaggioli, *History of New Zealand and Its Inhabitants,* first published 1895 (Dunedin: University of Otago Press, 2000, 308–09). Vaggioli was an Italian monk who lived in New Zealand in the 1880s. He strongly disapproved of the intermarriage of Catholics and Protestants in New Zealand and of the relaxed relationships between Catholics and Protestants in wider society.
86 Sister Mary Louis Keighron to My Own Darling Sis, 26 July 1903. GH3/5/6, DA.
87 King, *God's Farthest Outpost*, 275.
88 Len Richardson, 'Politics and political change', in Geoffrey Rice (ed.), *The Oxford History of New Zealand* (Auckland: Oxford University Press, 1992), 218–19.
89 Erik Olssen, 'Towards a new society', in Rice (ed.), *Oxford History of New Zealand*, 270–71.
90 E.R. Simmons, *A Brief History of the Catholic Church in New Zealand* (Auckland: Catholic Publications Centre, 1978), 87.
91 Erik Olssen, *Building the New World: Work, politics and society in Caversham, 1880s–1920s* (Auckland: Auckland University Press, 1995), 245.

92 Congregational Records. DA.
93 Sister Mary Bertrand McLoughlin to Mother Mary Margaret, 21 March 1921. GH3/6/10, DA.
94 Sister Mary Peter Slattery to Mother Mary Pius, 25 June 1924. GH3/6/18, DA.
95 Ibid.
96 Sister Mary Cecily Mulcahy to Mother, 17 November 1924. GH3/6/20, DA.
97 Sister Mary Cecily Mulcahy to Mother, 20 November 1925. GH3/6/27, DA.
98 Sister Mary Cecily Mulcahy to Mother Prioress, 27 March 1925. GH3/6/24, DA.
99 Sister Mary Cecily Mulcahy to Mother, 17 November 1924. Sister Mary Cecily Mulcahy to Mother Mary Pius, 1925. GH3/6/28, DA.
100 Sister Mary Cecily Mulcahy to Mother, 17 November 1924.
101 Sister Mary Cecily to Mother Prioress, 21 February 1927. GH3/6/29, DA.
102 Chronological description of foundations, 1 April 1909, 30 November 1910, 20 October 1911, June 1912. GH5/5/41, DA.
103 Chronological description of foundations, 25 April 1920. GH5/5/41, DA.
104 Chronological description of foundations, 12 March 1921. GH5/5/41, DA.
105 Cited in Pilkington, *We See What You Mean …: A history of St Dominic's School for Deaf Children and the Catholic Deaf Ministry in New Zealand* (Palmerston North: St Dominic's School for the Deaf Historical Society Inc., 2008), 125.
106 Pilkington, *We See What You Mean.*
107 Congregational Annals, 6 February 1929. CA1, DA. The novitiate building is now home to the Catholic Pastoral Centre, officially opened 21 May 1995.
108 Congregational Annals, 2 May 1937. CA1, DA.
109 Ibid. Commonly referred to as 'Albertus Magnus'.
110 *Dominican Star* (Dunedin: New Zealand Tablet, 1947), 20. M1/DA.
111 Sister Mary Dominica McKay to Sisters, 4 September 1942. C1/3/45, DA.
112 Sister Mary Dominica McKay to Sisters, 13 April 1942. CR1/2/76, DA.
113 Sister Mary Reginald Quilter to Sisters, 22 February 1935. CR2/1, DA.
114 Ibid.
115 Sandra M. Schneiders, *Prophets in their Own Country: Women religious bearing witness to the gospel in a troubled Church* (New York: Orbis Books, 2011), 41.
116 Ian Pool, Arunachalam Dharmalingam & Janet Sceats, *The New Zealand Family from 1840: A demographic history* (Auckland: Auckland University Press, 2007), 166–216.
117 Hans Mol, *The Fixed and the Fickle: Religion and identity in New Zealand* (Pilgrims South Press: Dunedin, 1992), 79.
118 Triennial Report on St Dominic's Priory, Dunedin 1940–42. CL4/1, DA.
119 Ibid.
120 Triennial Report on St Dominic's Priory, Dunedin, 1954–56. CL4/6, DA. Triennial Report on St Dominic's Priory, Dunedin, 1957–59. CL4/7, DA
121 Triennial Report on St Dominic's Priory, Dunedin, 1940–42. This report discusses the strain on space and staff in the boarding school, which had made it 'impossible to maintain proper discipline'.
122 Dominican Hall Annals, 1948–81. RA5, DA.
123 Dominican Hall Material. F15, DA.
124 Quinquennial Report to Rome, 1948–1952. [illegible] DA.
125 Father McArdle to Mother Mary Tarcisius, [illegible] March 1952, quoted in Congregational Annals, March 1952. CA1, DA.
126 Ibid.
127 Maureen O'Hanlon, Personal Profile, 2011. DA.
128 Triennial Report on St Dominic's Priory, Dunedin 1940–42.
129 Triennial Report on St Catherine's Priory, Invercargill, 1944. CL4/2, DA.
130 McCarthy, *Star in the South*, 277.
131 Mother Mary Philomena McCarthy to Sisters, undated. CR1/2/101, DA.
132 Carmel Walsh, Interview, 24 October 2010. DA.
133 Sandra Winton, Interview, 27 January 2011. DA.
134 Ibid.
135 Ibid.
136 Paddy McCann, Interview, 18 March 2011. DA.
137 Joan Hardiman, Interview, 25 July 2011. DA.
138 Raewyn Benzie, Interview, 4 September 2011. DA
139 Newsletter, March 1964. COM1/3, DA.
140 Newsletter, October 1964. COM1/3, DA.
141 Mary Horn, Interview, 17 March 2011. DA.
142 Newsletter, July 1965. COM1/3, DA.
143 Newsletter, June 1965. COM1/3, DA.

144 Newsletter, August 1965. COM1/3, DA.
145 Mission Formation Committee Report 2006. CH3/19, DA.
146 Acts of the Special General Chapter of the Congregation of the New Zealand Dominican Sisters, 26 December 1968–18 January 1969. CH, DA.
147 Triennial Report of Dominican Priory, Henderson, 1977. CL4/13, DA.
148 Triennial Report of Dominican Hall, 1977. CL4/13, DA.
149 Triennial Report of Convent of Our Lady of the Sacred Heart, 1977. CL4/13, DA.
150 Triennial Report of St Dominic's Convent, Feilding, 1971. CL4/12, DA.
151 Triennial Report of St Dominic's Priory, 1974. CL4/12, DA.
152 Triennial Report for St Dominic's Convent, Northcote, 1969–71. CL4/11, DA.
153 Triennial Report of Santa Sabina Convent, North East Valley, 1974. CL4/12, DA.
154 Mother Jordan McCormick to Sisters, 16 December 1970. CL7/2/31, DA.
155 Ibid.
156 Father Vincent de Couesnongle to Brothers, 6 January 1975. CL8/1/14, DA.
157 The Mission to the New Hebrides: A Summary of points submitted by the Sisters, 1979. F18/1/7, DA.
158 Discernment re: New Hebrides. F18/1/2, DA. Letters from sisters volunteering for the New Hebrides mission. F18/1/1, DA.
159 St Catherine's Convent, Walarano Annals, 1980. F18/5/1, DA.
160 *Walarano News*. F18/5/1, DA. Judith McGinley, Interview, 29 April 2011. DA.
161 Sandra Winton, Forward, 1984/1. COM3, DA.
162 Notes on Vanuatu, July 1984. C7/7/27, DA.
163 Mary Horn to Sisters, 21 June 1988. C8/11/28, DA.
164 Forward, 1986/4, 41. F18/9/12, DA.
165 Triennial Report of St Dominic's Priory, Dunedin, 1980. CL4/14, DA.
166 Administrator, St Joseph's Cathedral to Sister Mary Constance Quinn, 18 November 1980. C7/4/2, DA.
167 'Catholic Education. Dunedin City', 1975. CL8/1/8, DA.
168 Carmel Walsh, Interview, 24 October 2010. DA.
169 The Private Schools Conditional Integration Act, passed in 1975, more than 100 years since Bishop Moran had first begun his impassioned campaign for state aid to Catholic schools, allowed church schools to retain their special character while receiving government funding. By the late 1980s most church schools were integrated.
170 Triennial Report of St Dominic's Priory, Dunedin, 1980. CL4/14, DA.
171 Raewyn Benzie, Notes on the History of the Novitiate Building. GH5/5/3, DA.
172 Ninth General Chapter of the New Zealand Dominican Sisters, 1980–81. CH, DA.
173 Mary Horn, Interview, 17 March 2011. DA.
174 Quoted in *Asia Pacific Dominican Women Newsletter*, 1997/2. DF3/6, DA.
175 Meeting of the General Council, 10–12 May 1981. CL7/3/32, DA. Negotiations regarding the Priory, 6 July 1981. CL7/3/38, DA.
176 General Information, 1981. CL7/3/41, DA.
177 Heritage New Zealand Pouhere Taonga, 'St Dominic's Priory (Former)': www.historic.org.nz/TheRegister.
178 General Information 1981, 1982. CL7/3/56, CL7/3/59, DA. Margaret Quinn to Sisters, 9 September 1982. CL7/3/70, DA.
179 Margaret Quinn to Sisters, 20 March 1983. CL7/3/78, DA. General Information, April 1983. CL7/3/79, DA.
180 *Otago Daily Times*, 12 December 2009, 4.
181 Judith Anne O'Sullivan, Interview, 28 September 2010. DA.
182 St Brigid's Community Report, Dunedin, 1987–90. CL4/16, DA.
183 Sandra Winton, Interview, 27 January 2011. DA.
184 Report of York Place Community, Dunedin, 1987–90. CL4/16, DA.
185 Ibid.
186 Sister Mary Gerardine, Report, 1987–90. CL4/16, DA.
187 Raewyn Benzie, Interview, 4 September 2011. DA.
188 Tenth General Chapter of the New Zealand Dominican Sisters, 1986. CH, DA.
189 Leadership Team to Sisters, 21 September 1987. CL9/1, DA.
190 Raewyn Benzie, Interview, 4 September 2011. DA.
191 Janice Ogilvy, Interview, 16 March 2011. DA.
192 Mother Mary Constance Quinn to Sisters, 8 December 1976. CL7/1/51, DA.
193 Communication from the Leadership Team, April 1991. CL9/2, DA.

3. 'God stepped in': Becoming a Dominican sister

1 Judith McGinley in 'The hope that is within us', 1998. DA.

2 Questions to be asked before entering novitiate 1895–1939. NOV1/4, DA.

3 Questions to be asked before entering novitiate 1940–. NOV1/3, DA.

4 Sister Basil Geoffrey, Reminiscences, 2005–06, in Personal Profiles. DA.

5 Judith Anne O'Sullivan, Personal Profile, 2011. DA.

6 Sister Mary Genevieve O'Rourke, Personal Profile, 2011. DA.

7 Sister Getrude Fox, Interview, 24 January 2011. DA.

8 Mary Anna Baird, Personal Profile, 2011. DA.

9 Paddy McCann, Interview, 18 March 2011. DA.

10 Raewyn Benzie, Interview, 4 September 2011. DA.

11 Roxane Parkinson, Personal Profile, 2011. DA. Roxane Parkinson, Interview, 28 April 2011. DA.

12 Sister Mary Colman O'Sullivan in 'The hope that is within us', 1998. DA.

13 Anne O'Neil, Personal Profile, 2011. DA.

14 Susan Logan, Personal Profile, 2011. DA.

15 Barbara Dwyer, Personal Profile, 2011. DA.

16 Sister Loreto Meehan, Interview, 25 July 2011. DA.

17 Lorraine Challis, Personal Profile, 2011. DA.

18 Lorraine Challis in 'The hope that is within us', 1998. DA.

19 Patricia Hannan, Personal Profile, 2011. DA.

20 Ibid.

21 Carmel Walsh, Interview, 24 October 2010. DA.

22 Sister Marie Eugene Nicolson, Personal Profile, 2011. DA.

23 Catherine Tither, Personal Profile, 2011. DA.

24 Elizabeth Mackie, Interview, 11 November 2011. DA.

25 Joan Bennett, Personal Profile, 2011. DA.

26 Jacqui Ryan, Interview, 24 July 2011. DA.

27 *Book of Annals. Sion Hill Convent, Blackrock, Co. Dublin, Golden Jubilee, 1854–1904* (Dublin: Browne & Nolan, 1904), 307.

28 Congregation of New Zealand Dominican Sisters, Quinquennial Report to the Holy See 1953–1957. CL6/4/5, DA.

29 Mother Gabriel Gill to Archbishop Kirby, 1 December 1887. GH4/1/12, DA.

30 In 1870 Gill gave the Dominican mission to New Zealand a gold ciborium (a vessel for the communion host) 'in love of his beloved daughter Victoria'.

31 Mother Gabriel Gill to Archbishop Kirby, 2[illegible] April 1882. CH4/1/3, DA.

32 Mother Gabriel Gill to Archbishop Kirby, 2[illegible] November 1887. GH4/1/[illegible], DA.

33 Sister Mary Agatha Carroll, Deceased Sisters File S1, DA. Sister Mary Agatha died in July 1895 at the age of 28. Her parents were joined at the funeral by members of the Town Council, the Otago Harbour Board and the Charitable Aid Board, and the flag was flown at half-mast at the Town Hall.

34 Questions to be asked before entering novitiate, 1895–1939. NOV1/4, DA.

35 Mima originally took the name Sister Mary Liguori. When an Australian Dominican sister named Liguori hit headlines by 'leaping the wall' into the arms of her lover, the New Zealand sister changed her name to Alphonsus.

36 Sister Alphonsus Falconer, Deceased Sisters File S2, DA.

37 Sister Dominic Swindale, Interview, 25 July 2011. DA. Sister Dominic's mother died of cancer when she was a postulant. Janet would have left the convent to go home – 'they'd feel so happy to see me walking up the path to look after her' – but Mother David said 'No, it's taken you a long time to get here,' and Janet's younger sister went home and took responsibility instead.

38 Sister Madeleine McAleese, Interview with Mary Scally, December 2011. Private papers, Sister Madeleine McAleese.

39 Sister Gertrude Fox, Interview, 24 January 2011. DA.

40 Sister Maria McDonald, Personal Profile, 2011. DA.

41 Sister Mary Columba McHugh, Personal Profile, 2011. DA.

42 Sister Marie Eugene Nicolson, Personal Profile, 2011. DA.

43 Roxane Parkinson, Interview, 28 April 2011. DA.

44 Joan Bennett, Personal Profile, 2011. DA.

45 Jan Ogilvy, Interview, 16 March 2011. DA.

46 Sandra Winton, Interview, 27 January 2011. DA.

47 Judith Robinson, Interview, 24 January 2011. DA.

48 Helen Bergin, Interview, 24 October 2010. DA.

49 Patricia Hannan, Personal Profile, 2011. DA.

50 Mother Mary David Stark, Address on Dominican Order, undated. CL7/4/5, DA.

51 Rule and Constitutions of the Sisters of St Dominic, Sion Hill, 1858. CON1/8, DA.
52 Constitutions of the Congregation of the New Zealand Dominican Sisters, 1989, 23. DA.
53 Ordinations of the Congregation of the New Zealand Dominican Sisters, 1989, 7. DA.
54 Constitutions of the Congregation of the New Zealand Dominican Sisters, 1939. CON1/8, DA.
55 Mary Horn, Interview, 29 April 2011. DA.
56 Rule and Constitutions of St Dominick, for the use of the Religious Community of St Dominick's Priory, Dunedin, New Zealand, 1908, 27. CON1/2A, DA.
57 Ibid., 3.
58 Ibid., 27.
59 The profession and clothing ceremonies for choir and lay sisters were largely the same; the only difference, which signified lay sisters' lower status, was that the Veni Creator was spoken for lay sisters' ceremonies and sung for choir sisters.
60 Sister Marie Therese, 'A few memories of St Theresa's novitiate building'. GH5/5/3, DA.
61 Congregational Annals, 4 September 1929. CA1, DA. The women received at this ceremony were Ada Sligo (Sister Mary Damian) Ita Maloney (Sister Mary Brigid), Catherine Nolan, (Sister Mary Amata), Kathleen Treacy (Sister Mary Edna), Bea Cribbin (Sister Mary Columbanus), Margaret Brennan (Sister Mary St Anne), Kathleen Dooley (Sister Mary Oliver), Pauline Dunne (Sister Mary Teresita), May Lowe (Sister Mary Candice), Honor Smith (Sister Marie Therese), Bridie Butterly (Sister Mary Declan), Josephine Kearns (Sister Mary Veronica).
62 Janice Ogilvy, Interview, 16 March 2011. DA.
63 'Public to hear sisters' vows', undated unattributed newspaper clipping. CL7/2, DA.
64 Sister Marie Therese, 'A few memories'.
65 Ibid.
66 Sister Maria McDonald, Personal Profile, 2011. DA.
67 Sister Mary Columba McHugh, Personal Profile, 2011. DA.
68 Sister Basil Geoffrey, Reminiscences, 2005–06, in Personal Profiles. DA.
69 Lorraine Challis, Personal Profile, 2011. DA.
70 Roxane Parkinson, Interview, 28 April 2011. DA.
71 Barbara Dwyer, Personal Profile, 2011. DA.
72 Loreto Meehan, Interview, 25 July 2011. DA.
73 Maureen Connolly, Personal Profile, 2011. DA.
74 Maureen O'Hanlon, Personal Profile, 2011. DA.
75 Mary Concannon, Personal Profile, 2011. DA.
76 Sister Mary Adrienne White, Personal Profile, 2011. DA.
77 Mary Anna Baird, Personal Profile, 2011. DA.
78 Raewyn Benzie, Interview, 4 September 2011. DA. Life in other Dominican novitiates around the world was very similar in this period. The South African Dominicans also struggled to integrate the practicalities of studying and teaching with the ideal of isolation and spiritual development. South African sisters who were novices in the 1940s and 50s describe the novitiate as a process to be endured. Kathleen Boner, *Dominican Women: A time to speak* (Pietermaritzburg: Cluster Publications, 2000), 101–02.
79 Janice Ogilvy, Personal Profile, 2011. DA.
80 Janice Ogilvy, Interview, 16 March 2011. DA.
81 General Council Notes, 22–24 August 1976. CL8/3/1, DA.
82 Correspondence. C7/4/80, DA.
83 Jacqui Ryan, Interview, 24 July 2011. DA.
84 Constitutions of the Congregation of the New Zealand Dominican Sisters, 1989. DA.
85 This figure includes local and Irish postulants and professed sisters who emigrated from Ireland to join the New Zealand Congregation.
86 Rules and Constitutions of St Dominick, 1908, 35.
87 Sister Mary Cecily Mulcahy to Sion Hill, 13 March 1924. GH3/6/14, DA.
88 Mother Mary Peter Slattery to Mother, 25 June 1924. GH3/6/18, DA.
89 Sister Mary Cecily Mulcahy to Mother, 2 July 1924. GH3/6/19, DA.
90 Sister Mary Cecily Mulcahy to Mother Prioress, 21 February 1927. GH3/6/29, DA. Clara Steinmayer (Sister Mary Teresita), who had travelled out with Gerty and Kathleen, also had 'lung problems'. The doctor would not pass her for holy profession, so she left the community in 1925.
91 Sister Mary Cecily Mulcahy to Mother, 17 November 1924. GH3/6/20, DA.
92 Sister Mary Cecily Mulcahy to Mother, 26 March 1925. GH3/6/2, DA. Bishop James Whyte to Mother Pius, 18 March 25. GH3/6/23, DA.
93 Sister Mary Cecily Mulcahy to Mother, 22 June 1925. GH3/6/24, DA.

94 Sister Mary Ceslaus to Mother Prioress, 21 February 1927. GH3/6/29, DA.
95 Quinquennial Report of the Congregation of the New Zealand Dominican Sisters, 1933–37. CL6/4/1, DA.
96 Quinquennial Report of the Congregation of the New Zealand Dominican Sisters, 1943–47. CL6/4/3, DA.
97 Judith Graham, *Breaking the Habit. Life in a New Zealand convent 1955–1967*, 2nd edn (Dunedin: Longacre Press, 2006), 71.
98 Ibid., 79.
99 Ibid., 82.
100 Ibid., 89.
101 Ibid., 91–92, 132–47.
102 Sister Mary David Stark, Visitation 1967. CL5/3, DA.
103 Mary Horn, Interview, 17 March 2011, DA.
104 Kathleen Thomson, Personal Profile, 2014. DA.
105 The Interim Constitutions of the Congregation of the New Zealand Dominican Sisters, 1976. CON1/4, DA.
106 Constitutions of the Congregation of the New Zealand Dominican Sisters, 1989, 40–41.
107 Ordinations of the Congregation of the New Zealand Dominican Sisters, 1989, 16–17. DA.
108 Barbara Menzies, private communication with author, 9 May 2014.
109 Ibid.
110 Ibid.
111 Communication from the Leadership Team, Christmas 1995. CL9/2, DA.
112 Kathleen Thomson, Personal Profile, 2014, DA.
113 Barbara Menzies, private communication with author, 9 May 2014.

4. 'A total gift of your life': From enclosure to immersion

1 Mary Augustine McCarthy, *Star in the South: The centennial history of the New Zealand Dominican Sisters* (Dunedin: St Dominic's Priory, 1970), 16. Related by Mother Mary Michael (Margaret) McCarthy (1860–1956). Mother Michael was a white novice at Sion Hill when she responded to Bishop Moran's request for mission sisters; she travelled with him when he returned to New Zealand in 1881.
2 Rule and Constitutions of St Dominick, for the use of the Religious Community of St Dominick's Priory, Dunedin, New Zealand, 1908, 5. CON1/2A, DA.
3 Ibid., 20.
4 Sister Mary Gabriel Gill to Bishop Kirby, 1 April 1884. GH4/1/4, DA.
5 Ibid.
6 Book of Permissions, St Dominic's Priory, Dunedin, 1894–1916. C1/1, DA.
7 Book of Permissions, St Dominic's Priory, Dunedin, 1921–33. CR2/6, DA.
8 Father Finbar Ryan to Mother Prioress, 16 May 1931. CR1/2/41, DA.
9 Sister Mary Reginald Quilter to Sisters, 22 February 1935. CR2/1, DA.
10 Sister Mary Reginald Quilter to Sisters, 18 December 1937. CR2/1, DA.
11 Ibid.
12 Sister Mary Reginald Quilter to Sisters, 21 March 1939. CR2/1, DA.
13 Sister Mary Reginald Quilter to Sisters, 6 December 1939. CR2/1, DA.
14 Sister Mary Dominica McKay to Sisters, 28 January 1940. C1/3/27, DA.
15 Acts of the Second General Chapter of the Congregation of the New Zealand Dominican Sisters, 2[illegible]–24 December 1939. CH, DA.
16 Acts of the Fourth General Chapter of the Congregation of the New Zealand Dominican Sisters, 2[illegible] December 1950–2 January 1951. CH, DA
17 Acts of the Fifth General Chapter of the Congregation of the New Zealand Dominican Sisters, 2[illegible] December 1956–3 January 1957. CH, DA.
18 Quinquennial Report of the Congregation of the New Zealand Dominican Sisters to the Holy See 1953–57. CL6/4/5, DA.
19 Triennial Report on St Catherine's Priory, Invercargill, 1956. CL4/6, DA.
20 Sister Mary Adrienne White, Personal Profile, 20[illegible] DA.
21 Judith Graham, *Breaking the Habit. Life in a New Zealand convent 1955–1967*, 2nd edn (Dunedin: Longacre Press, 2006), 22.
22 Ibid., 45.
23 Marie Twomey, Personal Profile, 2011. DA.
24 Joan Bennett, Personal Profile, 2011. DA.
25 Nola Gleeson, Interview, 17 March 2011. DA.
26 Acts of the Sixth General Chapter of the Congregation of the New Zealand Dominican Sisters, [illegible] December 1962–3 January 1963. CH, DA.

27 Acts of the Eighth General Chapter of the Congregation of the New Zealand Dominican Sisters, 26 December 1974–15 January 1975. CH, DA.
28 Patricia Hannan, Personal Profile. DA.
29 Mother Mary David Stark, Visitation Book 1964. CL5/3, DA.
30 Newsletter, July 1965, August 1965, COM1/3, DA.
31 Acts of the Special General Chapter of the Congregation of the New Zealand Dominican Sisters, 26 December 1968–18 January 1969. CH, DA.
32 Acts of the Second Session of the Special General Chapter of the Congregation of the New Zealand Dominican Sisters, 31 December 1969–11 January 1970. CH, DA.
33 Interim Handbook of the New Zealand Dominican Sisters, 31 January 1970. CON1/11, DA.
34 Mother Mary Jordan McCormick to Superiors, 31 January 1970. CL7/2/20, DA.
35 Visitation of St Dominic's Priory, Dunedin, 10 June 1970, Book of Visitation, 1970–74. CL5/4, DA.
36 Visitation of St Catherine's Priory, Invercargill, 20–28 September 1971, Book of Visitation, 1970–74. CL5/4, DA.
37 Acts of the Eighth General Chapter.
38 The Interim Constitutions of the Congregation of the New Zealand Dominican Sisters, 1976. CON1/4, DA.
39 Lorraine Challis, Personal Profile, 2011. DA.
40 Lorraine Challis in 'The hope that is within us', 1998. DA.
41 Roxane Parkinson, Interview, 28 April 2011. DA.
42 Judith Anne O'Sullivan, Personal Profile, 2011. DA.
43 Margaret Quinn, Interview, 11 November 2011. DA.
44 Sister Judith Anne O'Sullivan to Council, 15 December 1977. C7/1/47, DA.
45 Sister Mary Elizabeth Mackie to Sisters, 2 November 1981. CL7/3/51, DA.
46 Sister Raewyn Benzie to Sister Margaret Quinn and Councillors, 1 October 1981. C7/5/4, DA.
47 Raewyn Benzie, Interview, 4 September 2011. DA.
48 Report of Dominican Priory, Teschemakers, 1980. CL4/14, DA.
49 Ambrose Loughnan, *Full Circle to God* (Ohoka: Loughley Books, 2000), 184.
50 Teschemakers Community Report, 1987–90. CL4/16, DA.
51 Ibid.
52 Tenth General Chapter of the New Zealand Dominican Sisters, 1986, 14. CH, DA.
53 Sister Mary St Anne Brennan in 'The hope that is within us'.
54 Sister Mary Declan Butterly in 'The hope that is within us'.
55 Constitutions of the Congregation of the New Zealand Dominican Sisters, 1989. DA.
56 Sister Mary Clare Timpany in 'The hope that is within us'. See also Waiheke Convent Files. RA1, DA.
57 Margaret Butler in 'The hope that is within us'.
58 Helen Bergin in 'The hope that is within us'.
59 May Street Community Report, 1987–90. CL4/16, DA.
60 Cecily Sheehy, Interview, 25 July 2011. DA.
61 Remits of the Second Session of the Special General Chapter, 1969. CL7/2/15, DA. Acts of the Eighth General Chapter.
62 Mai Duignan to Prioress General, 28 April 1972. CL7/2/75, DA.
63 Communication from the Leadership Team, 1 April 1989. CL9/1, DA.
64 Sister Susan Logan to Mother Constance Quinn, 9 May 1978. C7/2/12, DA.
65 Maureen O'Hanlon, Personal Profile, 2011. DA.
66 Anne O'Neill to Sisters, 19 April 1998. F20/1/4, DA.
67 Private conversation with author, Hampton Hermitage, Dublin, 3 September 2011.
68 Anne O'Neill and Barbara Dwyer, Evaluation 2002. F20/2/20, DA.
69 Communication from the Leadership Team, 5 October 1989. CL9/1, DA.
70 Sister Mary Leonie Parry in 'The hope that is within us'.
71 Raewyn Benzie, Interview.

5. 'Beauteous order': The rule

1 Rule and Constitutions of St Dominick, for the use of the Religious Community of St Dominick's Priory, Dunedin, New Zealand, 1908, 5. CON1/2A, DA.
2 Bishop Moran to Sisters, undated. CR1/2/12, DA.
3 William A. Hinnebusch, *Dominican Spirituality: Principles and practice* (Washington: The Thomist Press, 1965), 7. As Hinnebusch expressed it, 'Constant fidelity to the rule imposes considerable self-control on the religious, demands constant scrutiny of conscience, and whole-hearted obedience to rule and authority. This regime leads to a more perfect exercise of many

virtues. Thus it restrains the natural impetuosity of his senses and emotions, establishes peace in his soul, and nourishes his fraternal charity, a prime requisite for contemplation and apostolic activity.'

4 Sister Mary St Peter Slattery to Sisters, November 1899. CR1/2/14, DA.

5 Sister Mary Cecily Mulcahy to Mother, 30 June 1912. GH3/5/31, DA.

6 Sister Mary Louis Keighron to Mother, 26 June 1910. GH3/5/22, DA.

7 The Rule of St Augustine and the Constitutions of the Congregation of the New Zealand Dominican Sisters, 1939, 49. CON1/8, DA.

8 Ibid., 51.

9 Ceremonial of the Irish Dominican Congregation, Cabra, 1950, 9–10. PL1/17B, DA.

10 Customary of the New Zealand Dominican Sisters, 1–2. GH5/11/7, DA.

11 Ceremonial of the Irish Dominican Congregation, 4.

12 Sister Catherine Mary to Sister Mary Augustine, 28 May 1995. GH5/5/1, DA.

13 Ceremonial of the Irish Dominican Congregation, 111–27.

14 Cecily Sheehy, Interview, 25 July 2011. DA.

15 Judith Anne O'Sullivan, Personal Profile, 2011. DA.

16 Maureen Connolly, Personal Profile, 2011. DA.

17 Carmel Walsh, Interview, 24 October 2010. DA.

18 Patricia Hannan, Personal Profile, 2011. DA.

19 Sister Mary Catherine Hughes to Mother Mary Clare Elliot, 26 December 1872. GH3/2/8, DA.

20 Congregational Annals, Book 1: 1871–1910. CA1, DA.

21 Ibid.

22 Rule and Constitutions of St Dominick, 1908.

23 Sister Mary Leonie Parry, Personal Profile, 2011. DA.

24 Sister Mary di Pazzi Miscall to Mother Mary Philomena McCarthy, 26 October 1955. CR1/2/108, DA.

25 Minute Book of the First General Chapter of the Dominican Nuns of the Province of Otago, 1893–94.

26 Rule and Constitutions of St Dominick, 1908. CON1/2A, DA.

27 Only for the Salve Procession after Compline and the weekly Libera did the lay sisters join the choir sisters for the Divine Office.

28 Rule and Constitutions of St Dominick, 1908.

29 *Souvenir of the Novitiate* (New York: Benziger Brothers, 1879), 155.

30 The Rule of Saint Augustine, 1939.

31 Bluff Convent, 7 December 1936, Visitation Records. CL5/1, DA.

32 Milton Convent, 10 December 1936, Visitation Records. CL5/1, DA.

33 Lawrence Convent, 11 December 1936, Visitation Records. CL5/1, DA.

34 St Catherine's Priory, Invercargill, 9 November [illegible], Visitation Records. CL5/1, DA.

35 St Catherine's Priory, Invercargill, 19 September [illegible]. Visitation Records. CL5/1, DA.

36 Triennial Report on St Dominic's Convent, Northcote 1950. CL4/3, DA.

37 Northcote Convent, 21 March 1956, Visitation Records. CL5/2, DA.

38 Sister Mary Declan Butterly, Deceased Sisters Files S1, DA.

39 Ibid.

40 Sister Alban McCaughan, Interview, 29 July 2011. DA.

41 Nola Gleeson, Interview, 17 March 2011. DA.

42 Ibid.

43 Rule and Constitutions of St Dominick, 1908, 5.

44 Rule and Constitutions of the Sisters of St Dominic, Sion Hill, 1858, 3, CON1/8, DA.

45 Triennial Report on Queenstown Convent, 195[illegible]–59. CL4/7, DA.

46 Nola Gleeson, Interview, 21 August 1940. DA.

47 'Sisters recall life in the Novitiate', clipping from *Dunedin Diocesan News*, undated. GH5/5/2, DA.

48 Maureen O'Hanlon, Personal Profile, 2011. DA.

49 Sister Mary St Joan Terry, 'This is your life'. DA.

50 Roxane Parkinson, Interview, 28 April 2011. DA.

51 Paddy McCann, Interview, 18 March 2011. DA.

52 Joan Hardiman, Interview, 25 July 2011. DA.

53 Rule and Constitutions of St Dominick, 1908.

54 Sister Mary Reginald Quilter to Sisters, 11 October 1938, Queenstown Convent Correspondence. CL[illegible]1, DA.

55 Mother Mary David Stark to Superiors, 16 July [illegible]8. CL7/4/12, DA.

56 Mother Mary Jordan McCormick to Superiors, 2[illegible] June 1969. CL7/2/11, DA.

57 Customary of the New Zealand Dominican Sisters, 3

58 Sister Mary Reginald Quilter to Sisters, 21 March 1939. CR2/1, DA.

59 Customary of the New Zealand Dominican Sisters, 2

60 Customary of the New Zealand Dominican Sisters, 3 5–6.

61 Patricia Hannan, Personal Profile, 2011. DA.
62 Sister Mary Francis Lister, Personal Profile, 2011. DA.
63 Cecily Sheehy, Interview, 25 July 2011. DA.
64 Madeleine McAleese, Personal Profile, 2011. DA.
65 Bernie Chenye, Personal Profile, 2011. DA.
66 William A. Hinnebusch, *The History of the Dominican Order*, vol. 1 (New York: Alba House, 1965), 84. In 1220 the first General Chapter inserted a prologue in the Dominican customary: 'the prelate shall have power to dispense the brethren in his priory when it shall seem expedient to him, especially in those things that are seen to impede study, preaching, or the good of souls, since it is known that our Order was especially founded from the beginning for preaching and the salvation of souls. Our study ought to tend principally, ardently, and with the highest endeavour to the end that we might be useful to the souls of our neighbours.'
67 Ibid.
68 Simon Tugwell, *The Way of the Preacher* (London: Darton, Longman & Todd, 1979), 86.
69 The Rule of Saint Augustine, 1939, 39–40.
70 Rule and Constitutions of St Dominick, 1908.
71 Mother Mary David Stark, Visitation Report, 1967. CL5/3, DA.
72 Rule and Constitutions of the Sisters of St Dominic, 1858, 1–3.

6. Freedom: Community life since the Second Vatican Council

1 Patricia Hannan, Personal Profile, 2011. DA.
2 Judith McGinley, Interview, 29 April 2011. DA.
3 Mary Horn, Interview, 17 March 2011. DA.
4 Roxane Parkinson, Interview, 28 April 2011. DA.
5 Interview with Sister Loreto Meehan, www.dominicans.org.nz
6 Mother Mary David Stark, Visitation Notes, 1964. CL5/3, DA.
7 Mother Mary David Stark, Visitation Notes, 1967. CL7/3, DA.
8 Mother Mary David Stark to Superiors, 31 January 1967. CL7/4/59, DA.
9 Mother Mary David Stark, Visitation Notes, 1967.
10 Acts of the Special General Chapters of the Congregation of the New Zealand Dominican Sisters, 26 December 1968–18 January 1969. CH, DA. 'It is not a breach of silence for sisters to speak in the course of their work; a distinction should be made between general silence and profound silence, and between silence of the cloister and charity of the apostolate. Normal, friendly relations between the sisters and between sisters and children should be maintained.'
11 The venia could only be imposed after a serious fault against the rule, and was never to be used to punish elderly sisters. Accidental breakages were to be reported to the superior with an apology, but the sister responsible no longer had to kneel when apologising.
12 Mother Mary Jordan McCormick to Superiors, 30 January 1969. CL7/2/, DA.
13 Acts of the Special General Chapters, 26 December 1968–18 January 1969.
14 Triennial Report for St Patrick's Priory, Teschemakers, 1969–71. CL4/11, DA.
15 Triennial Report of St Dominic's Convent, Feilding, 1971. CL4/11, DA.
16 Triennial Report on St Catherine's Priory, Invercargill, 1974. CL4/12, DA.
17 Mother Mary Jordan McCormick, Visitation Notes, 15-17 June, 7 July 1970. CL5/4, DA.
18 Mother Mary Jordan McCormick, Visitation Notes, 27–30 June 1970. CL5/4, DA.
19 Mother Mary Jordan McCormick to Sisters, 16 December 1970. CL7/2/31, DA.
20 Mother Mary Jordan McCormick, Visitation Notes, 1971. CL5/4, DA.
21 Assessment of Strengths and Weaknesses, 1973. CL7/2/84, DA.
22 Cecily Sheehy, Interview, 25 July 2011. DA.
23 Acts of the Eighth General Chapter of the New Zealand Dominican Sisters, 26 December 1974–15 January 1975, CH, DA.
24 The Rule of Saint Augustine and the Interim Constitutions of the Congregation of the New Zealand Dominican Sisters, 1976, 11. CON1/4, DA.
25 Mother Mary Constance Quinn, Visitation, 9–16 July 1976. CL5/5, DA.
26 Sister Mary Elizabeth to Sisters, 30 March 1981. CL7/3/25, DA.
27 *Perfectae Caritatis*: www.vatican.va/archive/hist_councils/ii_vatican_council/documents/vat-ii_decree_19651028_perfectae-caritatis_en.html
28 Acts of the Special General Chapters, 26 December 1968–18 January 1969.

29 Mother Mary Jordan McCormick to Superiors, 9 March 1969. CL7/2/4, DA.
30 Customary of the New Zealand Dominican Sisters. PL1/7, DA.
31 Mother Mary Jordan McCormick to Superiors, 16 June 1970. CL7/2, DA.
32 Mother Mary Jordan McCormick to Superiors, Main Events 1970. CL7/2/33, DA.
33 Mother Mary Jordan McCormick, Visitation of St Dominic's Convent, Northcote, 7 July 1970. CL5/4, DA.
34 Mother Mary Jordan McCormick to Sisters, 22 June 1972. CL7/2/62, DA.
35 Acts of the Eighth General Chapter of the New Zealand Dominican Sisters, 26 December 1974–15 January 1975. CH, DA.
36 Sister Mary Constance Quinn, Directions to Superiors, 1975. CL7/1/1, DA.
37 Margaret Quinn, Interview, 11 November 2011. DA.
38 Barbara Menzies, private communication with author, 2014.
39 Ibid.
40 Sister Kathleen Thomson to Mother and Sisters, 15 February 1977. C7/1/46, DA.
41 Sister Marie Eugene Nicolson to Mother and Sisters, 25 September 1978. C7/2/15, DA.
42 Ninth General Chapter of the New Zealand Dominican Sisters, 1980–81, 6. CH, DA.
43 Constitutions of the Congregation of the New Zealand Dominican Sisters, 1989, 15. DA.
44 Sister Mary Alban McCaughan, Interview, 29 July 2010. DA.
45 Sister Dominic Swindale, Interview, 25 July 2011. DA.
46 Sandra Winton, Interview, 27 January 2011. DA.
47 Janice Ogilvy, Interview, 16 March 2011. DA.
48 Raewyn Benzie, Interview, 4 September 2011. DA.
49 Sister Mary Gertrude Fox, Interview, 24 January 2011. DA.
50 Sister Maria McDonald, Personal Profile, 2011. DA.
51 Sister Mary Columba McHugh, Personal Profile, 2011. DA.
52 Mother Mary Jordan McCormick to Sisters, 5 May 1974. CL7/2, DA.
53 Mother Mary Constance Quinn to Sisters, 16 August 1976. CL7/1/43, DA.
54 Sister Mary Constance Quinn to Sisters, 9 September 1980. CL7/3/10, DA.
55 Sister Margaret Quinn to Sisters, 19 May 1981. CL7/3/31, DA.
56 Margaret Quinn, Interview, 11 November 2011. DA.
57 Raewyn Benzie, Interview, 4 September 2011. DA.
58 Margaret Butler, Interview, 28 April 2011. DA.
59 Sister Dominic Swindale, Interview, 25 July 2011. DA.
60 Sister Mary Gertrude Fox, Interview, 24 January 2011. DA.
61 Constitutions of the Congregation, 1989, 5.
62 Ibid., 18.
63 Collation of Community Reports, 1987–90. C[illegible]/16, DA.
64 Raewyn Benzie, Interview, 4 September 2011. DA.
65 Janice Ogilvy, Interview, 16 March 2011. DA.
66 Mary Horn, Interview, 17 March 2011. DA.
67 Mary Anna Baird, Interview, 4 September 2011. DA.
68 Sister Dominic Swindale, Interview, 25 July 2011. DA.
69 Sister Loreto Meehan, Interview, 25 July 2011. DA.
70 Mike Noonan, 'Kindling the empty space : How we pray in the Dominican Family Community', in Neil Darragh (ed.), *Journeying into Prayer* (Auckland: Accent Publications, 2012), 27–29.
71 Sandra Winton, Interview, 27 January 2011. DA.
72 Ibid.
73 Carmel Walsh, Interview, 24 October 2010. DA.
74 Helen Bergin, 'Praying: A Dominican way', in Darragh (ed.), *Journeying into Prayer*, 42.
75 Patricia Hannan, Personal Profile, 2011. DA.
76 Roxane Parkinson, Interview, 28 April 2011. DA.
77 Sister Dominic Swindale, Interview, 25 July 2011. DA.

7. Money, men and power: The New Zealand Dominican sisters as part of a worldwide web

1 Congregational Annals, Book 1: 1871–1910. CA1, DA.
2 First Dogmatic Constitution on the Church of Christ, First Vatican Council.
3 Dean Burke's Sermon at the Pontifical Mass celebrating the Golden Jubilee of the Dunedin Diocese, *Dominican Star* (Dunedin: New Zealand Tablet, 1921), 41. M1, DA.
4 Bishop Moran, 2 October 1870. GH3/2/1, DA.
5 Sister Mary Francis Sullivan to Mother Mary Clare Elliot, 17 March 1871. GH3/2/4, DA.
6 Ibid.

7 Sister Mary Gabriel Gill and Sisters to Bishop Moran, 23 July 1892; First General Chapter of the Dominican Order in Otago to Bishop Moran, 27 December 1893, Minute Book of the First General Chapter of the Dominican Nuns of the Province of Otago, 1893–1894. CH1/1, DA.

8 The Bank of New Zealand, Account Books: Right Rev. P. Moran Trust Account Victoria Gill, Right Rev. P. Moran Trust Account Convent Building Fund. Bishop Moran's Diaries, DDA.

9 Bishop Moran to Mother Gabriel Gill, 25 April 1893. C2/6/5, DA.

10 14 January 1894, 22 January 1894, 7 April 1894, Book of Permissions, St Dominick's Priory, Dunedin, 1894–1916. C1/1, DA.

11 29 December 1894, Book of Permissions. C1/1, DA.

12 Bishop Moran to Mother Gabriel Gill, 25 March 1894, C2/6/22; Mother Gabriel to Mother Bertrand McLoughlin, Easter Sunday 1894. C2/6/12, DA.

13 15 January 1893, 15 April 1893, Minutes of the General Council. CL1/2, DA.

14 Minute Book of the First General Chapter of the Dominican Nuns of the Province of Otago, 1893–94. CH1/1, DA.

15 27 September 1894, Book of Records, St Dominic's Priory, 1894–96. RA5, DA.

16 Bishop Moran, Concluding Words and Last Advice to the Chapter. GH5/11/10, DA.

17 Bishop Moran to Sisters, 9 January 1894. CR1/2/8, DA.

18 *New Zealand Tablet,* 14 July 1876, supplement to 1; 6 October 1876, 10.

19 Mother Mary Gabriel Gill to Sion Hill, 7 November 1871. GH3/2/5, DA.

20 Mother Mary Gabriel Gill, 8 June 1895. GH3/4/27, DA.

21 Sister Mary de Ricci Kirby to Uncle Kirby, 29 July 1879. GH4/2/6, DA.

22 Sister Mary de Ricci Kirby to Uncle Kirby, 13 April 1873. GH4/2/2, DA.

23 Tobias Kirby to Mother Gabriel Gill, 3 December 1884. GH3/4/21, DA. As Kirby explained, the Pope was happy to approve 'this pious work so important for the religious education of youth in the Diocese of Dunedin, and for keeping them aloof from anti-Catholic schools'.

24 Sister Mary de Ricci Kirby to Uncle Kirby, 8 July 1872. GH4/2/1; January 1875, GH4/2/3. DA.

25 Archbishop Kirby to Mother Gabriel Gill, 4 July 1893. C2/6/20, DA.

26 Mother Mary St Peter Slattery and Council to Bishop Verdon, 27 August 1896. C2/7/5, DA.

27 Bishop Verdon to Mother Mary St Peter Slattery, 21 August 1896. C2/7/4, DA.

28 Mother Mary St Peter Slattery to Sisters, 7 September 1896. C1/3/12, DA.

29 Mother Mary St Peter Slattery and Council to Bishop Verdon, 27 August 1896. C2/7/5, DA.

30 Bishop Verdon to Mother Mary St Peter Slattery, 1 September 1896. C2/7/6, DA.

31 Mother Mary St Peter Slattery and Council to Bishop Verdon, 6 September 1896. C2/7/7, DA.

32 Minutes Book of the General Council, 5 September 1896. CL1/2, DA. Archbishop of Melbourne to Dominican Sisters, 30 October 1896. C2/7/9, DA.

33 Bishop Verdon to Mother Mary St Peter Slattery, 17 October 1898. C2/12/12, DA. Bishop Verdon to Mother Mary St Peter Slattery, 21 June 1902. C2/9/2, DA.

34 Mother Mary St Peter Slattery to Dr Kelly, 30 January 1899. C2/8/1, DA.

35 Sister Mary Louis Keighron to Mother, Easter Monday 1903. GH3/5/5, DA.

36 Mother Mary Cecily Mulcahy to Mother, 26 February 1924. GH3/6/13, DA. Mother Mary Cecily Mulcahy to Mother, 7 January 1924. GH3/6/12, DA. See also Bishop James Whyte to the Dominican Sisters. GH6/4/3, DA.

37 The Rule of St Augustine and the Constitutions of the Congregation of the New Zealand Dominican Sisters, 1939, 217–20. CON1/8, DA.

38 Sister Mary John to Sisters, 2 March 1955. CR1/2/103, DA.

39 Mother Mary Philomena McCarthy to Sisters, 28 March 1955. CR1/2/104, DA.

40 Carmel Walsh, private communication with author, 5 November 2014.

41 Minutes Book of General Council, 12 July 1975. CL1/7, DA.

42 Minutes Book of General Council, 6 February 1976. CL1/7, DA.

43 Accounts for the New Zealand foundation. GH3/1/1, GH3/1/2, DA.

44 Mother Mary Gabriel Gill to Sion Hill, 9 August 1892. GH3/1/11, DA.
45 Mother Mary Gabriel Gill to Sion Hill, undated. GH3/3/7, DA.
46 Mother Mary St Peter Slattery to Sion Hill, 14 February 1908. GH3/5/20, DA. Mother Mary St Peter Slattery to Sion Hill, 5 January 1909. GH3/5/21, DA.
47 For example: Mother Mary Gabriel Gill to Sion Hill, 21 May [1880?]. GH3/3/1, DA. Sister Mary Louis Keighron to Sion Hill, 31 October 1904. GH3/5/13, DA. Sister Mary Louis Keighron to Sion Hill, 3 June 1912. GH3/5/30, DA.
48 Sister Mary Louis Keighron to Sion Hill, 3 February 1903. GH3/5/4, DA.
49 Sister Mary Cecily Mulcahy to Sion Hill, 30 June 1912. GH3/5/31, DA. Sister Mary Cecily Mulcahy to Sion Hill, 12 February 1913. GH3/5/33, DA.
50 Sister Mary Cecily Mulcahy to Mother Mary Gonzales, 21 March 1924. GH3/6/15, DA.
51 Sister Mary Catherine Hughes to Mother Mary Clare Elliot, 28 December 1882. GH3/4/24, DA.
52 Mother Mary Gabriel Gill to Sion Hill, 30 April 1872. GH3/2/6, DA.
53 Sister Mary Francis Sullivan to Sion Hill, 25 November 1880. GH3/2, DA.
54 Ibid.
55 Sister Mary Francis Sullivan to Sister Mary Pius, 1 July 1879. GH3/2/11, DA.
56 Sister Mary Agnes Rooney to Mother Mary Clare Elliot, 1872. GH3/2/7, DA.
57 Sister Mary Francis Sullivan to Mother Mary Clare Elliot, 17 July 1878. GH3/2/10, DA.
58 Sister Mary Louis Keighron to Sion Hill, 3 February 1903. GH3/5/4, DA.
59 Sister Mary Louis Keighron to Sion Hill, 22 July 1906. GH3/5/16, DA.
60 Sister Mary Louis Keighron to Sion Hill, 5 March 1911. GH3/5/26, DA.
61 Sister Mary Louis Keighron to Sion Hill, 22 February 1904. GH3/5/8, DA.
62 Sister Mary Raymond McGrath to Sion Hill, 28 May 1920. GH3/6/5, DA.
63 Sister Mary St Peter Slattery to Sion Hill, 14 February 1908. GH3/5/20, DA.
64 Sister Margaret Mary Coffey to Mother Mary Clare Elliot, 11 August 1920. GH3/6/7, DA.
65 *Dominican Star: Golden Jubilee, 1871–1921* (New Zealand Tablet: Dunedin, 1921), 35. M2/5, DA.
66 The history of the status debate has been well covered in several scholarly texts. See Kathleen Boner, *Dominican Women: A time to speak* (Pietermaritzburg: Cluster Publications, 2000) and M.R. MacGinley, *Ancient Tradition – New World: Dominican Sisters in Eastern Australia 1867–1958* (Strathfield: St Pauls Publications, 2009).
67 MacGinley, *Ancient Tradition*, 162–70.
68 Papal Decree, 15 September 1903, included in The Rule of Saint Augustine and the Constitutions of the Congregation of the New Zealand Dominican Sisters, 1939, 106–07. CON1/8, DA.
69 MacGinley, *Ancient Tradition*, 172.
70 Mother Mary Raymond McGrath to Mother Mary Pius, 12 December 1919. GH3/5/35, DA.
71 Sister Mary Bertrand McLoughlin and Councillors to Dongarra, 24 November 1920. GH3/6/9, DA.
72 Rose O'Neil, *A Rich Inheritance: Galway Dominican nuns 1644–1994* (Galway: Dominican Sisters, 1994), 140–44.
73 MacGinley, *Ancient Tradition*, 229.
74 Sister Mary Teresa Lynch to Vocals, 30 October 193[illegible]. CR1/2/37, DA.
75 Congregational Annals, Book 2, 369–70. CA1, DA.
76 Father Finbar Ryan to Mother Prioress, 10 August 1932. CR1/2/42, DA.
77 Petition to Holy See for approval of Constitutions, 1933. CON2/5/1, DA.
78 The visit of the Master General, 1967. GH6/9/[illegible], DA.
79 Address by the Master General to the Dominican Mothers General, Rome, 22 November 1969. CL7/5/6, DA.
80 Father Aniceto Fernandez Alonso to the Sisters of the Order. CL7/5/7, DA.
81 The Changing Role of the Dominican Woman. DF2/1/1, DA.
82 New Zealand Dominican Sisters' Report on the Basic Charter of the Dominican Family. DF2/3/1, DA.
83 Dominican Family in New Zealand. DF2/3/1, DA.
84 General Secretariat of the Dominican Family, General Chapter of Rome, 1983, Commission XV: Dominican Family. DF2/3/1, DA. The Bologna Document on the Dominican Family, 1983. DF2/3/1, DA.
85 Combined Council Meeting Dominican Sisters and Fathers, May 1984. DF2/2/5, DA.

86 Dominican Family in New Zealand.
87 Leadership Team Report 2006. CH3/19, DA.
88 Administrative Notes. CL7/2/31, DA.
89 Mother Mary Constance Quinn, Meeting of Major Superiors, Rome, 6–13 November 1975. CL8/1/29, DA.
90 Communication from the Leadership Team, 18 February 1995. CL9/2, DA.
91 Sister Judith Anne O'Sullivan to New Zealand Dominican Congregation, 14 June 2001. DF2/7/1, DA.
92 Leadership Team Communications, 1996. CL9/3, DA.
93 Dominican Asia Pacific Regional Conference, Teschemakers, New Zealand, November 1987, Forward 88/1. DF3/1/1, DA.
94 Second Dominican Conference on Justice and Peace for the Asia Pacific Region, Hong Kong, 26–30 September 1988. DF3/3/10, DA.
95 Asia Pacific First Joint Conference of Dominican Superiors and Formators, Philippines, 29 November –4 December 1991. DF3/5/2, DA.
96 Asia Pacific Dominican Family Conference on the Rights of Women and Children, 23–29 November 1991. DF3/7/1, DA.
97 Mary Anna Baird, 'Justice and peace in the Asia Pacific region', *Dominican Family Newsletter*, July 2000. DF2/6/1, DA.
98 Dominican Family Asia Pacific Justice, Peace and Care of Creation Conference, Taiwan, 20 October 2006. DF3/5/1, DA.
99 MacGinley, *Ancient Tradition*, 289–91.
100 Communication, October 2011, No. 5. DA.
101 Statutes of the Federation of Dominican Sisters in Oceania, 8 March 2014. DA.
102 Constitutions of the Congregation of the New Zealand Dominican Sisters, 1989, 11. DA.
103 Ibid., 29.
104 Roxane Parkinson, Interview, 28 April 2011. DA.
105 Mary Horn, Interview, 17 March 2011. DA.
106 Margaret Quinn, Interview, 11 November 2011. DA.
107 Raewyn Benzie, Interview, 4 September 2011. DA.
108 Cecily Sheehy, Interview, 25 July 2011. DA.
109 Matthew Fox, *A Spirituality Named Compassion*, 2nd edn (Rochester, Vermont: Inner Traditions, 1;999), 36–65.
110 Bernadette Cheyne, 'Women in mid-life: Psychological and spiritual development' (MA thesis, Fordham University, 1980), 107.

8. A women's world: Internal structures of authority

1 Calls from Chapter 2011. DA.
2 The Rule of Saint Augustine and the Constitutions of the Congregation of the New Zealand Dominican Sisters, 1939, 123–24. CON1/8, DA.
3 Sister Mary de Ricci Kirby to Uncle Kirby, November 1882. GH4/2/10, DA.
4 Sister Mary Francis Sullivan to Mother Mary Clare Elliot, 12 August 1883. GH3/4/20, DA.
5 Ibid.
6 Sister Mary Louis Keighron to Mother, 5 June 1904. GH3/5/11, DA.
7 Sister Mary Louis Keighron to Mother, 4 April 1904. GH3/5/9, DA.
8 Minutes of the General Council, 1871–94. CL1/2, DA.
9 Minutes of the General Council, 1907–21. CL1/3, DA.
10 Sister Mary Gabriel Gill to Sisters. GH3/2/3, DA.
11 Sister Mary Gabriel Gill to Mother Mary Clare Elliot, 16 June 1882. GH3/4/12, DA.
12 Book of Records, St Dominic's Priory, 1894–96. RA5, DA.
13 Visitation of Helensville Convent, 19–20 September 1947, Visitation Records. CL5/1, DA.
14 Visitation of Lawrence Convent, 29 October 1953, Visitation Records. CL5/2, DA.
15 Visitation of Teschemakers Convent, 3 November 1964, Visitation Records. CL5/3, DA.
16 Visitation Records. CL5/5, DA. 'Visitation: strengthens union and charity, encourages more perfect observance of the Constitutions and gives each sister an opportunity to speak freely on matters which concern her personal welfare or the general good.'
17 Reflection on Visitation, 1997. CL5/8, DA. Even in the late 1990s visitation was still occasionally used for the 'correction of abuses'. The Congregation had moved to a shared model of leadership and a democratic understanding of authority, but visitation remained a valuable process for articulating expectations and applying standards.
18 Minute Book of the First General Chapter of the Dominican Nuns of the Province of Otago, 1893–94. CH1/1, DA.
19 Ibid.
20 Mother Mary Jordan McCormick to Sisters, 16 December 1970. CL7/2/31, DA.

21 The Rule of Saint Augustine and the Interim Constitutions of the Congregation of the New Zealand Dominican Sisters, 1976, 44. CON1/4, DA.
22 Sister Loreto Meehan, Interview, 25 July 2011. DA.
23 Sister Margaret Quinn, Interview, 11 November 2011. DA.
24 Acts of the Special General Chapter of the Congregation of the New Zealand Dominican Sisters, 26 December 1968–18 January 1969. CH, DA.
25 Sister Margaret Quinn to Sisters, 18 September 1981. CL7/3/46, DA.
26 Meeting of the General Council, 10–12 May 1981. CL7/3/32, DA.
27 Ibid.
28 Teschemakers Community to Mother Constance and Council, 9 March 1980. C7/2/57, DA.
29 Sister Margaret Quinn to Sisters, 13 February 1983. CL7/3/76, DA.
30 Sister Margaret Quinn to Sisters, 10 November 1983. CL7/3/88, DA.
31 St Brigid's Community to Council, 29 January 1986. C7/4/100, DA.
32 St Brigid's Community Report, 1987–90. CL4/14, DA.
33 Henderson Dominican Convent Report, 1987–90. CL4/14, DA.
34 Tenth General Chapter, 1986. CH, DA.
35 Ibid.
36 Ibid.
37 Mary Horn, Interview, 17 March 2011. DA.
38 Communication from the Leadership Team, January 1987. CL9/1, DA.
39 Communication from the Leadership Team, 1 April 1989. CL9/1, DA.
40 Visitation, 1988. CL5/6, DA.
41 Chapter Reports, August 2010. DA.
42 Congregational Communication, October 2010, No. 27. DA.
43 Dunedin Regional Meeting. CL5/6/4, DA.
44 Communication, May 2014, No. 26. DA.
45 Declarations before profession 1936–76. NOV1/12, DA.
46 Mother Mary David Stark to Sisters, 16 July 1958. CL7/4/10, DA.
47 Mother Mary Jordan McCormick to Sisters, 16 December 1970. CL7/2/31, DA.
48 Constitutions of the Congregation of the New Zealand Dominican Sisters, 1989, 6. DA.
49 Ibid., 7.
50 Ibid., 8.
51 Ordinations of the Congregation of the New Zealand Dominican Sisters, 1989, 9. DA.
52 Ibid., 10
53 Constitutions of the Congregation, 11. DA.
54 Ibid., 12
55 Barbara Menzies, private communication with author, 2014. Comment made in a lecture to the novices in 1974.
56 Congregational Communication, November [illegible] No. 21, DA.
57 Barbara Menzies, private communication with author, 2014.
58 Ibid.
59 Susan Healy, 'The theology colleges and the Māori', MA thesis, University of Auckland, 1988.
60 'Pakeha repentance nun in the media hot seat', [illegible] September 1993, undated newspaper clipping. DA.
61 Communication from the Leadership Team, April 1991. C_9/2, DA.
62 Mary Horn, Interview, 17 March 2011. DA.
63 'Sisters and friars protest to PM', Christchurch Press, 10 November 2007, 2.
64 Congregational Communication, March 2010, No. 23. DA.
65 www.dominicans.org.nz/issues

9. Love of learning: Dominican Sisters as students and teachers

1 Fifteenth General Chapter, 28 December 2005–3 January 2007, 6. CH3/21, DA
2 Sister Mary de Ricci Kirby to Uncle Kirby, November 1882. GH4/2/10, DA.
3 Sister Mary Francis Sullivan to Mother Mary Clare Elliot, 29 January 1885. GH3/4/25, DA.
4 Bishops to Religious Congregations, 4 August 1894. C2/12/–, DA.
5 15 June 1895, Book of Permissions, St Dominic's Priory, Dunedin, 1894–1916. C1/1, DA.
6 Barbara Bell to Mother Prioress, 14 December 1904. GH6/4/2, DA.
7 1 April 1907, Book of Permissions, St Dominic's Priory, Dunedin, 1894–1916. C1/1, DA.
8 Sister Mary Louis Keighron to Sister, 2 April 1911. GH3/5/27, DA.

9 Sister Mary St Joan Terry, 'This is your life'. DA. Congregational Annals, Book 2: 1911–37. CA1, DA. Sister Catherine Mary to Sister Mary Augustine, 28 May 1995. GH5/5/1, DA.
10 Sister Mary Reginald Quilter to Sisters, 21 March 1939. C1/3/23, DA.
11 Sister Mary Gertrude Fox, Interview, 24 January 2011. DA.
12 Congregational Annals, Book 2.
13 Acts of the First General Chapter of the Congregation of the New Zealand Dominican Sisters, 20 December 1933–02 January 1934. CH, DA.
14 Sister Mary Dominica McKay to Sisters, 27 May 1942. CR1/2/77, DA.
15 Bishop Kavanagh to Mother Prioress, 27 October 1950. CR1/2/95, DA.
16 Brenda Fitzgerald, Interview, 26 January 2011. DA.
17 Dorothy Pilkington, *We See What You Mean …: A history of St Dominic's School for Deaf Children and the Catholic Deaf Ministry in New Zealand* (Palmerston North: St Dominic's School for the Deaf Historical Society Inc., 2008) 235, 238.
18 Judith Robinson, Interview, 24 January 2011. DA.
19 Triennial Report for St Dominic's Priory, Dunedin, 1957–59. CL4/7, DA.
20 Sister Mary Madeleine McAleese, Eulogy for the Requiem of Sister Mary Augustine McCarthy, Deceased Sisters Files. S3, DA.
21 Mary Horn, Interview, 17 March 2011. DA.
22 Margaret Butler, Interview, 28 April 2011. DA.
23 Mother Mary David Stark to Sisters, 2 May 1960. CL7/4/22, DA.
24 *Evening Star*, 30 November 1962, 8.
25 Mother Mary David Stark, Memo, 4 July 1964. DA.
26 Sister Mary Elizabeth Mackie, Impressions of Sion Hill, September 1962. GH3/8/6. DA.
27 Judith McGinley, 'The Dominican Sisters' response to Vatican II', *New Zealand Tablet*, undated clipping. GH6/10/10, DA.
28 *Otago Daily Times*, 5 December 1968, 3.
29 Judith McGinley, Interview, 29 April 2011. DA.
30 Education Trust Fund for Dominican Sisters, 1971. F2/3/4, DA.
31 The Interim Constitutions of the Congregation of the New Zealand Dominican Sisters, 1976. CON1/4, DA.
32 C.H. Irwin to Helen Bolger, 5 February 1973. C6/1/5f3, DA.
33 C.H. Irwin, 21 March 1973. C6/1/54, DA.
34 Margaret Quinn, Interview, 11 November 2011. DA. See also Mother Mary Constance Quinn to Sisters, 9 September 1975. CL7/1/21, DA.
35 Teschemakers Convention, 1979. AM3/3, DA.
36 Mosgiel Summer School, 1992–93. AM3/4, DA.
37 Communication from the Leadership Team, April 1991. CL9/2, DA.
38 Communication from the Leadership Team, August 1991. CL9/2, DA.
39 Chapter Reports, August 2014. DA.
40 Quoted in *Otago Witness*, 27 May 1871, 3.
41 Thomas Dunn and others to Bishop Moran, 25 June 1875, Bishop Moran Correspondence 1871–94. DA.
42 Bishop Moran to Sisters, 9 January 1894. C2/6/3, DA.
43 Mother Mary Gabriel Gill, Teaching Notes. GH1/4, DA.
44 Mother Mary Gabriel Gill, Notes on Lectures intended for Teachers, 10 July 1894. GH1/4/8, DA.
45 Rule and Constitutions of St Dominick, for the use of the Religious Community of St Dominick's Priory, Dunedin, New Zealand, 1908, 10. CON1/2A, DA.
46 Congregational Annals, Book 1: 1871–1910. CA1, DA.
47 Sister Mary Francis Sullivan to Mother Mary Clare Elliot, 17 March 1871. GH3/2/4, DA.
48 Mary Augustine McCarthy, *Star in the South: The centennial history of the New Zealand Dominican Sisters* (Dunedin: St Dominic's Priory, 1970), 65.
49 Mother Mary Gabriel Gill, Teaching Notes.
50 'Dominican Priory and College, Dowling Street, Dunedin', in *Cyclopaedia of New Zealand, vol. 4: Otago and Southland* (Christchurch: The Cyclopaedia Company, 1905), 171.
51 Mother Mary Gabriel Gill, Teaching Notes.
52 School Customs. GH6/6/2, DA.
53 Ibid.
54 See for example Reorganisation of School, 1959. CL7/4/18, DA.
55 Sister Mary Francis Sullivan to Sister Mary Pius, 1 July 1879. GH3/2/11, DA.
56 Bishop Moran to Mother Mary Clare Elliot, 8 September 1882. GH3/1/10, DA.
57 Sister Mary de Ricci Kirby to Uncle Kirby, 10 August 1887, GH5, DA.
58 Ibid.
59 Quoted in *Otago Witness*, 6 May 1871, 9.
60 Sister Mary Francis Sullivan to Sion Hill, 30 April 1880. GH3/3/7, DA.

61 Sister Mary Gabriel Gill to Sion Hill, 30 April 1872. GH3/2/6, DA.
62 Sister Mary Columba Fagan to Sister Mary Gertrude Dooley, 31 July 1882. GH3/4/14, DA.
63 New Zealand Bishops to Mother Prioress, 29 July 1892. C2/12/3, DA.
64 Mother Mary Gabriel Gill, Examination of the Catholic Schools in Dunedin. C1/3/9, DA.
65 Quoted in Congregational Annals, Book 1: 1871–1910. CA1, DA.
66 'St Dominic's College', *New Zealand Tablet,* 21 December 1899, 5.
67 The Rule of Saint Augustine and the Constitutions of the Congregation of the New Zealand Dominican Sisters, 1939, 98–99. CON1/8, DA.
68 Ibid., 92.
69 Triennial Report on St Mary's Convent, Kaikorai, 1944. CL4/2, DA.
70 Triennial Report on St Catherine's Priory, Invercargill, 1944. CL4/2, DA.
71 Triennial Report on St Catherine's Priory, Invercargill, 1950. CL4/4, DA.
72 Minutes Book of General Council, 14 December 1958. CL1/5, DA.
73 Newsletter, 1962. F16/1/4, DA.
74 Joan Hardiman, Interview, 25 July 2011. DA.
75 Report on Convent of Our Lady of Perpetual Succour, Milton, 1944. CL4/2, DA.
76 Triennial Report of St Dominic's Convent, Helensville, 1947. CL4/3, DA.
77 Triennial Report on St Catherine's Priory, Invercargill, 1950.
78 Mother Mary David Stark, The Dominican Order and its Work in New Zealand, 1959. CL7/4/16, DA.
79 Gertrude Fox, Notes on Music Tuition, c. 1980s. GH5/10, DA.
80 Mother Mary David Stark to Sisters, Summary and Interpretation of the Pope's Address to Catholic Elementary Teachers. CL7/4/3, DA.
81 Ibid.
82 Mother Mary David Stark to Mothers, 31 January 1967. CL7/4/59, DA.
83 Mother Mary Jordan McCormick to Sisters. CL7/2/22, DA.
84 Acts of the Special General Chapter, First Session 26 December 1958–18 January 1969, Second Session 31 December 1969–11 January 1970. CH, DA.
85 Acts of the Eighth General Chapter of the New Zealand Dominican Sisters, 26 December 1974–5 January 1975. CH, DA.
86 The Rule of Saint Augustine and the Interim Constitutions of the Congregation of the New Zealand Dominican Sisters, 1976, 24–25. CON1/4, DA.
87 Triennial Report on St Dominic's College, Henderson, 1980. CL4/14, DA.
88 Cecily Sheehy, Interview, 25 July 2011. DA.
89 Raewyn Benzie, Interview, 4 September 2011. DA.
90 Roxane Parkinson, Interview, 28 April 2011. DA.
91 Mary Horn, Interview, 17 March 2011. DA.
92 'Roman Catholic population: Unprecedented rise', *Otago Daily Times*, 13 May 1968, 5.
93 Elizabeth Mackie, Address at Congregational Meeting, January 1974. GH6/10/4, DA.
94 See correspondence and other material relating to integration in AM4/1, DA.
95 Elizabeth Mackie, Address at Congregational Meeting, January 1974. GH6/10/4, DA.
96 Gertrude Fox, Interview, 24 January 2011. DA.
97 Apostolate in Country Areas: Education, 1977. CL8/2/4, DA.
98 Lawrence Annals, 1981. RA8, DA.
99 Apostolate in Country Areas: Education, 1977.
100 Extract from Minutes of Meeting held at Feilding, 1[illegible] and 17 May 1977. F9/7/1, DA.
101 Questions discussed at meeting re: Teschemakers closure. F9/7/2, DA.
102 See correspondence and related material in F9/7, DA.
103 Sister Mary Constance Quinn to Sisters, 27 October 1980. CL7/3/13, DA.
104 Amalgamation notes. GH6/8, DA.
105 St Dominic's College, Henderson, Works to be carried out by the proprietor in relation to the integrated school. AM4/1/15, DA.
106 Communication from the Leadership Team, April 1998. CL9/3, DA
107 Mother Mary Constance Quinn, Meeting held at Dominican College, Teschemakers, 24 June 1977. F9/7/4, DA.
108 Elizabeth Mackie, Address at Congregational Meeting, January 1974.
109 Sister Mary Louise to Parliamentary Candidates, 5 September 1975. CL8/1/20, DA. Sister Mary Louise to Sisters, 23 September 1975. CL8/1/21, DA.
110 Pilkington, *We See What You Mean*, 329–89.

111 Maureen O'Hanlon, Interview, 19 July 2011. DA.
112 See Dominican Hall correspondence and related material in F15, DA.
113 Janice Ogilvy, Interview, 16 March 2011. DA.
114 Helen Bergin, Interview, 24 October 2010. DA.
115 Raewyn Benzie, Interview, 14 September 2011. DA.
116 Judith McGinley, Interview, 29 April 2011. DA.
117 www.challenge2000.org.nz/about-us
118 Paddy McMann, Interview, 18 March 2011. DA.
119 Helen Bergin, Address to Fourteenth General Chapter, 2003. CH3/1/4, DA.
120 Jane Tolerton, *Convent Girls: New Zealand women talk to Jane Tolerton* (Auckland: Penguin, 1994), 98–99.
121 Ibid., 120–21.
122 Paddy McCann, Interview, 18 March 2011. DA.
123 Barbara Menzies, private communication with author, 2014.
124 Paddy McCann, Interview, 29 April 2011. DA.
125 Mary Anna Baird, Interview, 4 September 2011. DA.
126 www2.verdoncollege.school.nz/special-character
127 www.stdoms.ac.nz
128 Loreto Meehan, Interview, 25 July 2011. DA.
129 Communication, October 2014, No. 29. DA.
130 Father Finbar Ryan to Mother Prioress Teresa Lynch, 16 May 1931. CR1/2, DA.

10. God seekers: A community of preachers

1 Helen Bergin & Peter Murnane, 'The living word of God: The preacher's task', *Tui Motu*, August 2006, 18–19.
2 Sandra Winton & Elizabeth Mackie, 'Veritas and the search for truth', *Tui Motu*, March 2006, 18–19.
3 Mother Mary David Stark to Sisters, 19 July 1961. CL7/4/27, DA.
4 Sister Mary Jordan McCormick, The Contribution expected of Religious, 11 May 1979. CL8/4/5, DA.
5 Ibid.
6 Sister Margaret Quinn to Sisters, 2 August 1986. CL7/3/144, DA.
7 Mary Ann Wiesemann-Mills, 'Standing up straight: A self-reflective resource for United States Dominican women on the charism of preaching' (1996), 1, 2. DA.
8 Fourteenth General Chapter, 3–8 January 2003. CH3/1/4, DA.
9 Fifteenth General Chapter, 28 December 2006–3 January 2007. CH3/21, DA.
10 Chapter Reports, August 2010. DA.
11 Helen Bergin, 'The triune God as liberating God: Edward Schillebeeckx's recent theology of the Trinity', STD thesis, Catholic University of America, 1994, 308–09, 348.
12 Margaret Quinn, Interview, 11 November 2011. DA.
13 Joan Hardiman, Interview, 25 July 2011. DA.
14 Elizabeth Mackie, Interview, 11 November 2011. DA.
15 Jacqui Ryan, Interview, 24 July 2011. DA.
16 Acts of the Eighth General Chapter of the New Zealand Dominican Sisters, 26 December 1974–15 January 1975. CH, DA.
17 Chapter Reports, 2014–15. DA. Judith Robinson, Interview, 24 January 2011. DA.
18 Chapter Reports, 2014–15. DA.
19 Chapter Reports, August 2012. DA.
20 Chapter Reports, 2014–15. DA.
21 www.iec.org.nz/g_korimako
22 www.dominicans.org.nz/dominican-laity-newsletter-10
23 Judith Robinson, Interview, 24 January 2011. DA.
24 Chapter Reports, 2014. DA.
25 Sister Mary Reginald Quilter, Dispensation, 15 April 1937. C1/2/22, DA.
26 Margaret Butler, Interview, 28 April 2011. DA.
27 Nola Gleeson, Interview, 17 March 2011. DA.
28 Maureen Connolly, quoted in *Newsletter of the Federation of Dominican Sisters in Oceania*, June 2014. DA.
29 Ibid.
30 Paddy McCann, Interview, 18 March 2011. DA.
31 Brenda Fitzgerald, Interview, 26 January 2011, DA.
32 www.hospicenorthshore.org.nz/About+Hospice/Our+Team/Sister+Bernie+Cheyne
33 Sandra Winton, in 'The hope that is within us', 1998. DA.
34 Communication from the Leadership Team, October 1991. CL9/2, DA.
35 Lorraine Challis in 'The hope that is within us', 1998.
36 Sister Mary Gertrude Fox, Interview, 24 January 2011. DA.
37 Forward, 1984/1. COM3, DA.
38 Ibid.
39 Mary Horn, 'The "Fingerprint of God": Truth through art', in Gabrielle Kelly & Kevin Saunders (eds),

Dominican Approaches in Education: Towards the intelligent use of liberty (Adelaide: Australian Theological Forum Press, 2007), 292–301.

40 Mary Horn, *Pilgrimage*, exhibition catalogue, 2009, 27. DA.

41 Mary Dominica Horn, '"New hope for our time": A reflection on the Letter to the Romans Chapter Eight', BTheol dissertation, University of Otago, 1985, 7.

42 Margaret Butler, Interview, 28 April 2011. DA.

43 Margaret Butler, 'Praying with the Bible in one hand and the newspaper in the other', in Darragh (ed.), *Journeying into Prayer*, 76.

44 Margaret Butler in Congregational Communication, April 2011. DA.

45 Sister Cecily Sheehy in 'The hope that is within us', 1998. DA.

46 Susan Logan to Brenda Fitzgerald, 22 July 1998. DF3/2/7, DA.

47 http://word.op.org/author/dominicans.

48 Winton and Mackie, 'Veritas', 18–19.

49 Ninth General Chapter of the New Zealand Dominican Sisters, 1980–81. DA.

50 Mother Mary David Stark to Sisters, 19 December 1963. CL7/4/43, DA.

51 Sister Margaret Quinn to Sisters, 20 October 1[illegible]. CL7/3/72, DA.

52 Sister Margaret Quinn, Report to the Tenth General Chapter, August 1986. CL7/3/145, DA.

53 Father Vincent de Couesnongle, undated. CL8[illegible]/14, DA.

54 www.nzcatholic.org.nz

55 Sandra Schneiders, *Prophets in their Own Country: Women religious bearing witness to the Gospel in a troubled Church* (New York: Orbis Books, 2011), [illegible]–8.

56 Leadership Team Reflection, Congregational Communication, September 2009, 3. DA.

57 Chapter Reports, 2014. DA.

58 Chapter Call, Seventeenth General Chapter of the New Zealand Dominican Sisters, 2014–15. DA.

Glossary

annalist sister responsible for keeping a narrative record of significant events in the convent year by year

apostolate referring generally to the work or mission of the apostles, and specifically to the different spheres of Christian mission such as teaching, healthcare, preaching, etc.

cappa cloak worn over the habit

capuce short, rounded shoulder cape

Catharism religious movement that spread through parts of southern Europe between the 12th and 14th centuries, denounced by the Catholic Church as heretical

coif headpiece of the habit, consisting of close-fitting cap with veil attached

creation spirituality modern religious movement drawing on ancient traditions, based on a God-centred cosmology that honours creation as a blessing

customary (n.) written guide to a religious order's customs and traditions

discernment the process of determining God's will, or seeing the truth in a certain situation

gnosticism religious movement characterised by a conviction that matter is evil; adherents seek salvation through spiritual understanding rather than faith

guimpe stiffly starched cloth covering the neck and shoulders of the habit

horarium daily schedule of those living in a religious community

infirmarian sister who worked in the convent infirmary caring for sisters suffering from ill health, and for the elderly in the community

kaikaranga woman with the role of making the ceremonial call to visitors onto a marae at the start of a pōwhiri; a role based on status, traditionally given to the eldest sister in the hapū or whānau

liturgist sister responsible for leading the community through the rituals of formal worship

ordinary (n.) person in a position of religious authority whose power to exercise that authority is permanently connected with the office they hold (as opposed to delegated authority)

profession formal process for admitting an individual into a religious order by means of public vows

reception formal ceremony at which a postulant became a novice, receiving the full habit and also receiving the religious name by which she would henceforth be known

religious (n.) a member of a religious order; a nun, sister, friar or monk

rule the system of government, way of life and discipline of a religious order; usually referring to one of several papally approved medieval rules that were subsequently adopted by other orders

scapular symbolic apron covering the back and front of the habit

tāngata whenua the people of the land, the indigenous inhabitants

vocation a divine call to religious life

Bibliography

Archives

Archives of the Congregation of New Zealand Dominican Sisters, Dunedin

A Arts
AM Apostolates and Ministry
C Correspondence
CA Congregational Annals
CEL Celebrations
CH General Chapters
CL General Council – Leadership Team
COM General Communications
CON Constitutions
CR Conventual Records
DA Dominican Archives
DDA Dunedin Diocesan Archives
DE Dominican Exhibition
DF Dominican Family
F Foundations
FL Financial/Legal
GH Historical
L Leadership
M Magazines
NOV Novitiate
P Photographs
PL Prayer and Liturgical Life
R Regions
RA Regional Annals
S Deceased Sisters Files
SHA Sion Hill Archives
V Videos/Tapes/Films

Dunedin Diocesan Archives

Bishop Moran's Diaries
Bishop Moran's Correspondence, 1871–84

Sion Hill Archives, Dublin

Jubilee Album, 1904
Assorted New Zealand memorabilia and photographs

Interviews

Conducted by Susannah Grant

Mary Anna Baird
Raewyn Benzie
Helen Bergin
Margaret Butler
Brenda Fitzgerald
SM Gertrude Fox
Nola Gleeson
Joan Hardiman
Mary Horn
Susan Logan
Elizabeth Mackie
Paddy McCann
SM Alban McCaughan
Judith McGinley
SM Loreto Meehan
Jan Ogilvy
Maureen O'Hanlon
Judith Anne O'Sullivan
Roxane Parkinson
Margaret Quinn
Judith Robinson
Jacqui Ryan
Cecily Sheehy

SM Dominic Swindale
Carmel Walsh
Sandra Winton

Personal profiles

Mary Anna Baird
Joan Bennett
Lorraine Challis
Bernadette Cheyne
Mary Concannon
Maureen Connolly
Barbara Dwyer
SM Gertrude Fox
SM Basil Geoffrey
Molly Griffin
Patricia Hannan
SM Frances Lister
Susan Logan
Elizabeth Mackie
SM Madeleine McAleese
S Maria McDonald
SM Columba McHugh
SM Loreto Meehan
S Marie Eugene Nicolson
Jan Ogilvy
Maureen O'Hanlon
Anne O'Neill
SM Genevieve O'Rourke
Judith Anne O'Sullivan
Roxane Parkinson
SM Leonie Parry
Margaret Quinn
Kathleen Thomson
SM Catherine Tither
Marie Twomey
SM Adrienne White

Theses and unpublished papers, Dominican Archives, Dunedin

Bergin, Helen F., 'The triune God as liberating God: Edward Schillebeeckx's recent theology of the Trinity', STD thesis, Catholic University of America, 1994.

Cheyne, Bernadette I., 'Women in mid-life: Psychological and spiritual development', MA thesis, Fordham University, 1980.

Collins, J.M., 'Hidden lives: The teaching and religious lives of eight Dominican sisters, 1931–61', MEd thesis, Massey University, 2001.

Concannon, Mary, 'Spiritual direction in the life and writings of Saint Catherine of Siena and its significance for women spiritual directors', Diploma in Spirituality thesis, Pontifical Gregorian University, Institute of Spirituality, Rome, 1985.

Finlay, Gemma, '"Ephphatha" – Be opened', DRE thesis, National Pastoral Institute of Religious Education, Australia, 1980.

Healy, Susan, 'The theology colleges and the Maori', MA thesis, University of Auckland, 1988.

Heath, Margaret M., 'Elements of the spiritual patrimony of the New Zealand Dominican Sisters with particular reference to preaching the Word of God', MA thesis, St Paul University, Ottawa, 1992.

Horn, Mary Dominica, '"New hope for our time": A reflection on the Letter to the Romans Chapter Eight', BTheol dissertation, University of Otago, 1985.

'One hundred years on the hill 1912–2012, St Mary's Catholic Church and School Kaikorai', unpublished book of memories, Dunedin, 2013.

Parkinson, Sister Mary Denise (Roxane), 'The Rosary: Its place in liturgical spirituality', thesis, Pontificium Institutum Regina Mundi, Rome, 1968.

Schneiders, Sandra, 'That was then … this is now: The past, present and future of women religious in the United States', Women and Spirit Lecture, Saint Mary's College and University of Notre Dame, 24 September 2011.

Wiesemann-Mills, Mary Ann, 'Standing up straight: A self-reflective resource for United States Dominican women on the charism of preaching', 1996.

Periodicals and newspapers

New Zealand Tablet
Otago Daily Times
Otago Witness
Press
Tui Motu

Published sources

Annals of the Dominican Convent of St Mary's Cabra 1647–1912 (pub. details unknown), 1912.

Arnold, Rollo, 'The patterns of denominationalism in later Victorian New Zealand', in Christopher Nichol & James Veitch (eds), *Religion in New Zealand Society* (Wellington: Victoria University, 1980), 76–110.

Bergin, Helen, 'Praying: A Dominican way', in Neil Darragh (ed.), *Journeying into Prayer* (Auckland: Accent Publications, 2012), 39–46.

Bergin, Helen & Peter Murnane, 'The living Word of God: The preacher's task', *Tui Motu*, August 2006, 18–19.

Bermisa, Leonila, 'Women in the Church', in Luisa Campos (ed.), *Women's Rights Are Human Rights* (Rome: Dominican Sisters International and the International Commission of Justice and Peace, 2003).

Boner, Kathleen, *Dominican Women: A time to speak* (Pietermaritzburg: Cluster Publications, 2000).

Bonniwell, William R., *A History of the Dominican Liturgy* (New York: Joseph F. Wagner, 1944).

Book of Annals. Sion Hill Convent, Blackrock, Co. Dublin, Golden Jubilee, 1854–1904 (Dublin: Browne & Noland, 1904).

Burley, Stephanie & Katherine Teague, *Chapel, Cloister and Classroom: Reflections on the Dominican Sisters at North Adelaide* (Adelaide: St Dominic's Priory College, 1993).

Butler, Margaret, 'Praying with the Bible in one hand and the newspaper in the other', in Neil Darragh (ed.), *Journeying into Prayer* (Auckland: Accent Publications, 2012), 75–82.

Cahill, Barbara, *Dominic: The preacher* (London: Darton, Longman & Todd, 1988).

Campos, S Luisa (ed.), *Women's Rights are Human Rights* (Rome: Dominican Sisters International and the International Commission of Justice and Peace, 2003).

Coburn, Carol K., 'An overview of the historiography of women religious: A twenty-five-year retrospective', *US Catholic Historian*, vol. 22, no. 1, 2004, 1–26.

Collins, Jenny, 'Strategies for survival and success: Dominican teachers 1931–61', *History of Education Review*, vol. 33, no. 1, 2004, 1–13.

Cyclopaedia of New Zealand, vol. 4: Otago and Southland (Christchurch: The Cyclopaedia Company, 1905).

Darragh, Neil (ed.), *Journeying into Prayer* (Auckland: Accent Publications, 2012).

Davidson, Allan, *Christianity in Aotearoa: A history of church and society in New Zealand* (Wellington: Education for Ministry, 1991).

Delaney, Mary Veronica, *Gracious is the Time: Centenary of the Sisters of Mercy, 1850–1950* (Auckland: Sisters of Mercy, 1952).

Drane, Augusta Theodosia, *The Spirit of the Dominican Order*, 2nd edn (London: R. & T. Washbourne, 1910).

Duggan, Maura, *In Search of Truth: Journeys of nineteenth century Irish Dominican women* (Dublin: Linden Publishing Services, 2010).

Fitzgerald, Sarah, *Open Minds, Open Hearts: Stories of the Australian Catholic Deaf Community* (Lidcombe: CCOD, 1999).

Fitzgerald, Thomas P., *The First Hundred Years: Dominican Friars in Australia, New Zealand, Solomon Islands & Papua New Guinea* (Hindmarsh: Dominican Fathers South Australia Inc., 1998).

Foley, Nadine (ed.), *Journey in Faith and Fidelity* (New York: Continuum, 1999).

Goulter, Phyllis Mary, *Sowers and Reapers: A short history of the Society of the Sacred Heart in New Zealand* (Auckland: Society of the Sacred Heart, 1982).

Graham, Judith, *Breaking the Habit: Life in a New Zealand convent 1955–67*, 2nd edn (Dunedin: Longacre Press, 2006).

Gulley, Mary (ed.), *Centenary of Sisters of St Joseph of Nazareth, Wanganui, New Zealand* (Whanganui: Sisters of St Joseph, 1980).

Hall, Bernadette, 'The words that get up', in Mark Williams (ed.), *The Source of the Song: New Zealand writers on Catholicism* (Wellington: Victoria University Press, 1995), 155–67.

Hellwig, Elizabeth, 'Up she gets, for up she must! An account of a journey from Kingstown, Ireland to Maitland, Australia in 1867 during the age of sail' (Strathfield: Dominican Sisters of Eastern Australia and Solomon Islands, 2001).

Hinnebusch, William A., *Dominican Spirituality: Principles and practice* (Washington: The Thomist Press, 1965).

Hinnebusch, William A., *The History of the Dominican Order*, vol. 1 (New York: Alba House, 1965).

Hogan, Stanislaus M., *The Dominicans* (Dublin: Juverna Press, 1934).

Horn, Mary, 'The "Fingerprint of God": Truth through art', in Gabrielle Kelly & Kevin Saunders (eds), *Dominican Approaches in Education: Towards the intelligent use of liberty* (Adelaide: Australian Theological Forum Press, 2007), 292–301.

Horn, Mary, 'Questing for God', in Neil Darragh (ed.), *Journeying into Prayer* (Auckland: Accent Publications, 2012) 161–66.

In God's White-Robed Army: The chronicle of the Dominican Sisters in Rhodesia (Cape Town: Maskew Miller, 1947).

Jackson, H.R., *Churches and People in Australia and New Zealand 1860–1930* (Wellington: Allen & Unwin with Port Nicholson Press, 1987).

James, Ruth Marchant, *Fields of Gold: A history of the Dominican Sisters in Western Australia* (Doubleview: Dominican Sisters of Western Australia, 1999).

Kealy, Maire M., *From Channel Row to Cabra: Dominican nuns and their times 1717–1820* (Dublin: Columba Press, 2010).

Kelly, Gabrielle & Kevin Saunders, *Dominican Approaches in Education: Towards the intelligent use of liberty* (Adelaide: Australian Theological Forum Press, 2007).

Kempis, Thomas A, *The Imitation of Christ* (London: Burns Oates & Washbourne, 1915).

King, Michael, *God's Farthest Outpost: A history of Catholics in New Zealand* (Auckland: Penguin, 1997).

Little Manual of Novices, trans. by E. McMahon (New York: D. & J. Sadlier & Co., 1880).

Loughnan, Ambrose, *Full Circle to God* (Ohoka, New Zealand: Loughly Books, 2000).

McCabe, Honor, *A Light Undimmed: The story of the Convent of Our Lady of Bom Sucesso, Lisbon, 1639–2006* (Dublin: Dominican Publications, 2007).

McCarthy, Mary Augustine, *Mother of the Missions: Mother Mary Gabriel Gill OSD (1837–1905)* (Dunedin: St Dominic's Priory, 1989).

——, *Star in the South: The centennial history of the New Zealand Dominican Sisters* (Dunedin: St Dominic's Priory, 1970).

McCoy, E.J., 'Petre churches', in Francis Porter (ed.), *Historic Buildings of New Zealand: South Island* (Auckland: Methuen, 1983), 150–59.

MacGinley, M.R., *Ancient Tradition – New World: Dominican Sisters in Eastern Australia 1867–1958* (Strathfield: St Paul's Publications, 2009).

McKinnon, Malcolm (ed.), *New Zealand Historical Atlas* (Auckland: David Bateman, 1997).

Mol, Hans, *The Fixed and the Fickle: Religion and identity in New Zealand* (Dunedin: Pilgrims South Press, 1992).

Moran, Patrick, *History of the Catholic Church in Australasia* (Sydney & Melbourne: Frank Coffee & Co., 1896).

Munro, Jessie, *Letters on the Go: The correspondence of Suzanne Aubert* (Wellington: Bridget Williams Books, 2009).

Munro, Jessie, *The Story of Suzanne Aubert* (Auckland: Auckland University Press & Bridget Williams Books, 1996).

Nichol, Christopher & James Veitch, *Religion in New Zealand Society* (Wellington: Victoria University, 1980).

Noonan, Mike, 'Kindling the empty space: How we pray in the Dominican Family community', in Neil Darragh (ed.), *Journeying into Prayer* (Auckland: Accent Publications, 2012), 23–37.

Northey, Helen, *Living the Truth: The Dominican Sisters in South Australia 1868–1958* (Adelaide: Holy Cross Congregation of Dominican Sisters, South Australia, 1991).

O'Hanlon, *M Assumpta, Dominican Pioneers in New South Wales* (Sydney: The Australian Publishing Company, 1949).

Olssen, Erik, 'Towards a new society', in Geoffrey Rice (ed.), *The Oxford History of New Zealand* (Auckland: Oxford University Press, 1992), 254–84.

O'Neil, Rose, *A Rich Inheritance: Galway Dominican nuns 1644–1994* (Galway: Dominican Sisters, 1994).

O'Regan, Pauline, *A Changing*, first published 1987 (Wellington: Bridget Williams Books, 1995).

O'Sullivan, Dominic, *Faith, Politics and Reconciliation: Catholicism and the politics of indigeneity* (Wellington: Huia, 1995).

Pilkington, Dorothy, *We see what you mean ...: A history of St Dominic's School for Deaf Children and the Catholic Deaf Ministry in New Zealand* (Palmerston North: St Dominic's School for the Deaf Historical Society Inc., 2008).

Pochin Mould, Daphne D.C., *The Irish Dominicans: The Friars Preachers in the history of Catholic Ireland* (Dublin: Dominican Publications, 1957).

Pool, Ian, Arunachalam Dharmalingam & Janet Sceats, *The New Zealand Family from 1840: A demographic history* (Auckland: Auckland University Press, 2007).

Power, Anne Marie, *Sisters of St Joseph of the Sacred Heart: The New Zealand story, 1883–1983* (Auckland: The Sisters, 1983).

Rafter, Pat, *Never Let Go: The remarkable story of Mother Aubert* (Wellington: A.H. & A.W. Reed, 1972).

Richardson, Len, 'Politics and political change', in Geoffrey Rice (ed.), *The Oxford History of New Zealand* (Auckland: Oxford University Press, 1992), 201–29.

Roach, Kevin, 'The growth of Roman Catholicism in New Zealand', in Christopher Nichol & James Veitch (eds), *Religion in New Zealand Society* (Wellington: Victoria University, 1980), 111–36.

Schneiders, Sandra M., *Prophets in their Own Country: Women religious bearing witness to the Gospel in a troubled Church* (New York: Orbis Books, 2011).

Simmons, E.R., *A Brief History of the Catholic Church in New Zealand* (Auckland: Catholic Publications Centre, 1978).

Smith, Susan, *Call to Mission: The story of the Mission Sisters of Aotearoa New Zealand and Samoa* (Auckland: David Ling Publishing, 2010).

Smyth, Geraldine (ed.), *Distance Becomes Communion: A Dominican symposium on mission and hope* (Dublin: Dominican Publications, 2004).

Souvenir of the Novitiate (New York: Benziger Brothers, 1879).

Strevens, Diane, *MacKillop Women: The Sisters of St Joseph of the Sacred Heart Aotearoa New Zealand 1883–2006* (Auckland: David Ling, 2008).

——, 'Some issues around writing the histories of Catholic religious congregations for women in Aotearoa New Zealand', in Geoffrey Troughton & Hugh Morrison (eds), *The Spirit of the Past: Essays on Christianity in New Zealand history* (Wellington: Victoria University Press, 2011), 69–82.

Tolerton, Jane, *Convent Girls: New Zealand women talk to Jane Tolerton* (Auckland: Penguin, 1994).

Trotter, Ann, *Mary Potter's Little Company of Mary: The New Zealand experience, 1914–2002* (Wellington: Bridget Williams Books & Little Company of Mary, 2003).

Troughton, Geoffrey & Hugh Morrison, 'Introduction: Perspectives on Christianity and New Zealand history', in Geoffrey Troughton & Hugh Morrison (eds), *The Spirit of the Past: Essays on Christianity in New Zealand history* (Wellington: Victoria University Press, 2011), 11–24.

Tugwell, Simon, *The Way of the Preacher* (London: Darton, Longman & Todd, 1979).

van der Krogt, Christopher J., '"The evils of mixed marriages": Catholic teaching and practice', in Geoffrey Troughton & Hugh Morrison (eds), *The Spirit of the Past: Essays on Christianity in New Zealand history* (Wellington: Victoria University Press, 2011), 142–5[illegible].

Vaggioli, Dom Felice, *History of New Zealand and its Inhabitants*, first published 1895 (Dunedin: University of Otago Press, trans. and republished 2000).

Vicaire, M.H., *Saint Dominic and His Times* (London: Darton, Longman & Todd, 1964).

Walgrave, Valentine, *Dominican Self-Appraisal in the Light of the Council* (Chicago: The Priory Press, 1968).

Walsh, Carmel, '"To do for God what the miners do for gold": Dominican Sisters of Aotearoa New Zealand', in Geraldine Smyth (ed.), *Distance Becomes Communion: A Dominican symposium on mission and hope* (Dublin: Dominican Publications, 2004), 119–27.

Williams, Mark (ed.), *The Source of the Song: New Zealand writers on Catholicism* (Wellington: Victoria University Press, 1995).

Wilson, J.J., *The Church in New Zealand: Memoirs of the early days* (Dunedin: New Zealand Tablet, 1910).

Winton, Sandra & Elizabeth Mackie, 'Veritas and the search for truth', *Tui Motu*, March 2006, 18–19.

Websites

word.op.org/author/dominicans
www.beingfrank.co.nz/how-the-mighty-have-fallen
www.challenge2000.org.nz/about-us
www.dominicans.org.nz
www.hospicenorthshore.org.nz/About+Hospice/Our+Team/Sister+Bernie+Cheyne
www2.justice.govt.nz/ministerial-review/documents/submissions/7-145-1+New+Zealand+Dominican+Sisters
www.iec.org.nz/korimako
www.historic.org.nz/TheRegister
www.nzcatholic.org.nz
www.stdoms.ac.nz
www.vatican.va/archive/hist_councils/ii_vatican_council/documents/vat-ii_decree_19651028_perfectae-caritatis_en.html
www2.verdoncollege.school.nz/special-character

Index

Page numbers in **bold** *refer to illustrations.*